Joseph Clark: A Popular Victorian Artist and his World

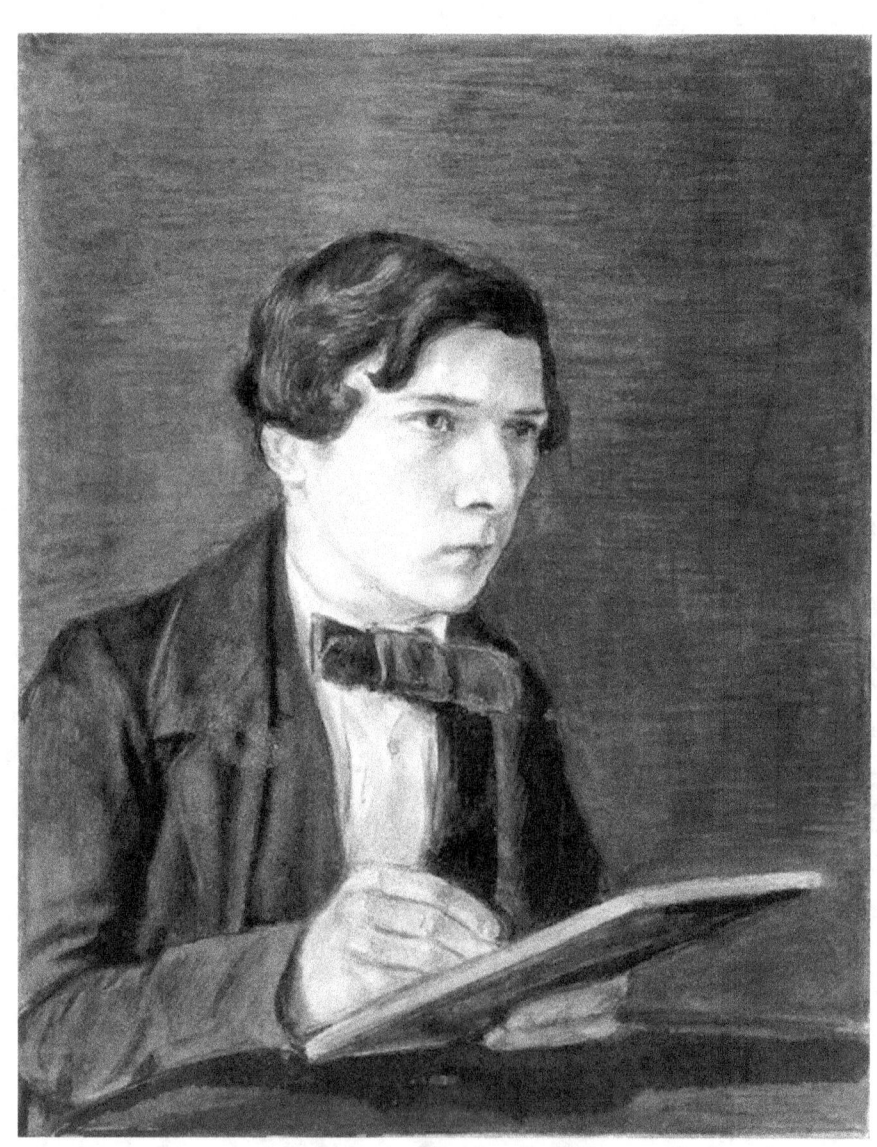

Self-portrait: Joseph Clark mid-1850s
(Courtesy Victoria and Albert Museum)

Joseph Clark

A Popular Victorian Artist and

his World

ERIC GALVIN

PORTWAY PUBLISHING

First published in 2016 by
PORTWAY PUBLISHING
89 Portway, Wells,
Somerset BA5 2BR
ericgalvin4@gmail.com
jclark1834.website

ISBN 978-1-910388-25-9

PORTWAY PUBLISHING is an imprint of CARRIGBOY.
Typesetting and design by CARRIGBOY, www.carrigboy.com
Printed by CreateSpace.

For Teresa Galvin,
my wife, and our daughters
Sarah and Jen

Contents

Preface

Growing up in the 1950s in Holloway, North London, I heard much about 'Uncle Joe' and 'Cousin Joe' – Joseph Clark (1834–1926) and Joseph Benwell Clark (1857–1938) respectively. I knew they were my maternal grandfather's uncle and cousin; and that both were artists. There were also several prints of their work in the house.

Who were these people? This book started as an attempt to find out. I found myself concentrating on the life and works of Joseph Clark who exhibited over 100 oil paintings at the Royal Academy (RA) between 1857 and 1916; and a further 70 at the Royal Institute of Oil Painters (ROI) after 1883. His pictures also went to seven International Exhibitions between 1862 and 1910.

This book will be of interest to several audiences. Art Historians and students will find a full coverage of Joseph's life, the works he exhibited, the response of critics and the impact of his family life, his religious faith and changes in society on his selection of subjects. It will also be of interest to general readers wanting to know more about nineteenth century life and art. It offers a good understanding of a neglected group of Victorian and Edwardian artists. It will also interest many local and family historians in the approach I took to combining genealogical sources and contemporary press coverage to produce a good idea of Joseph's life and works.

The picture that emerges is of a cultured, well-educated 'gentleman' committed to using his art to bring the hope and solace he found in his faith to others in difficult circumstances. He chose to do this by portraying ordinary people in everyday settings. Joseph enjoyed great public and critical acclaim at the start of his career. This faded as new styles and critical viewpoints gained acceptance in the final quarter of the nineteenth century but in time he became, in the eyes of some critics, the 'grand old man of British art'.

Others saw his work in the British genre tradition; mostly family scenes set in rural households, as sentimental, out of touch with the reality of daily life and overly deferential to the landed gentry and the aristocracy. As I put together this book, it was clear that these criticisms were wrong. In addition to family scenes in oils, he produced outdoor scenes, portraits, religious works and some inspired by national occasions. He provided illustrations for a range of magazines; many of them dealing with non-conformist and temperance themes aimed at families or children. All his work demonstrated high-level drawing and compositional skills. A full assessment of his output shows that he presented the daily lives of people living in distress and poverty in ways the reflected the tastes of the growing numbers of middle class art patrons. This appreciation is fundamental to understanding how his sixty-year career fits into the Victorian art world.

It emerges that Joseph hoped that reflection on the narratives embedded in his works would help people viewing them to realise that small acts of kindness would ease the situation of people in distress. At the same time, he hoped those facing misfortune and misery would know they are not alone, help them reflect on the positive aspects of their lives and sustain hope for the future. These ambitions are central to understanding his approach to the the educative role of art in nineteenth century society. They also explain why he did not embrace the art styles that emerged during his career that focused on a particular instant in time rather than a narrative; moved from detail towards broad impressions of a scene; and focused on the artist's reactions rather than those of the viewer.

Many books about Victorian and Edwardian art cover a few well known 'celebrity painters'. Some of these were members of the wealthy nineteenth century artistic elite. Others had gained notoriety through their radical political or moral views, unconventional or scandalous lifestyles or used innovative techniques in a succession of avant-garde styles. As such, these books do not offer a full or balanced view of the lives and works of the growing number of professional artists active during Joseph's career. In 1861, there were 4,600 professional artists in England and Wales. By 1881, there were 11,000. Almost all were men working in London.

This book offers a good starting point for anyone wanting to go beyond 'celebrity artists' to understand the work of the 'middling sort' of professional artists of Joseph's generation. 'Middling' in that they achieved some public and critical recognition for their works, earned reasonable incomes and enjoyed a modest position in society. Many of them were popular with contemporary art lovers but neglected by twentieth century art critics and educators. Consequently, their work faded from the public's memory.

The book has three sections. The first covers Joseph's early life and education. He spent his childhood in Cerne Abbas, Dorset, and attended the school in Dorchester run by William Barnes, the Dorset dialect poet and friend of Thomas Hardy, that advertised itself as turning 'boisterous boys into young gentlemen'. After exploring his decision to become a professional artist, it concludes with his experiences while at Leigh's Academy and the Royal Academy Schools in London.

The second section deals with his career as an artist. It starts by showing how the art world of the late eighteen fifties worked and which practices, institutions and trades were important for a young artist. It continues with chapters dealing with the three key phases in his career. Each looks at the key influences on his work – his family life; his strong Christian faith founded on the teachings of Emanuel Swedenborg; changing fashions and beliefs in the art world; and new ways of bringing art to wider and more diverse audiences. These chapters also cover the works he exhibited and the critical and press coverage they received.

The final section offers an overview of Joseph's works. It was in many respects the most difficult to write. When I started, I imagined that it would be relatively straightforward to draw up a reasonably accurate list of his works. I was wrong. The chapter on Joseph's works describes why it was so hard to identify a reliable list of his works and presents an overview of the works we know about and the themes he covered over the decades. The conclusions are tentative, as we have no more than a title for about half of the works that went to the RA and ROI and patchy knowledge about other works he produced. The location of many of his exhibited works is unknown and we have images of only a quarter of them. The final chapter examines how his body of work stands up to scrutiny against critical frameworks available during his lifetime and subsequently.

As Joseph did not write about his approach to art or reactions to changing fashions in the art world, the analysis in this book draws on books about Victorian art; articles and illustrations in specialist magazines, original archive materials and newspaper reports about Joseph's works and the changing art scene. I also drew on genealogical sources to explore how the experiences of his extensive family refreshed his youthful understanding of the reality of life for people in different sections of society and in different generations. These sources also allow us to understand more about the people who sat for the portraits he exhibited and those who bought his works. Again, this information is patchy but adds significantly to our understanding of his place and that of similar artists in the art world. Likewise, local history sources add to our understanding of the impact of the communities where Joseph lived and worked – Cerne Abbas and Dorchester in Dorset; Christchurch and Winchester in Hampshire; St Pancras, Holloway and several areas in North West London.

I hope this book will contribute to a wider understanding of Joseph's work, his aims as an artist and continued relevance in the twenty first century. More widely, it offers a good starting point for anyone wanting to understand the 'middling sort' of professional artists of Joseph's generation. These artists contributed so much to shape Britain's cultural life in the decades before the Great War. Modern critics acknowledge their invaluable contribution to understanding how ordinary folk lived, their dress, their household furnishings and family relationships. Many seemingly fail to appreciate the continuing potential of nineteenth century genre works to speak to twenty first century audiences.

I am grateful for help from so many people and institutions listed in the acknowledgements who accompanied me on my journey of discovery through the libraries, archives and websites used in preparing this book. My particular thanks go to distant relatives who supported my work and allowed me to use their own research. These include Graham Clark for access to his extensive research and helpful challenges to my initial interpretations of the facts he collected; Rosemary Chiles, Joseph Clark's granddaughter, for access family pictures and recollections; Peter Benwell Clark gave invaluable insights drawn on his extensive collection of original documents; and Richard Neal for his knowledge of the pictures ascribed to Joseph. All provided helpful comments and suggestions on successive drafts of this book. I dedicate this book to my immediate family who helped in so many ways.

All errors or omissions are mine and for these I apologise. I welcome comments, corrections or amendments from readers.

Notes on the text and images

I have called Joseph Clark, Joseph throughout the text. Likewise, I chose to call his mother Susan Clark although she appears as Susannah in several documents.

I have used many quotes from nineteenth century books and press cuttings, and have retained the original spellings, punctuation, usage and grammar. These often differ from twenty first century conventions. Some readers may find this disconcerting but they give a stronger flavour of the period in which they were written. I apologise to those readers who find this distracting.

The images contained in this book come from a wide range of sources. Many appeared originally in newspapers, exhibition catalogues and books produced using technologies less advanced than those available today. Some of the sources used are poor or damaged versions of the originals. Again, these may irritate some readers but on balance, each adds to the overall value of the work to students and others. In a few cases, modern images are available on the internet but the copyright owners were unable or unwilling to give permission for their use in this book. I have not used images where licence fees would have added significantly to the overall price of this work.

I have converted historical values to contemporary terms using the 'economic status' approach as defined on the Measuring Worth website. All comparisons are with 2013 prices and income levels. This measures a subject's income or wealth relative to a wage or more general income, such as the wage rate of workers in manufacturing or per-capita Gross Domestic Product. Occasionally the 'historic Standard of Living' measure offers a better representation of change over time. This measures a subject's income or wealth against the cost of a 'fixed' bundle of consumer goods and services (the Cost and Prices Index or Retail Price Index) or the cost of all goods and services (the Gross Domestic Product deflator). These indicators are increasingly unreliable as we push back into earlier centuries. Thus, these measures provide only a broad indicator of wealth or income at different points in the past.

The illustrations used in this book come from a variety of sources and consequently are variable in their quality. For the most part illustrations are associated with the relevant stages in Joseph's career (Chapters 6, 7 and 8 respectively) with some family pictures and pictures relating to the 'art world' at the end of Chapter One. There is a list of illustrations for ease of reference.

PART I

Family Life
&
Education

ONE

Childhood and Family Life

One hundred and eighty years ago, Cerne Abbas was full of the news that Susan Clark had gone into labour. The household in Abbey Street was delighted when a boy was delivered safely on 4th July 1834, but also fearful. Joseph was Susan's tenth child, but four older siblings had died before he was born.

The Jesuits say that if they have a child for the first seven years of life they will show you the man he will become. This chapter describes the first seven years or so of Joseph's life with his parents, in the wider family circle and in the local community. These all made important contributions to his development and practice as a professional artist.

At the time, Cerne Abbas was a rapidly growing prosperous market town serving nearby villages. The nearest big towns were Dorchester and Sherborne. Most of the town belonged to George Pitt-Rivers (1810–1866), 4th Baron Rivers of Sudeley Castle, who when not in London was based at Rushmore Lodge, Berwick St. John, Wiltshire. He was a member of governments led by Sir Robert Peel and the Lords Aberdeen, Palmerston and Russell between 1841 and 1866.

Joseph's parents

William Henry Clark Snr., Joseph's father, was born in 1793. The Universal British Directory of 1793 shows Joseph's grandfather, trading as a Watchmaker and Linen Draper. His mother, Susan, was christened in Cerne Abbas in January 1790. She was the only child of Thomas Shepherd and Mary Down.

In August 1818, William Henry and Susan married at St Andrew's Holborn (Plate 1). Although both were shown in the register as being 'of this parish', this was a temporary address used to allow them to marry close to family friends in the capital.

They were not the first members of the Clark family to celebrate important events in London. Graham Clark's (2013) research shows that Joseph's aunt, Mary Clark married James Coombs (also from Cerne) in London in 1804; Robert Clark, his uncle, married Mary Day of Cerne Abbas at St Mary's, Newington in January 1811; and Grace Philips (born Mullett and a relative of Joseph's maternal grandmother) had her daughter baptised there in 1817. Grace's husband, James Philips was a witness at William Henry and Susan's wedding. Another witness at the wedding was Frances Chubb from Evershot who later married Benjamin Swaffield who managed the 'home farm' on the Chatsworth Estate in Derbyshire when Joseph's brother, Edwin, was apprenticed in the early eighteen fifties.

This all suggests that Joseph came from a cosmopolitan family in frequent contact with a wide circle of distant relatives and friends in London. This must have widened Joseph's horizons well beyond those available to him in a small rural community like Cerne Abbas.

Another important aspect of the family's links with London was the New Church based on the teachings of Emanuel Swedenborg, the eighteenth century scientist, philosopher and theologian. As will be seen later, these links began in the 1790s with Joseph's Grandfather. Joseph's father was an active member of the Swedenborg Society by the 1820s and Susan's obituary mentions that he introduced her to Swedenborg's beliefs early in their married life. As there was no New Church within easy reach of Cerne Abbas, they became 'isolated receivers'; that is to say people living outside established congregations. The nearest congregations to Cerne were in Bath, Bristol and Salisbury. Isolated believers often continued to worship in the Church of England and Joseph's father became a churchwarden at St Mary the Virgin, Cerne Abbas, in 1834. The Swedenborg Society records show William Clark of Cerne Abbas as a subscriber in 1839, 1841 and 1845; although this was probably Joseph's brother, William Henry Jnr. Joseph's mother was an annual subscriber between 1845 and 1853 (from Cerne Abbas), 1855 and 1862 (from London), and in 1863 and 1866 (from Christchurch in Hampshire). The Society published and circulated copies of Swedenborg's voluminous works in English.

William Henry and Susan's belief in Swedenborg's teachings, with its distinctive revelations about the 'after life', helped the family cope with the loss of several children. Joseph became a strongly committed member of the New Church. Its teachings inspired the distinctive tone and treatment of tough subjects in many of his paintings. Childhood illness, separation, old age and death became recurrent themes in Joseph's work.

During their first sixteen years of marriage William Henry and Susan had 10 children; of whom only four survived to adulthood. The children who survived until Joseph's birth in 1834 were:

- **William Henry Jnr**, the second son, generally known as Harry, born in 1821. After his father's death, he ran the drapery business with his mother until the end of the 1840s. He married Christiana Anne Benwell Ellisdon at Shoreditch in March 1846 and their first three children (Christiana, William and Annie) arrived before Joseph moved to London in 1852. William Henry Jnr. ran the drapery business until his death in 1896 after which it passed to his unmarried daughter Christiana – the subject of one of Joseph's early portraits.

- **Mary Susan**, the first daughter arrived in November 1822. She married James Payn in Cerne Abbas on 21 September 1852 and they moved to Christchurch to run a drapery business. Their first son, William James, was baptised on 19th August 1853, in Christchurch as were their subsequent children.

- **Charlotte Francis** (b.1827) survived until 1838 when she died aged 11 and **Emma Elizabeth** (b.1831) who died at the age of 20 in 1852.

- **Edwin John** (b.1833) grew up in Cerne and as already mentioned, was an 'agricultural pupil' at the Duke of Devonshire's Chatsworth Estate in Derbyshire in the 1851 census. He married Martha Sarah Ellisdon, sister of his sister-in-law, in 1859. He ran a large farm near Christchurch at the time of the 1861 Census but later returned to Cerne Abbas to run The New Inn. He was also a part-time Excise Officer and a church warden until his death in 1876.

The children who died in infancy before Joseph was born were Thomas (b.1819), Robert (b.1824); Francis Charlotte (b.1825) and Thomas (b.1829).

In the eighteen twenties William Henry Snr., now a married man with young children, began to take charge of his father's drapery, thread manufacturing, spinning and linen weaving interests while his brother, Robert concentrated on the watch and clockmaking business. Two further generations of his family were to run the drapery business in Cerne Abbas until it closed in the early twentieth century. One grandson, John Clark became a senior export manager in Pawson and Lief's, a large wholesale drapers based in St Paul's Churchyard in the City of London and another, Clement, was a traveller for the same firm criss crossing the country selling drapery goods, ladies silk underwear and similar products to local retailers. John's daughter, Tess, worked in senior sales roles in the household furnishing departments of large Drapery Stores in Holloway, Kentish Town and the West End until her marriage in 1941. So five generations of the family worked in various aspects of the drapery trade for over one hundred and fifty years.

Two aspects of the drapery business gave Joseph important insights into two areas valuable as he built his reputation as a professional artist. First, drapers needed a good eye for colour in different types of fabric and of colour combinations needed to produce attractive styles for fashion conscious ladies. Second, good class drapers needed the sensitivity to deal with the vagaries of taste amongst the growing numbers of middle class patrons of their businesses. These aspects of the drapers' trade were also important in the clock making business run by Joseph's uncle, Robert Clark.

Evidence of this transfer of William Clark's business interests to his sons can be seen in the rate assessments made by the Overseers of the Poor and the lists of jurors drawn up by the Churchwardens. The references to W. Clark in the 1820's in these documents and trade directories need to be treated with great care. Certainly by 1825 when the qualification for jurors changed to stipulate that they should be men, aged 21 to 60 with a freehold worth more than £10 a year (£7,300), the references are to William Henry Clark Snr. Typically there were between 25 and 30 men each year on Cerne's juror lists drawn from an adult male population of around 400.

In December 1825, William Henry Snr took possession of the house on the corner of the Market Place and Abbey Street under a copyhold agreement. This gave him security of tennure so long as he paid the ground rent. This is almost certainly the house where Joseph was born. At roughly the same time he bought the lease for a 3 acre meadow near the Tucking Mill on the road to Upcerne for which he paid £300 (£2,500).

Another indicator of the scale of William Henry Snr's business interests comes in a press report of the hurricane that hit the town in 1828:

> … Mr. Clark's dowlas factory was then visited by this terrible whirlwind, which possessed sufficient power to force down the roof and one of the side walls; but the fall of the roof being impeded by an apple tree, the work people, of whom about a dozen were at the time engaged in the building, were providentially saved …
>
> **Dorset County Chronicle and Somersetshire Gazette**, 11 Dec. 1828 –
> reprinted as 'Dorset a Hundred Years Ago' in the
> **Dorset County Chronicle and Somersetshire Gazette**, 6 Dec. 1928.

Dowlas is a plain cloth, similar to sheeting, but coarser, made in several qualities, used chiefly for aprons, pocketing, linings and overalls. The finer types were sometimes made into shirts for workmen, and occasionally used for heavy pillow-cases. The numbers employed suggest the business supplied a wide area with products geared to the needs of poor agricultural communities.

William Clark's will dated 25 April 1832, exactly three months before he died, contained some unusual provisions, perhaps hinting at tensions between his sons. First, unusually for the time, he made William Henry Snr, the younger of his two sons, the sole executor. Perhaps, he felt that he had displayed more of his own entrepreneurial spirit that had driven his businesses. The will also specified that Robert should, within 12 months, build a wall without any windows or openings overlooking the yard that was to pass to William Henry Snr.

William's estate was valued at almost £2,000 (around £2.9m). It is probable that he had already settled money on his children as they married and arranged the transfer of several properties to William Henry Jnr. If this is the case then his estate in 1832 was smaller than in the 1820s.

After William Clark's death, the drapery and watch making businesses ran separately within a formal partnership between Robert and William Henry Jnr. It is unclear how this benefited the businesses and it was dissolved formally on 16 June 1835.

The 1830's were a profitable time for a natural entrepreneur like William Henry Snr. After the land purchase in 1825, he bought £500 of 3½% Government Stocks in 1830 (£688,000). So at the time of Joseph's birth, his father was a wealthy enterprising businessman contributing to community life.

It was around this time that William added tailoring to the services offered in the retail drapery business. This, together with the dowlas factory, created the capability for William Henry Snr's successful bid in 1837 for the lucrative and prestigious contract to supply clothing for the newly constructed Cerne Union Workhouse. The workhouse opened in 1837 with space for 130 residents from the town and nearby parishes. The union supplied clothing for both Workhouse residents and those receiving 'outdoor relief'. These were poor people receiving money while remaining in their own homes. The Union's minute book lists the agreed prices for each item supplied by William Henry Clark Jnr:

Table 1. Prices paid in 1837 by Cerne Union for clothing supplied by W.H. Clark, snr.

Item	Price (1837)	Price (2013)
Stout coloured counterpanes	3s 0d	£11.50
Stout brown smocks (pair)	3s 11d	£15.10
Jacket & trousers (5–10 year olds)	7s 3d	£27.90
Jacket, waistcoat & trousers (5–10 years)	8s 3d	£31.70
Jacket, waistcoat & trousers (10–15 years)	10s 3d	£39.40
Men's jacket, waistcoat and trousers (suit)	25s 0d	£97.10
Women's stout stockings (pair)	1s 3d	£4.81
Worsteds (yard)	2s 2d	£8.33
Flannel shrouds(yard)	6d	£1.92
Children's pocket handkerchefs (dozen)	3s 0d	£11.50
Blue stripped cotton for aprons (yard)	1s 3d	£4.81
Blue stripped cotton for shirts (yard)	11 ½d	£3.72
Grey cloth (yard)	3s 2d	£8.65

In September 1837 the Union's Guardians decided that people dying in the workhouse or whilst on 'outdoor relief' should be interred on the fourth day after their decease unless the surgeons ordered otherwise. William Henry Snr's offer to provide a pall at 30 shillings (about £115) was accepted. A pall was the cloth, often of velvet, for spreading over a coffin, bier, or tomb.

The family's involvement in the administration of the Poor Law provided a youthful Joseph with an insight into the lives of the poorer families in the area. These family links with the poor law system continued well into the twentieth century as Joseph's nephew, Frank Clark, held several local public service roles concurrently including being the vaccination, school attendance and relieving officer for the area. Joseph's own interest in the plight of the poor and the elderly is demonstrated by his work as a deacon in the Swedenborgian Church, and in several paintings of the residents of the St Cross Hospital in Winchester and of 'waifs and strays' in various institutional settings.

The sight of candles illuminating many windows in the town in June 1838 had a lasting impact on Joseph's four-year old mind. The Morning Post reported this celebration of Queen Victoria's coronation on 28th June 1838:

> CERNE ABBAS: The coronation was celebrated here with great éclat. The day was ushered in by firing a royal salute from the tower; a merry peal of bells and a band playing. At five o'clock the streets presented a scene of greatest animation; the streets were decorated with evergreens; Abbey

Street in particular was covered with laurels &c; triumphal arches were erected in various parts of the town; numerous banners were displayed, bearing inscriptions 'Long Live Victoria', 'Victoria may thy reign be long and prosperous'. At half Past 10 o'clock, the church bells summoned the inhabitants to attend divine service. Our worthy pastor Rev. J Davis explained the Coronation Service, there was also a service in the afternoon. During the morning fourteen tables were set up in a line from the top of Abbey Street to the Market Place. At half past two o'clock a procession walked round the town and proceeded to Abbey Street where an excellent dinner was served up; which after grace said by Mr Hillyer, the chairman; was taken by 840 persons consisting of the gentleman tradesmen and the poor of the town. The cloudless sky enhanced the beauty of the scene; the utmost harmony, peace and goodwill prevailed though the memorable day, which will be long remembered by the inhabitants of this loyal town. The evening concluded by Mr. T. Dunning Jnr inflating two beautiful balloons which ascended in a majestic manner. In the evening Mr. and Mrs. Hart entertained a select party at their house. Dancing commenced at an early hour, which was kept up with great spirit and the party separated highly delighted with the attention they had received. The following evening the females of the town drank tea in a booth fitted up for the purpose, after which dancing commenced and was kept up with great animation until a late hour.

Morning Post, 7 July 1838

In 1838, William Henry Snr acquired the Market House and planned to rebuild it. Two years later in 1840 it was insured for £400 (almost £31,500). In 1839, the Dorset County Chronicle carried an advertisement showing William Henry Clark Snr. as the local agent for the Crown Life Insurance Company of Blackfriars, London. Its not clear when this aspect of his business life started although many traders in small towns held such agencies to supplement their incomes. In 1861, his son, William Henry Jnr was acting in a similar role for the Sun Alliance Insurance Company.

William Henry Snr's business interests had bought him into regular contact with drapers from elsewhere including many in London. This range of contacts is shown by the witnesses and trustees of his will. These were Thomas Shepperson, William Orchard and Joseph Dyson – all using a business address at 27 Cheapside, London while the trustees were his close friend William Ellisdon (of Dalston) and G. Wadman of Yeovil (probably the George Wadman shown as a silk weaver in the 1841 census. Others in his household were associated with the drapery trade).

William Henry Snr, Susan and their children maintained strong links with London. A critical strand in these links was their close relationship with William and Sarah Ellisdon's family living in Dalston, now part of the London Borough of Hackney. William Ellisdon was born in Upper East Smithfield in 1798 and was a woollen draper at the time of his marriage to Sarah Lovelock Benwell on 27 January 1822 at St Pancras Old Church. Sarah Benwell was born on 18 April 1790 in Kingsclere, Hampshire.

William and Sarah Ellisdon's first child, Christian Anne Benwell Ellisdon, was born in October 1822 and christened at St Luke's church, Sydney Road, Chelsea. William and Sarah's seven other children were all christened at St Pancras Old Church. Later William became a commercial traveller alongside his role as a retail draper. Two of their daughters married Joseph's brothers; Christian Anne Benwell Ellisdon married William Henry Clark Jnr in 1846 and Martha Sarah married Edwin Clark in 1859.

A year after William Henry Snr's death, Sarah Ellisdon and her son Philip were staying with Susan Clark in Cerne Abbas on 6th June 1841 (Census night). This was the first census in which Joseph appears. On the same night Joseph's sister – the eleven-year old Emma Elizabeth was staying with

Sarah Ellisdon's other children (Christian, Emma, John and Martha) at the fashionable Cumberland Terrace in London's Regent's Park under the care of Rachel Benwell. Rachel was Sarah Ellisdon's sister and carried a family name which was to be used as a middle name by later generations of Clarks including Joseph Benwell Clark whose paintings, drawings and book illustrations are sometimes confused with Joseph's work. Philip Ellisdon was again staying in Cerne Abbas twenty years later on 7th April 1861, also a Census night, and was a draper's assistant. By 1871 he was a draper in Christchurch, Hampshire living with his sister, Emma. By 1901 he was a patient at the Christchurch infirmary, part of the Christchurch Union Workhouse, where he died in 1903.

Both the Clarks and the Ellisdons developed close ties with Christchurch. William Ellisdon died there in 1876. William Henry Clark Snr's daughter, Mary Susan, moved there after her marriage in 1852; Susan, his wife, moved there when her health deteriorated in the early eighteen sixties accompanied by Joseph. Joseph stayed there after Susan's death until he married in 1868. Joseph's continuing ties with Hampshire inspired several of his paintings, including 'A Hampshire Dairyman – Scalding out' exhibited at the Society of Painters in Oil Colours in 1886 and several secenes set in St Cross Hospital in Winchester.

In 1838, Charlotte Francis, Joseph's 11 year old sister died. This bought him, for the first time, face to face with the impact of the death of a child on a family. Joseph returned to the subject of childhood illness and death in several paintings, including his most renowned work 'The Sick Child' first exhibited at the Royal Academy in 1857.

Two years later, in 1840 when Joseph was six, his father died of consumption, now known as pulmonary tuberculosis. William Henry Snr. inspired trust and great confidence from many friends, acquaintences, business partners and customers. He was executor for at least three people, including his father. His wife, Susan was an equally warm and well liked person despite her stern appearance in surviving photographs. This warmth comes out clearly in her obituary and in William Henry Clark (son of Robert)'s letters from America with fond references to 'Aunt Clark'.

William Henry Snr's death was a devastating blow to the Clark family. It bought to an end the steady rise in the family's fortunes, financially and socially, that started when his father moved to Cerne in 1780. In his last years William Henry Snr achieved a great deal despite his declining physical and mental health. He had been an energetic, innovative and intelligent man who was also a deep thinker as evidenced by his lifelong interest in the writings of Emanuel Swedenborg. The loss of William Henry Snr's entrepreneurial drive had a wider impact on the town during its long economic decline. While the family continued to prosper for a while, its wellbeing was increasingly constrained by the town's decline. This decline was intensified by the town's isolation from the railway network exacerbated the impact of successive economic depressions.

In February 1840, just prior to his death, William Henry Clark Snr transferred by an indenture of assignment, all his stock in trade and effects to James Crane, gentleman, of Cerne Abbas, and to William and Samuel Dingley of Sherborne, drapers. This was done upon trust for the benefit of all William's creditors and all persons indebted to him were asked to pay their debts to James Crane, or Samuel and William Dingley. Most probably William was consolidating his affairs and this may have included closing the dowlas mill. By 1840, small scale manufacturing operations in areas without easy access to a railway were no longer economically viable.

When William Henry Snr died payment for much of the work on rebuilding the Market House was outstanding and accordingly a valuation undertaken. This gives a good idea of the scale of William Henry Snr's ambition and works completed before his death. It details work on framing the roof, floor joists and internal partitions, laying floors, extensive finishing works in the shop and house, making and installing sash windows and doors, panelling, architraves, chimneypieces including one marble chimneypiece, works on the staircase, plastering, painting and some oak grained finishes. As well as the shop, other rooms mentioned were the office, parlour, dining room, bedrooms, attic and cellar. In 1840, William Henry Snr held Stocks worth £1,600 (approaching £1.9m).

It appears from the June 1841 census that Susan and family had by then moved into the Market House. When William Henry Jnr married Christian Ellisdon in March 1846 they set up house across the road. Susan remained in the Market House until the middle of 1850, when she moved out and William Henry Jnr and Christian's family moved in.

Evidently William Henry Snr had enormous confidence in his wife, Susan who proved extremely capable when she took over the drapery business running it with her son, William Henry Jnr. They traded as 'Susanna Clark and Sons' until their 'drapery' partnership was dissolved on 29 September 1849.

Joseph's wider family and their friends

William Henry Snr's father – William Clark (1750–1832) was the 'patriarch' of the family. He came from the small village of Wraxall, 7 miles west of Cerne, but does not appear in Cerne Abbas records before his marriage in Cattistock to Mary Mullett on 17 July 1780. As Mary signed the register she was one of the minority of women of her generation who could read and write. Only 40% of women were able to sign the wedding register in the second half of the eighteenth century; fewer in rural areas. The witnesses to William and Mary's wedding were Joseph Mullett (Mary's brother) and John Strange her first cousin who lived in Cerne Abbas at the time. Might John have played a part in bringing the couple together and their decision to live in the town?

In time they had at least six children and 33 grandchildren – Joseph's uncles, aunts and cousins. William and Mary's first child, also named Mary, was christened in Wraxall while the second daughter, Charlotte was christened in Cerne Abbas in 1782 and a third, Elizabeth followed in 1784. Their first son, William Henry arrived in 1786 but he died aged 2 in 1789. A second son, Robert, was born in 1789 and a further son, also named William Henry, Joseph's father, was born in 1793. Unusually for the age, we know something of William's physical appearance. The Somerset and Dorset Family History Society (nd) transcription of the Malita Ballot lists drawn up just after William Henry Snr's birth shows '*William Clark – watchmaker – as having 5 children and being some 5 feet 5 inches tall*'.

William's early training in the 1760s was as a long-case clock and watch maker. His surviving works in the Dorset Clock Museum or offered in recent auction sales shows that he and his son, Robert (Joseph's uncle), were both talented designers and producers of long-case clocks. Success depended on design and sales skills going well beyond the technical skills used in making clocks. They designed the intricate mechanisms and the finely engraved dials, hands and cases. The mechanical components used would normally have been ordered from specialist suppliers, virtually 'off the shelf'. William and Robert each produced at least one '400 day clock' demonstrating the high level skills which few clockmakers possessed at the time. Clocks were very much a luxury item with fashions changing every few years and the customers were demanding well to do middle class people generally closely engaged in approving the designs of the custom-made items they purchased from William. They were similar in approach and manner to the people who started to patronise fine art in the early nineteenth century.

William appears in the churchwarden's accounts for the first time in 1780 when he received 2s 6d (about £180) for 'Brass collar, Nutt and Screw for the dial' on the church tower clock. During the early 1780s the church clock and its chimes caused endless problems and expense for the Churchwardens. Eventually they installed a new clock and dial for which John Foord recieved a total of £12 0s 7d (£16,600); Joseph Thomas – for dials £14 10s 1d (£20,100) and William Clark £8 8s 3d (£11,600) – a total of £34 18s 11d (£47,700). After 1785 William recieved a regular salary of two guineas a year (around £3,000) to maintain and repair the clock. This arrangement continued until the early 1790s. Thereafter William seems to have repaired the clock as the need arose rather than having a fixed annual salary. By 1815, Robert Clark was involved in clock repairs and this continued until his death in 1864.

William Clark and his family appeared frequently in the Cerne Abbas churchwardens' accounts not just as a business man paid for work on the clock but also as a resident of some standing. In 1786 he bought two seats in church for 1s 0d (£70.20) and three further seats in 1793 for Mary, Charlotte and Robert for 1s 6d (£90.20). In 1819, following a meeting of people who were *'Proprietors and Claimants of Pews, and sittings'* in the church such as William Clark, the churchwardens agreed to build new pews and sell them for life at 2s 6d for each sitting (£92). William bought 4 new seats in Pew 7 for 10s 0d (£369.10), two seats in Pew 19 for *'Wm and Susan Clark'* (Joseph's parents) for 5s 0d (£185.05) and one in Pew 19 for *Mary Sheppard* (Susan's mother) for 2s 6d (£92.30).

Graham Clark (2013) shows that William's first property was the house and shop on the corner of Abbey Street and the Market Place, transferred to him on 4 July 1792. The payment to the Pitt-Rivers estate was £6 (about £7,500). He would also have paid a fee to the former copyholder in order to occupy the property. In December 1825 this property was surrendered and granted to William Henry Clark Snr.

Although William's initial training was as a clockmaker he had diversified into other activities. Several other middle class families in the town had similarly diverse business portfolios at the time. The initial stimulus for William may have been simply that there was insufficient work locally as a clockmaker to support his growing family; alongside the realisation that as his sons grew to manhood they needed to be support themseleves.

As we have seen his first venture beyond clockmaking was as a linen draper. It would be a mistake to see drapery as a simple retail business with a limited range of linen goods. Across the country in rural areas tradespeople undertook a range of services for others regardless of the title over the 'shop door'. A good impression of the life of a village shopkeeper comes from Thomas Turner's 'The Diary of a Village Shopkeeper' (1754–1765). David Vasey (1998), editor of The Folio Society edition of the diary, says in the introduction:

> "To keep a village shop in mid-eighteenth century England was literally to be a jack-of-all trades. The first edition of the diary defined the mercer as 'grocer, draper, haberdasher, hatter, clothier, druggist, ironmonger, stationer, glover, undertaker, and whatnot."

This was the world in which William Clark grew up; a world that was changing rapidly. By the time William became a shop keeper thirty years later specialisation was growing apace but William almost certainly carried out about half of the trades given in Vasey's list. By 1811, Holden's Directory in the Dorset History Centre, shows that William had diversified 'up the supply chain' from retail drapery into thread manufacture. Later we will see that he had an early interest in manufacturing shown by the patent he took out in 1806. Sadly there was no diarist in Cerne in the eighteenth century equivalent to Thomas Turner, but Catherine Davies' diary from 1820-21, kept in the Dorset History Centre, has a single brief entry refering to a visit to Clark's to look at the millinery available. It's a pity that she did not have more to say about the shop, the assistants or the outcome of the visit.

William Clark acquired the leasehold for a second property on 27 March 1796 paying £12.12s (about £9,250). It was large, also on the Market Place and extended through to Back Lanes. In time, William Henry Snr established large spinning and weaving shops specialising in linen thead in this property.

By the end of the eighteenth century, William was one of the more prosperous men in the town. In the 1798 land tax returns he was required to pay 19s 9d (£1,030). As twenty Cerne residents had assessments larger than William, he was far from being the wealthiest person in the town but nevertheless his family were well off. Another, somewhat later, indicator of the family's increasing prosperity and status can be seen from the 1807 Poll Book. William was one of just 12 electors in a town with about 800 people at a time when the right to vote depended on wealth, property holding, income and gender. William had clearly moved up the town's 'Rich List'.

This period saw two further developments that were to have a important impact on the Clark family. These were the move into manufacturing and the growing interest in the teachings of Emanuel Swedenborg. Both probably involved William Clark's friend and business associate, James Bugby.

Research by the artists' family and others shows that in 1790, James Bugby was a school teacher, sacking manufacturer and clock maker living in New Alresford near Winchester, with his wife and growing family. This was a difficult year as he was declared bankrupt. He next appears in Yeovil in 1803 – probably living in South Petherton. It is not clear when Joseph and William met but by 1806 William Clark was granted in association with Joseph Bugby letters patent for 'Improvements in a Machine for spinning Hemp, Flax, Tow and Wool'. It is not clear whether machines using the invention were made in any numbers or where they were used. Clearly William was combining his experience of the drapery trade and knowledge of mechanics gained as clock maker to improve processes in fabric making.

It may be that Joseph Bugby introduced William Clark to Swedenborg's writings. Joseph Bugby may have played a significant role in Robert Clark's life. Robert may have been apprenticed to a London clockmaker in 1803. In January 1811 he married Mary Day of Cerne Abbas at St Mary's, Newington, then in Surrey but today part of the London Borough of Southwark. By 1814, they were living in South Petherton and he was working as a clock and watch maker, perhaps in association with James Bugby. Might Robert have been involved in manufacturing spinning machines using the 'Clark/Bugby' patent? Robert returned to Cerne Abbas in 1825, the year of Joseph Bugby's death. By 1826, he had taken full responsibility for maintaining St Mary's church clock in Cerne from his father. He extended his business to include manufacturing silverware alongside clock making.

William Clark's standing in the community was reflected and enhanced by his daughters' marriage partners who came from well other off local families. In 1801 Charlotte married James Stroud of Cerne Abbas. As the town's millers the Strouds were prosperous. In September 1804 James Stroud witnessed the wedding of Mary Clark to James Coombs in London. James Coombs came from an established family of maltsters, brewers and drapers, and was described as a mercer at the time of his marriage. Elizabeth married Henry Hopkins in 1813. When Henry died two years later his freehold property in Buckland Newton and personal estate were valued at £450 (£480,000). Later, she married William Collier from a prosperous Piddletrenthide family who had a variety of occupations including carpenter, shop keeper, miller and farmer. When William Collier's father died in 1826, his personal estate was £800 (£977,000). The marriages of William Clark's daughters show that Joseph's wider family had achieved a good social standing across the county as well as strong links with London. It is unclear how frequently they travelled to the capital or corresponded with their distant friends. Although travel to London was expensive the family seems to have visited the capital fairly frequently, perhaps when business documents needed signing, for weddings or other social occasions.

Some feel for the extent of William Clark's wealth comes from an assessment carried out in 1826 for '*the necessary Relief of the Poor, and for other purposes in the several Acts of Parliament mentioned, relating to the Poor of the Parish of Cerne Abbas in the County of Dorset*'. The rate was set as One Shilling in the Pound for the Year 1826. This shows that William and William Henry Clark Snr held twelve rateable properties. William Henry Jnr. held three properties and a fourth was occupied by James and Charlotte Stroud. Seven other properties were occupied by people unrelated to the Clark family; presumably providing a sizeable rental income.

Table 2. Clark family properties, 1826.

Property	Tenant
House and Garden	Joseph Adams
House and Garden	William Clark Snr.
House	Thomas Coward
House (Corner of Abbey St & Market Place)	William Clark, Jnr.
Land, Weaving House and Factory	William Clark, Jnr.
Land (purchased in 1825 for £300)	William Clark, Jnr
Malthouse	James and Charlotte Stroud
House	John Childs
Cottage	George Hislock
Cottage	George Mills
Cottage	John Sprankin
Cottage	Joseph Whiteham

It is clear that both Joseph's father and grandfather were resourceful, ambitious and enterprising men. They had mastered the technical and commercial aspects of their original trades and diversified into associated fields. They participated in and benfited from the town's economic growth and new technologies available in the early nineteenth century commonly known as the 'industrial revolution'. During his childhood Joseph gained valuable insights into the practical application of design, fashion awareness, acute appreciation of colours and strong customer skills. These were also vital attributes for an aspiring artist.

So at the time of Joseph's birth, the result of the efforts of his grandfather and father meant that his wider family held prominent positions in a busy town whose population had grown by just under 50% in the previous 30 years. Their standing extended well beyond the Cerne Valley with close associates in around Yeovil, Sherborne and London. This meant that Joseph was well aware of the world beyond the confines of his home from an early age creating the wider view of life that underpinned his subsequent career and lifestyle choices.

Though rapid by today's standards, Cerne's growth was significantly less than that of towns and cities in the industrial North and Midlands – and of London. What was the town like in the eighteen thirties and forties?

The local community

Cerne Abbas (plate 2) developed from a medieval settlement around its Abbey that, after the dissolution of the Monasteries in 1539, passed eventually into the Pitt-Rivers Estate. Almost all the references in the press to Lord Rivers in connection with Cerne Abbas refer to his role as patron responsible for nominating candidates to become the 'perpetual curate' or vicar of the parish church.

As in many similar estates, day-by-day control rested with the estate's steward supported by local bailiffs who arranged for the collection of rents, transfer of tenancies and registration of properties. On the quarter days, the church bells were rung and tenants went to the New Inn to pay their rent and receive in return a beer voucher worth 3*d* (96p). The Bragg family ran the New Inn and in 1849, Ellen Bragg married Joseph's cousin, Nathaniel Clark. Edwin his uncle ran the New Inn during the 1860s and 1870s. During his childhood, Joseph would have been familiar with these 'quarter day' events and the celebrations accompanying them, not least the exchange of 'beer vouchers'.

The largely Georgian façades of many homes in Cerne known to Joseph as a child concealed much older buildings. The Abbey's destruction created a ready source of dressed stone used extensively as the town expanded in the seventeenth and eighteenth centuries. The impact of this can be seen in a brief report on the domestic architecture in Dorset:

> "At Cerne Abbas, besides a noble Church, are remains of the ancient Abbey, particularly a gateway and apartment over it. We find also barns and other fragments of antiquity, in various parts the village."
>
> **Salisbury and Winchester Journal,** 15 September 1828

The town's eighteenth century expansion rested largely on the prosperity of the brewing trade that in turn depended on the excellent quality of its water filtered through the surrounding chalk hills. By the end of the century the town had fourteen inns and its beer was sent across the country and exported to North America. A house in Abbey Street is said to have been inhabited by one of George Washington's uncles.

Joseph's extended family had a wide range of business interests including milling, brewing and several specialist leather making trades. They operated several of the 30 or so, mainly craft based, small businesses appearing in Trade Directories in the early nineteenth century. These businesses were concerned with housing (mainly construction trades), feeding (butchers, bakers, innkeepers and grocers) and clothing (drapers and hatmakers) the people of Cerne Abbas and nearby villages; and the six large farms in the parish provided most of the raw materials they needed. Larger concerns such as William Henry Clark Snr's dowlas works drew their raw materials from a much wider area. As a market town, Cerne Abbas had several professional people: surgeons, teachers, boarding school proprietors and a solicitor. There were regular market days and two fairs a year.

Despite the growth and progress seen in the late eighteenth and early nineteenth century some things had not changed. A good example of this is the deferential relationship between the town and its owner, Lord Rivers. This is evident from a report of his visit to Cerne Abbas in 1844 when Joseph was nine years old:

> "Cerne Abbas.—The inhabitants of our town were much gratified on Sunday last visit from Lord and Lady Rivers, who drove from Dorchester to attend Divine service at our church. His Lordship who has been making a brief sojourn this county, paid us also a visit on the preceding Thursday, and took the opportunity of inspecting the newly erected schools, and the large plot of ground appropriated by him to the allotment system. His Lordship was accompanied to the latter place by the Rev. Mr. Waugh, Mr. Hodges and other gentlemen of the committee, who explained the arrangements which had been made for carrying into effect this most admirable system encouragement and assistance the poor. His Lordship appeared to be much pleased, with all which the committee had done, and assured them his cordial approval and continued patronage. … The whole town of Cerne together with the patronage of its living, and an immense domain around it, have long been the family possession of his Lordship and his ancestors, but excepting this and a brief visit on a former occasion, such event as the one we are recording has not occurred within the last 50 years. It regarded therefore, and we hope with reason, as the commencement nearer and more frequent personal intercourse than has hitherto existed between Lordship and his family and his numerous tenantry in this county, a circumstance that cannot fail source of satisfaction on the one hand, and of advantage on the other. During the Sunday, Lord and Lady Rivers staid with the Rev. Mr Waugh, at the Vicarage House … it is rumoured that his Lordship has been inspecting Kingston House and Park, now in the market—with the view making it one of his future residences."
>
> **Sherborne Mercury** 22 June 1844

Doubtless Joseph, who was a pupil at William Bench's school at the time, would have witnessed many of the scenes reported in the newspaper. It is unlikely that Joseph would have gained any significant insight into the lives of the aristocracy from his time in Cerne as Lord Rivers' interests were military, political and scientific rather than cultural; and he rarely visited Cerne.

The deference shown by the Sherborne Mercury's reporter was facing a growing challenge at the time. Change was afoot but not without a lot of controversy and some violence. In the eighteen thirties, just before Joseph's birth, rural unrest came to a head in Dorset. The 'swing riots' started with the smashing of newly introduced threshing machines held to be a cause of much poverty for agricultural workers. These riots were akin to the better known earlier 'luddite' attacks in the Midlands and North when spinning frames were broken. Joseph's uncle, Robert Clark, as a member of the local militia, helped to put down the Swing Riots in Buckland Newton, 4 miles from Cerne. Lord Digby of nearby Minterne petitioned Parliament for a reward for the local militia. As a result, Robert was paid £10, (around £7,500). The Swing Riots had many causes but but were essentially about the progressive impoverishment and dispossession of the English agricultural workforce over the previous fifty years. Eventually the farmers agreed to raise wages while the church and some landlords reduced the tithes and rents – but many farmers reneged on the agreement and the unrest continued.

Many saw political reform as the only solution to the unrest and this led to the Great Reform Act of 1832. Under this Act, Parliamentary constituency boundaries were redrawn to eliminate the 'Rotten Boroughs' in the gift of the aristocracy and to increase somewhat the proportion of people entitled to vote. However, this was not enough on its own.

In February 1834, another symptom of continuing unrest occured in Tolpuddle about eleven miles from Cerne Abbas, following a 40% reduction in agricultural wages from 10s (£41) to 6s (about £24) a week. The 'Tolpuddle Martyrs' were six agricultural labourers convicted of swearing a secret oath as members of the Friendly Society of Agricultural Labourers. Though a friendly society, this had many features of contemporary trades unions that were outlawed during an earlier period of unrest at the end of the eighteenth century. All six were transpored to Australia. They quickly became popular folk heroes and 800,000 people signed a petition calling for their release. In 1836, they were released and four returned to England. Today they are iconic heroes of the early trades union movement.

Beyond these rare outbursts, crime was not a serious problem in Cerne Abbas in the eighteen thirties. Contemporary press reports of court proceedings show a small but steady flow of Cerne Abbas residents being found guilty of relatively small scale crimes, mainly the theft of food and easily sold low-value items. For example, the Salisbury and Winchester Journal reported that at the Dorset Midsummer Quarter Sessions held in the week of Joseph's birth, Mary Terrell of Cerne Abbas was sentenced to three months imprisonment with hard labour for stealing linen cloth. Was this taken from the Clark family? The volume of crime seems to have increased somewhat in the 'hungry forties' but its nature remained the same. In this period the poor in many rural communities were impoverished and living close to absolute poverty. Many moved to distant growing cities or to Britain's growing empire. Charles Dickens describes graphically the situation encountered by many migrants moving to London. More widely contemporary realist literature, such as Elizabeth Gaskill's 'North and South', describes the flow of people from rural communities in the South to rapidly growing urban areas in the North; and the hardship many suffered before and after their move.

Queen Victoria came to the throne in the first year of a major economic recession that by 1842 had put a million and a half unemployed workers and their families (in a total population of sixteen million) on some form of poor law relief. Violence broke out and pressure grew for the repeal of the Corn Laws. These dated from 1815 as a measure to levy high import duties to protect British cereal producers from low cost overseas competition. The effect was to keep corn prices high when many people were desperately poor and short of food. The problem was worse in Ireland where famine spread following the outbreak of potato blight affecting their use as food for both humans and livestock. The situation there intensified as many Irish farmers exported grain to England where the Corn Laws gave them far higher prices. In time, the potato blight spread to England including to farms in the Cerne valley. The situation became unsustainable and following the repeal of the Corn Laws in January 1846, import duties were reduced in stages until their complete abolition in January 1849.

Some ameloriation to the plight of the poor came from Cerne"s allotment system established in the eighteen thirties as described in a letter to the editor of the Devizes and Wiltshire Gazette in 1852:

> "The allotment system was introduced into the parish of Corsley in 1846, by the present much-respected Rector, the Rev. James Hay Waugh, M.A., on his entering into residence when appointed to the living. The reverend gentleman has had much experience to bring to the working of the allotment system, having been one of the first to introduce it into Dorsetshire, under the sanction of the Right Hon. Lord Rivers, his lordship having granted about 20 acres of good land for the purpose in the parish of Cerne Abbas, of which parish Mr. Waugh was then Vicar, which was found by judicious management to produce a great amount good and it is but right to state that the condition of the poor of all conditions in Cerne Abbas was much improved during his residence there, that at the last allotment rent audit, which he presided over in that place, an Address, signed by the inhabitants of all classes over 18 years of age, was presented him, expressive of their unqualified approbation of the way in which had discharged the duties of his responsible and sacred office, the noble and by the noble and generous example he had always set before them, being always foremost to relieve the wants of the distressed, by administering food to the hungry, clothing to the naked, and consolation to the sick and dying."

Devizes and Wiltshire Gazette 4 November 1852

The Clarks, like others living in rural communities, gained much of news about current events beyond the town from local carriers, the stage coaches stopping at the New Inn, occasional personal letters from their friends and relatives in London and the emerging local press. In particular, they needed to keep abreast of the latest trends in fashions and technical developments affecting the clockmaking and drapery businesses.

The Dorset County Chronicle first appeared in the 1820s and, like similar provincial newspapers at the time, carried a mix of local, national and international news. In the week Joseph was born, the paper carried editorials on recent debates in the British Parliament; the newly elected Chamber of Deputies in France; and growing political dissent in Spain. This breadth of interest in a local paper is rare in local papers in the early twenty first century. As would be expected in a largely agricultural community there were also detailled reports of the prices fetched for livestock and arable crops in markets across the South West. There were also long, often verbatim reports of trials at the Assizes and numerous advertisements. Amongst other subjects advertised that week were the county horticultural show; opportunities for girls under 15 who were members of the Church of England to become apprentice hairdressers; the reopening of various schools after the early summer break; patent medicines and the sale of a phaeton and two 7 year old horses. We have no way of knowing whether the Clark family took this or any other paper, but if they did they would have been well informed by the range and detail of developments in the outside world.

During Joseph's early childhood personal travel and trade depended on horses and the Turnpike road between Dorchester, Sherborne and Yeovil. This was used by local carriers; the stage coaches with names such as 'John Bull' and the 'Duke of Wellington' linking the town with Weymouth, Dorchester, Sherborne, Yeovil and Bath; and privately owned coaches, wagons and horses. Regular carrier services linked the town with Bristol, Dorchester and Weymouth.

In the 1820s the road was being improved:

"Parliament has received the Royal Assent for making a turnpike road from Cerne Abbas to Charminster and from the former to Totnell Corner near Sherborne and another road, branching out of the last road, through Lion's Gate, extending into present road leading from Dorchester to Sherborne. This measure will be a great accommodation to the neighbourhood and to the public in general, particularly during the Winter season, as the present road leading from Sherborne to Dorchester is in some parts (near to Cerne) occasionally rendered impassable by snow, whilst in the Vale, travelling is not thereby impeded, and through it at all times of the year. The roads will in future be found pleasant to persons with carriages, as they are nearly-level from Charminster to Sherborne, with impediments to prevent travelling expeditiously. All the landholders have very liberally-given a portion of their lands to widen the road and have subscribed handsomely to enable the measure to be prosecuted; with effect."

Hampshire Chronicle 3 May 1824

and the work took two years

"A new turnpike-road (formed under the superintendence of Mr. McAdam) is now finished and opened from Sherborne to Cerne Abbas, and from thence to Dorchester, by which road all hills are avoided, and a sheltered and safe journey through the Vale secured, without the risk exposure to snow or other casualties."

Bath Chronicle and Weekly Gazette 18 May 1826

John McAdam was the famous Scottish born surveyor and road engineer who developed a revolutionary new approach to road building whilst working for the Bristol Turnpike Trust in 1816. His innovation involved remaking roads with crushed stone bound with gravel on a firm base of large stones. This was the hailed as the greatest advance in road construction since Roman times and it became known as 'macadamisation', or, more simply, 'macadam'.

The Turnpike Trust ceased operating in 1876. Joseph and his family knew these roads well as William Henry Jnr and Robert Clark used them to transport their raw materials and finished goods.

A sense of the stage coach services using the new road can be gained from the advertisement for the 'Red Rover' published in Sherborne just six weeks before Joseph's birth:

"SUPERIOR TRAVELLING BRISTOL AND BATH. The Public are most respectfully informed, that the fast, favourite, four-inside post coach, The Red Rover, leaves the above Hotel every Tuesday, Thursday, and Saturday mornings, at half-past seven o'clock, through Dorchester (Antelope), Cerne Abbas, Sherborne (Half-Moon), Yeovil (Greyhound), Mudford, Marstou Magna, Queen Camel, Sparkford Inn, Castle Cary, Shepton Mallett, Old Down (in time for the Wells, Glastonbury, Bridgewater, and Taunton Coach), arriving at the Plume Feathers Hotel, Wine Street, Bristol, at five o'clock, in time for the Coaches to Birmingham and Liverpool: and arriving at the White Lion Hotel, Bath, half past five, in time for the Mails and Evening Coaches to London."

Sherborne Mercury 26 May 1834

The turnpike and stage coaches carried the expensive and somewhat unreliable Royal Mail which was supplemented by the Penny Post (31 pence) linking Dorchester and Cerne Abbas set up in February 1827. This became part of the the national penny post system in May 1840 under Sir Rowland Hill's reforms of the Royal Mail making postal services cheaper, faster, more secure and easier to use. In part this was a response to rising literacy rates and the growing needs of industry and commerce.

Communications between Cerne Abbas and the rest of the country were to change during Joseph's childhood. Earlier proposals involving his grandfather, William Clark, for a canal through Cerne Abbas had failed to gain approval. The 1830s and 1840s were of time great excitement about the growing railway system. Joseph was born just four years after the opening of the world's first passenger railway between Manchester and Liverpool. When he was two years old his family was associated with proposals for the Bath and Weymouth Great Western Union Railway passing through the centre of Cerne Abbas. The proposers of the railway claimed it offered the prospect of reducing coal prices in Cerne by around 60%. Most of the capital was to come from Bath but five shares were held in Cerne Abbas including one held by Joseph's father. Strong opposition from landowners along the proposed route led to the abandonment of the plan.

This decision proved to be a tipping point in the fortunes of the town and proved catastrophic as Cerne Abbas that remained isolated from the railway network. This isolation hastened the onset of the century-long decline in Cerne's economic fortunes during which its population fell by 50% and most of its businesses closed. The impact of this decline on the appearance of the town was captured graphically by Sir Frederick Treves (Treves 1906) when he wrote:

> "There was a time when Cerne was a stately place. It is humble enough now. … On entering the Main Street of Cerne it is evident that some trouble has fallen on the abbey town. It is silent and well nigh deserted. Sad to tell Cerne Abbas is dying, and has already fallen into a state of herbitude. … Nothing, however went well for long in Cerne after the last monk slinked out of the Abbey. One enterprise failed after another. … When the railways made their brutal advance into Dorset the heart of Cerne gave way utterly. … The place, however, is empty and decaying and strangely silent. Grass is growing in the streets; many houses heve been long deserted, many have their windows boarded up, or are falling into listless ruin. … There are quaint old shops with bow windows, but the windows are empty of everything but a faded red curtain while over the door in very dim paint, are traces of a name …"

Sir Frederick Treves, was best known as the surgeon to who operated on King Edward VII in 1902 just days before the original date planned for the coronation. He, like Joseph, was educated at William Barnes' school, although they were not contempories. So during the first seventy years of Joseph's life the town had been transformed from a bustling expanding market centre into a shadow of its former self. In 1919, the combined impact of town's economic decline, death duties and the Great War led the Pitt-Rivers family to sell its interests in he town.

This decline had a profound impact on the prospects for the younger members of the Clark family, including Joseph; most of whom left the area. On 25 March 1904, Alice (Joseph's niece) wrote to her brother, John Clark in London, saying:

> "The school gets smaller and smaller, there seems to be no money anywhere in the family. I wonder if it will ever be any better. I am sure it can't be much worse. There is that consolation …"

She was a teacher at the village school. The railway eventually reached Dorchester from Winchester and London in 1847. When the line from Bristol to Dorchester arrived in 1857, the last stage coach services serving Cerne Abbas stopped. No railway ever came to Cerne.

Implications for Joseph's life and work

Early family, religious and community life are important influences in the professional development of many artists; both as an inspiration for becoming an artist and the subjects depicted in their works. Joseph was no exception.

It is dificult to analyse precisely the ways in which the family tragedies affected Joseph's early development. It is reasonable to assume that at an early age he developed a strong sense of his own mortality and the transient nature of personal and family relationships – and perhaps led to periods of insecurity and depression affecting his career. The family's experiences may have strengthened his religious beliefs; as did his time at William Barnes' school.

Joseph's early experience in a small rural community gave him a strong sense of the ups and downs of daily life faced by people in different classes and conditions. Today he is best known for pictures of rural family scenes informed by his observations of life in the cottages of Cerne Abbas – and later refreshed by occasional visits and time spent in Hampshire. Throughout his career he also produced scenes of middle class life presumably drawning on his engagement with the extended Clark family, the Ellisdons and his wife's family. Speaking to the Women's League of Swedenborg House in the 1950s, Joseph's daughter recalled his love of Dorset (Drummond 1950). She mentions his memories of 'cowslip gatherings', 'nutting' and fearsome tales of the famous Cerne Giant. The giant is a large rather rude figure cut into the chalk hillside. She also reflected on his lifelong closeness to his mother.

While most of his best known works are set in the homes of relatively well off working and middle class households, he also depicted people in much less fortunate circumstances. Did these works showing the lives of elderly people and children in poverty draw on his family's close connections with Cerne's Poor Law Union, the conditions he saw during the 'hungry forties' in Dorset or later as a deacon in the Argyle Square Church.in London?

The other dimension of the impact of Joseph's early life on his career, already mentioned briefly, was the contact with middle class customers who became important demanding art patrons during Joseph's career. Many had similar family backgrounds to the Clarks and Ellisdons or were the second or third generation descendants of skilled artisans and mechanics living in the second half of the eighteenth century and running their own businesses. Some were highly innovative exploiting new technologies and markets to become extremely wealthy art patrons. Their grandsons acquired the classical education necessary to be regarded as 'gentlemen' – a privilege previously restricted to upper class families. Some of their sisters went to schools – such as those depicted in William Thackery's 'Vanity Fair' – but many remained at home developing the necessary social accomplishments including drawing and water colouring from 'a governess' or their mother. Joseph saw this progression in his own family as his all but one of his nephews moved to become teachers, doctors and businessmen working in the growing cities and overseas, mainly in Britain's colonies.

Jeffrey Sachs (Sachs, 2010) makes the point that the way in which these well off families spent their money changed during Joseph's career. Initially the families with artisan roots lived modestly and devoted any 'surplus' income to philanthropic causes; although a few built up fine art collections that became the core of new collections in the new national and provincial art galleries. As the nineteenth century progressed many wealthy families engaged in 'conspicuous consumption' and gave less to philanthropic causes. This switch had an important impact on the art market towards the end of the nineteenth century.

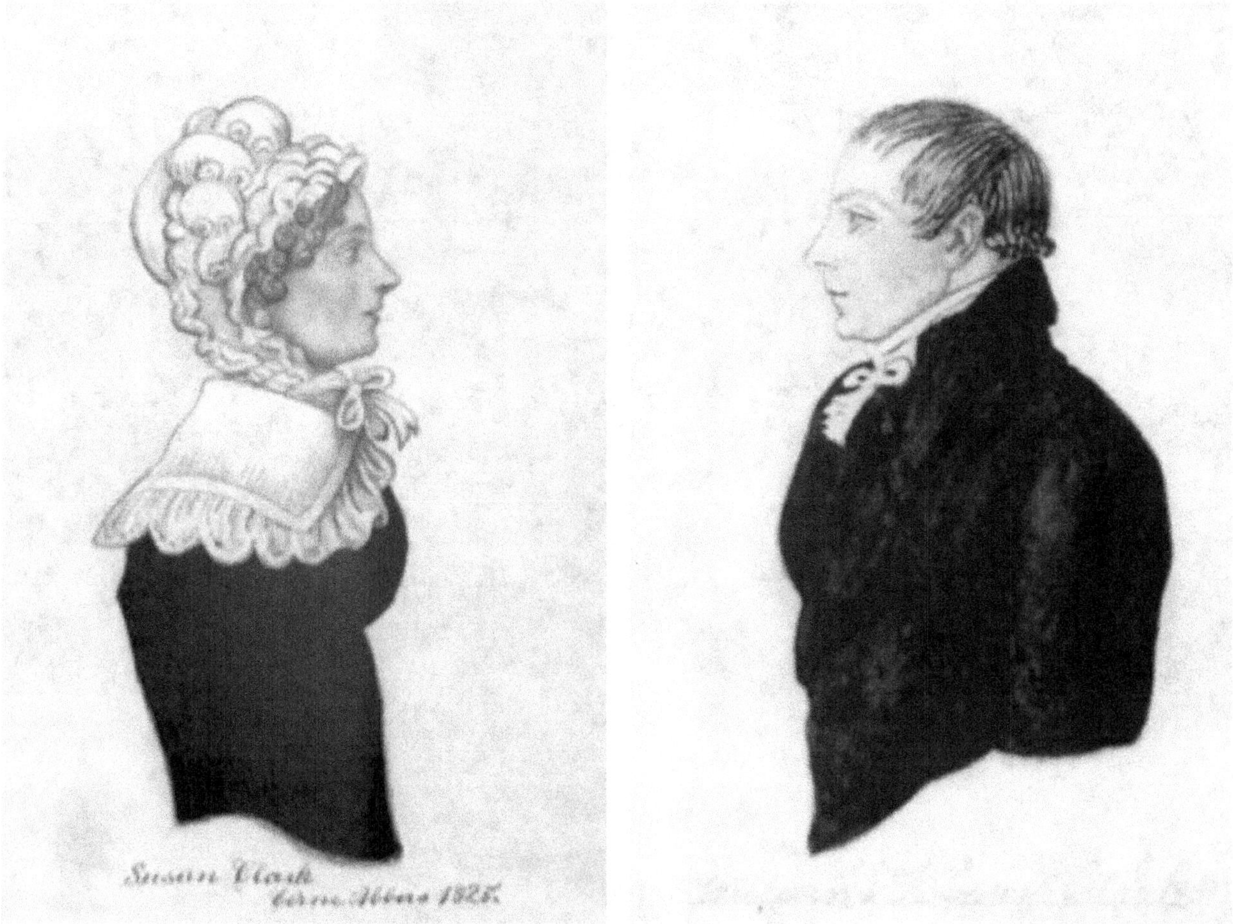

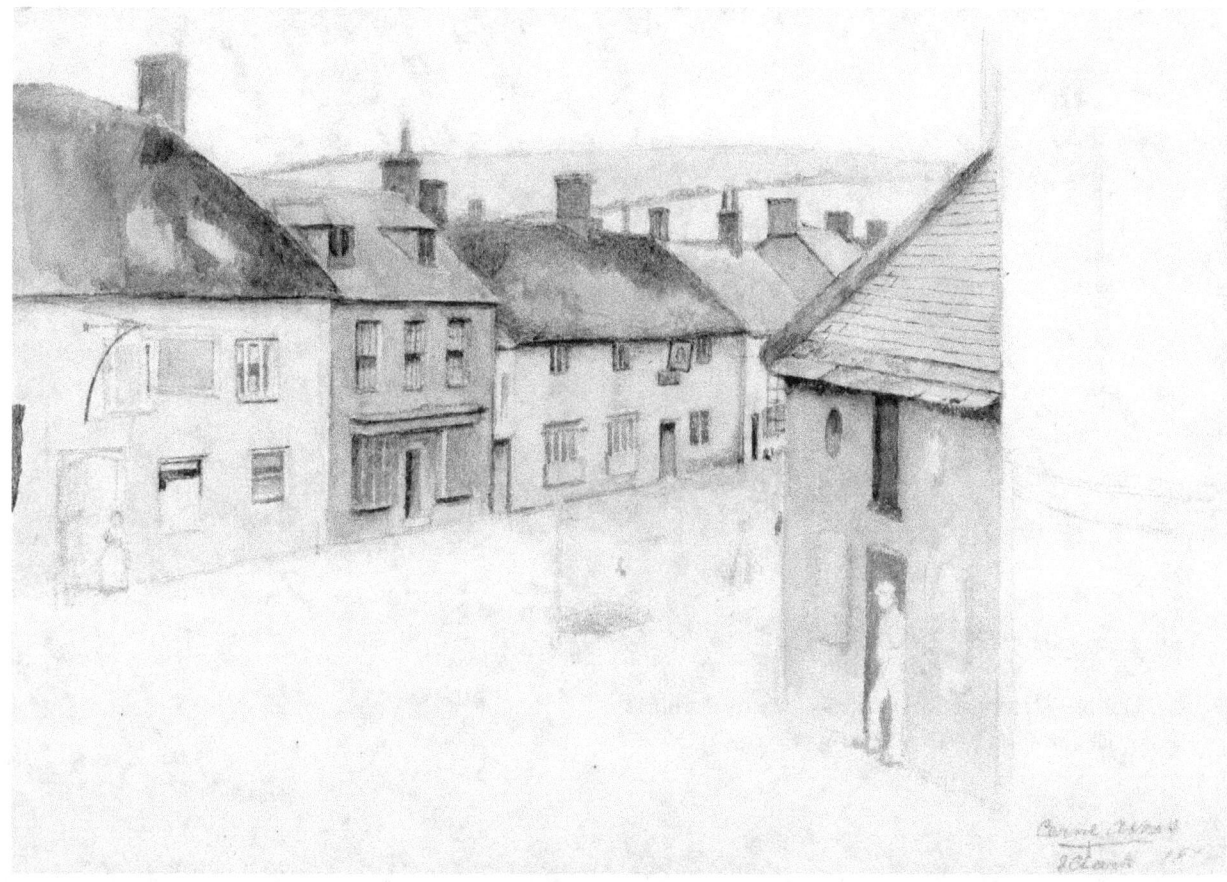

Plate 1. Joseph's parents (1825). (Courtesy the artist's family)

Plate 2. Joseph Clark's Water Colour of Cerne Abbas (1870s). (Courtesy of the Victoria and Albert Museum)

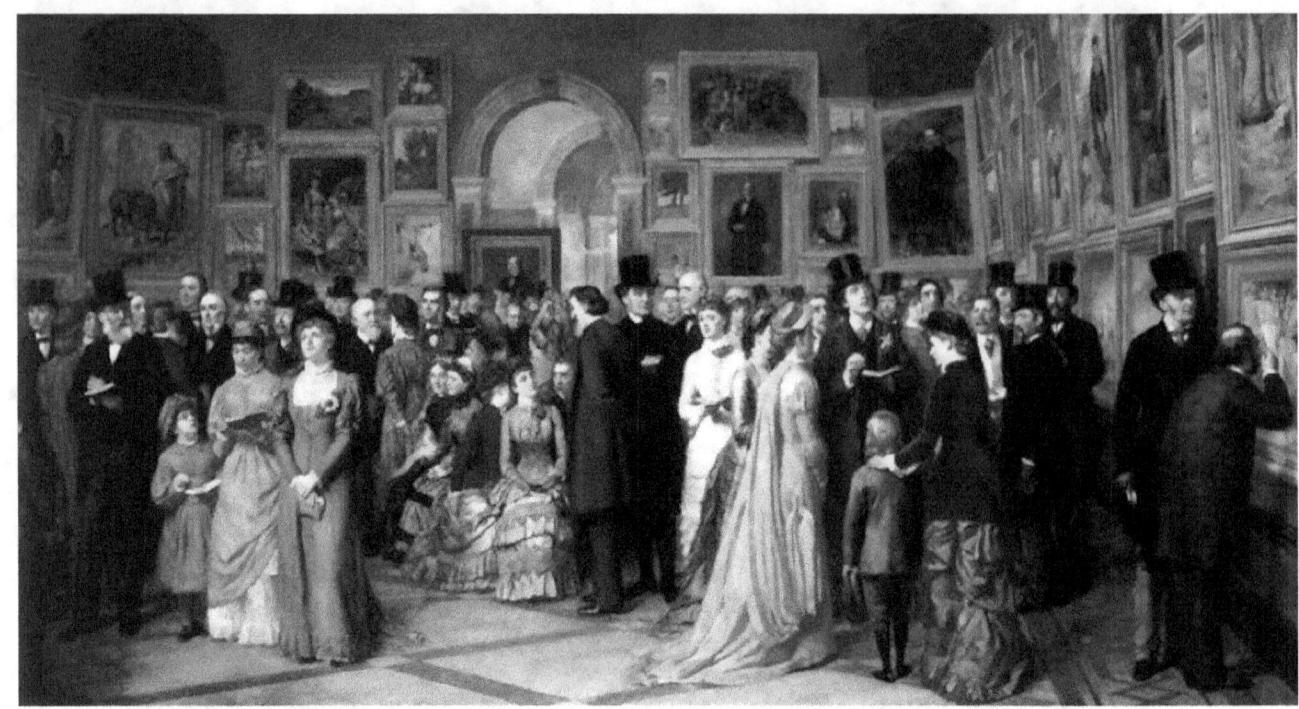

Plate 3. 'A private view 1881' (exhibited at the RA 1883) William Frith. (Source: Wikipedia Commons)

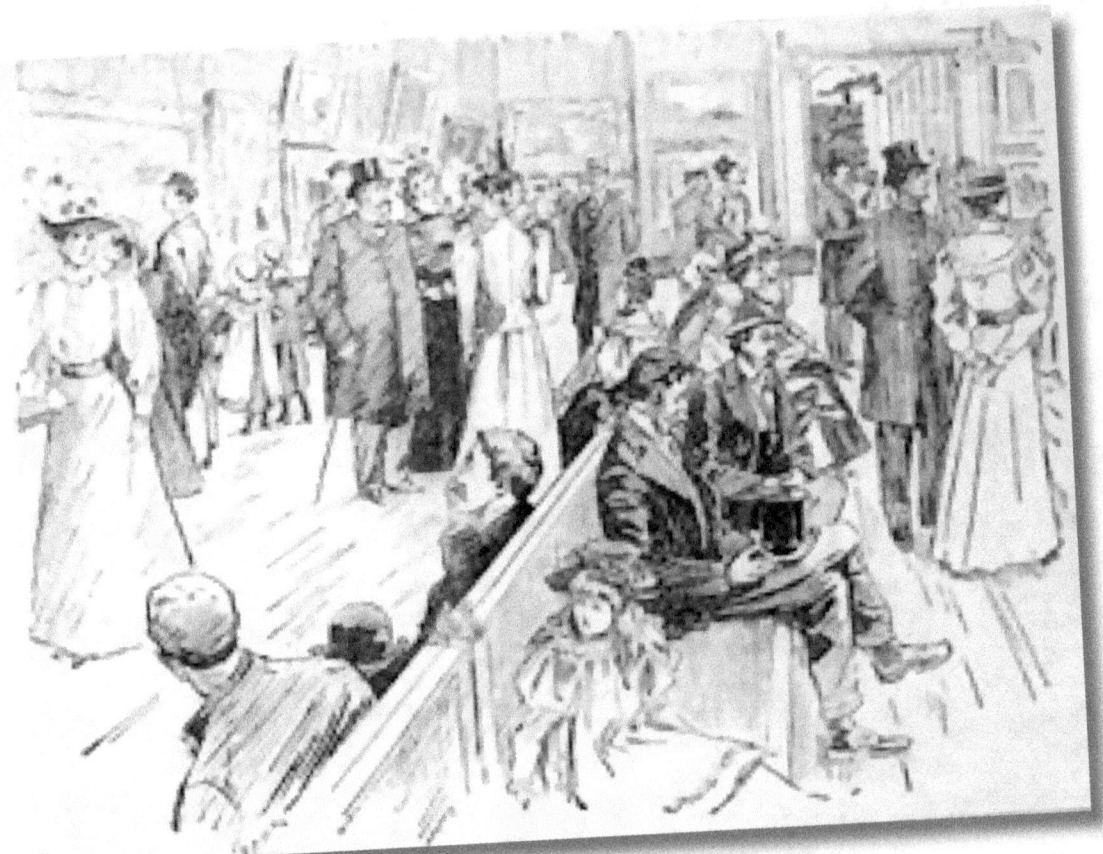

Plate 4. 'Our New National Gallery: Inspecting the Pictures at Millbank'. (Source: The Daily Graphic, 1897)

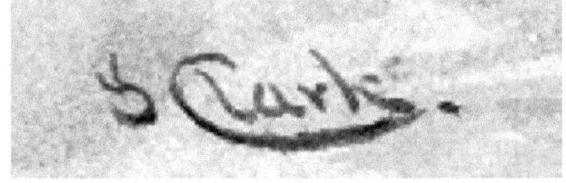

Plate 5. Joseph's signature
from Sketch for oil painting 'The Word of Life' (1881).
(Courtesy Victoria and Albert Museum)

TWO

General Education

J oseph's formal education was his first step away from the family environment and Cerne Abbas. As his parents were cultured, literate and numerate, they probably taught him the rudiments of reading, writing and arithmetic at an early age.

In the 1840s there were no legal requirements for children to attend school. It was a further thirty years before school attendance became compulsory under the Elementary Education Act 1870. In the first half of the nineteenth century there was a significant growth in the number of local schools and the proportion of children who received several years schooling. Although private schools existed in Cerne Abbas from the late 18th century, the National School in Duck Street did not open until 1844 as part of the network of schools run by the 'National Society for Promoting the Education of the Poor in the Principles of the Established Church in England and Wales'. From 1833, the government made grants to the Society; although these were accompanied by inspections and increasing control from London. Today, Cerne's National School is part of the state system as a 'Church of England' school.

In large part, the Society' efforts and those of the smaller British and Foreign School Society created the first near-universal system of elementary education in England and Wales. On average children attended school for between five and six years. Nationally, the number of 'day scholars' rose from just over 600,000 in 1818 to 1.3 million 1833 and 2.1 million 1851. Over this 30 year period the total population grew by about 50% while the number of 'day scholars' rose by about 220%. R.K. Webb (1963) commented on the impact on the overall level of literacy in the early to mid nineteenth century when he wrote:

> "In so far as one dare generalize about a national average in an extraordinarily varied situation, the figure would seem to run between two-thirds and three-quarters of the working classes as literate, a group which included most of the respectable poor who were the great political potential in English life."

So, Joseph was part of the first generation in English history to have a significant level of education and high literacy levels. This was important in Joseph's career choice in that it helped create a ready market for the growing numbers of illustrated papers that carried many images of fine art works. This expanded the market for prints and increased the incomes of professional artists.

William Beach's school

Joseph described his first school in the early eighteen forties as a 'dame school'. None of the surviving records refer to a 'dame school' as such. Of the two schools appearing in the records the best candidate was the one in Duck Street run by William Beach. He taught both boarding and day scholars. In December 1827, William Beach from Dorchester took over 'Thomas Pittman's Academy' that had opened in 1825. Vivien and Patrica Vale (2000) quotes (without a citation) that he hoped that:

> "…his experiment in the instruction of youth, and a strict attention to the duties of his profession, to obtain the confidence of those persons who may be induced to place young gentlemen under

his care. Their domestic comfort, morals, health and general mental improvement (to) be objects of his unceasing solicitude."

In 1829 William Beach advertised in the Dorset County Chronicle:

> "ACADEMY, CERNE ABBAS. Mr Beach presents his most grateful thanks to his numerous Friends, for the very liberal support he has received since the commencement of his School, and hopes by continuance of his exertions, to merit their future favour and patronage. The duties of the School will be resumed on Monday, July 20th."

Dorset County Chronicle 2 July 1829

At the time of the 1851 census, the school had eighteen boarders aged between 8 and 16 as well as day pupils. Their average age was 11 and all came from Dorset. William Beach remained in Duck Street until 1858, when the academy moved to The Lodge at the east end of the village. In the 1871 census, Beach's academy had just four boarders. In the early 1850s William Beach became the Clerk to the Guardians for the Cerne Poor Law Union and registrar of marriages; possibly to supplement his income as the demand for fee-paying elementary education declined as the national schools gained a good reputation.

Vivien and Patrica Vale (2000) also report that in 1864 in an advertisement William Beach spoke about his academy as:

> "… his classical, mathematical and commercial school at which young gentlemen are trained not only for business persuits but for situations in several Departments of Government as well as the Legal and Medical professions."

Later that year the academy closed and he appeared at the Exeter Court of Bankrupcy at the suit of his bankers and the owners of The Lodge. His total debts were £1,798 (£154,100).

William Barnes' school

In 1845 Joseph, then aged 11, was ready to move onto a school offering a more demanding and substantial curriculum attractive to an ambitious middle class family. He became a pupil at the school at 40 South Street, Dorchester run by William Barnes. This was advertised and run to *'give boys the skills and attainments need to be accepted as a 'young gentleman'*. Barnes was the renowned Dorset dialect poet who, while Joseph was a pupil, was studying for his degree with the intention of taking 'holy orders'. A few years later this school was described in the 1852–3 Directory of Cornwall, Devon, Dorset and Somerset as *'William Barnes Gents Classical and commercial boarding and day school'*.

As the daily carrier from Cerne Abbas in the 1840s took 1½ hours each way, Joseph lived in Dorchester; almost certainly as one of about 20 borders at Barnes' school. He studied divinity, English, geography, geology, and both English and Roman history; and benefited from William Barnes' liberal and flexible educational philosophy.

We do not have details of the cost of Joseph's tuition at William Barnes's school but Trevor Hearl (1996) in his 'William Barnes – The schoolmaster' has an intriguing entry *'half year tuition of Master Clark in dancing £2 2s od'* (£179). Sadly the reference does not specify which Master Clark received dancing lessons; there was another unrelated pupil named Clark at the time.

A good idea of the costs and books supplied for Joseph's use comes from an account signed by William Barnes for Thomas and William Crick held in the Dorset History Centre. The cost of their board and schooling was £13 19s od (about £1,260). The bill breaks down the total for both pupils:

Table 3. Cost of education and board at William Barnes School.

Items	Cost
Board and Tuition	£11 10s 0d
4 Copy Books	3s 0d
4 Exercise Books	3s 0d
4 Note Books	1s 0d
Books etc	10s 6d
French	£1 1s 0d
Latin (for the younger brother)	10s 6d

The books supplied were Darley's Trigonometry (3s 6d) for Thomas and a copybook, latin grammar, latin dictionary and pens, pencils etc. (7s 0d) for William. They were living with their widowed mother at the time of the 1851 census. This account suggests that the total cost of Joseph's education at William Barnes' school probably amounted to about £45 (£3,500) for three academic years.

The books, paper, pens and pencils used by Joseph and his fellow pupils probably came from the booksellers and stationers founded by George Clark, William Barnes' long term friend and publisher. Both William Barnes and George Clark were on the jurors list for Dorchester, St Peter's in the 1840s. Both George and his son Thomas died in the spring of 1846 and the business had passed into other hands. There are several slight indications that George Clark and his relatives knew the Clarks of Cerne Abbas, abut none of a direct family relationship between them.

Lucy Baxter (1887), William Barnes' daughter, described his general approach to education:

"His theory was that minds should be trained and not crammed; that the school curriculum ought to contain the germs of all the knowledge which the man would require in after life. … The importance of science … [and] its value in developing the reason and observation. … [were important in the education offered] … His object was to induce the boys to wish for more knowledge. This was done by a daily lecture taking the first hour of the day. … William Barnes's system of moral training was as unique as it was successful. No obligatory tasks, no caning (except solely, and seldom, for lying), no restriction and restraints, except only the natural consequences of wrong-doing. … This method was proved by practical use to be more efficacious than all the canings and impositions in the world. … The conscience being the true ruler of the soul, moral influence of the mind, and self-interest governing the world career."

From this it is easy to see where Joseph acquired the self discipline, commitment and dedication needed to sustain a steady flow of good quality work over seven decades. He also gained a grounding in Latin and the classics regarded as essential for a gentleman and for admission to the Royal Academy Schools.

During Joseph's time in Dorchester, William Barnes was a prominent opponent of the Southampton and Dorchester Railway's plans to cut through Maumbury Rings; a Neolithic Henge and Roman Amphitheatre in Dorchester. This opposition did not stop Barnes from taking his pupils to hunt for fossils in the railway excavations as part of their science lessons. It is tempting to think that Joseph may have been part of these expeditions but there is no direct evidence for this. Somewhat later Barnes was involved in a campaign to stop the Great Western Railway from cutting through Poundbury; the Roman site where a cutting was replaced by a tunnel. These campaigns led to the formation of the Dorset County Museum where Barnes became one of its first secretaries.

Lucy Baxter (1887) refers to her father's active interest in art as a keen amateur sketcher. It went beyond this with articles published in The Art Journal and in Macmillian's Magazine during the period while Joseph was at the Royal Academy School and his early career. Trevor Hearl's (1966) book suggests that Barnes fostered Joseph's aptitude for art. Joseph's youngest daughter, Margaret Drummond (1950), spoke about Barnes's drawing classes and their great influence on his ambition to become an artist. Drawing was widely seen as an essential accomplishment for gentlemen and young women at the time.

This was not the first time William Barnes offered encouragement to a budding artist. Another well known Victorian artist from Dorset, Albin Martin (b.1812 or 1813) was also a pupil of William Barnes. In 1851 he migrated to New Zealand where he became an artist, farmer and politician. Eighty two of his works, almost all landscapes of the West Country, Italy or New Zealand, are in the Auckland Art Gallery. We have no way of knowing whether he corresponded with his schoolmaster or visited him whilst Joseph was a pupil. As Barnes kept in touch with many of his former pupils he probably knew of Albin's plans and of his experience as a professional artist.

William Barnes' wife, Julia, managed the business side of the school allowing her husband time to study for his Bachelor of Divinity degree at St. John's College, Cambridge and later for his ordination in 1850. Each year she arranged for the redecoration of the school and for a constant stream of repairs to be undertaken. The frequent need for repairs suggests the school was a boisterous community. A few years after Joseph left Barnes' school in 1848, a young apprentice architect moved next door to William Barnes. He was Thomas Hardy who regarded Barnes as his mentor.

After Julia's death in 1852 the school's fortunes declined, but not before producing an unusual number of pupils who achieved eminence in their professions. Joseph is one of these high achieving former pupils.

Joseph acknowledged Barnes' influence as several of his works use quotations from Barnes's poems for their titles. These include 'Jeanes Wedden Day in Mornen' (1879), 'Farmer's Woldest Dater' (1908) and 'Wedden morn' (1909). Rosemary Chiles's (2010) book contains a copy of a letter from Joseph to William Barnes; this confirms that they remained in touch for at least 30 years after Joseph left school. On 12th July 1878, Joseph wrote:

> "Dear W Barnes
> Your kind letter reached me this morning from Holloway and in reply I wish to thank you for the encouraging manner in which you view my attempt to illustrate one of your dearest little poems. I have often felt that many of them contain subjects that are very congenial to me in the branch of art I have chosen – and although this has been the first attempt at illustrating them, I trust that it will be by no means the last.
> With kind regard(s)
> I am, Dear Mr Barnes
>   Your affectionate
>   Old pupil
>   J Clark"

After William Barnes became Rector of Winterbourne Came in 1862 the school was sold to George Philip de Winton. After returning to Cerne Abbas in retirement in the 1920's, Joseph Benwell Clark (Joseph's nephew) recalled that he and his brother Frank attended GP de Winton's school. Both were boarders on Census Night 1871. Joseph Benwell Clark contributed to the cost of the William Barnes' statue in Dorchester and viewed it at the London studio of the sculptor, Roscoe Mullins.

John Betjeman, the former Poet Laureate and the first secretary of the Victorian Society, spoke warmly of Barnes' poetry in a radio broadcast in March 1951 describing his *"humble craftsmanship"*. By this Betjemin meant that Barnes did not try to be *'fine or deep; to scan the universe or listen to the pulse of the universe'*. Rather he was held to be *'content with his own parish and the nearest town setting down what he saw and heard'*. Betjamin ascribed Barnes' continuing popularity to his simplicity and humbleness of his approach. Did Joseph consciously adopt a similar approach in developing his style and choice of subjects or had he simply absorbed it in his day to day studies and life as a boarder? Barnes was a polymath. He was a poet, tutor to Thomas Hardy, mathematician, linguist, amateur inventor, and an artist who published hundreds of engravings. When Barnes died in 1886 his obituary read:

> "There is no doubt that he is the best pastoral poet we possess, the most sincere, the most genuine, the most theocritan; and that the dialect is but a very thin veil hiding from us some of the most delicate and finished verse written in our time."
>
> **Saturday Review** 1886

Some of Joseph's works can be seen as a visual depiction of the sentiments expressed in Barnes' poetry. So it is tempting to see Joseph Clark, William Barnes, and Thomas Hardy as partners in the most significant contribution from Dorset to English cultural life in the second half of the 19th and early 20th centuries. H.F.V. Johnstone's (1961) article 'Joseph Clark of Cerne Abbas – The artistic counterpart of William Barnes' in the Dorset Yearbook for 1961–62 hints at this possibility. When E.M. Forster said of William Barnes that 'to read him is to enter a friendly cottage where a family party was in full swing.' he might almost have been describing many of Joseph's paintings.

A false start

After finishing his general education at Barnes' school, Joseph followed his older brother, Edwin, in becoming an apprentice – a common career path for middle class families with artisan roots. The younger sons, such as Edwin and Joseph, were apprenticed into trades where they might be expected to progress to solid middle class positions without undermining or being in direct competition with the eldest brother in the drapery business.

Edwin trained at the Duke of Devonshire's Chatsworth estate in Derbyshire and was living with the Benjamin Swaffield, Head Baliff in Edensor Village at the time of the 1851 Census. Benjamin came from Chilborough in Dorset and in 1829 married Frances Chubb who had been a witness at William Henry Snr and Susan Clark's wedding a decade earlier. Francis died in February 1832. In 1836 Benjamin married Frances Watkinson at Brampton Church, a few miles from Chatsworth. In addition to Edwin Clark, their household also included two agricultural labourers, George and Joseph Bridle recorded as being from 'Wotton' in Dorset. Glanvilles Wootton is a small village five miles north of Cerne and there was a large family called Bridle living at Godmanston in the 1841 census, just three miles south of Cerne Abbas. Clearly, the links between the Clarks and the Swaffields opened the way for Edwin's apprenticeship although the Chatsworth Estate archives have no records of the apprentices in the middle of the nineteenth century to confirm this.

Joseph went to train with a chemist and druggist at St Neots in Huntingdonshire although it is not clear why this occupation was chosen, how the specific opportunity was selected or how long he stayed in St Neots. One possibility for the choice of career was that Joseph's family saw retail pharmacy as a coming trade offering the prospects of a respectible and worthwhile profession. The state began to regulate pharmaceutical retailing with the Apothcaries Act 1815 and consideration of a Sale of Poisons Bill in 1818. In 1841 the Pharmaceutical Society was founded with about a thousand members, associates and apprentices. It gained a Royal Charter in 1843 recognising its educational aims and gave it powers to regulate entry to the profession.

Robson's Trade Directories for Huntingdonshire published in 1839 and Kelly's Directory for 1854 show that there were three retail chemists in St Neot's. The most likely candidate as the pharmacy where Joseph started his apprenticeship was Samuel Sprigg who lived in Market Square, probably 'above the shop'. In 1851 he was 43 and was employing an apprentice, presumably Joseph's successor, who came from Essex close to the area where Joseph's Elisdon relations lived. They may have known of the opportrunity in St Neot's and recommended Joseph. Neither of the other chemists employed an apprentice at the time of the 1851 census.

Seemingly unsuited to pharmacy and because of homesickness Joseph returned to Cerne. However his training as a chemist, however rudimentary, may have helped him to understand the chemistry behind new pigments and paints coming onto the art market in the middle of the nineteenth century.

The 1851 census does not record any occupation for Joseph's sister, Mary Susan aged 28. Perhaps Mary, like other young women of a similar social standing in Victorian Britain, remained at home until they married. The younger sister, Emma Elizabeth is also shown without any occupation. Sadly she died within a few months of the census night.

Influence on Joseph's life and work

This phase in Joseph's life also made a profound impresson on his life and career. His schooling gave him a good grounding in the classics, science and possible contacts in the art world that marked him out as a 'gentleman' in the making. William Barnes may well have influenced Joseph's style, especially on the choice of genre subjects, and advised on how to progress his artistic ambitions. Certainly Joseph's work, like that of Barnes, has been widely appreciated over several generations. They both concentrated on homely subjects and characters firmly located in the Dorset countryside of the mid-nineteenth century. Their focus was on the lives and experiences of respectable working people.

This period was a difficult and unsettling time for Joseph. He coped with his unsuccessful spell as an apprentice in Huintingdon, the death of his sister Emma Elizabeth (his third experience of death in his close family), the marriage of Mary Susan and her departure for Christchurch. It would not have been surprising if this sapped his confidence and added to his uncertainty about his future.

THREE

Career choices

After returning from St Neots, Joseph Clark was unclear about what to do with his life. There were no opportunities for him as a younger son in Cerne Abbas. We have little direct evidence about how or when Joseph and his family decided that he should become a professional artist. The general questions facing the mid nineteenth people wanting to become an artist are described in detail by Paula Gillett (1990). She highlights the main factors in such decisions as the general sentiment about art in England and its implications for the social status of the potential artist; the quality of art education available; the fit between the family's values and beliefs and the artistic lifestyle; the extent of the young person's natural talent; the financial rewards offered by a career as a professional artist; and the ways in which art might develop in a volatile market.

General sentiment about professional artists

The first question concerns the general feeling about professional artists. Gillett (1990) argues that much of English society in the first half of the nineteenth century was not just apathetic toward art but actively hostile towards it. At the end of the eighteenth century fine art made only a limited impact on the lives of most middle and working class families. This changed as new technologies made images of the most celebrated works widely available alongside rapidly rising literacy rates.

Another important driver of the change in public attitudes was a linked series of reforms to the management of major art institutions called 'The Institutionalisation of the Arts in Early Victorian England' by Charles Saumarez Smith (2009). These reforms started about twenty five years before Joseph made his career choice. In that period, the world of fine art, its study and practice, suddenly came within the scope of Parliament to organise, finance, supervise and control. These changes were led by two key public servants, Charles Eastlake and Henry Cole. They were forerunners of the the later reform of the civil service itself, culminating in the the sweeping away of patronage following the Northcote-Trevelyan Report of 1854. Both had a strong moral purpose and understood the wide social, political and educational value of art. Accordingly, they thought art needed to be taken away from the traditional connoisseurs and used as an instrument of social and economic policy. But their view was not rigidly utilitarian as they took a strong and idealistic view of the arts as a source of moral, intellectual and religious uplift in improving society. Some of their reforms feature in later chapters.

Improved access to fine art stimulated a vigorous debate about the status of professional artists reflecting society's preoccupation with class differences and social standing. In the absence of an effective social security system and the imprisonment of debtors, financial instability threatened a family's standing and very survival. Charles Dickens, Anthony Trollope and Elizabeth Gaskill all describe the consequences of financial failure. Gillett (1990) uses the term 'status anxiety' to capture this preoccupation for many families and offers examples of leading artists who feared lowering their family's status in society. An example from later in the nineteenth century is Edward Burne-Jones who reportedly changed his name from Ned Jones to safeguard his son's position as part of the Prince of Wales's social circle. She argues, as did many leading artists of the time, that few artists were ever accepted fully in 'society' and were seen as 'being in trade'; while those who came from aristocratic families found it difficult to escape charges of dilittantism.

The status aspects of the decision were probably not decisive as Joseph's family were well established and accustomed to being regarded as 'in trade' by longer standing and higher status families. The Clarks were proud of the social and economic status achieved by their family in the previous generation. Equally, by the time Joseph made his decision to become a professional artist, painting had become a respectible occupation ousting previous associations with poverty and lowness in behaviour and character. That said, Martin Myrone's contribution to David Bindman's (2008) collection of essays on the History of British Art (1600–1870), points to lingering prejudices that being an artist was an effeminate occupation and, if not that, at least an occupation for *'naughty people'*.

Another positive element in building public esteem for art was the emergence of public art galleries. The Foundling Hospital Collection in London dates from 1740 when William Hogarth donated a painting to commemorate King George II's signing of the Hospital's Charter. Encouraged by Hogarth, many other leading artists, including Thomas Gainsborough, Thomas Hudson, Allan Ramsay, Joshua Reynolds, Louis-François Roubiliac and John Michael Rysbrack gave works for display to the general public to raise money for Britain's first home for abandoned children. Their donations became Britain's first public art collection. Visiting the gallery and appreciating fine art became an important element in what became known as the 'cult of sensibility' towards the end of the eighteenth century. This was an important step away from fine art being the exclusive realm of royal, religious and aristocratic art patrons.

By the middle of the nineteenth century there were more opportunities for the public, especially in London, to see good quality art following the foundation of the National Gallery in Trafalgar Square in the 1820s. We do not know whether Joseph's family and their friends in London took advantage of these opportunities but Joseph's granddaughter, Rosemary Chiles, recalls being told that Joseph visited the Great Exhibition of 1851. Did the quality of the work on show and the warm reception it gained contribute to his career choice and its acceptance by the family?

In this respect, his choice may also have been influenced by the growth of the 'celebrity status' accorded to leading members of the Royal Academy including John Constable (1776–1837) and William Turner (1775–1851). After 1848, leading members of the Pre-Raphaelite Brotherhood (PRB) became celebrities as did several other Royal Academicians specialising in genre subjects in the early eighteen fifties. The rising sales of works by these artists came, in part, from 'conspicious consumption' by the rising generation amongst families leading lives increasingly remote from either their family's artisan origins or from the lives of people working in their factories, mines, docks and country estates.

The term 'professional artist' was something of a misnomer. It is unclear whether professional status was important to Joseph and his family. The mid-nineteenth century was a period in which many occupations aspired to the status enjoyed by the traditional liberal professions of divinity, law and medicine. Certainly art as practiced in the mid nineteenth century fell well short of the definition of a profession offered by Beatrice and Sidney Webb (1917) as a '... *vocation founded upon specialised educational training, the purpose of which is to supply objective counsel and service to others, for a direct and definite compensation, wholly apart from expectation of other business gains*'. Essentially this means having a formal professional association, a systematic widely agreed abstract conceptual and practical knowledge base, lengthy institutionalized training, individual autonomy at work, a strong vocational culture with codes of ethical behaviour, colleague oversight and control, and freedom from direct state regulation of its activities. These usually led to members of a profession being a cohesive and exclusive elite group with social standing and good incomes.

The recognition of an occupation as a profession in Britain usually resulted in the granting of a Royal Charter and legislation-giving members of the profession exclusive rights to supply specific services. How far did artists live up the Webb's criteria? Linda Peterson (2004) in her review of Julie Codell's study of life writing by artists between 1870 and 1910 says:

"In this masterful study, Julie Codell argues for the pivotal role of life writing in the achievement of professional status for Victorian artists. Codell suggests that public self-presentation in a wide range of autobiographical genres—not only full-length memoirs and posthumous family biographies, but also interviews, mini-biographies in periodicals, and biographical dictionaries and histories of British art—made a crucial difference in the Victorian artist's ability to distinguish himself (or herself) from less desirable stereotypes (the failed Romantic genius, the bohemian, the degenerate) and to reach equity with other professions. For Victorian artists, this meant presenting themselves as 'gentlemen and ladies whose material success and public appeal became representative of English cultural domination and superiority'."

Codel (2004) argues that artists unlike authors tended to be sociable and accustomed to working in congenial groups. This in her view derived from the long tradition of professional schools, a tendency to share large studios, having strong links with galleries and participating in numerous exhibitions. Authors tended to work alone and with only infrequent contact with other writers. Indeed many French artists visiting Britain during Joseph's lifetime envied the discretion and freedom from Government control enjoyed by English artists. Therefore, some aspects of the criteria were met but not all of them.

One aspect of this congeniality amongst artists imported from France was the artists' colony. In the middle of the eighteen fifties Frederick Hardy established the Cranbrook colony in Kent. This offered mutual support and the opportunity to develop new artistic themes and styles. The artists and their families formed strong bonds and were active in the local community, often playing a philanthropic role. They employed local people as models and their spacious well-kept local cottages appeared in many paintings. Their well-balanced compositions used good colour harmonies to offer a romanticised view of the countryside and sentimental images of bucolic simplicity. The Cranbrook style remained enormously popular until the end of the century. Thomas Webster, one of Joseph's teachers was a member. Later, a similar and much better known group of artists with a similar approach lived at Newlyn near Penzance in Cornwall. These colonies were another expression of the gregarious nature of the art world.

This gregariousness amongst artists may have been difficult for Joseph. His bouts of insecurity and tendency to be somewhat shy would have been a barrier to his professional progression.

The quality of art education available

Gillett (1990)'s second question was whether the quality of art education available in England was sufficient to sustain a successful career. When Joseph was considering his future, the Royal Academy (RA) was the leading provider of art education. It was over 60 years old and its educational provision, described in detail in the next chapter, was essentially that laid down by Sir Joshua Reynolds, its first President in the 1780s.

Its provision had been under increasing criticism from many practising British artists, industry, commerce, the military and the Government itself. The burst of innovation and economic development commonly known as the 'Industrial Revolution', created a strong and rising demand for high-order technical drawing skills from the mining, engineering and other science based businesses and Government itself to support the military and administration in the expanding empire, especially in India, Africa and the Caribbean.

Unfavourable comparisons with the German approach to technical and artistic education, training and apprenticeships were highly influential. In 1836 the report of a Parliamentary Select Committee on Arts and Manufacturers made many recommendations in line with the general reformist nature of Lord Melbourne's government. One recommendation was to open a School of Design through which *'the direct application of the arts to manufacturers should be deemed an essential element'*. In response, the Government School of Design opened in 1837 at Somerset House, London. In 1841, as part of a government led drive to promote local schools of design, the College became the Central School of Design. This trained teachers for the provincial design schools as well as direct instruction in drawing, designing and modelling geared to the requirements of trade and manufacture. They also promoted the benefits of a wider appreciation of art by supporting 'art unions', new powers for local authorities to raise a 'rate of up to 1 penny in the pound to establish art galleries; and modest reforms to the Royal Academy Schools (RAS) where Joseph learned his trade.

Despite these reforms artists continued to criticise the quality of fine art education in Britain feeling it to be greatly inferior to that available in France. Richard Redgrave, one of Joseph's teachers at the RAS, recalled that Daniel Maclise when writing from Paris in 1844 said:

> "My belief is that we in London are the smallest and most wretched set of snivellers that ever took pencil to hand and I feel that I could not mention a single name with full confidence, were I called upon to name one of our artists in comparison with one of their."

Reynolds (1966) reports that Richard Redgrave continued his campaign in his reflections on the 1855 Paris Exhibition when he wrote:

> "To pass from the grand salons appropriated in Palais de Beaux Arts to the French and Continental works, into the long gallery of British pictures, was to pass at once from the midst of warfare and its incidents, from passion, strife and bloodshed, from martyrdoms and suffering, to the peaceful scenes of home."

Likewise, Charles Landseer reportedly said *'If people only knew as much about painting as I do they would never buy my paintings.'*

A decade later, Richard Redgrave and his brother Samuel Redgrave (1866) reflected on the nature of training for artists in Britain:

> "It is a peculiarity of art that many men enter the profession entirely self-taught; and these men both within and without the Academy; are largely indebted to their professional brethren for much generous assistance. It is thus alone that true art can progress, every rising genius creating by his originality a new field for himself, not tending in the way of others, but increasing the spread of art to the common advantage of all its professors."

Continued criticism of art education led to a further Parliamentary inquiry in the early eighteen sixties. This time more substantial changes to the RAS and the continued development of art as a practical and academic subject in higher education were proposed. Although these came too late to influence Joseph's initial training, they resulted in a growth in the number of artists with high level drawing skills entering the market as professionally trained artists, engravers, illustrators and critics. These changes, especially the growing competition from the rising generation, had profound implications for Joseph's career that were simply unimaginable at the time Joseph made his basic career choices.

There were other sources of art education beyond the direct control of government or the Royal Academy (RA). These included several important private art schools preparing young men for entry to the RAS where women were not admitted until the 1860s. Joseph attended one of these schools where tutors offered support to aspiring artists principally in drawing and water-colouring skills. While some of this was directed towards professional development, much of it, especially that for young women, was about acquiring skills seen as essential for cultured young adults in middle and upper class society.

Family values, religious belief and a career in art

Another question that arose for Joseph and his family was whether life as a professional artist would be compatible with his strong Christian values. As we have seen Joseph and his parents were strong adherents to the teachings of Emanuel Swedenborg.

Alain de Botton (2012) highlights an important role for art in societies facing a decline in the overall level of religious faith similar to that seen in nineteenth century England. He wrote:

> "[Things start to become clear] … when we consider the relationship between the decline in the teaching of scripture and the rise in the teaching of culture. When religious belief began to fracture in Europe in the early nineteenth century, anguished questions were raised about how, in the absence of a Christian framework, people would manage to find meaning, understand themselves, behave in a moral fashion, forgive their fellow humans and confront their own mortality. And in answer, it was proposed by an influential faction that cultural works might henceforth be consulted in place of the biblical texts. Culture could replace scripture.
>
> The hope was that culture might be no less effective than religion (which was understood to mean Christianity) in its ability to guide, humanize and console. Histories, paintings, philosophical ideas and fictional narratives could all be mined to yield lessons not far removed in their ethical tenor and emotional impact from those taught by the Bible. One would be able to have meaning unburdened by superstition."

An an educated and cultured family, the Clarks would have been aware of the general thrust of the anti-clerical spirit of the age although, as committed Christians, they are unlikely to have approved of the emerging secular thinking. Joseph seems to have been a serious minded young man and as such would have been attracted by a career in art as a way of communicating his deeply held religious convictions and their implications for realtionships within society. From the start of his career, Joseph clearly bought into the view of one function of art was as an educative force within society supporting people in times of distress and encourage others to be take small steps to offer consolation and help. His wider family, like many other similar families, appreciated the potential of fine art, especially genre works, as a moral teacher as noted by Julian Treuherz (1999) to '*convey values of piety, charity, hard work, innocence of children and young love, and the sanctity of family life*'. They evidenced this appreciation in their developing support for Joseph's decision to become a professional artist.

Alain de Botton (2012) says it was clear to many Christians that simply including culture into educational programmes was not the full answer to challenges they faced from scientific method and enlightenment thinking. This realisation, although not necessarily understood in these terms, may have given Joseph a further impetus for embarking on an artistic career.

Joseph's decision coincided with the launch of a long running campaign to make public art collections more easily available to the general public. This advocated both lowering admission fees at certain times in the week and opening galleries at times when working people could visit them. At the time when most working people worked a six day week this the implied that galleries should open on Sundays, something resisted by strict Sabitarians. Several leading New Church members were active supporters of this campaign.

Not everyone agreed. William Wordsworth (1844) was sceptical of the benefits of widening access to galleries and museums. In December 1844 as part of his ultimately unsuccessful campaign against building a railway from Kendal to Windermere in the English Lake District, he wrote:

"The scope of the main argument, … was to prove that perception of what has acquired the name of picturesque and romantic scenary, is so far from being intuitive, that it can be produced only by a slow and gradual process of culture; and to show as a consequence, that the humbler ranks of society are not and cannot be in a state to gain material benefit from more speedy access than they now have to this beautiful region. Some of our opponents dissent from this latter proposition, though the more judicious of them readily admit the former; but then overlooking not only positive assertions, but reasons carefully given, they say 'As you allow that a more comprehensive taste is desirable, you ought to side with us'; and they illustrate their position, by reference to the British Museum and National Picture Gallery. 'There' they add, 'thanks to easy entrance now granted, numbers are seen, indicating by their dress and appearance their humble condition, who, when admitted for the first time, stare vacantly around them, so that one is inclined to ask what bought them hither? But a impression is made, something gained that may induce them to repeat the visit until light breaks in upon them, and they take an intelligent interest in what they behold Persons who talk thus forget that, to produce such an improvement, frequent access at small cost of time and labour is indispensible. …"

Financial security

The next question would have been about the financial security of an artistic career. For all aspiring professional artists, especially those from a family engaged in commerce, this was about whether the artist would be able to support themelves and, in time, a young family.

The first strand in this would have been whether Joseph had the talent, ability and drive to make a success of an artistic career. As we have seen, Joseph came from a family with a tradition of producing and selling intricate artifacts with highly decorative qualities. His talent was encouraged while at William Barnes' school and by his brother's cutter, called David, in the drapery and tailoring business – a trade that depended to a significant extent on a strong appreciation of decorative skills, colour, artistic qualities and an eye for fashion. We do not know who this cutter was though he clearly influenced the decision about Joseph's career. The 1851 Census shows no tailor's cutters in Cerne but there were two drapers assistants to William Henry Clark Jnr. One was Thomas Fernley aged 18, the son of a weaver from Frome in Somerset. The other was Fanny Skermeall born in St Pancras aged 17. There is nothing in the census and other genealogical records to suggest that either had any particular knowledge of the art world. Whoever this person was, they were said to have had some knowledge of the art world and to have advised an art education in London. There were no Davids living in Cerne at the time.

The second strand is financial in its nature. Joseph knew that the demand for works by 'living artists' had grown rapidly in the eighteen forties, partly in response to the tastes of urban middle class art patrons. Fort the first time the 1851 census showed that over half the population lived in urban areas. Many had grown up in the countryside and were attracted by rural scenes produced by artists specialising in contemporary genre. An extreme example of the financial rewards open to leading artists in the 1850s came somewhat later in 1858. William Frith's 'Derby Day' (1858) exhibited at that year's RA Summer Exhibition sold for £3,750 – equivalent to about £2.4m.

A third dimension was the consequences of failure to succeed in the art world. Joseph's home life gave him a good sense of how to manage his personal finances. He also knew that the wider family had the resources to support anyone in difficulty. Joseph's father had left his estate in trust for Susan and her surviving children – William Henry Jnr, Edwin, Mary Susan, Emma Elizabeth and Joseph. Joseph's share depended on the continued success of the family drapery business. The conclusion is that while finaical considerations were important they were far from decisive in Joseph's career choice.

What sort of art should Joseph produce?

Once Joseph and his family had agreed that he should become a professional artist, he needed to decide the type of works to produce. To answer this definitively he needed to understand developments in the art world during the first half of the nineteenth century as well as his own views on the purpose of art. Inevitably such decisions were provisional until he had acquired the basic skills, familiarised himself with the culture of the artistic community and understood current 'insider' thinking about art market trends. As Joseph seems not to have spent much time exploring various possibilities as it seems likely that his decision to specialise in genre was taken at an early stage in his artistic development.

The eighteenth Century inheritance

The leading eighteenth century artists, William Hogarth and Joshua Reynolds, influenced Joseph's choices in different ways. The subjects Joseph chose and their treatment can be seen as building on Hogarth's concern with depicting ordinary people albeit treating them with much greater sympathy, compassion and understanding. Reynold's impact came through the emphasis he placed on attention to fine detail and mastery of the techniques, especially those used during the renaissance and by 'Old Masters' of later centuries.

David Bindman (2008) says that in the second half of the eighteenth century William Hogarth was widely viewed as the first British artist of international renown since the reformation two hundred years earlier. His work remained inspirational for young artists wanting to give their work a spiritual and moral dimension until the end of the nineteenth century. Hogarth frequently captured the tension between vice and virtue in many situations faced by ordinary people. Alongside this he was also noted for savagely satirical depictions of London life, often with highly subversive undertones. Andrew Graham-Dixon (1996) regards Hogarth as the *'guilty conscience of the eighteenth century given to extreme moralising showing that the Protestant imagination was alive and well.'* Hogarth's true legacy was to transform professional artists from subserviant 'servant cum tradesmen' into independently minded crafts people earning their own living largely freed from the domination by overbearing patrons. This created an environment in which artists developed a growing sense of duty to express their own personality, beliefs and perspective on life in their works alongside the challenge of meeting market demands. This allowed Joseph to follow his personal ideas as an independently minded artist.

Beyond that, Andrew Graham-Dixon (1996) views eighteenth century art as understated and well matched to the tone of the age. In his view, mediocre artists worked cautiously and did not enhance their sitter's image. They portrayed their subjects as self-important and confident, as many were. Sir Joshua Reynolds went well beyond this as he specialised in portraits and other works in the 'Grand Style' that sought to idealise the imperfections of reality. One important element in his impact on later generations came from the lectures he gave, and subsequently published, as the first President of the Royal Academy. These lectures formed the basis of the syllabus followed at the RAS by Joseph and others well into the second half of the nineteenth century.

The British School

Hogarth's presence on the international art stage led other nations to take British art seriously and this in turn generated a new confidence in its quality at home. So too did the role taken by Reynolds in the RA's foundation as nurturing practical skills in the classical tradition. This, coupled with the long isolation from the continent between the French Revolution and Napoleon's defeat in 1815, created conditions in which a distinctively British School of Art emerged. This isolation created a generation of aristocratic art patrons who had not formed their artistic tastes through the 'Grand Tour'. Instead they learned to appreciate British art and its preoccupations as seen in the works of Constable, Turner and their contemporaries. The growth of empire in the first half of the century facilitated cultural exchanges beyond Europe, especially with the Orient, that gave a distinctive flavour to the British School.

Once peace returned, opportunities arose for patrons and artists to seek inspiration in Paris which had replaced Rome as the foremost art centre in the early nineteenth century. Renewed exposure to continental art led to a gradual decline of confidence in the British School from the eighteen twenties onwards. This intensified as railways made it easier and less expensive for British artists and patrons to experience continental art for themselves. The rising generation of artists questioned the proficiency of older British artists and developed a strong feeling that British Art was being compromised by materialism and commercialism.

Andrew Graham-Dixon (1996) feels that by the middle of the century '*Victorian conservatism had infected* [art] *with a drowsy dullness of escapism and the tedium of moral earnestness*'. The works could be seen as '*society's attempt to stay sane*' in the face of the chaotic world bought about by industrialisation and imperialism.

Genre tradition in Britain

There was a growth of interest and the social acceptability of genre works in the 1830s and 1840s continuing a trend starting around 1800. Andrew Graham-Dixon (1996) says that these decades saw a rising demand for paintings showing real people in contemporary dress with mothers, fathers and children doing ordinary things. This built on the genre tradition in Holland and Belgium several centuries earlier, and the prominence enjoyed by the French realists in the eighteen forties. Andrew Graham-Dixon (1996) sees Willkie as portraying '*plain lives highlighted by a Wordsworthian sentimentality*'.

Andrew Wilton (2009), a visiting fellow at Tate Britain, in a review of David H. Solkin's (2008) book 'Painting out of the Ordinary: Modernity and the Art of Everyday Life in Early Nineteenth-century Britain', describes this process in detail when he wrote:

> "During the 18th century painting was famously divided into five 'branches of art': the most elevated was history, and below it came portraiture and landscape. Genre painting, the depiction of scenes from ordinary life, came a poor fourth, only just above still-life painting. Around 1800, a noticeable change occurred: scenes of everyday life began to be fashionable; and they maintained their place of importance among the branches of painting throughout the first half of the 19th century—and indeed, beyond. There were several reasons for this, including the curious fact that the libidinous and luxury-loving Prince Regent, shortly to become George IV, collected and even commissioned genre subjects. He patronised a young artist, David Wilkie, who arrived on the London scene in 1806, bringing from his native Scotland an inspired new interpretation of the subject matter of the 17th-century Netherlandish masters Jan Steen, the two David Teniers, and Adriaen and Isaac van Ostade.

The excitement caused by Wilkie's first submission to the Royal Academy, 'Village Politicians', signaled not only a new talent but a general sense that new kinds of subject matter needed to be addressed. The affairs of the common man, woman and child were suddenly seen to be legitimate matter for the painter's brush – an insight owing, in large part, to the 'sentimental' movement that had been growing in Britain under the influence of Rousseau and the philosophers of the Scottish Enlightenment. In addition, the Napoleonic Wars were drawing all strata of society into a general conversation about Britain's role in the world and the position of those strata in a system that was coming under considerable stress. After the wars were over, in 1815, that stress increased: an economic slump and all the discontents that follow a long-drawn-out war created new tensions and the decades that followed were famously unsettled, with rioting in the countryside, battles over Parliamentary reform and the growth of radical politics as a vocal force.

These were subjects with which artists might legitimately concern themselves, and Wilkie provided a language they could use. What had happened was that the genre painters had adopted the traditional formulas of history painting, in which a dramatic situation is narrated through the expressions and gestures of heroic characters, in order to tell stories about ordinary people – what one writer in 1809 called 'the epic of common life'. The perception that 'ordinary folk' represented an important aspect of the national life imbued Wilkie's pictures, and those of his fellow genre-artists, with a significance that carried this 'branch' of painting triumphantly through the first half of the century and into the second.

David Wilkie gave genre a greater psychological depth and narrative content than had been seen previously. Contemporary critics thought many of Joseph's early works had a strong story line and displayed great sensitivity for their subjects. Wilkie's interest in the expression of humankind's inner psychic experience also pointed the way towards the preoccupations of many artists well into the twentieth century. Early critics of Joseph saw him as a potential successor to Wilkie.

Both David Wilkie and William Mulready, another of Joseph's teachers, showed their concern for their subjects in small scale works known as cabinet paintings, presenting wonderful detail reflecting their subject's homespun philosophies. Their milder forms of domestic genre gradually gave way to a harsher aesthetic during the 'hungry forties' with its rampant unemployment and social unrest. In this period artists such as G.F. Watts and Richard Redgrave produced works which were as dark in mood and colour as the events they portrayed. Their approach demonstrated that individual incidents could give expression to universal problems. It is often said that this shift of perspective responded to the tastes of the new middle class art buyers, including many industrialists and prosperous merchants, who favoured pictures they could easily understand and with which they could relate. This created a natural market for Joseph given his middle class background.

Reynolds (1987) makes the point that by the middle of the century Wilkie's interest in the life of the rural peasant began to give way to the cosier middle class urban milleau. Richard Redgrave was one of the first to follow his lead while retaining his keen interest in social problems while others kept to light hearted themes. Later as the enthusiasm for the PRB's approach waned and the economic boom of the 1850s gathered pace, social realism moved in a more poetic direction led by artists including Henry Wallis and Thomas Faed. Faed's work is said to display a sugary texture designed to interest but not challenge the public giving it a powerful capacity to achieve public approval.

England's leading mid–century realist was William Frith, yet another of Joseph's teachers. His work focused on 'pleasant interludes in middle class life'. His most influential work, 'Margate Sands' was exhibited in 1854, the year Joseph became his student. Paintings in this strand of the genre tradition often favoured outdoor scenes with large numbers of figures bought together, for example at the seaside, boating on the Thames or at race meetings, offering a large number of separate narratives. Frith also responded to the vogue in both Britain and France for works showing crowded railway stations. Joseph, like many others, could not afford the investment of time and materials in works on this scale.

Turner (1906) recalled the position of contemporary genre art in the middle of the nineteenth century when he wrote:

> "Genre painting was, and still is, the most profitable vocation for a painter; not the genre painting of Hogarth's famous satires but an enfeebled and genteel imitation of the pictures of the Dutch school … and the subjects chosen are tame and common-place. … Lacking the realism of Teriers, the broad merriment of Franz Hals nor the satiric humour of Steen or Terbourg.
>
> Only Willkie, Leslie, Mulready and Collins rise above the mediocrity and through their keen observation and sense of humour enjoy a reputation which is far higher than they would claim on their artistic merits.
>
> Over the last thirty years, a great change has come over the English School. A far higher standard of technical excellence has been achieved and a deeper and closer insight into natural trust has been attained."

He ascribed this change to the influence of the PRB and noted a renewed confidence in the quality of British Art recovered. Though not mentioned by Turner (1906), Joseph's works exhibited this technical excellence.

Subject matter in mid nineteenth century genre works

The subjects depicted in genre works reflected the emerging values of the early Victorian period including belief in the sanctity of the home; the God-given duty of mankind to pursue a good active life; the importance of piety; and the goal of self-improvement. The dominant theme in genre works was childhood covering issues such as the duties of parents and children in a celebration of what was seen as the 'golden age of childhood', at least for middle and upper class children but not for large working class families living in poverty. Children were often the main protagonists but their actions were underpinned by adult values such as discipline, love, industriousness, child bearing and gender roles. Many depict parental pride and esteem for the achievements of their children. Around one third of Britain's population in the middle of the nineteenth century were children.

Other important themes occuring frequently in genre works in the middle of the nineteenth century included:

- Respect for religion and the love of God, especially through works showing families at prayer (particularly the grace said before meals)
- Charity towards neighbours – widely defined
- Respect for authority of all types in the home, local communities, the state and the church; and for social traditions coupled with implied social criticism and a feeling for reform; church going; education; and greater refinement, virtue and intelligence.
- Working families receptive to religion in an age of growing intellectual doubt amongst middle and upper classes
- Conflict in relationships between rich and the poor
- a strong feeling for the countryside as both a peaceful retreat from busy urban lives and as a symbol of a healthy integrated community with responsive landlords and employers.

As will be seen in later chapters many of Joseph's works touched on these themes and were filled with incident and meticulous detail. They depended on stylistic detail and calculated emotion for their popularity. The Art Journal in 1864 referred to genre as featuring *'trivial incidents both pleasant and unpleasant; and as being sparkling, perspicuous and persuasive'*. The ill-health and death of children often presented in terms of Christian endurance and acceptance was a fairly frequent theme in genre paintings. Many people with a twenty first century sensibility see such works as unfeeling, uninvolved and distant.

Andrew Graham-Dixon (1996) highlighted the view of many genre artists that their fundamental purpose was to stir the social conscience of people and inform them of the realities of life for the poor in an increasingly fractured society. In this, they shared Benjamin Disraeli's view of the world as set out in his novels, especially Coningsby (1844) and 'Sybil, or The Two Nations' (1845) that Britain was comprised of:

"Two nations between whom there is no intercourse and no sympathy; who are as ignorant of each other's habits, thoughts, and feelings, as if they were dwellers in different zones, or inhabitants of different planets. The rich and the poor."

Each artist had his own 'take' on how genre was developing and the issues they wanted to highlight as society adapted to problems and issues within a new sensibility derived from 'Enlightenment' and scientific thinking. Some sought to stimulate collective action to tackle emerging problems while others, including Joseph, focused on individual personal steps of kindness to ease distress.

Richard Redgrave (1866) stressed the moral worth of Genre paintings in their ability to 'stimulate compassion for social injustice'. He and others sought to display a clarity of anecdote and a simplicity of moral appeal that stimulated such compassion. Reynolds (1987) saw these as the characteristic strength and weakness of mid-Victorian genre painting. Late nineteenth and twentieth century critics often confused highlighting the sentiment experienced by people in different situations with excessive sentimentality.

This concern for social justice fitted well with the public mood in the middle of the nineteenth century. Scandals of child labour and lethal working conditions revealed in many official enquiries during the 1840s stirred the public's conscience. In literature, similar themes emerged in the works of Charles Dickens, Benjamin Disraeli, Elizabeth Gaskill and, to some extent, Anthony Trollope. The public mood responded to social realism in contemporary literature and art, and became receptive to measures to regulate conditions in factories, working hours, and the employment of children and pregnant women.

Andrew Graham-Dixon (1996) noted that in some respects genre paintings were an ancestor of twenty first century 'soap operas' in their concentration on ordinary people facing moral dilemmas and for the most part embracing contemporary values. Today's values differ but the message is the same; the heroes come through by embracing society's dominant values and the villains come to a 'sticky end'.

The educative element in British genre painting owes something to the ideas Prince Albert bought to Britain in 1839 including the thinking of the Nazarene school and of German Art more widely. The Nazarene school founded in Vienna in the first decade of the nineteenth century when students left the Academy to found the Brotherhood of St Luke. They hoped to return to art which embodied spiritual values using bright colours drawing their inspiration from artists of the late Middle Ages and early Renaissance. In some senses they were forerunners of the Pre-Raphalites in their use of medieval techniques. The Prince had a strong belief in art's didactic function; a belief shared by Sir Charles Eastlake who was President of the Royal Academy while Joseph was a student.

Before Joseph became an art student, two further developments contributed to the style he adopted.

French influences

During the eighteen forties and fifties, some French artists came to see themselves as being in opposition to romanticism; the philosophy dominating French arts and letters in the late 18th and early 19th centuries. They believed in an ideology of 'objective reality' and rebelled against what they saw as the exaggerated emotionalism of the romantic movement. Truth and accuracy became their chief goals and many of their paintings depicted people at work or in domestic settings. Generally they rendered everyday characters, situations, dilemmas and objects in a 'true-to-life' manner discarding theatrical drama, lofty subjects and classical forms favoured by the romantics. Realism in 19th century art was paralleled by similar movements in drama, literature and opera.

Gustave Courbet was the most influential French Realist and his work 'A Burial at Ornans' produced in 1849–50 was the first statement of the Realist style. Its agenda was taken forward by the Brabizon School from 1849 emphasising the close observation of nature, and by the Hague School from about 1860. Another leading French realist, Pierre Édouard Frère became the leader of the 'sympathetic art' movement; a vein of Realism which portrayed the lower classes sensitively with dignity and charm and glorifying the simplicity of their lives and work. Most of his paintings deal with the life of the kitchen, the workshop and the dwellings of the humble; and many with the pleasures and little troubles of the young. These works did not solicit pity but rather portrayed his subjects with a sense of sincerity and simplicity. Part of his popularity in England after 1855 flowed from John Ruskin's support. Several newspaper critics in the 1850s and 60s drew favourable parallels between Joseph's early works and those of Frere and Courbet.

A third French artist, Theophile-Emmanuel Duverger produced realist paintings noted for their remarkable charm, often portraying children in domestic settings such as the schoolroom or nursery. His paintings received much acclaim at the Paris Salons between 1846 and 1882. He also exhibited in London; and his success and that of Frère may have encouraged Joseph to place children at the centre of so many of his works. The success of the French realists encouraged several of Joseph's teachers to exhibit genre works; a development that in its turn deepened his commitment to genre as his prefered style and steered his choice of subject matter.

Pre-Raphaelite Brotherhood

The launch of the PRB manifesto in 1848 alerted the public to the ferment in the art world just as Joseph was thinking about his career. The leading members of the brotherhood were William Holman Hunt, Dante Gabriel Rossetti, John Everett Millais, William Michael Rossetti, James Collinson, Frederic George Stephens and Thomas Woolner.

Four key declarations capturing their early doctrines were that an artist should:

- have genuine ideas to express,
- study nature attentively,
- sympathise with what is direct and serious and heartfelt in previous art to the exclusion of what is conventional and self-parodying and learned by rote; and most indispensable of all,
- produce thoroughly good pictures and statues.

These principles were deliberately non-specific in their content as the PRB wished to reinforce the artist's personal responsibility to determine their own ideas and methods of depiction. That said their principal intention was to reform art by rejecting the mechanistic approach adopted by the 'Mannerist' artists who succeeded Raphael and Michelangelo. They thought the classical poses and elegant compositions of Raphael in particular had corrupted academic art teaching giving rise to the term 'Pre-Raphaelite'. Timothy Hilton (1970) reports that William Michael Rossetti thought the RA in following the lead set by Sir Joshua Reynolds gave rise to work that was *'lax or skimped in the process of painting … and hence … anything or person of a commonplace or conventional kind'*. They believed that the RAS 'visitor system' added to the laxness in its approach to education and training. Instead the PRB wanted a return to the abundant detail, intense colours and complex compositions of fourteenth century Italian art.

Many PRB works drew their inspiration from medieval themes and literature; or from the Bible and Shakespeare. This emphasis on medievalism alarmed some of the more fundamentalist Protestant elements in the Church of England who were fearful of a 'return to Rome' following the re-establishment of the Roman Catholic hierarchy in England and Wales in 1850. They linked the PRB's interest in medieval themes to the ambitions of the Oxford Movement of High Church Anglicans arguing for the reinstatement of lost Christian traditions of faith and their inclusion into Anglican liturgy and theology. This was an important element in the wider debate on religion during Joseph's lifetime alongside the impact of Darwin's work on evolution.

The PRB's members showed the natural world in detail using bright colours and sharp focus techniques on a white canvas. In their attempt to revive the brilliance of colour found in the fourteenth century, Hunt and Millais developed the use of thin glazes of pigment over a wet white ground in the hope that the colours would retain jewel-like transparency and clarity. Their emphasis on brilliant colours was partly a reaction against the excessive use of bitumen by artists, such as Joshua Reynolds and David Wilkie that produced unstable areas of muddy darkness. These bright colours also reflected the growing impact of the new science of chemistry on the art world. Traditionally artists had mixed their own colours but by the middle of the nineteenth century, new more stable colours were coming onto the market. Although, this was not without hostility from more traditional members of the art establishment, the RA appointed its first professor of chemistry.

The PRB's work and principles were highly controversial until Ruskin's intervention in the debate in May 1851 after which their approach came to dominate critical discussion during Joseph's time as a student. The cohesion of the Brotherhood and its influence started to wain after 1850. Hunt and Millais moved away from direct imitation of medieval art to stress the realist and scientific aspects although Hunt continued to emphasise the spiritual significance of art. He sought to reconcile religion and science by making accurate observations and studies of locations in Egypt and Palestine for his paintings of biblical subjects. After 1860, Millais adopted a looser style influenced by Joshua Reynolds's work and writings.

Many consider the PRB to be the first real avant-garde or experimental art movement in British art. Leslie Williams (1997) offers a detailed examination of the critics' response to the early works of the PRB from a radical, sometimes Marxist, perspective. The essence of this was that the PRB challenged the established order in several important respects. In his view, they used a detailed treatment of the background as well as the foreground whereas many critics at the time held that a proper, praise-worthy painting should differentiate between the more important and less important areas of a canvas. A radical interpretation was that this was undermining the hierarchical relationships were seen as central to the Victorian social order. This was highly subversive in the light of contemporary events in Europe, coming so soon after 1848, 'the year of revolutions'.

Many PRB works and some in the British genre tradition, depicted solitary female figures suggestive of an alternative role for women in society going beyond the conventional subordinate status regarded as the norm at the time. Their works also contained elements for which there was no precedence in the Old Masters or elsewhere. Critics schooled in traditional modes of thought found these hard to accept and saw members of the PRB as 'juvenile' whose art had relapsed into infancy or as 'diseased needing treatment'. Their works also challenged the traditional relationship of the older, wiser reviewer to the younger, less experienced painter. Accordingly some critics ranged themselves on the side of righteousness and railed against 'puerility,' 'morbid infatuation' and 'monkish follies.'

Samuel Carter Hall's Art-Journal (1845) which regarded itself as the voice of the Victorian art establishment proclaimed: '*Conservative by education, habit, and principle, we shrink from the idea of aiding the adversaries of any established institution*'. Arguably, to weaken the Royal Academy was to weaken the power of conservatism and bring on the revolution. The political sensibilities of the early Victorian art world help explain why the members of the PRB and John Ruskin were attacked with such vigor.

Elizabeth Prettejohn (2008) in her article on the 'PRB and the Painting of Contemporary Life' in David Bindman (ed) (2008), said that the PRB manifesto and John Ruskin's later intervention had taken time to find their full expression in portraying contemporary life, largely because the PRB had looked back to earlier Dutch and French influences. John Lucas Tupper's (1850) piece in the 'The Germ' highlighted the difficulties inherent in finding a new pictorial model to achieve this. He argued forcefully that artistic creation must come from life around us and artists should not take the easier route of taking on the poetic associations of subjects from the past. In his view, every artist must acknowledge the best and most creative ideas come from his own times. The Germ was a magazine for the early Pre-Raphaelites. Tupper described himself as a 'physiological Diagramist' in the 1851 census and was the son of the publisher of The Germ (G.F. Tupper). Ford Maddox Brown amongst others responded to this challenge in his works 'An English Afternoon' (1854), 'The Last of England' (1855) and 'Work' (1865).

New technologies

David Bindman (2008) identifies another important development in the art world before Joseph made his career decisions. This was the emergence of much improved printing techniques.

Originally, printmakers used wooden blocks. A German amateur artist, Ludwig von Siegen, invented the mezzotint process in the middle of the seventeenth century. This produced better quality and richer prints using half tones. There was prolonged craze for mezzotint collecting lasting from the mid eighteenth century to the twentieth century. In a further development, aquatint techniques used copper or zinc plates marked by acid to etch a design and rosin to create tonal effects. Publishers needing large numbers of prints or newspaper illustrations used steel plates. These developing technologies played a pivotal role in spreading an appreciation of contemporary art to the middle and working classes in the middle of the century. These new approaches allowed artists meet demands from a rapidly growing audience and take their work to large numbers of people. Many of Joseph's works circulated widely as prints during his lifetime and many continue to be available through internet print shops.

Further decisions

Once the main decisions about Joseph's career were taken, two others followed that were to have a profound impact on his life and that of his mother.

First, it was decided that Joseph should have the best art education and training avilable in England. They chose Leigh's Academy and subsequently the RAS as described in the next chapter.

The second was that Joseph's mother, Susan, and the family servant Jane Scard should accompany him to London.

Susan's decision was not simply about her wish to support her youngest son as he moved towards adult life. The fact that Joseph was her youngest child, his unhappy experience as an apprentice retail pharmacist in Huntingdonshire and that he was unmarried may have been significant factors in her decision. She may also have felt the need to escape the many unhappy memories of Cerne Abbas associated with the death of her husband, father and several children. Especially pressing was the death of Joseph's sister, Emma Elizabeth, in the summer of 1851. By then her eldest surviving son, William Henry Jnr. was running the drapery business in Cerne Abbas and had two young children of his own. The other son, Edwin, was training to become an estate manager in Derbyshire and was unlikely to return to Cerne Abbas. Her surviving daughter, Mary Susan, was about to marry James Payn and they were planning to set up home in Christchurch. Finally, she may have wanted to move closer to the Ellisdons and other friends of her own generation in London.

It is unclear whether the initial decision was intended to be a permanent move or simply to support Joseph as he established himself in London. The exact date of the move is unclear. At the time of the March 1851 Census, Joseph and Susan were still in Cerne Abbas. Research by Graham Clark (2013) into the records of the Cerne Abbas' Overseer of the Poor Rates shows Susan Clark as the sole occupier of the family home on the corner of the Market Place and Abbey Street until the list dated 26 March 1853. By the time of the next list on 29th June 1853 the house is described as 'not occupied'. As Joseph started at Leigh's Academy in the summer of 1852 this may mean that final decisions about Susan's future may not have been made until there was some confidence in Joseph's capacity to settle in this career. So, she may have been living intermittently in Cerne Abbas until spring 1853 when she moved permanently to London.

Joseph stayed with William Ellisdon, his brother-in-law's father, in Englefield Road, Dalston when he started at Leigh's. By the time Joseph became a probationer at the RAS in July 1854, he was living at 6 Hawley Road in Kentish Town with his mother. The move to London proved to be Joseph's decisive break with Cerne Abbas. Although he did not return to live permanently in Cerne Abbas, he remained in close contact with his family there and visited the town from time to time; and in due course took holidays there with his wife and children.

FOUR

Formal Artistic Education

Many young men intending to become professional artists in the middle of the nineteenth century aimed to enter the RAS. Usually they undertook a preliminary period of study at one of the 'preparatory' institutions coaching students to gain entry to the RAS. Joseph was no exception. He had a choice between two main schools – Leigh's in Newman Street just off Oxford Street and Sass's in Bloomsbury.

Sass's Academy

Henry Sass (1788–1844) established the first of these two schools in 1818. Its past students included John Millais and William Frith. As the school prospered Henry Sass entertained the intelligentsia of the day and was friends with Sir Edwin Landseer, William Etty and J.M.W. Turner. Two years before his death Sass passed the directorship of the school to Francis Stephen Cary (1808–1880). Sass was forward thinking and admitted women students from 1832. One of these, Henrietta Ward (1832–1924), went on to found her own art school for women. William Frith recalls his two years as a student boarder at Sass's, where he learned the rudiments of drawing by laborious exercises. This was so resented by one student that he drew a hanged man in the middle of his effort; he was expelled. The UCL Bloomsbury Project (nd) identified an advertisement for Sass's from 1840:

> "School of Design, 6 Charlotte Street, Bloomsbury. Established for the Education of Artists, and Instruction of Amateurs in the Principles and Practice of Drawing, Painting, Modelling, &c, &c; and possessing the most complete arrangements as a Probationary School to the Royal Academy. The Gallery and Studii, an extensive collection of Casts from the Antique Paintings and Drawings, and in the Library, on Works of Art, and Folios of Prints from the Old Masters. There is a separate Establishment for Ladies, and private Studii for those who may desire them. The Gallery is at all times open to inspection, and the Professor may be consulted, and Prospectuses obtained upon application at the above address, any day from twelve to three."

> **Literary Gazette, and Journal of the Belles Lettres**, 5 December 1840

Leigh's Academy

The other main preparatory school for the RAS was Leigh's Academy that originated when a group of students from the Government School of Design unable to tolerate the academic restrictions imposed on them, began to work as a separate class in Dickenson's Drawing Gallery at 18 Maddox Street. In 1848, their school moved to Newman Street with James Leigh as Principal. Leigh's was an unorthodox institution differing from the Government School in providing a broader curriculum, admitting women, not having strict entrance requirements, charging lower fees and adopting teaching methods based on the atelier system used in France rather than the rigorous prescriptivism favoured at the RAS and elsewhere. He allowed male and female students into life classes, had a relaxed teaching

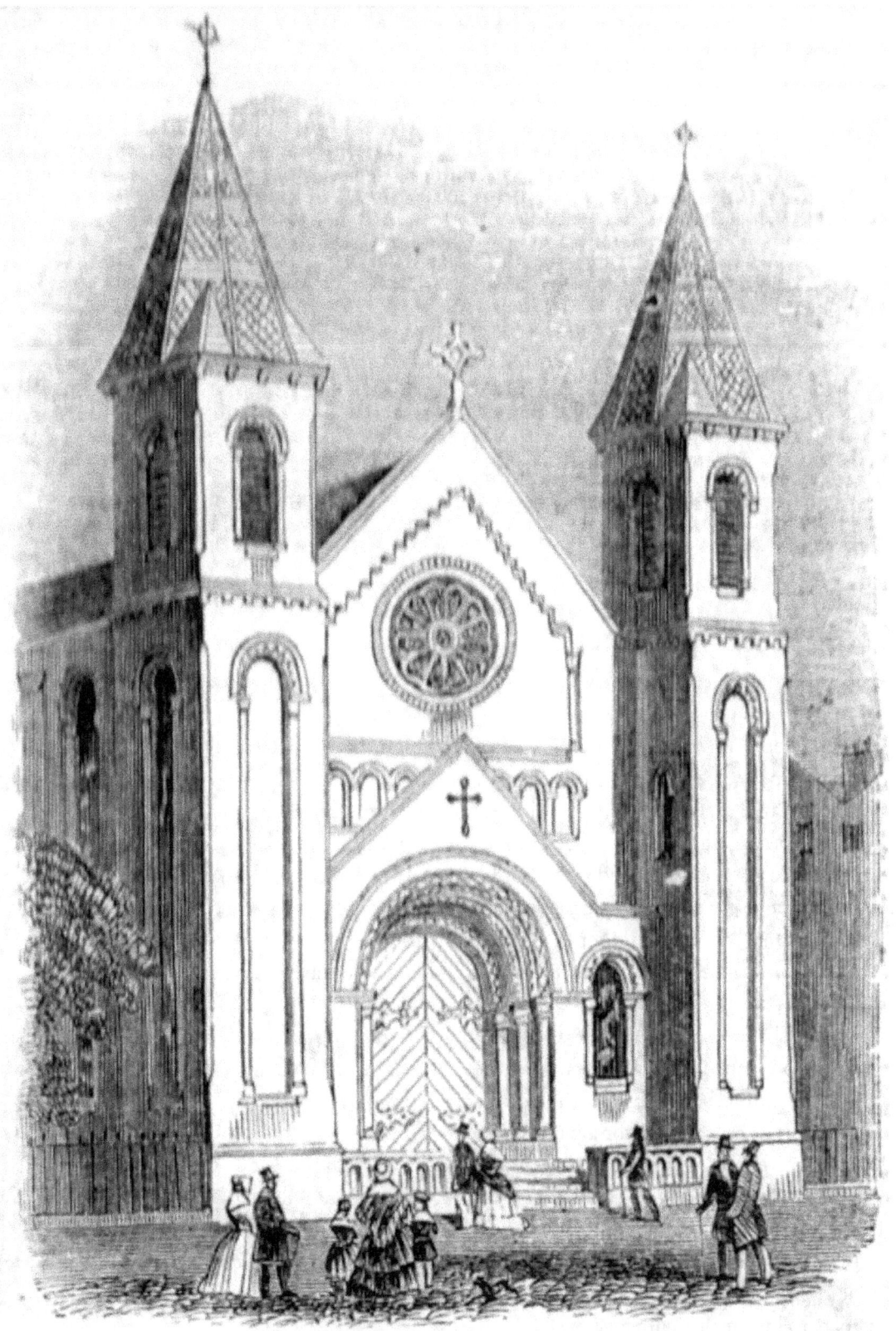

NEW CHURCH, ARGYLE-SQUARE.

1. 'New Church, Argyle Square' (1844). From Illustrated London News 31 August 1844.
(Courtesy of the Swedenborg Society)

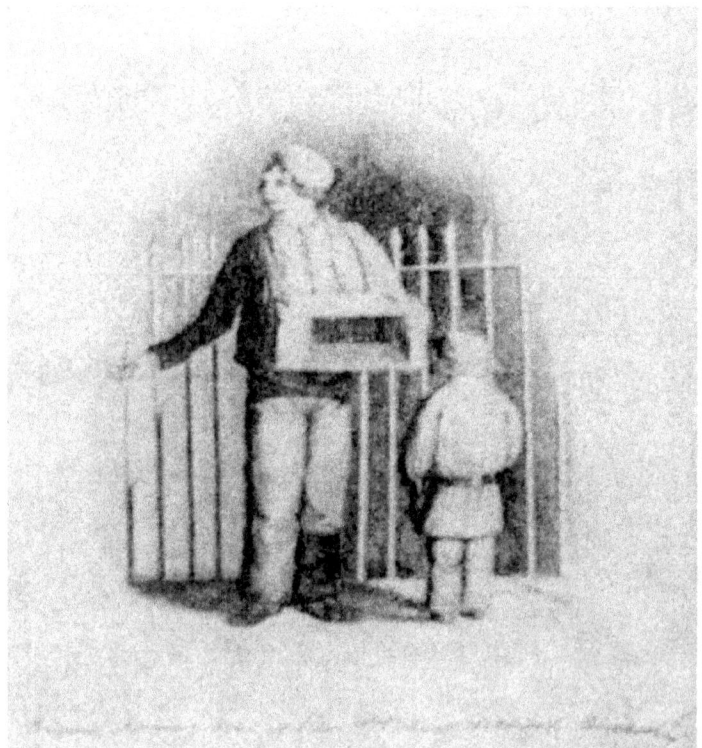

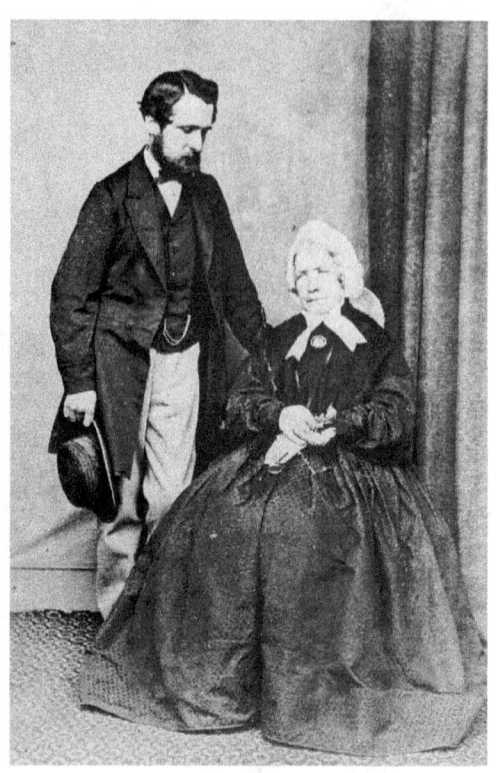

2. Drawing by Joseph Clark while at William Barnes'
school 1845–1848. (Courtesy the artist's family)

3. Joseph Clark and his mother – late 1850s.
(Courtesy the artist's family)

style and fostered high student morale. Many distinguished artists received their early training at Leigh's academy including Frederic Leighton, Philip Calderon, Edward Poynter and Walter Crane.

Under the atelier system, students were encouraged to be experimental in their approach and to form fraternities in which small groups discussed each other's work and learned through a process of critical reflection. An experienced professional artist often led these groups mirroring the educational models used in trade apprenticeships. This promoted practical independent learning focused on the student's personal experience rather than simply reciting the 'right answers' provided by the instructor.

Joseph attended Leigh's between 1852 and 1854. He would have experienced

- 'Sight-Size' methods of drawing and painting that reproduced an object exactly as it appears to the artist on a one to one scale using a variety of measuring tools including strings, sticks, mirrors, levels and plumb bobs. This promoted extremely accurate and realistic drawings recording exact dimensions in preparation for a painting.
- 'Comparative measurement' methods required proportional accuracy primarily using the naked eye while allowing the artist to vary the size of the image created.
- Illusions often taught in conjunction with advanced compositional theory that lead the viewer into believing an image is accurate. As it is not necessary to copy the subject accurately to achieve a successful illusion, this allows the artist to experiment with many options while retaining what appears to be a realistic image.

Paula Gillett (1990) mentions that, Alfred Walter Bayes (1860) the graphic designer, painter, illustrator, photographer and Joseph's contemporary, kept a journal while a student at the school in which he ruminates on a variety of styles and idioms as part of the process of finding his own artistic identity. It has not been possible to locate his journal.

Thomas Heatherley took over the school when Leigh died in April 1860. It is, today, the oldest independent art school in London and among the few to focus purely on portraiture, figurative painting and sculpture. Unfortunately, Heatherley's archives do not contain any documents about Leigh's Academy from the eighteen fifties.

Royal Academy Schools (RAS)

In July 1854 Joseph and three fellow students from Leigh's progressed to the RAS as probationers.

A combination of education, developing a professional culture and exhibiton lay at the heart of the Academy's vision since inception in 1768 as the first institution to provide professional training for artists in Britain. Later, this combination set RAS apart from other arts organisations and provided the foundation upon which it came to dominate the London art scene in the 19th century. When Joseph became a student, the RAS occupied the East Wing of the recently completed National Gallery in Trafalgar Square. George Dunlop Leslie (1914) who became a probationer three months before Joseph set out his recollections of the RAS in his memoirs *'The Inner Life of the Royal Academy'*. He describes the East Wing as crowded and inconvenient but praised the invigorating culture it stimulated amongst the students; and compares it favourably to Burlington House where the RAS has been since 1868. Leslie was the son of an Acadamician and went on to become an ARA in 1868, RA in 1876 and Senior RA in 1919.

The RAS's formal training programme was modelled on that of the French Académie de Peinture et de Sculpture modified to reflect the ideas of Sir Joshua Reynolds. In his fifteen Discourses delivered to students between 1769 and 1790, Reynolds (1841) stressed the importance of copying the Old Masters, and of drawing from casts and life models. He argued that such a training produced artists capable of creating works of high moral and artistic worth.

When Joseph entered the schools its basic programme was set out in the Academy's Laws (1854). Its aims were to *'promote the means of studying the human form in respect of anatomical knowledge and taste of design … through the study of the best remains of Ancient Sculpture and in the study of living models … to which has been added a school of painting'*. The laws also specified the stages through which students passed, the roles of the key people involved in their development and general rules of conduct. All instruction in RAS was free but with probationers and students paying for their own materials.

The hours of attendance varied between schools but were normally for six days a week. Students had three vacations a year – a fortnight at Christmas, some time (varied annually) in March and about three weeks between 1st September and Michaelmas. The early autumn break reflects the medieval tradition in the ancient universities of allowing students time off to participate in gathering in the harvest.

The laws outlined the code of conduct to be followed by Joseph and his fellow students. Highlights included:

> Every student on his admission will be furnished with a copy of the laws … with which he is expected to make himsef thoroughly acquainted that he may at no time plead ignorance, in excuse for any violation of them.

They go on to list specific rules which included:

- Each student must enter his name in the book every time he attends
- No student shall wear his hat in the Schools
- Students shall maintain silence during lectures
- No student shall take away, deface or damage any casts or other property.

The penalties for breaching these rules are not specified, except expulsion for damaging casts in the Antique School or failing to produce the work required in the Life School.

Leslie (1914) offers a rather different picture of discipline in the RAS. He recalls that when William Dyce, the 'visitor' or teacher, left the room dispine would break down. On one occasion, it started with students pelleting classmates with small balls of modelling clay and progressed through a rather unsuccessful game of cricket (because the modelling clay stuck to the bat) to a dramatic performance using the models's props. This all came to an end when Bob – the school porter – entered the room. The following morning William Dyce called the students a *'set of boobies who could not be trusted'*; and the day after he apologised to the students for his intemperate language. It is likely that Joseph was one of these boobies; perhaps even a ring leader in the cricket match given the Clark family's strong interest in the game.

The RAS laws governing admission said that applicants *'should be of such a proficiency as will enable him to draw or model well prior to admission'*. For people wanting to become painters had to submit a chalk drawing two feet high of an undraped antique statue for consideration by the Academy's Council at their January or July meetings – and a reference attesting that it was the work of the applicant. An average of 20 probationers were admitted each January and July.

Joseph was accepted as a probationer in July 1854 as one of twenty nine young men, including about ten intending architects and sculptors. The RA archives provide details of who provided the recommendation for entry for about half of Joseph's contempories. Joseph was one of four probationers recommended by J.M. Leigh.

'Painting' probationers entered the Antique School conducted by the Keeper – the Acadamician responsible for the day-to-day running of the RAS. Leslie (1914) recalls that Charles Landseer, the Keeper between 1851 and 1873, was a slightly deaf good-natured man with a loud staccato voice who found it difficult to keep order amongst the boisterous students and as a result a 'curator' was appointed to maintain discipline.

Each probationer had three months to deliver a set of at least six finished drawings of groups or figures prepared within the Academy. The times of the probationer's attendance were between ten in the morning and three in the afternoon. Probationers also had to obtain certificates from the Keeper verifying that they had undertaken these works and that they had attended the required lectures; one full course in perspective and two consecutive programmes of lectures. Signed registers provided the evidence for the Keeper's Certificate.

Joseph clearly progressed as expected as his work was presented to the Academy's Council on 19th December 1854. The RA archives show that he was one of nine probationers admitted to the Life School on that occasion; and the only one of the four probationers from Leigh's admitted in the previous July. The progression was marked by the receipt of an ivory ticket from the Keeper. Students were admitted for a nine year term; this being an eligibility rather than a course length in the modern sense. Few students spent the full nine years at the RAS. The Council members participating in the decision to admit Joseph were Sir Charles Eastlake (President), Charles Cockerell, Frederick Pickersgill, William Marshall, William Frith, Abraham Cooper, Thomas Webster and Philip Hardwick (the Academy's Treasurer). This procedure bought rising talents to the attention of the leaders of the profession at an early stage. Most later participated in Joseph's education acting as 'Visitors' during 1855 or 1856. Joseph started as a full student in early 1855 and as he progressed through the two schools and came into contact with four groups of office holders.

The Painting School

In the Painting School, the students painted entire fully clothed figures, often in historical costumes, reflecting an important strand in British art in the late eighteenth and early nineteenth century.

The Life School

The Life school was open from ten in the morning until three in the afternoon; and again from five till seven in summer (and eight in winter).

The Life School Visitor set the model who was required to maintain the pose for two hours. RAS used a number of different models in the Life School who were reasonably well paid, judging by the amounts shown in successive minutes of Council meetings. G.D. Leslie (1914) recalls that time was kept by a large hourglass. When a model signalled the need for a rest the hour glass was laid on its side and returned to the upright position once the pose had been resumed. Typically a model sat for three or more nights. Wallis (1957) describes Frith's experiences of the Life School a few years before Joseph was a student there. At the time it was held in the central cupola of the National Gallery, known as the 'pepperpot' by the students. The model posed at one side of the room with students in a semicircle working opposite with positions determined by ballot.

Wallis (1957) says that Frith recalled that he once observed that a nude female model in an apparently easy pose had tears falling down her cheeks. Some months later a very respectable looking model was refered to him by a friend. He recognised her as the tearful model who on questionning said that she had posed 'that way' to keep her father out of prison for a debt of £3 10s 0d (about £300) but had not done so again.

The Academy Laws (1854) showing some sensitivity to the situation of female models said *'None but a member of the Academy or Students of the Life Schools shall be admitted when a female model is sitting'*. Joseph, unlike some of his younger contemporaries, was allowed to draw from female models as the laws went on to say *'nor shall any student under twenty years of age (unless he be married) be allowed to study.'* from a female model.

Each year students in the Life School had to present a Certificate of Attendance from the Keeper along with a drawing or painting from a live male model. If approved by Council the student was permitted to continue for a further year.

The President

The President of the Academy whilst Joseph studied there was Sir Charles Eastlake who displayed both the attributes needed by any President of the Academy as identified by Frith and included in Wallis (1957). In his view the President needed to be both a successful artist and a successful orator. The skills of oratory allowed the President to mix with the 'great and the good' whose influnce was necessary for the continued success of the Academy. Oratorical skills were also necessary for the President's address to the students on the 'Prize Day' held annually on 11th December, the anniversary of Sir Josuha Reynolds's birth. Frith saw success in oratory in terms of being learned, eloquent and not too long. Many Presidents published their collected annual addresses but Eastlake seems not to have done so making it difficult to know what Joseph might have learned from him and thus his influence on Joseph's work. Each prize day medals were awarded to the most promising students but Joseph did not receive any medals during his time as a student.

Visitors

Each year, the Council appointed eighteen 'visitors', nine each for the life and painting schools – although some served in both schools simultaneously. The visitors were Royal Academicians (RA) who attended for a month, setting the models and examining and instructing the students. Most had themselves studied at the RAS. The Council believed this system gave students access to wider range of skills, interests and points of view than would have been available if tuition came from a single full-time teacher. It avoided undue influence by any particular visitor or promotion of specific point of view. Visitoirs also helped students to absorb the 'professional culture' necessary for success in the art world and gave them a growing network of colleagues able to offer support as their careers developed. Visitors also facilitated access to private art collections and introduced promising students to potential patrons and art dealers.

Not everyone thought the visitor system worked well. Stuart Macdonald (1970) wrote of the *'wise neglect of the Visitors in the 1850s'*; and quotes a contemporary view that 'from old men such as these we derived little or no benefit in our studies'. Some of the visitors were equally sceptical. William Frith (1877) in his 'My autobiography and Reminiscences' wrote

> "A newly elected RA finds himself elected into offices for which he may or may not be suited. He becomes a teacher in the Life and Painting Schools … It is well known that some of our best painters are the worst teachers. Landseer used to say 'There is nothing to teach'. I have heard one of the most eminent Academicians say – in answer to reproaches for his neglect in not attending at the Painting School – 'What would be the good? I don't know anything; and if I did I couldn't communicate it' Maclise said to me, when as a student I was copying a picture by Reynolds, 'I can't teach you anything. I am here to take a lesson myself'.
>
> It certainly appears to me that the system of what is called teaching by visitors is altogether wrong; as, from the varied and often contradictory character of the advice tendered, the student finds himself in a condition of helpless bewilderment."

The list of visitors working in the schools while Joseph was a student gives some insight into the experiences and styles that helped shape Joseph's approach later in his career; and gave him the opportunity to develop a network of influential colleagues.

The visitors during Joseph's student days, omitting sculptors, were:

Abraham Cooper (1787–1868) ARA 1817, RA 1820 and a leading painter of racing, battlefield and historical subjects. Today he is best known for his cabinet pictures of contemporary genre subjects, often of mothers with children.

William Dyce (1806–1864) Probationer 1825, ARA 1844, RA 1848 A painter of portraits and religious subjects. With Redgrave he played a leading role in reforming art education and in shaping the cirriculum followed by Joseph.

William Powell Frith (1819–1909). ARA 1845, RA 1852. He exhibited at the RA from 1840 to 1902. After the PRB launched its manifesto he recognised that his only chance of acquiring lasting fame was through paintings of modern life (Reynolds 1987).

Solomon Alexander Hart (1806–1881) Exhibited RA (1826–1881); ARA 1836; RA 1840; Visitor 1855 then Librarian. He specialised in historical and biblical genre works on a large scale.

Charles Robert Leslie (1794–1859) RAS 1811 (Two silver medals); ARA 1821; RA 1826. He specialised in historical genre works and wrote a Handbook for Young Painters.

Daniel Maclise (1806–70) RAS 1828, exhibited RA (1829–1870), ARA 1835, RA 1840. Offered but declined the RA Presidency (1865). He painted portraits and historical genre works from literary sources, many with a harsh and dull colouring. He may have influenced Joseph's palette that attracted frequent press criticism from the early 1860s onwards.

William Mulcready (1786–1863) RAS 1800, exhibited RA (1814–1862), ARA 1815, RA 1816. A major genre painter in the style of Wilkie. His close relationship with the leading genre painters in the first half of the century makes it likely that Joseph would have been especially open to his ideas and suggestions.

William Henry Pickersgill (1782–1875) RAS 1805, ARA 1822, RA 1826, Librarian 1856–64. Pickersgill was an eminent portrait painter.

Richard Redgrave (1804–1888) RAS 1826, exhibited RA (1825–1883) ARA 1840 and RA 1851. From 1840 onwards he concentrated on contemporary social subjects and pioneered the switch from Wilkie's style to the expression of domestic emotions.

Sir William Charles Ross (1794–1860) RAS 1808 (Silver medal 1810), ARA 1838, Knighted 1842, R.A 1843. He was an eminent painter of minatures.

Thomas Webster (1800–1886) Exhibited RA 1823–1879: RAS (gold medal 1824); ARA 1840; RA 1846. A popular and prosperous genre painter especially of school children with some portraits early in his career.

Over half of the RAS visitors in the mid eighteen fifties were associated with contemporary genre. Joseph followed the path they created in featuring children at the heart of the action in the narrative embedded in their works. As Joseph did not have the resources or reputation needed to produce large-scale works, he concentrated on small-scale works with no more than a handful of figures. Several visitors also had a strong reputation for portraits that also had a place in Joseph's repertoire.

The average age of visitors was fifty-seven – two were under fifty and three in their seventies. Typically, they had been full Academicians for just under twenty years with five having served for over thirty years. Eight became academicians in their thirties and six in their forties. This means that the views they conveyed to the students drew on their experience in the eighteen thirties and forties. Reynolds (1953) believed that their writings demonstrated that they adhered to the commonly held view in early nineteenth century; that art styles could be arranged in decreasing degrees of excellence from 'high art' through historical works to portraits, landscape and paintings of contemporary scenes to still life studies'.

Professors

In addition to regular practical work in the schools, probationers and students attended regular lectures given by the Academy's four professors. Each had to deliver six lectures a year. Charles Robert Leslie (1860) refers to a letter of 2nd November 1847 in which he wrote:

> "Since I wrote this letter I have been elected Professor of Painting to the Royal Academy, by a unanimous vote. My business will be to deliver six lectures annually, which will be rather an amusement than a trouble, and for which I shall receive £60 — £10 for each lecture."

£10 in 1847 is around £800. C.R. Leslie (1856) published his lectures under the title 'A handbook for young painters'.

The professors working between 1855 and 1857 were:

Painting – **Solomon Alexander Hunt** (1806–1881) who was also a Visitor.

Perspective – **John Prescott Knight** (1803–1881) was a student from 1823 and exhibited between 1835 and 1881 at the RA and at the British Institution. He became an ARA in 1836, RA in 1844, Secretary (1847–1873) and Professor of Perspective (1852–1860).

Sculpture – **Sir Richard Westmacott (Snr.)** (1775–1856). Sculptor. Studied under his father before going to Rome to study under Antonio Canova. Returning to London he set up his own studio and brass foundry. He became an ARA in 1805, RA in 1811, Professor of Sculpture in 1827 and was knighted in 1837.

Anatomy – **Richard Partridge** (1805–1873). A surgeon who rose to be President of both the Royal College of Surgeons and the Royal Medical and Chirurgical Society. He was a skilled draughtsman, having taken drawing lessons from his brother, John Partridge, and an able lecturer and teacher. He was the professor of anatomy at the Royal Academy from 1852 to 1873.

George Dunlop Leslie (1914), Joseph's contemporary, recalls that Richard Partridge was the most popular professor amongst students during his time in RAS. Partridge was assisted on his lecturing platform by a male model named Westall, who would sit in the nude, demonstrating the muscle groups. The platform itself was decorated with 'gruesome anatomical diagrams' and the RA's skeleton 'swinging from a ring in its skull'. Partridge also allowed students to visit him at the Kings College Hospital in the early mornings so they could watch and draw dissections. He believed this helped students to improve their understanding of anatomy and thereby their figure drawing skills. Partridge also encouraged visits to RAS by former students, in particular the leading members of the PRB.

Students were unlikely to have had much contact with the three associate professors. Their biographies suggest that although they had a good knowledge of ancient history, antiquity and ancient literature respectively, they may have been appointed largely because of their power and influence amongst politicians and the social elite, perhaps fulfilling a role occupied by trustees of large predigious charities in the 21st century. The three associate professors in the mid 1850s were Sir Robert Inglis MP (Professor of Antiquity), Harry Hallam (Professor of Ancient History) and Thomas Babington Macaulay, 1st Baron Macaulay (Professor of Ancient Literature).

Joseph's experience

Joseph, like other students of the time, sold his works at minor exhibitions and auctions. Some students also undertook rapidly produced works, known as 'pot boilers', exclusively for commercial reasons rather than from any artistic impulse or academic purposes. The highest price Joseph received for a 'potboiler' at auction during his student days was £4 17s 6d (£3,180). We do not have details of this or other 'pot-boilers' he produced whilst a student. Some students saw a steady flow of new works as essential in building their reputation, especially amongst the middle classes who were avid buyers of contemporary genre.

Shortly after Joseph became a full time professional artist, the Academy Council decided to prohibit the sale of student works undertaken in the RAS. In part, this reflected the view that the commerciality of the art market endangered standards while some more elevated members saw 'pot boilers' as deeply demeaning to the profession. A century earlier, James Boswell (1791) records that Dr. Johnson rebuked similar 'ivory-tower' attitudes in literature with his comment that *'no man but a blockhead ever wrote, except for money'*. Did this apply equally to painters of Joseph's generation?

As noted earlier, Joseph was admitted to RAS for nine years but like most of his contemporaries did not attend for anything like this length of time. We do not know exactly when Joseph stopped attending the life and painting schools and associated lectures; or whether this was sharp change in his life or a more gradual transition. It appears that after the critical success of his first exhibited work in 1857, he concentrated on producing works for exhibition and sale.

While the RAS provided support in developing a high level of technical skills, a good understanding of the underlying philosophy to contemporary art, a grounding in the classics and a range of contacts in the art world, Joseph needed to do much more to establish his reputation as a serious professional artist. In a sense all professional artists in the nineteenth century had embarked on a lifetime of learning as will be apparent in the later chapters.

PART II

Working Artist

FIVE

Getting Started in the Art World

Becoming a professional artist in the nineteenth century required Joseph Clark to make several important choices once he had developed his technical skills and formed important contacts amongst leading artists. As already noted in Chapter 3, when Joseph made his career choice, he saw the potential of genre works to communicate his values and beliefs to a wide audience while earning a reasonable income. His art education confirmed this choice.

Continuing his professional development

Joseph had embarked on a lifetime of continual professional development by viewing high quality work by others in galleries and exhibitions; understanding how the art market worked; building his reputation with art patrons, buyers and critics; reading critical reviews; and harnassing the talents and support of a network of material suppliers, models and engravers.

Joseph was not alone in his decision to become a professional artist. When he was starting out, there were some 4,643 Artists in England and Wales according to the 1861 census. Twenty years later, the total had reached over 11,000. In both years, the great majority of these artists were male, and lived and worked in London.

The art market was in flux in the middle of the nineteenth century, reflecting the growth of the middle class art patronage, London's growing role as the principal global art-trading centre and changing technologies. The central question for the new artist was how to bring their work to the attention of potential buyers, critics and connoisseurs. To answer this question, they needed to know how the art market worked, who the key participants were (patrons, critics, dealers, auctioneers, models and others) and how to maximize their income.

This chapter looks at how Joseph and his contemporaries approached this at the start of their careers. Later chapters trace subsequent developments in the art world and Joseph's response.

How did the art world work?

It would be wrong to think that there was a single art market in nineteenth century England. Rather the art world had a diverse range of institutions, each with its distinctive ethos and experiences for artists, buyers and others. It is convenient though simplistic to identify two main art worlds, each made up of distinctive, often antagonistic, institutions, and an emerging third art world that came to dominate academic thinking about art before the end of Joseph's career.

The first was the 'traditional' fine art world adhering to the values, styles, subjects and traditions originally set by the classically educated well travelled aristrocratic art patrons of the eighteenth and early nineteenth centuries.

By the middle of the nineteenth century a second 'realist' art world was well established catering for the needs of middle class patrons who tended to favour modest 'cabinet' sized works dealing with familiar subjects; and embodying their values and livestyles in paintings displaying high level technical skills.

Just over the horizon was a series of 'avant garde' art movements concentrating on works trying to capture the artists immediate response to the inner essence of their subjects using innovative methods. Each of these worlds used new materials and technologies, albeit in different ways and contexts.

During his time at Leigh's and the RAS, Joseph and his fellow students immersed themselves in the traditional fine art world; absorbing its values; understanding and keeping up with market trends; learning about the high profile controversies of the day; and establishing potentially valuable networks helping his career and artistic ambitions. What did they find?

Access to high calibre art

As a professional artist, Joseph experienced the wide range of high calibre art available in London.

Permanent collections

Weale's (1854) handbook of London lists about 40 permanent displays of fine art in a variety of settings open to the public. These were spread across the capital but congregated in the elegant prosperous parts of the West End including Piccadilly, Park Lane and Carlton House Terrace.

There were several distinct types of collection on view with almost half in the 'town' houses of the aristorcracy. Few allowed unrestricted public access. In some cases admission was by means of a letter of introduction from a well known 'artist or distinguished personage'. Joseph had ready access to such introductions through RAS 'visitors'. Elsewhere, housekeepers in the London homes of aristocratic families had a profitable 'sideline' in showing visitors the houses and their art treasures when 'the family' was not in residence. This also happened in the aristrocracy's country houses; something seen in Jane Austen's novels and reenacted in several National Trust properties.

Access to art in both town and country properties was far from easy as mentioned by James Stourton and Charles Sebag-Montefiore (2013) in their work on British art collectors. Angus Trumble (2013) in his review of this book in the Times Literary Supplement writes:

> "Referring in 1844 to great English country houses with notable collections of Old Master paintings, Anna Jameson wrote: 'I know not for my own part, more than one or two isolated instances in which admission was refused to an artist or stranger who came properly introduced, or whose name was known'. On his epic tours of inspection in the 1830s, however, Dr Gustav Waagen was often tormented by key-jangling housekeepers hovering at his elbow, poor light, and out-of-date lists, inventories and wall diagrams. Accessibility was a problem, and information often scarce."

In London, a further five collections in houses belonging to well-to-do private citizens were open to the public. Works from the royal art collection were on display in Buckingham Palace, Kensington Palace, Hampton Court, Windsor Castle and St James Palace. Here, in the early part of Victoria's reign, access was easier than to aristocrats' homes and no charge was made. Later access was restricted in part because of attempts on Victoria's life.

High calibre art was also shown in various public collections including the National Gallery, British Museum and Dulwich Galleries. Two educational institutions had galleries open to the public: University College and the Government School of Drawing. Beyond this, other public bodies shared their art collections with the public. These included The Guildhall, The Banqueting House on Whitehall, Chelsea and Greenwich hospitals (homes for retired ex-military men); and the Foundling and Bridewell Hospitals. Contemporary Art could also be seen in the recently constructed Parliament buildings, and in many of the capital's Churches and Cathedrals. Ecclastical collections were in addition to those listed by Weale (1854).

General directories were not the only source of information about art collections available to Joseph and his contempories. Anna Jameson (1842 and 1844), a well known feminist and lady of letters, prepared detailed guides and catalogues of works in the principal collections. In her 1844 guide to private collections, she said:

> "I have at least endeavoured to be accurate. I say, endeavoured, for as to achieving complete accuracy, those alone can tell who have tried how difficult is the mere attempt; those alone who have tried what it is to hunt a fact, misstated, through a dozen volumes – to trace a name misspelled – to ascertain a date – to decide between opposing authorities – to compare disputed points – or, hardest of all! to knock down a charming theory or a pretty story with a dry row of figures – to take from some favourite picture its pretension to authenticity, and stick a doubt or a lie on the face of it."

At roughly the same time, Mrs Russell Barrington (1906) reports that the young Frederic Leighton, aged 15, wrote to his mother giving his impressions of various London galleries.

> "… I will now tell you rapidly what I have seen; Vernon gallery, very much gratified; Dulwich Gallery, very much disappointed; British Institution, ditto; National Gallery, pictures magnificent, locality disgraceful, I must make another visit there; Royal Academy, on the whole, satisfactory; British Museum, very fine; Mogford's Collection, very indifferent; Marquis of Westminster (Mr. Laing), very fine indeed; private collection (through interest of Mr. Moffat) delightful; Windsor, Vandyke, superb; Lawrence, a wretched quack."

So it is clear that Joseph and his contemporaries starting out as professional artists had a wealth of good art from which they could draw inspiration, generate new ideas, learn new techniques and meet others in the art world.

London's 'Exhibition culture'

The galleries listed by Weale (1854) were permanent art venues. Most of the works on display had stood the test of time. For the aspiring professional artist, further inspiration and access to the art buying public came from temporary exhibitions, mostly of contemporary works; though there were occasional retrospective shows somewhat similar to today's 'block busters'.

The number and size of these temporary exhibitions grew in importance through the second half of the nineteenth century with a dramatic rise in the number of exhibition societies, galleries, artists' professional societies and sketching clubs. They became known as London's 'exhibition culture'. Some idea of the scale of this comes from *The Western Daily Press* (10 April 1876) that suggested some 16,000 paintings were shown in London each year. A University of Glasgow (2006) study documented over 3,000 exhibitions and 900 galleries operating in London between 1878 and 1908. The numbers in the late eighteen fifties when Joseph started out were smaller though still substantial.

As well as being good places to see contemporary art, the major exhibition societies also offered a range of other services for professional artists, art buyers and the public.

The Royal Academy (RA) was the elite society maintaining its leading position in Victorian England. Other societies saw themselves as providing an alternative by offering exhibition spaces freed from the 'bureaucratic constraints' imposed by the Academy's view of art, its traditions, and old fashioned ways of working. Consequently successive generations of young artists tried to challenge the RA's standing. Many of the newer exhibition societies had open memberships and held regular public exhibitions; although several introduced rigorous selection, processes intended to uphold the quality of work on display. The major societies provided a good platform for young artists to establish their reputations. Several offered drawing classes, studios where patrons could sit for their portraits, and lectures and debates on various aspects of art and culture. Some specialised by medium (watercolour, drawing, photography, etching or decorative art) and others catered for groups marginalised by the RA's rules including water colourists, photographers and women. Joseph had links with several exhibition societies.

Although Joseph exhibited at the RA throughout his career, he did not became an Academician or Associate. Membership was limited to forty-two artists drawn from the leading sculptors, printmakers and architects as well as painters. The election of new Academicians took place each February until 1881 and thereafter twice yearly; with the numbers elected depending on the death or resignation of existing incumbents. Candidates for full membership came from the Associates (ARAs). After 1866, there was no upper limit on the number of ARAs but a minimum number was set at twenty. Until 1876 when the minimum number rose to thirty, there were few new ARAs.

The RA does not have records of any discussions prior to the nomination or election of new academicians or associates. Seemingly, existing academicians did not nominate Joseph for election. There are several possibilities why this might have happened. The obvious one is that academicians did not consider his work to be of sufficient quality to justify nomination. This is unlikely as he had works accepted for almost every Summer Exhibition between 1857 and his formal retirement in 1910. As described in later chapters, he was also the first artist to have two paintings acquired by the RA using the Chantrey Bequest funds. Another possibility is that he refused to allow his name to go forward. Some family members recall he refused a state honor towards the end of his life. A third interesting possibility is that he was born at the wrong time. As most ARA appointments came to artists in their early forties, Joseph might have expected to be a candidate around 1875. In the early eighteen seventies Joseph was a newly married family man, probably somewhat reserved and possibly disinclined to spend the time or energy on the 'RA's internal politics' needed to become an associate. Interestingly, few artists born between 1825 and 1834 ever became associates. In fact, only eight artists born in this decade became associates compared to twenty born between 1835 and 1844. Only three of Joseph's contemporaries at the RAS became RAs.

Early in his career, Joseph exhibited regularly at the 'British Institution for Promoting the Fine Arts in the United Kingdom' widely known as the British Institution. A committee of art buyers and prominent critics selected around 500 works for display each year and awarded prizes; with surplus funds used to buy paintings for the nation. In addition to daytime opening, there were private showings in the evenings, allowing exhibitors to meet potential patrons, critics and collectors. Many saw it as a stepping-stone towards having works accepted by the RA. Many waited years before exhibiting at the RA, although it took Joseph just three months.

Several sources suggest that Joseph was also involved in organisations catering for water colourists, especially the New Water-Colour Society founded in 1831, in competition with the older Royal Watercolour Society. Both challenged the RA's refusal to accept watercolours as serious art and held their exhibitions at the same time as the RA. There is no hard documentary evidence of Joseph's participation in their exhibitions although his friend, Francis Oliver Finch exhibited regularly as will be seen in the next chapter.

The other main exhibition society was the Society of British Artists based in Suffolk Street. Joseph did not exhibit there until 1865 and exhibited three further works before becoming a member in 1875.

Following James Whistler's appointment as its president in 1876, Joseph resigned. Its standing with middle class art lovers is apparent from this report from 1875:

> "The Society of British Artists seems to be the favorite resort of the Art Union prize holders, furnishing no less than 88 pictures, or about 4 to 1 from the Academy, which afforded only 28. The new British Institution comes next in popularity, supplying just one more than the Academy; the Crystal Palace Gallery 11, the Water Colour Societies, 6 and 9 respectively, and other exhibitions only one each."
>
> **London Daily News** 12 August 1875

The number of exhibitions and the fraught relationships between them led to intense competition. The Illustrated London News on 7th June 1856 reported that there were six important exhibitions open to the public at the same time. These were those of the New Society of Painters in Water Colours; Society of British Artists; the Royal Society of Painters in Water Colours; the National Institute of Fine Arts, the Royal Academy; and a temporary Exhibition of the French School of Fine Arts. A good list of exhibitions can be found on the University of Glasgow's Faculty of Arts website (nd). Joseph seems to have restricted himself to the British Institution and the Society of British Artists.

The growth in the number of societies and exhibitions through Joseph's career was a manifestation the public's strong interest in art and of the gregarious nature of the increasing number of painters, critics, auctioneers, material suppliers and gallery owners.

One-off exhibitions

Another source of potential inspiration, development and useful contacts for professional artists was a series of major one-off exhibitions. As mentioned earlier, we know Joseph attended the Great Exhibition of 1851. The large surplus it generated helped establish new fine art, engineering and technological museums in South Kensington.

Between May and October 1857, The Art Treasures of Great Britain exhibition took place in Manchester. It remains the largest art exhibition ever held in Britain with over 16,000 works on display. We do not know whether Joseph joined the 1.3 million visitors, many of them arriving on railway excursions arranged by Thomas Cook, the pioneering travel trade entrepreneur. The selection and display of works in the Art Treasures exhibition had a powerful influence on the municipal public art collections being established at the time, as well as on the National Portrait Gallery and emerging plans for the South Kengsington Museum (now the Victoria and Albert Museum).

Municipal Galleries

Mention has already been made of the powers given to local authorities in 1841 to raise local taxes to fund public galleries. Marina Vaizey (2015) 'In the Public Eye' review in Art Quarterly of Giles Waterfield (2015) 'The People's Galleries: Art Museums and Exhibitions in Britain 1800–1914' (Yale 2015) describes how local government used their powers through Joseph's lifetime who wrote that the:

> "… astounding spectrum of regional galleries that were initiated throughout Great Britain in an amalgam of philanthropic, idealistic, philosophical, commercial and self-serving reasons from the Age of Enlightenment through the industrial revolution until the beginning of the First World

War. By the end of the nineteenth century, every self-respecting city in the country had a public art gallery and museum.

… These extraordinary happenings were part of a new pattern of the mediation of culture in its broadest terms, moving from the private to a public sphere. … In 1888, Birmingham City Art Gallery drew a million visitors, a number greater than the city's population. The great and the good of the city were on record as working towards a 'beautify and civilise life' for all the people.

… Attitudes towards making permanent collections also varied. The promotion of the National School was important, while the new art galleries, that often bore the name of the chief patron, tended to host selling exhibitions for local art societies and local artists. Overwhelmingly popular as these ephemeral exhibitions might have been, and thus distracting from more solid aspirations, we are reminded that two primary purposes were paramount: to entertain and instruct.

… Originally, there were very few staff for these institutions, and very limited funds for the buildings themselves. … Throughout the period, a slow emergence of curatorial skills began to develop. By the 20th Century, the emphasis was on art for art's sake. … Throughout the 19th century the promotion of the National School and antipathy in the regions not only to the Old Masters but to anything foreign was a potent characteristic of of many of the new galleries, while the galleries themselves acted as a school room for the masses; both aspects were ferociously denounced by the metropolitan elite.

… the arguments – and tensions – of the period … are still being rehearsed today about social class, education, inclusion, access, art for art's sake, audiences and, above all, funding and money. In microcosm, these debates and discussions are about not only the role and obligation of government, central, regional and local, but of the obligations and role of different strata of society."

Joseph did not seem to make much impact on the new municipal galleries in promoting his works. He did, during one of his stays in Winchester in the 1880s, exhibit at a local exhibition. Today the majority of his paintings available for public viewing are in municipal galleries.

Building a reputation in the art market

All professional artists were anxious to build and maintain their reputation amongst critics, colleagues, patrons and the public.

One consequence of the 'exhibition culture' was the enormous attention paid to leading celebrity artists by the press. They became, in some respects, the equivalent of the show business and sports celebrities in the early twenty-first century. The 'A list' of artists were feted by the aristocracy and royalty; their works were collected by rich and powerful patrons; they received enormous fees; and their lives were subjected to frequent, extensive and sometimes intrusive press coverage. During Queen Victoria's reign there was a spectacular rise in the wealth and prestige of leading English artists and designers, particularly those living in London. Many of those at the peak of their careers lived lavishly in attractive suroundings indulging in the type of 'conspicuous consumption' seen amongst newly rich merchants and industrialists.

Russell James (2011) captures the broad range of lifestyles facing professional artists when he said:

"Long before Victoria died the nation's top artists, like modern pop stars, were fabulously rich, lived in mansions, and surrounded themselves with luxury. They were household names. Outside the top bracket, artists struggled or starved; some drank themselves to death, some overdosed on drugs, others died lonely and disillusioned. ... Some had tangled love affairs, a few of which were played out and lapped up by the public. And most artists, for all their dilettante lifestyle, worked far harder at their craft than they let on; many were more commercial than they let on; they had managers, agents, supporters and promoters; and they displayed their talents in prestigious venues. They were in the entertainment business."

This sums up the popular public stereotype of artists' lifestyles. Joseph was not a nineteenth century 'A-list' celebrity, a dilettante or involved in scandals. Nor was he the poverty stricken garrett dwelling struggling artist of popular imagination. As will be seen in later chapters, Joseph remained true to his 'middle class' origins throughout his career. This provided him a good income and a comfortable though not lavish lifestyle.

Changing patterns of Art Patronage

Traditionally, art purchases by royalty, wealthy aristocrats and the Church played a leading role in shaping the art market and sustaining the livelihoods of artists.

In Britain, the role of the church was much weaker after the reformation in the sixteenth century and the rise of puritanism in the seventeenth century. The demand for religious art revived somewhat during the rebuilding of City Churches after the Great Fire of London in 1666, the spread of non-conformist chapels in the eighteenth century and the opening of new Anglican churches and cathedrals in the nineteenth century. The role of aristocratic patrons declined in the early nineteenth century and that of wealthy middle class manufacturers, merchants and the Government grew in importance.

Queen Victoria and Prince Albert were committed art patrons adding many paintings and sculptures to the Royal Collection. In addition to purchases from leading artists, many from Continental Europe, they collected hundreds of watercolours and photographs of their growing family, the chief events of the reign, the places they visited and royal residences.

Trevor Hearl (1996) in describing a difficult time for William Barnes writes:

"1859 can be seen as a year of hope, as well as anxiety, and even the school had a moment of success. In January, Queen Victoria set a fashion by purchasing the work of his former pupil Joseph Clark who although only 25 had already exhibited at the Royal academy."

There is no citation for this reference and there is no record of this in the contemporary press, the Royal Archives or the Royal or Government Art Collections.

Victoria and Albert were keen amateur artists receiving instruction in drawing, painting and etching. Though Victoria was keen on art, she was more reserved about artists. In 1845, she advised King Leopold of Belgium to be *Beware of artists. They mix with all classes of society and are therefore most dangerous'*.

An artist's acceptance by wealthy private patrons in the traditional fine art market depended not just on talent and creativity but also on being accepted socially as a 'gentleman'. Being a 'gentleman' in the middle of the nineteenth century required both a good general education in the history and literature of anquity, and the means to live in a gentlemany style. Prior to 1860 few artists had the education or funds to gain social acceptance, though there were notable exceptions who moved easily in London 'society'. Wallis (1957) says William Frith was member of two clubs – The Athenaeum and The Garrick – where he was able to mix socially on equal terms with many potential art patrons. The RAS were unable to do much about the money needed to live as a gentleman but the curiculum followed by Joseph and his contemporaries included history with a strong emphasis on antiquity – in Joseph's case building on the foundation he received at William Barnes' school.

By the middle of the nineteenth century, important shifts in the pattern of art patronage were apparent to all:

> "The ground of art patronage – not long since a narrow and almost exclusive domain – is, year by year, expanding, and admitting a fresh class of occupants. They who, on the ground of position, assumed formerly to be authorities and influencers in the matter of Art are no longer the most forward to afford that real assistance without which the mere loan of a name to an association for the maintenance of a picture gallery, or to the superintendence of the decorations of a national palace, is little better than a dead letter. It is a striking enough feature of the times, that to the class which in some of the best ages of art contributed the impulse and the means on which it fed, we are again returning for the real nourishment of the eternal cause. The wealthy merchant, manufacturer and trader are now the artists' most constant and liberal patrons. The walls of the present [Royal Academy] Exhibition abound in the proofs of this fact; and many a private dwelling in our manufacturing districts of the North furnishes the means of renewing our acquaintance with works which were leading attractions of well remembered Exhibitions gone by."
>
> **Bulletin of the American Art-Union**, 1 July 1849

These shifts were clearly unwelcome to some associated with the traditional fine art market who demonised them as a 'democratisation of the art world'. As J.B. Atkinson (1862) pointed out in Blackwood's, a conservative leaning journal:

> "Patronage is now not solely in the sovereignty of the state or in the power of the church, but in the hands of the people. Palaces and churches in these days call for fewer pictures than the private dwellings of merchants and manufacturers."

Conservative minded critics in Blackwood's and the Art Journal found these changes in patronage particularly disturbing. Their attacks continued for over a quarter of a century. In 1868, the Art Journal claimed:

> "The power of the British Press has been as great as that of the Royal Academy, and it has been much more abused"

It linked this abuse by the press to the presence of a new uninformed audience for

> "… writing upon a subject the alphabet of which was unknown to general readers, an unintelligible jargon was substituted for knowledge, and the amount of technical slang was taken as the standard of critical acumen … empty phrases still characterized its method. … Formerly critics shook their heads at pictures and pronounced the 'carnations diluted,' or the 'empasto destitute of force'; that the handling wanted breadth, or that the chiaroscuro was imperfect, and people were expected to wonder at such knowledge and such skill. Now critics tell us, the Art Journal complained, that the pose is 'too pronounced,' or 'not pronounced' enough; the colour is not 'articulated'."

In other words, critics had exchanged the catchwords of the aristocratic connoisseur for a pretended knowledge to impress the new middle-class audience. One of the severest criticisms levelled by conservatives was that a work was vulgar, by which they meant not only that it was without taste but that it spoke too much to the people or on their behalf. Holman Hunt was a particular target. Although The Art Journal (1858) had to admit that Frith's 'Derby Day' was 'the picture of the season', it emphasised that its tone was 'vulgar and no supremacy of execution can redeem it'.

Rather than recognising opportunities for a new art, they saw only the democratic destruction of what they took to be an aristocratic culture in the fine arts. They saw the practice of exhibiting one's paintings to attract patronage as dangerous, for as Frederic Harrison (1888), explained in his 'A Few Words about Picture Exhibitions':

> "An Exhibition is necessarily more or less a competition, and a competition where for the most part the conspicuous alone catches the public eye. Il faut sauter aux yeux, and that in the eyes of the silly, the careless, the vulgar, in order to be popular."

Harrison also pointed out that exhibitions prevent the spectator from seeing paintings in their proper setting, and he refers to the French Salon with scenes of rape and murder as examples of the ends to which the need for exhibitionistic sensationalism had bought artists. The need to command public attention, according to J.B. Atkinson (1885) had made:

> "the arts pander to sensation, and like popular politics, obtain applause by realising through low expedients the greatest happiness of the greatest number ... [The Royal Academy] by increasing its 'exhibition space ... is acting the part of certain politicians who lower the franchise, let in the flood of democracy, and with the consequent multiplication of constituents, open additional voting booths."

Furthermore, as J.B. Atkinson (1862) observed, changes in patronage necessarily produced important changes in the kinds of work artists painted, for now ...

> "small cabinet pictures of homely subjects had become the general rule, while commissions for monumental art, history painting, and what the critics took to be other aristocratic forms became increasingly rare – so rare, in fact, that when Parliament decided to decorate the new House, it had difficulty in finding men who could properly execute these commissions."

He continued by complaining that

> "... art, in common with other products of genius, had descended from her high pedestal to become popular in sympathy and secular in spirit. ... Thus, the people, both for evil and for good, have, throughout Europe, grown into a power, and pictures, accordingly, are made to pander to the wants of a dominant democracy. Painters paint down to the level of the multitude."

Clearly Joseph was one of the culprits as many of his works were small cabinet pictures of homely subjects appealing to the multitude.

Three years later in Blackwood's review of 'The London Art-Season' Atkinson (1865) lamented that '*in these days too little of ideal beauty, too little of scholarly culture, too little of gentlemanly refinement*' traditional fine art cannot survive. It was not only the prevalence of homely portraiture and domestic scenes which troubled him, but also the fact that realist styles, including the Pre-Raphaelites, had triumphed. Two years later in 1867 he complained

> "Imagination, has well nigh been driven away from her favourite haunts, and ... the domain of art is now delivered over to the dominion of the senses."

Private patronage

Wealthy private patrons continued to play an important role in the Victorian art world through their purchases from dealers, at auctions, and by commissioning works direct from artists. At least three of their collections passed into public hands during Joseph's career to form the core of important national collections at the Tate Gallery, The Wallace Collection and the South Kensington Museum.

The closest most artists of Joseph's generation and standing came to benefiting from wealthy private patrons was through the commissioning of occasional portraits. As we will see later, Joseph exhibited several portraits of family members and acquaintances of a similar social standing to the Clark family. We cannot be certain about the precise role portrait painting played in developing his reputation as many portraits quickly become treasured family heirlooms and are not displayed publicly, sold in auctions or through dealers; or circulated through modern prints.

The growth of Government patronage

As the century progressed the Government took an increasing interest in art. Previously the state had intervened by granting royal charters to self governing organisations such as the Royal Academy. After the report of the Parliamentary Select committee in 1836, the Government developed a more interventionist stance so that by the eighteen eighties there were upwards of one hundred and thirty local art shools with at least three hundred thousand art students. This compares to just a thousand when Joseph was a student, mostly on fine art courses.

Another stimulus, mentioned earlier, for government's engagement with art was the need for high quality work to adorn the new Palace of Westminster following the destruction of the old Parliament buildings in the fire of 1834. In 1841, a Parliamentary Select Committee started to commission new paintings and sculpture. The committee's work continued to provide a stimulus for art during much of the eighteen forties and fifties.

The prominence given to fine arts at the International Exhibitions of 1851 and 1862 boosted the public expectation that Government would play a growing role in the arts. New public galleries and art colleges meant that, by the time Joseph was became a professional artist the Government, nationally and locally, was a major patron of the fine arts. Sadly none of his works found their way into National Collections and only a few into municipal galleries.

A new form of art patronage – Art Unions

A new form of art patronage emerged following the 1836 Select Committee report. They recommended setting up Art Unions as joint associations to buy contemporary art. Most art unions decided which works to buy but the Art Union of London (AUL) placed the decision in the hands of its members. The annual membership fee of a guinea (roughly £82), less administrative costs, went to individual members selected by ballot. They received a 'coupon' that could be exchanged for art works in five London exhibition societies – the Royal Academy, British Institution, Society of Artists and the Old and New Watercolour societies. In addition to the chance to win a 'coupon', each member received an annual report and at least one specially commissioned engraving a year. In London, members could opt to receive a medal mostly with images of great artists instead of a voucher as part of the AUL's policy of encouraging interest in the medallist's art and British die-engravers. Other prizes awarded from time to time included etchings, bronzes and Parian (porcelain) figures.

Unlike commercial sources, the AUL did not simply reproduce the most popular pictures of the day. Instead, its governing Committee sought to foster a taste for traditional fine art by distributing good quality prints of works it saw as the best examples of historical and literary painting. In a series of bound prints issued during the 1840s and 1850s. These combined a highly abstract outline technique with patriotically British subjects to promote a greater appreciation for 'simplicity of composition' and 'purity and correctness of drawing'. These stimulated the market for the technically competent realist works.

The Art Unions quickly became a simple and effective form of private art patronage for the middle classes. Joy Sperling (2002) in her 'Art cheap and good' reviews the history and impact of the AUL. In 1837, its first year, revenue was £480 (£36,900) which by 1842 had increased to almost £13,000 (£950,000) as its membership rose to 12,000. By 1850, there were thirty Art Unions in Britain and Ireland. The AUL's membership peaked at just over 20,000 in 1876.

William Thackeray writing in 1844 lamented that *'Alas, it is not for art they paint, but for the Art Union.'* The success of Art Unions resonated with the 'self-help' ethos of the era. Indeed Samuel Smiles, the Scottish radical, best known for his self-help writings, was a member of the AUL's governing council. The AUL's leadership came from a group of passionate young social reformers and Members of Parliament who wanted to harness the power of middle class and traditional aristocratic patrons. This policy seemed politically and culturally unassailable at a time of great political and social uncertainty. The AUL's leaders believed that significant economic, moral, social and cultural benefits would arise from introducing the middle and industrial classes to fine art. They saw art as a civilizing and refining force alongside Parliament's more utilitarian ambitions. This approach had helped to shape an art market that would be receptive to Joseph's educative ambitions and his strong religious and moral beliefs.

The AUL was successful in its dealings with members while it had mixed relationships with artists, institutions and publishers. This reflected the potential risks to their position from changes in the public's artistic tastes and buying habits. Its relationship with the RA was particularly problematic from the outset and many established critics, including John Ruskin, were actively hostile.

The primary challenge the AUL faced was the claim that it cultivated mediocre tastes and stimulated the production of mediocre art. Sperling (2002) points out most coupons were exchanged for works from RA or British Institution exhibitions; with historical works predominating amongst the larger prizes; and modest sized landscapes and genre paintings by relatively unknown artists for smaller prizes. We do not know if any prizewinners used AUL coupons to buy works by Joseph, although he undoubtedly benefited from the general stimulus given to the market for his type of work.

Richard Redgrave thought the AUL forced artists to produce small low-grade realist pictures appealing to its middle class members. Sperling's (2002) analysis of the thirty-four engravings offered between 1838 and 1859, shows that eighteen were from paintings by academicians and eighteen were of historical subjects, six of landscapes (including one by Turner and nine of contemporary genre (including two by Frith). Thousands of works of art were purchased; and many hundreds of thousands of visitors attended the annual exhibitions of works chosen by AUL winners; or received engravings of contemporary art. Alison Inglis (2011) highlights the AUL's influence in spreading good quality art well beyond London including Britain's colonies. However, she believed the long-term impact of the AUL on English art and the London art market to be relatively small.

Despite the AUL's commitment to a radical reform of the London art world, it failed. Like the art establishment, it could not visualise an independent middle-class taste going beyond the 'correct' traditional tastes of the aristocracy. However, for a brief period, it created a space in which aesthetics, economics, technology, and communication bought together the interests of the artistic elite and the new middle classes patrons. It was in this period that Joseph became a professional artist.

Art Criticism and writing

Ambrose Bierce (1842–1913) the American editor, journalist, short story writer and satirist once defined painting as '*the art of protecting flat surfaces and exposing them to the critic*'. In this he captured something of the pivotal role many thought critics played in the nineteenth century art world. Undoubtedly their role grew with rising newspaper readership; increased literacy rates; and rising 'disposible incomes' available to spend on 'luxury' goods, including art. In 1871, the Royal Academy recognised the growing importance of press critics when it introduced a Press Day ahead of the opening of the Summer Exhibition.

When Joseph became a professional artist there were three main strands in writing about art:

- The newspapers and general periodicals, including the relatively new illustrated magazines, focused on reports of exhibitions and other major events, especially those involving the 'A list' celebrity artists. As today journalists and the public loved confrontational arguments, novelty and stories of 'bad behaviour' by well known people. Although there was a good deal of scandal in the nineteenth century art world, none of it involved Joseph. However, as we will see later, two of his works featured strongly in the long running controversy over the RA's management of the 'Chantrey Bequest'.
- Some writers with a strong conceptual perspective wrote for the 'quality press' and specialist art journals. These writers like today's critics based their criticism on aesthetics or the theory of beauty in the hope of providing readers with a rational basis for appreciating art. Many of the writers were well known and many came from wealthy upper middle class backgrounds similar to those of private art patrons. For the most part they had a university education and some had travelled widely to the main art centres in Europe. Some moved between writing, academic positions and managing the new public galleries and collections. Fierce debates arose between these writers reflecting, in part, the fundamentaly different ideological perspectives of those favouring traditional fine art and realist art in the battle for the hearts and minds of the middle classes.
- Finally, there were large numbers of books on art-related subjects including many biographies of 'A list' celebrity artists; studies of masterpieces; lives of renaissance and later painters; manuals devoted to artistic techniques and iconography; and extensive treatises on aesthetic and critical theory.

Press criticism

At the start of Joseph's working life art critics wrote for a variety of media. Among the national papers extensive coverage of fine art appeared regularly in the Daily Telegraph, London Daily News, Manchester Guardian, Financial Times, Sunday Times and the London Standard as well as in the numerous widely read local and regional papers. A good example of the scale of the importance they gave to art can be seen in the coverage the London Daily News's afforded the 1869 RA Exhibition. This appeared on four successive Saturdays and totaled 10,000 words. While the art editors of the main papers were well known, many reports were unsigned making it difficult to establish the critic's credentials, trace their effect on public sentiment or establish their impact on individual artists. A number of general interest magazines, such as the Illustrated London News, Blackwood's, Punch and The Athenaeum, also covered art in some detail.

Newspaper critics commented regularly on Joseph's works throughout his career and their views are quoted in later chapters. We do not know what Joseph thought of critics generally or their views of his work. Artists of all generations have uneasy relationships with critics while recognising their impact on artists' reputations or potential patrons. Artists also felt that the views of people who have not experienced the rigors of an artistic training and the difficulty of translating concepts into pictorial representations were suspect.

In reading critics comments on Joseph's works and those of other artists, we need to be mindful that all critical judgements are provisional. It is commonplace in every age to take critics of earlier times to task for either favoring artists now long forgotten or for dismissing artists now rated highly. Perhaps Joseph's early works fall into the first category as they were favoured by his contempories but are now largely forgotten.

Imogen Hart (2014) in her review of Katherine Haskins's (2012) work on the Art Journal argues that prints influenced the reception of paintings in significant ways. She shows that prints built reputations, cultivated taste and mediated interpretation. The Art Journal played a central role in the Victorian art world by packaging 'art knowledge' and making it available in many middle-class homes. She also argues that The Art Journal's commitment to 'patronage-as-patriotism' bolstered the idea of an 'English School' by showcasing works by English artists, often those associated with the Royal Academy. As will be seen later, Joseph's early works appeared in the Art Journal and contributed to his career progression. Haskins (2012) argues that we can only understand the Victorian respionse to certain paintings if we take into account the way they were mediated by prints published in The Art-Journal.

Advice for young artists on critics

Painters of Joseph's generation were not short of advice about how to deal with critics. John Ruskin (1859) offered this advice to young artists on critics:

> "It may not be out of place to warn young painters against attaching too much importance to press criticisms as an influence to their fortunes. If sharp and telling, it is a disagreeable thing to look at, when just damp from the type; and it is certainly in an unpleasantly convenient form for one's friends to carry about in their pockets. But, ultimately it is quite powerless except so far as it concurs with general public opinion. I have never yet seen a bad picture crushed by criticism, much less a good one. The sale of a given work may, indeed be checked or prevented, but so it may by a whisper or a chance touch on the elbow. I have seen more mischief and definite injury done to property in ten minutes by an idle coxcomb amusing his party, than could possibly be done by all the malice in type than could be got into all the journals of a season. The printed malice only makes people look at a picture; the fool's jest makes them pass it.
>
> I repeat therefore, to the young painter, in all distinctness and completeness, this assurance: Do your work well, and no enemy can harm you. So soon as your picture deserves to be bought, it will be bought. If, indeed you want to live by your art before you have learned it; or to sell what you know to be worthless, by catching the fancy of the purchaser; or to display your own dexterity, instead of pleasing them: in each and all of these cases you must take the chances of you speculation, or the penalty of your presumption. There are, indeed, some things you may preach without presumption; only, do not expect to be paid for your sermons: for people will pay richly for being pleased – scarcely, if at all, for being rebuked."

Wallis (1957) in his edited version of William Frith's 'My Autobiography and Reminiscences' (1887) and his 'Further Reminiscences' (1888), highlights advice to young artists. Presumably, this advice featured in conversations with his students in the RAS.

"I would here advise all artists, young and old, never to read art criticism. Nothing is to be learned from it. Let me ask any painter if, when he wants advice on any difficulty in the conduct of his work, he would seek it from and art critic – No, I reply for him; he would apply to an artist friend. But though, as I believe, no advantage accrues in any case to an artist from public criticism, much undeserved pain is often afflicted, and even injury caused, by the virulent attacks that sometimes disgrace the press. For very many years – indeed ever since I became convinced of the profound ignorance of the writers – I have never read a word of art criticism."

Frith's daughter, Mrs. James Panton (1908), echoes this in her 'Leaves from a Life' when she tells us:

"Papa never read any criticisms, good, bad or indifferent, and remarked, very truly, that as long as his pictures sold as they did, what people said about them mattered nothing at all to him, and I am certain he said what he meant and thought. But I am sure that neither Ruskin nor Stephens, of The Athenaeum, could have had the least idea how their ridiculous censure pained his wife and family. … But Ruskin never hurt Papa, who had actually to give evidence in the celebrated Whistler – Ruskin case, in which Whistler was awarded a farthing damages."

Wallis (1957) reflects this point of view when he writes:

"Enduring, surely, at least in mellow retrospect, Frith's perfect faith in public approval, and his equally firm belief that all art critics were either knaves or fools, conceivably possessing some literary grace, but never in the least (so he was persuaded from youth) anything of the processes and problems of painting."

What did critics write about?

Attention to artistic technique or the fine details of a painting were comparatively rare in early Victorian press criticism. In practice, critics preparing reports of major exhibitions faced with hundreds of works could only mention a few. Even then, one sentence often mentioned several works by a single artist and many reports of major exhibitions focused on just 20 or 30 works. Occasionally critics used scurrilous invective to gain the reader's attention but generally, they contented themselves with a brief description of the painting, its subject or the narrative conveyed.

J.B. Atkinson (1859) clearly hated and feared John Ruskin as one who had created a *'civil war of opposing parties* [who] *threaten the empire of Art with hopeless anarchy'*. Atkinson, John Eagles and other conservatives clearly found the claims of Ruskin and the rising school of young painters particularly upsetting, in part because they themselves had led an earlier revolution in taste. John Eagles writing in Blackwood's Magazine championed poetic landscape as part of its attack on the traditional primacy of history painting and supported the claims of the cultured upper-middle-class man to patronise learned relatively informal art appropriate to his taste and position in life.

Right at the end of Joseph's career, Arthur Clutton-Brock (1919) offered a collection of essays on art including one on the function of critics. In this, he challenged the views of Sir Thomas Jackson (1835–1924), a leading architect, who saw critics as people who told people what to think based solely on their reputation. Clutton-Brock (1919) argues this is to misunderstand the role of art critics. In his view, critics have a general interest in art and their strength lies in their ability to express this interest. Although they offer judgments, the value of their criticism lies not in the judgment, but in its formation. Its real value lay in power of expression to provoke thought rather than to suppress it. In good criticism, judgment is implied rather than expressed. He saw the proper subject matter of criticism as the critic's experience of art. The best critics experienced art so intensely that their criticism is a spontaneous expression of this experience. The critic tells us what has happened to him and readers should expect to share a similar experience. None of the reports of Joseph's work came close to his model of critical excellence.

John Ruskin

John Ruskin (1819–1900) was the leading English art critic and writer of the Victorian era as well as being an art patron, draughtsman, watercolourist, prominent social thinker and philanthropist. He was hugely influential in the middle of the century. His work ranged from art and architecture to geology, myth to ornithology, literature to education, and botany to political economy. He wrote over 250 works reprinted in the 39-volume 'Library Edition', collected by his friends Edward Cook and Alexander Wedderburn, published between 1906 and 1912. In all his writings, he emphasised the connections between nature, art and society.

Ruskin came to widespread attention with the first volume of 'Modern Painters' issued in 1843. This extended essay was a defence of J.M.W. Turner's work in which he argued that the principal role of the artist is 'truth to nature'. From the 1850s, he championed the Pre-Raphaelites who he saw, as *'a new and noble school of art that would provide a basis for a thorough going reform of the art world'* while emphasising that *'art must be an expression of the artist's whole moral outlook'*. On the 24 May 1856 Punch published a short ditty:

> "I paints and paints,
> Hears no complaints
> And sells before I'm dry,
> Till savage Ruskin sticks his tusk in
> Then nobody will buy."

Many people offered advice to intending artists. One of the more entertaining items came from John Ruskin's response to an invitation to address art studernts in Chesterfield. It displayed his approach to art and money, and much else in contemporary life:

> "Characteristic letter from Mr. Ruskin. At a distribution of prizes to the art classes of Chesterfield, last night, Lord Edward Cavendish presiding, an extraordinary letter was read from Mr. John Ruskin, in answer to one asking him to deliver a lecture in that town. Mr. Ruskin says – 'I could not if I would go to Chesterfield, and doubt whether I would if I could. I do not hire myself out, like a brainless long-tongued puppet for filthy ducats. You want me to make money for you. Then you will tolerate advice. Hath not Chesterfield a steeple abomination, and is it not the home of that arch abomination-creator Stephenson? To him we are indebted for the screeching, howling, shrieking fiends, fit for pandemonium, called locomotives, that disfigure the loveliest spots of God's land.'
>
> After giving the students advice, Mr. Ruskin continued 'My good young people, this is pre-eminently the foolishest notion you can get into your empty little eggshells of heads – that you can be a Titian, Raphael, or Phidias. But because yon can't be great, that is no reason why you should not aspire to greatness. Don't study art because it will pay, and don't ask for pay because you study art. Art will make you all wiser and happier, and is worth paying for. This advice is better than money'."

Liverpool Mercury 12 November 1880

The steeple abomination is the famous crooked spire at the town's parish church. Today, the railway station forecourt has a statue of George Stephenson who pioneered passenger rail transport and spent his retirement in the town.

Who supported artists to produce and bring their works to market?

Many see art as the creation of an individual artist working alone. In reality, professional artists depend on a wide range of others to bring their creative ideas to the audience. The exhibition societies and art critics played an important role in this. Other collaborators included fellow artists; artist's material suppliers; models; dealers, auction houses, engravers and print makers.

We know little about Joseph's closest associates in the art world. Clearly, he knew his contemporaries at the RAS whether they became professional artists or moved into associated fields such as engravers and print makers. These included Henry Storey Marks, Samuel John Hodson, Philip Hermogenes Calderon and Francis Black most of whom became prominent members of the St John's Wood group; although there is no evidence that Joseph was part of this or any other group. We know he had close links with artists who were fellow Swedenborgians.

Artists' suppliers

With over 4,000 professional artists working in London in the eighteen fifties, and numerous amateurs, the demand for the 'tools of the trade' and materials was considerable. The Post Office London Directory for 1852 shows almost 100 businesses specialising in meeting the needs of artists, and many more who supplied artists' requisites alongside a wider range of products. Fifty of these specialists were picture frame makers and about thirty were 'artists colourmen'. In previous centuries artists, or more usually their apprentices, made and mixed the paints they needed. By the middle of the nineteenth century many artists bought their materials from specialist dealers although some 'traditionalists' continued to argue that better works came from artists who made their own pigments. Amongst the colourmen working in London were several brands that survive into the twenty first century including Windsor & Newton, Reeves and George Romney. Some of these businesses also supplied the wide range of pencils, brushes, crayons and charcoal; although there were a handful of specialist pencil and brush makers too. There was at least one specialist artists' canvass maker and two 'artists repositaries', presumably renting storage space and arranging safe carriage for paintings.

Models

Joseph, like others in his generation with a formal art training, had been taught to paint from life. This created a market for men and women of different ages and classes willing to endure long hours holding a specific pose as the artist struggled to bring his artistic conception to fruition.

Many artists recalled in later life the ardous nature of modelling. Russell James (2011) makes the point that relatively little attention has been devoted to the lives of artists'models apart from those working with the PRB. They may not have been ypical of the models used by artists like Joseph with more conventional lifestyles, ambitions and aspirations. Many models worked for several artists. Careful examination of Joseph's works show that some models appear in several works; some in works from different decades.

In the 1850s, the 'going rate' for professional models was around one shilling an hour (about £6.15 – roughly equivalent to today's Living Wage). Models came from a range of backgrounds and many had other occupations.

Frederick Goodall (1902) reflected on the importance of models, mishaps and the use of family members:

"No one but an artist knows the supreme importance of procuring the right model for a principal figure in a composition. Sir John Millais always seemed as if he secured his model before beginning the picture, as a rule, and sometimes the model suggested the subject. Millais never began his picture until he was perfectly sure of getting the right model for it and even the dress. ...

Then there was John Tropp, who had a baby drugged to keep it still. Of course, I would not have allowed him to do such a thing if I had known what he was about, much as I prefer a still infant. This was the incident. I was painting a sleeping infant on the lap of its mother, in one of my pictures. The baby was brought asleep to me, but after it had been asleep for a couple of hours I suddenly saw the mother looking anxiously into its face, and tears drop from her eyes. At last she exclaimed, 'I think John has given it too much sleeping stuff. That made me feel alarmed. I am afraid it won't wake anymore,' she said to me. But to our delight it did wake, squalled, and happily proved none the worse for the dose John had given it. This John Tropp was often in prison for begging in the streets ...

I must not forget that my sisters served me as models, for as a youth I never had a professional model at all. Our servants sat to me; so did the watchman who shut me in his box, and the turn-cock; in fact, any one I knew, including a young brother, who was very useful to me and posed well. My sisters, who had French blood in their veins, were most willing models, and many artists wondered where I got the French character in the faces. My mother's grandfather crossed the Channel as a refugee, being one of the first printers in colours in England. I daresay he printed the engravings that are so popular and so valuable at the present time. One of my sisters had a serious face, and the other a round and dimpled one. The latter could assume a laughing expression whenever I wanted it. But at the end of one day's sitting she complained that her cheeks were 'so tired with laughing,' and pressed them with a finger and thumb for a rest. I made it up afterwards by presenting the girls with a piano, which pleased them immensely. Other gifts reached them when I began to sell my pictures."

Frederick Goodall, born in 1822, received his first commission when he was sixteen from Isambard Kingdom Brunel, the engineer, for six watercolours of the construction of the Thames Tunnel at Rotherhide.

Generally Victorian artists, like the Old Masters, used family members, friends and work colleagues (especially apprentices) as models. Many artists used actors from local theatres, burlesques, music hall; soldiers; workhouse residents and the like. Joseph used family members in his work but there is no record of the other models he used or where they came from. However in the 1890's he produced several paintings set in St Cross, Winchester where the elderly people living there, notably Brother Nobbs, appeared in his works.

Wallis (1957) shows that William Frith used his daughters Alice, Fanny and Louisa for his 'English Archers, nineteenth century' exhibited at the RA in 1872. William Frith (1888) himself wrote extensively about artists' models. One source was the local workhouse:

"I am indebted to the workhouse for some very good elderly models. I am sorry to say that the freedom with which artists were allowed to select sitters from the 'asylum of poverty' no longer exists. We are shut out from all workhouses and the reason given is the impossibility of the 'inmates,' whether male or female, being able to pass the public-house on their homeward route, without leaving there much of their sitting money in exchange for drink. ... The masters of the workhouses that I visited had always been willing to assist in allowing me to select models from the great variety of characteristic faces abounding in their establishments. Till the old ladies and gentlemen proved beyond all doubt, by their frequent habit of returning drunk and abusive, that the indulgencies must be stopped."

Wallis (1957) also mentions Frith's use of a Mr. Bell as a source of models:

"Mr. Bell was very useful to me in procuring models. Few people have a more extensive acquaintance, especially amongst the female sex, than that possessed by Jacob Bell; and what seemed singular, was the most remarkable prettiness that distinguished nearly all these pleasant friends. I had but to name the points required, and an example was produced. 'What is it this time?' he would say 'Fair or dark, long nose or short nose, Roman or aquiline, tall figure or small: Give your orders. The order was given, and obeyed in a manner that perfectly astonished me. I owe every female figure in 'Derby Day', except two or three, to the foraging of [Mr. Bell]."

Oscar Wilde (1889) wrote a long essay on 'London models' and some of his key themes are captured in the following extracts:

"Professional models are a purely modern invention. ... As for the old masters, they undoubtedly made constant studies from their pupils and apprentices, and even their religious pictures are full of the portraits of their friends and relations ... the model, in our sense of the word, is the direct creation of Academic Schools... In Europe, however, it is different. Here we have plenty of models, and of every nationality, The English models form a class entirely by themselves. They are not so picturesque as the Italian, nor so clever as the French, and they have absolutely no tradition, so to speak, of their order. ... As a rule the model, nowadays, is a pretty girl, from about twelve to twenty-five years of age, who knows nothing about art, cares less, and is merely anxious to earn seven or eight shillings a day without much trouble. ... They accept all schools of art ... they merely desire that the studio shall be warm, and the lunch hot, for all charming artists give their models lunch. ...

As to what they are asked to do they are equally indifferent ... They career gaily through all centuries and through all costumes, and, like actors, are only interesting when they are not themselves. They are extremely good-natured and very accommodating ... They are very sensitive to kindness, respect, and generosity. When they are tired a wise artist gives them a rest. ... Then they sit in a chair and read penny dreadfuls, till they are roused from the tragedy of literature to take their place again in the tragedy of art. A few of them smoke cigarettes. This however is regarded by the other models as showing a want of seriousness, and is not generally approved of. They are engaged by the day and by the half-day. The tariff is a shilling an hour, to which great artists usually add an omnibus fare. The two best things about them are their extraordinary prettiness, and their extreme respectability. As a class they are very well behaved ... They usually marry well, and sometimes they marry the artist. In neither case do they ever sit again. For an artist to marry his model is as fatal as for a gourmet to marry his cook, the one gets no sittings, and the other gets no dinners. ...

On the whole the English female models are very naive, very natural, and very good natured. The virtues which the artist values most in them are prettiness and punctuality. Every sensible model consequently keeps a diary of her engagements, and dresses neatly. ... Nearly all of them live with their parents, and help to support the house.

As for the male models ... there is the true Academy model. He is usually a man of thirty, rarely good-looking, but a perfect miracle of muscles. In fact he is the apotheosis of anatomy, and is so conscious of his own splendour that he tells you of his tibia and his thorax, as if no one else had anything of the kind. As for the English lad of the same age he never sits at all. Occasionally also an artist catches a couple of gamins [boys who hang round in the streets] in the gutter and asks them to come to his studio. The first time they always appear, but after that they don't keep their appointments. They dislike sitting still, and have a strong and perhaps natural objection to looking pathetic. Besides they are always under the impression that the artist is laughing at them. …

One remarkable privilege belongs to the Academy model, that of extorting a sovereign [about £85] from any newly elected Associate or R.A. … They wait at Burlington House till the announcement is made, and then race to the hapless artist's house. The one who arrives first receives the money. They have of late been much troubled at the long distances they have had to run, and they look with strong disfavour on the election of artists who live at Hampstead or at Bedford Park, for it is considered a point of honour not to employ the underground railway, omnibuses, or any artificial means of locomotion. …

Model-painting, in a word, while it may be the condition of art, is not by any means its aim. It is simply practice, not perfection. Its use trains the eye and the hand of the painter, its abuse produces in his work an effect of mere posing and prettiness. It is the secret of much of the artificiality of modern art, this constant posing of pretty people, and when art becomes artificial, it becomes monotonous … We must, however distinguish between the two kinds of models, those who sit for the figure and those who sit for costume. The study of the first is always excellent, but the costume model is becoming rather wearisome in modern pictures. … However we must not blame the sitters for the shortcomings of the artists."

Art Dealers

As art patronage spread through a much wider section of society, artists faced an increasingly difficult task of making links with the large number of potential purchasers, including those who might be interested in commissioning family portraits. Inevitably matching artists and potential clients was a somewhat random process in which chance encounters and personal recommendations from mutual acquaintances played a part.

The eighteen fifties saw the emergence of commercial art dealers. They offered a range of services to both artists and purchasers that came to displace the rigidly codified market formed by state-sanctioned institutions such as the RA. Many aspects of this shift have been explored by the The London Gallery Project (2014) using 'big data' and Geographical Mapping Systems The new commercial dealers were distinct from both artist-run exhibition societies and shops selling art among other items of home décor or artists' supplies. This change opened up multiple pathways for artistic success (as measured in purely commercial terms) and exerted increased pressures on artists trying to steer their way through a complex, dense and rapidly changing art world. A recognisably modern gallery system with professional dealers and specialist exhibition spaces came to dominate the the art world.

The London Gallery Project (2014) and Harrison and Cynthia White's (1965) work on institutional change in the French Art market – showed that the British art market, particularly in London, was shaped by distinctive conditions. These included the new wealth created by Britain's rapid industrialisation, the strong Protestant preferences of many leading art collectors, the rise of theories justifying the commodification of art, and the tightly-knit, often overlapping, and mutually supportive social circles of artists, patrons, critics and dealers.

Although commercial dealers were displacing exhibition societies to some extent, it would be wrong to see their relationship as entirely hostile. Rather it was a story of mutual benefit. The London Gallery (2014) project demonstrates there was a close relationship between the location of commercial art galleries and of the Royal Academy and other exhibition societies. The West End, particularly Regent Street and Bond Street, was already a fashionable shopping area by the mid-nineteenth century and art dealers moved in among purveyors of other 'high-end' goods. Many of these galleries were new businesses; but some print sellers and frame makers started selling original paintings and relocated to the West End. There was also another growing concentration of art dealers in the City of London close to the offices of art patrons with a commercial or financial background.

In time, the large numbers of commercial galleries and exhibition societies in the West End came to share a common set of norms and practices. This blended the exhibition society traditions with the emerging retail practices of the later nineteenth century to create a new vibrant distribution network. This does not mean that all West End galleries worked in the same way, or carried the same degree of prestige. The best successfully combined the aura of aesthetic disinterestedness and commercial acumen that continues into the twenty-first century.

One artist who explored the possibilities of this synergy was William Frith. The London Gallery project (2014) describes how this was done:

> "The immense popularity of his major modern-life painting, 'Derby Day', at the Academy in 1858 made him a household name. Having achieved this level of success and … recognition, he chose to exhibit his next major modern-life painting, 'Railway Station' with a private dealer rather than at the Academy. The dealer Louis Flatou paid him £4,500 (£355,000) for the painting, sketches, and engravings rights, and later paid the artist an additional £750 (£59,260) to give up the right to exhibit the painting at the Academy. Both the enormous price and the decision to exhibit the painting with a dealer rather than at the Academy attracted significant press coverage, but Flatou used the Academy's prestige in other ways to promote the work. While he generally used an exhibition space in Cornhill [in the City of London], he exhibited the 'Railway Station' in 'a gallery prepared for it in the Haymarket, near to Mr. Hogarth's shop,' and, tellingly, close to the Royal Academy, then located at the National Gallery in Trafalgar Square. The exhibition at No. 7 Haymarket opened on Saturday 19th April, 1862, two weeks before the private view of the Academy exhibition, and Flatou even copied the famous installation of a protective railing in front of the painting that had been one of the most visible signs of 'Derby Day's success at the Academy in 1858."

The interplay between the RA and commercial gallery spaces was critical for Frith's success, although he continued to exhibit at the RA until the year before his death in 1909. While exhibition societies and galleries relied on one another to attract an audience, artists also played the different types of venues off against one another.

The London Gallery Project (2014) revealed a further important aspect of commercial dealers in its study of the Goupil firm. Though founded in Paris in 1829 it began expanding overseas in New York (1846), London (1857) and to other European capitals over the following twenty years. Originally, Goupil produced and sold prints but in the second half of the nineteenth century started selling original works. As well as selling to private buyers they also supplied public galleries including Leeds, Manchester and Preston in Britain and others abroad. This demonstrates the growing influence of dealers in shaping the tastes of the art buying public and sustaining the livelihood of favoured artists. Also asppearent is the 'internationalisation' of the art market as well as trading between art dealers before works reached the final buyer. Overall, the commercial galleries tended to concentrate on artists with an established reputation amongst wealthier patrons. Joseph and other 'middling artists' did not, as far as we can tell, use these galleries despite their overall impact on the art market.

Auction houses

The relationship between contemporary artists and auction houses is often indirect. Most auction houses deal in 'second hand' art works. In the late seventeenth century, the London Gazette began reporting auctions of artwork held in the coffee houses and taverns of London. Sotheby's opened in 1744, Christies appeared in newspaper advertisements from 1759 and Bonham's started trading in 1793. By the eighteen eighties, 'The Art Year' listed six major art auctioneers in London.

Wealthy new collectors untrammelled by 'collecting traditions' entered the market in the first half of the nineteenth century. They bought many works 'direct from the easel' or from the exhibitions reflecting their preference for contemporary art, watercolours as well as oils. However, from the middle of the century, auction houses began to handle the dispersal of fine art collections alongside the sale of the contents of artists' studios on their retirement or death. These large sales highlighted the financial gains from investing in contemporary art and artists' income. The boom in the demand for contemporary pictures peaked in the 1870s but declined steeply later in the century. Throughout the nineteenth century, the auction houses continued to cater for their traditional clientele interested in 'Old Masters'.

Like the art dealers, the main auction houses moved into new premises in the West End close to the RA and other exhibition societies. For example, Bonham's moved into a large site on Oxford Street in 1861. The plain Georgian shop premises were rebuilt with fashionable Italian façades.

Engravers

In the nineteenth century, engraving became central to bringing an artist's work to a wide audience. For many centuries, wood blocks were used to illustrate books and later for magazines and newspapers. Gradually engraving on metals of various types had become the dominant technology in this field.

In the early years of the nineteenth century, J.M.W. Turner, who reputedly made more money than any previous professional artist did, earned a significant portion of his income from engravings. Direct access to the middle-class market for engravings freed him from the RA's restrictions and wealthy art patrons. This allowed him to produce some of his best-known and most innovative works. Turner made his engravings from watercolors and drawings originally produced solely for reproduction.

Many followed Turner's lead, although later artists tended to produce engravings from previously exhibited works that had attracted public attention. Some, including Joseph, often sold their printmaking rights to illustrated magazines employing specialist engravers. By the middle of the nineteenth century, there was a large group of excellent draftsmen, including some of Joseph's contempories at the RAS, specialising in producing engravings and prints.

Book Illustrators

For artists without the resources to buy expensive oils or undertake speculative works without a patron, illustrating books offered a useful steady source of income. Many of important Victorian painters, including most of the PRB, provided wood engravings of designs for book illustrations. While Joseph did not act as a book illustrator, he allowed authors and publishers to use his works. He produced wood block illustrations of his works for the catalogues for the early exhibitions of the Society of Painters in Oil Colours from the early eighteen eighties. His nephew Joseph Benwell Clark, made a name for himself through this medium. Both recognised the shared interests of authors, artists and publishers in developing a mass audience for both the art and the literature.

From time to time, Joseph's works appeared as prints in newspapers, journals and, to some extent, in books about art. Towards the end of his career, he began to provide illustrations for a number of weekly 'improving' magazines for young people, mainly with temperance themes.

Later Years

This chapter has looked at the various players in the art market of the late eighteen fifties. As we have seen, the market had changed immensely during the previous decades and continued to do so throughout Joseph's career. The next three chapters deal with the main phases of that career. Each starts with a a discussion of the impact of the four main influences on Joseph's career – his family life, his religious faith, the art world and new technologies. Each chapter reviews his exhibited works and the critical response to them.

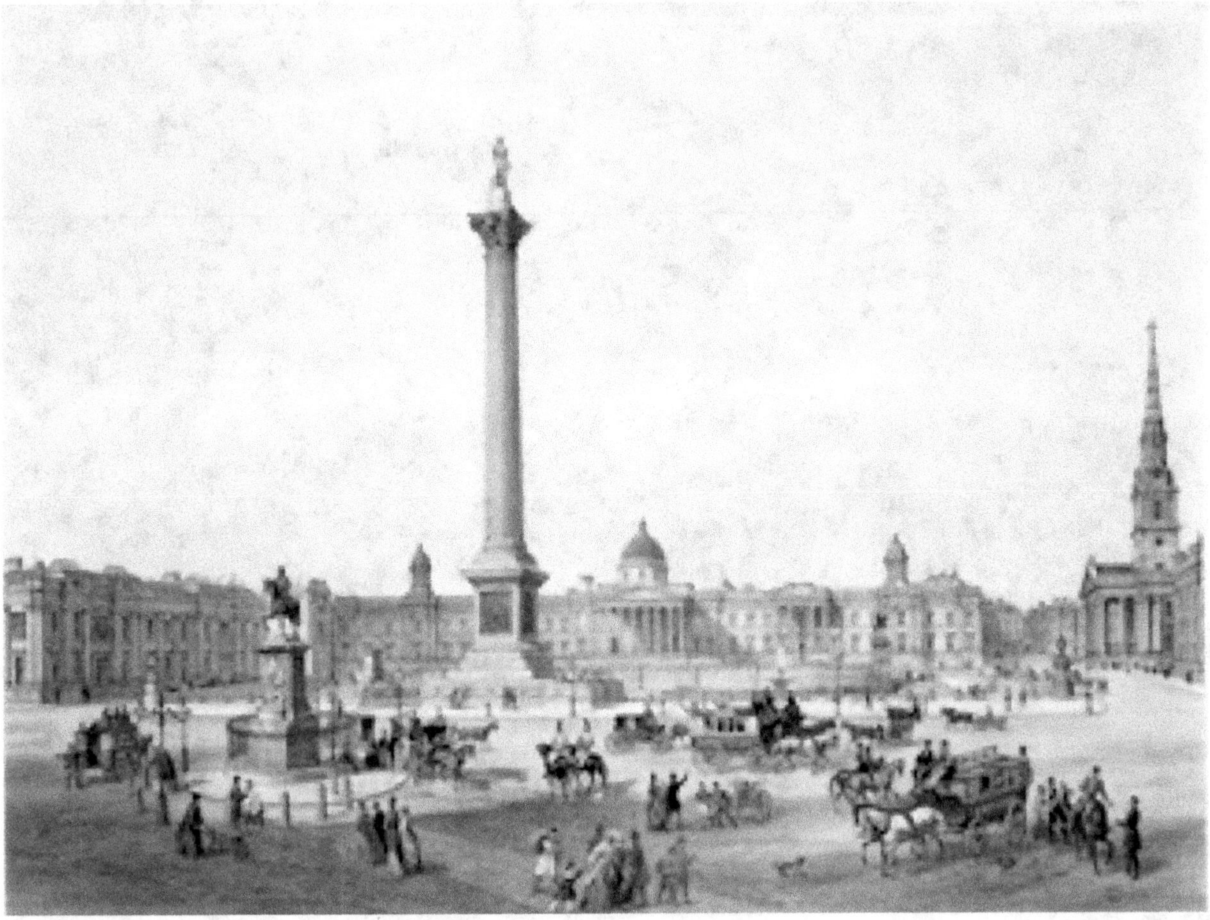

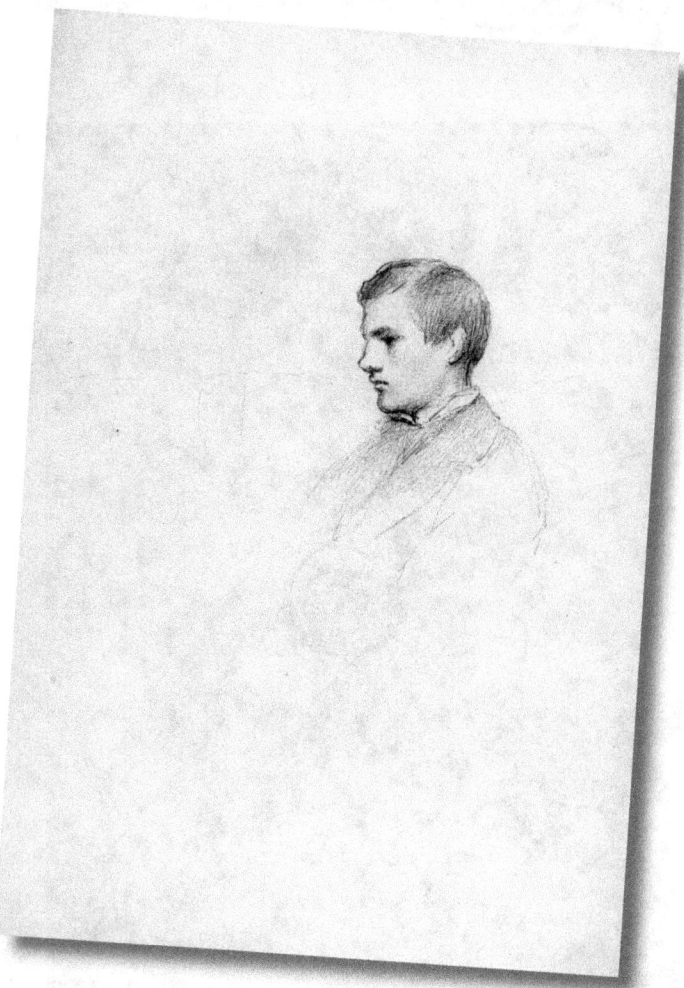

Plate 6. Trafalgar Square (1852). Showing the National Gallery – home to the Royal Academy Schools until 1868. Walker, E. (artist), Thomas Picken (lithographer), Day & Son (printers) and Lloyd (publishers). (Courtesy of the Victoria and Albert Museum)

Plate 7. Portrait of a Young Man:
Joseph Benwell Clark (1870s).
(Courtesy of the Victorian and Albert Museum)

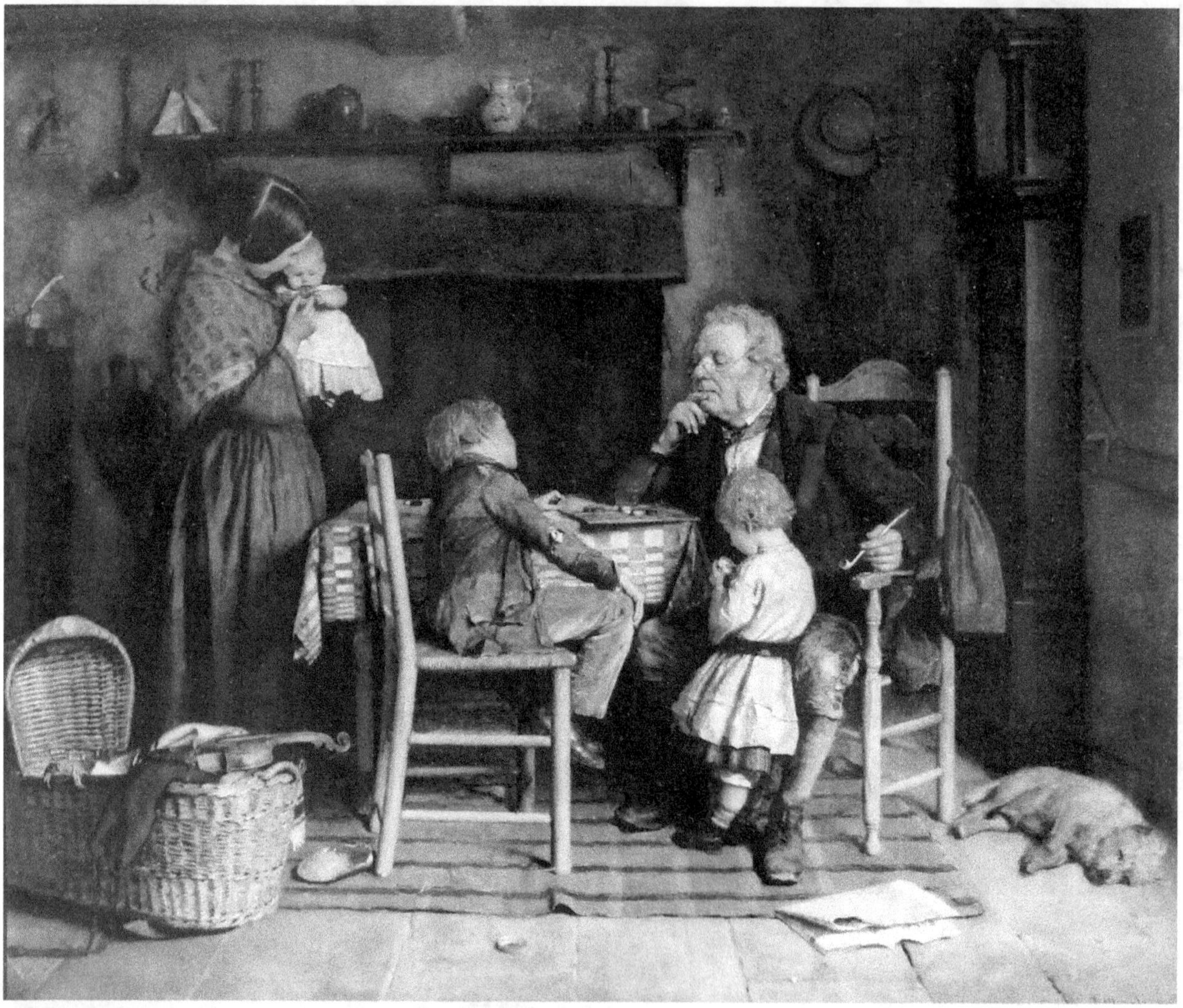

74b

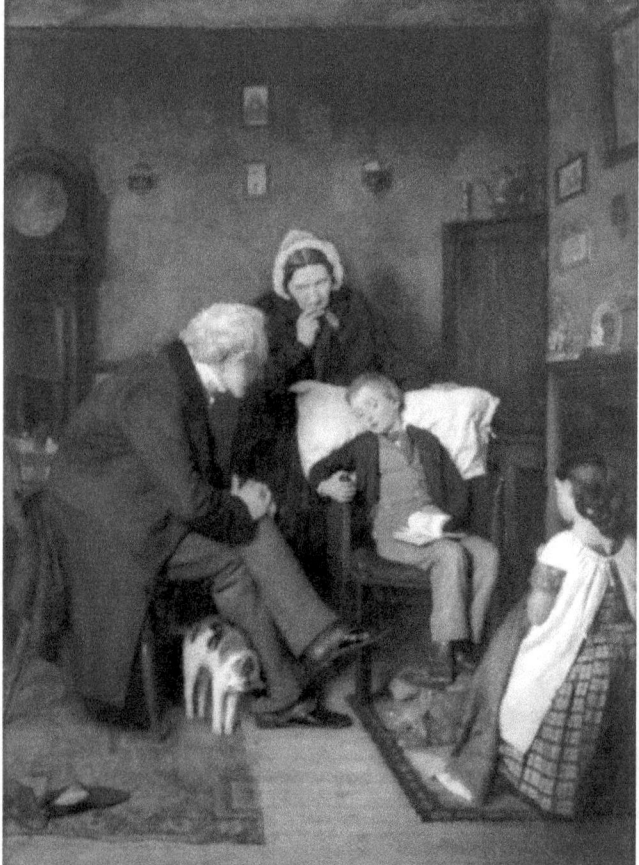

Plate 8. *(above)* 'The Draught Player' (1859). (Courtesy Sarah Galvin)

Plate 9. 'The Doctor's Visit' (1858) also known as 'The sick boy'. (Source: 'I am a Child' website)

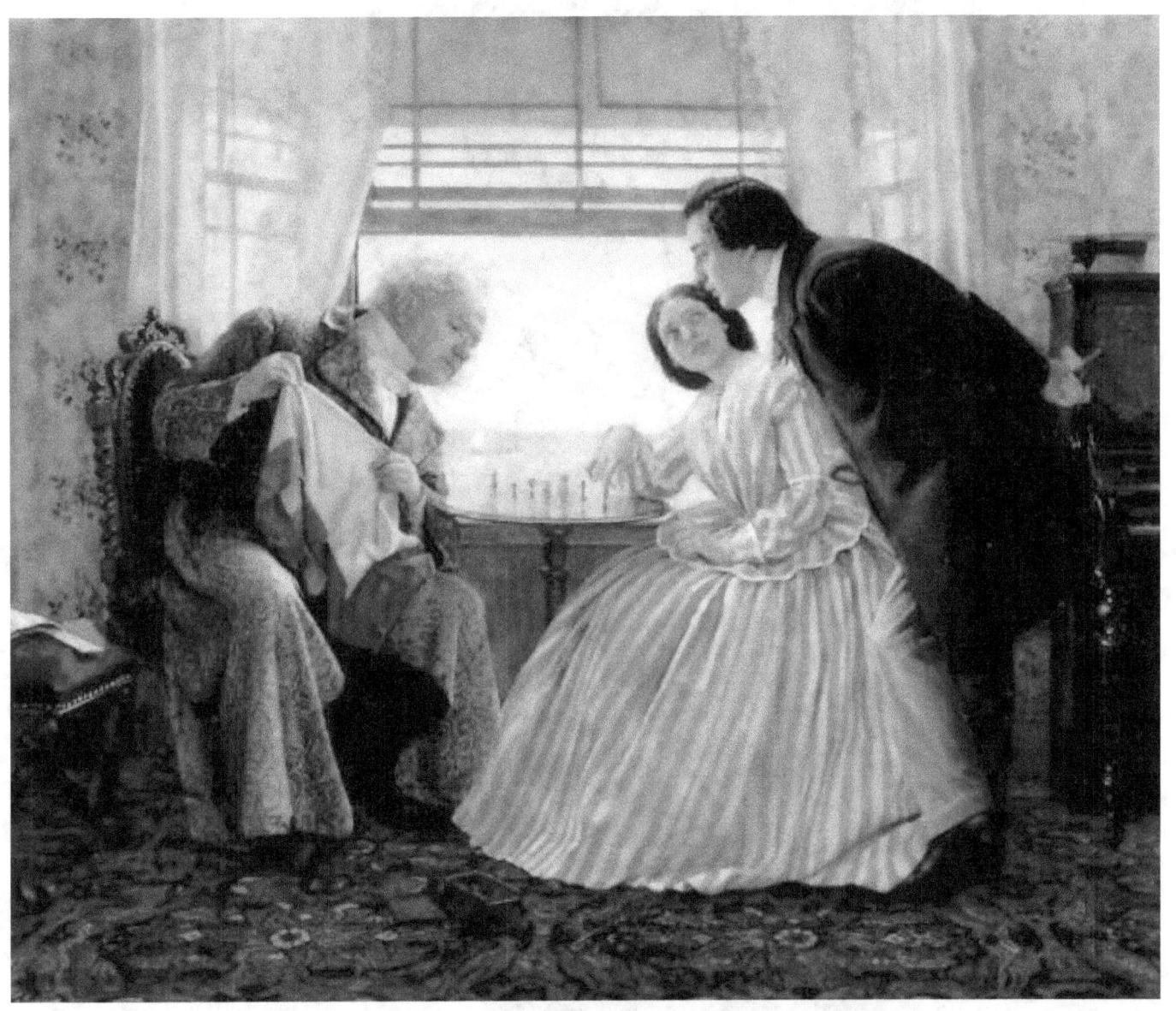

Plate 10. 'The Chess Players' (1860).
(© Peter Nahum At The Leicester Galleries)

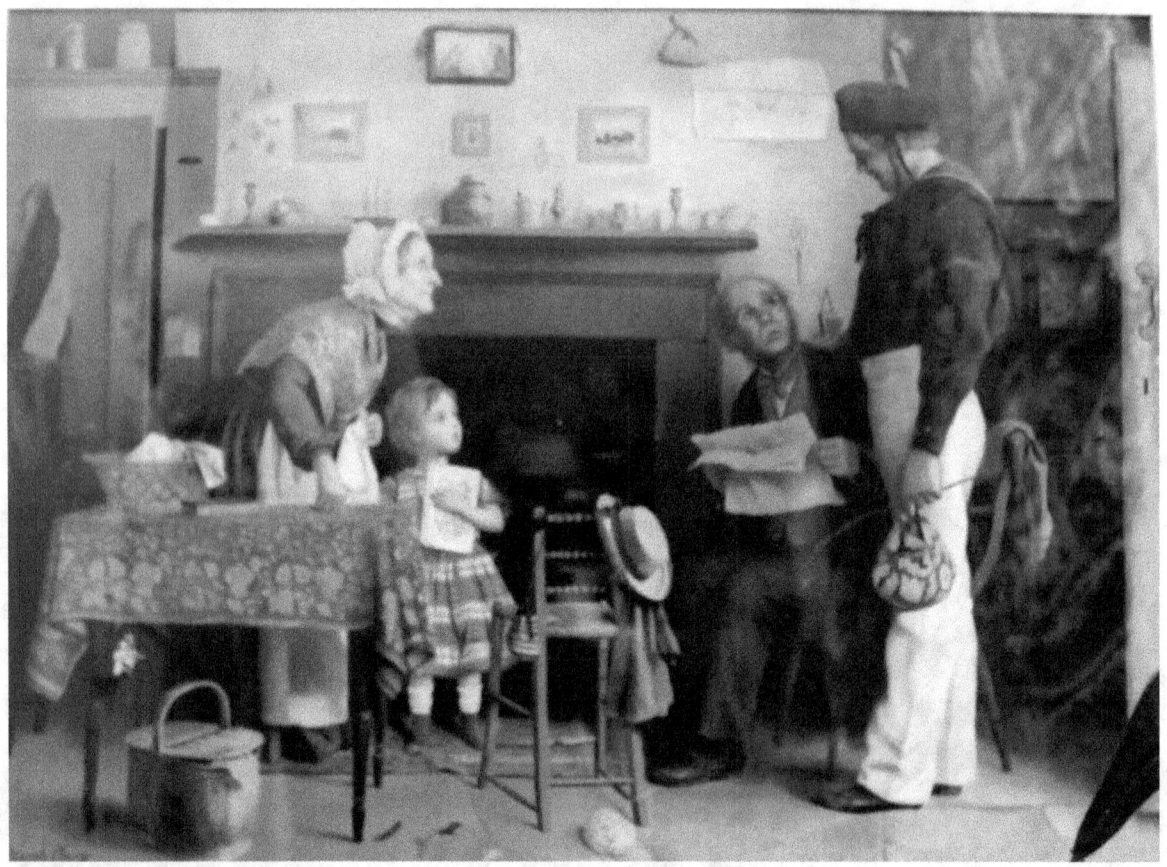

Plate 11. *(above)* 'Return of the Runaway' (1862). (Courtesy Sarah Galvin)

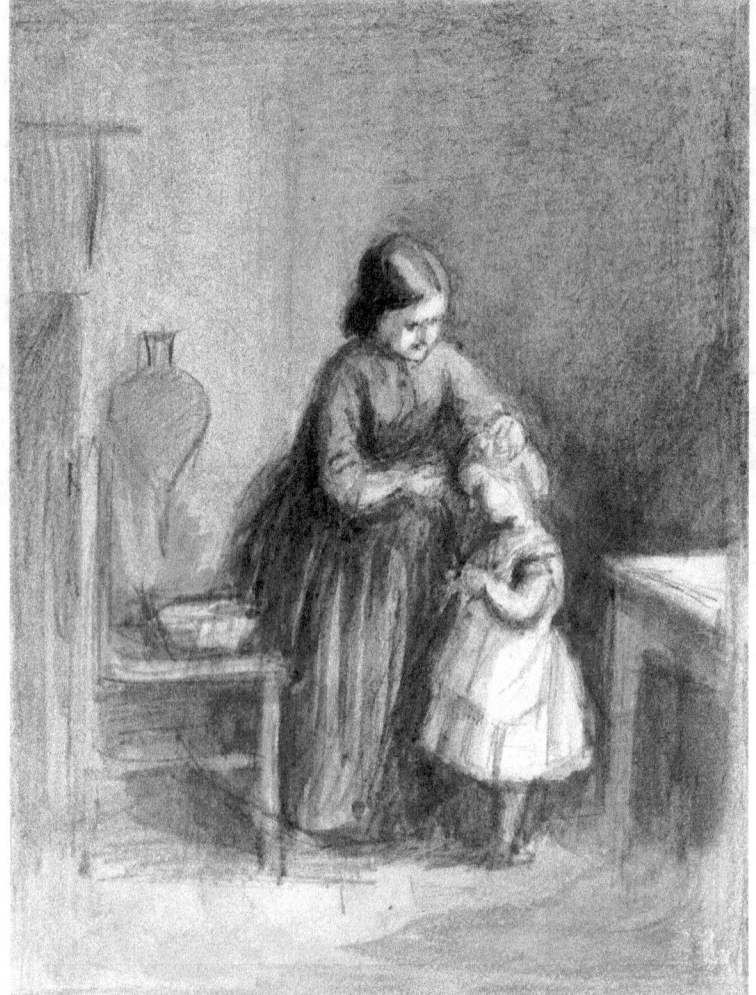

Plate 12. Mother washing little girl (*c.*1860). (Courtesy Victoria and Albert Museum)

Plate 13. Christina Mary Clark (1860).
(Courtesy Maas Gallery)

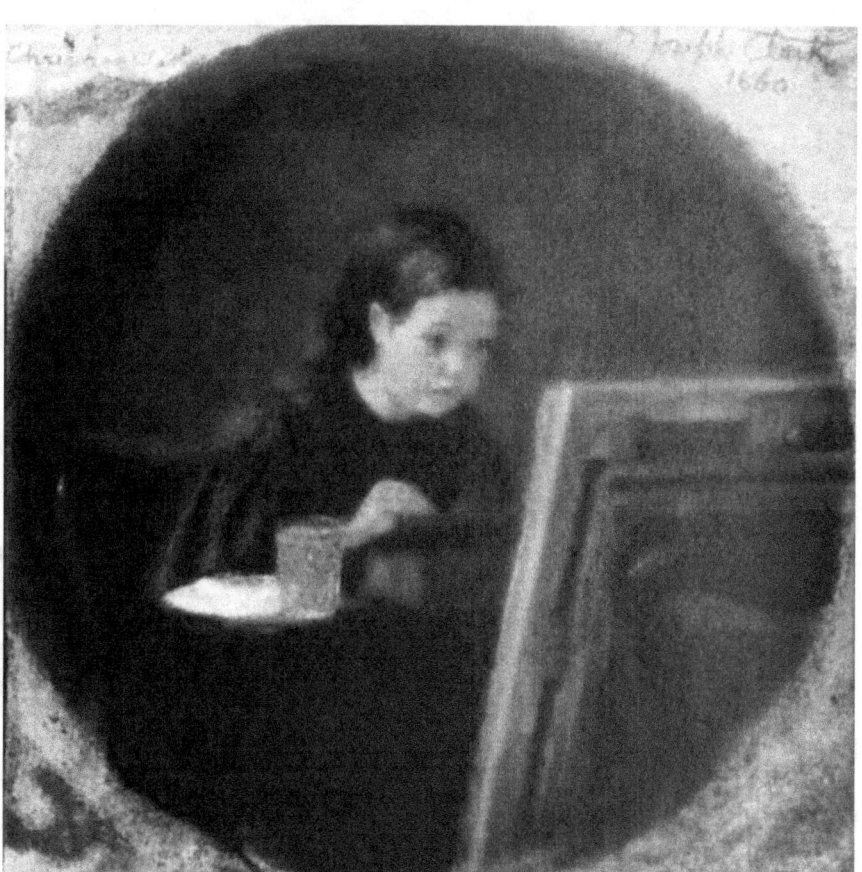

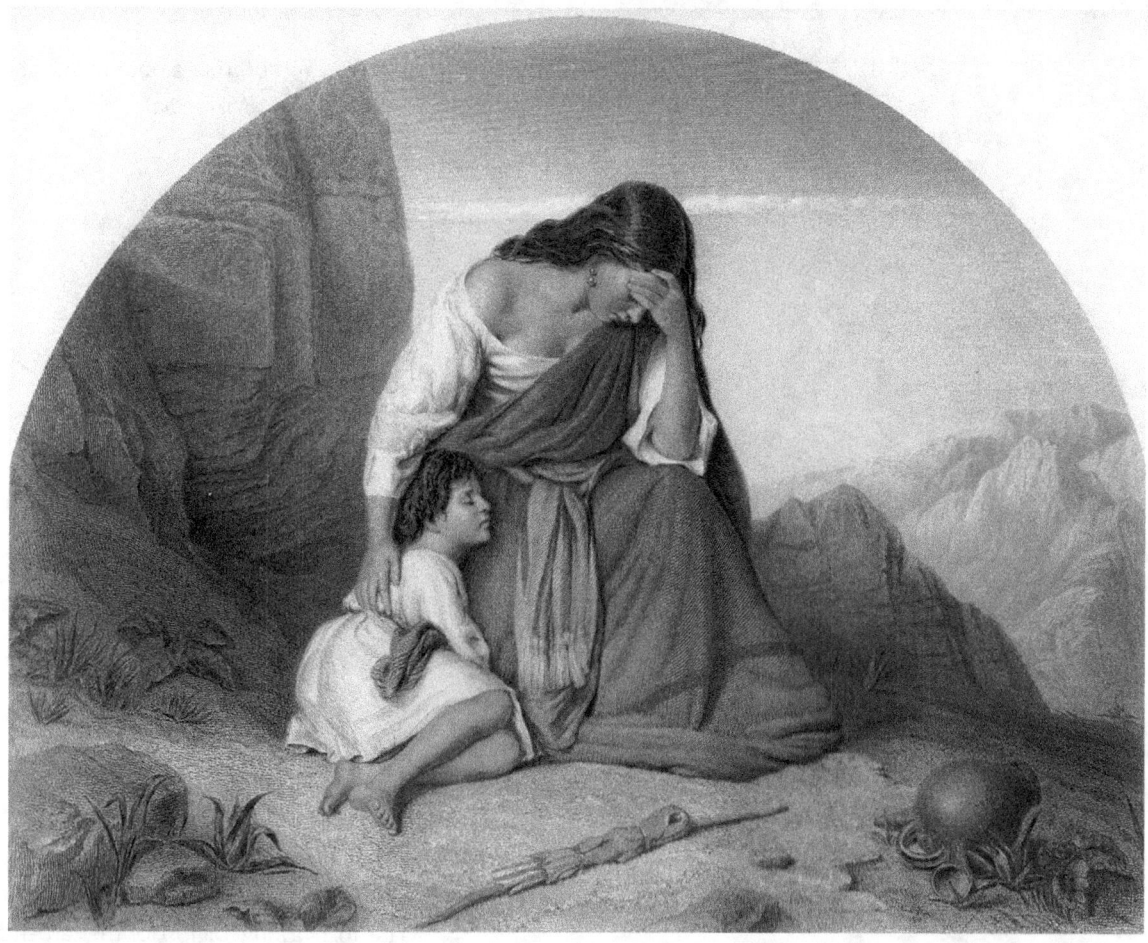

Plate 14. 'Hagar and Ishmael' (1860). (Courtesy the artist's family)

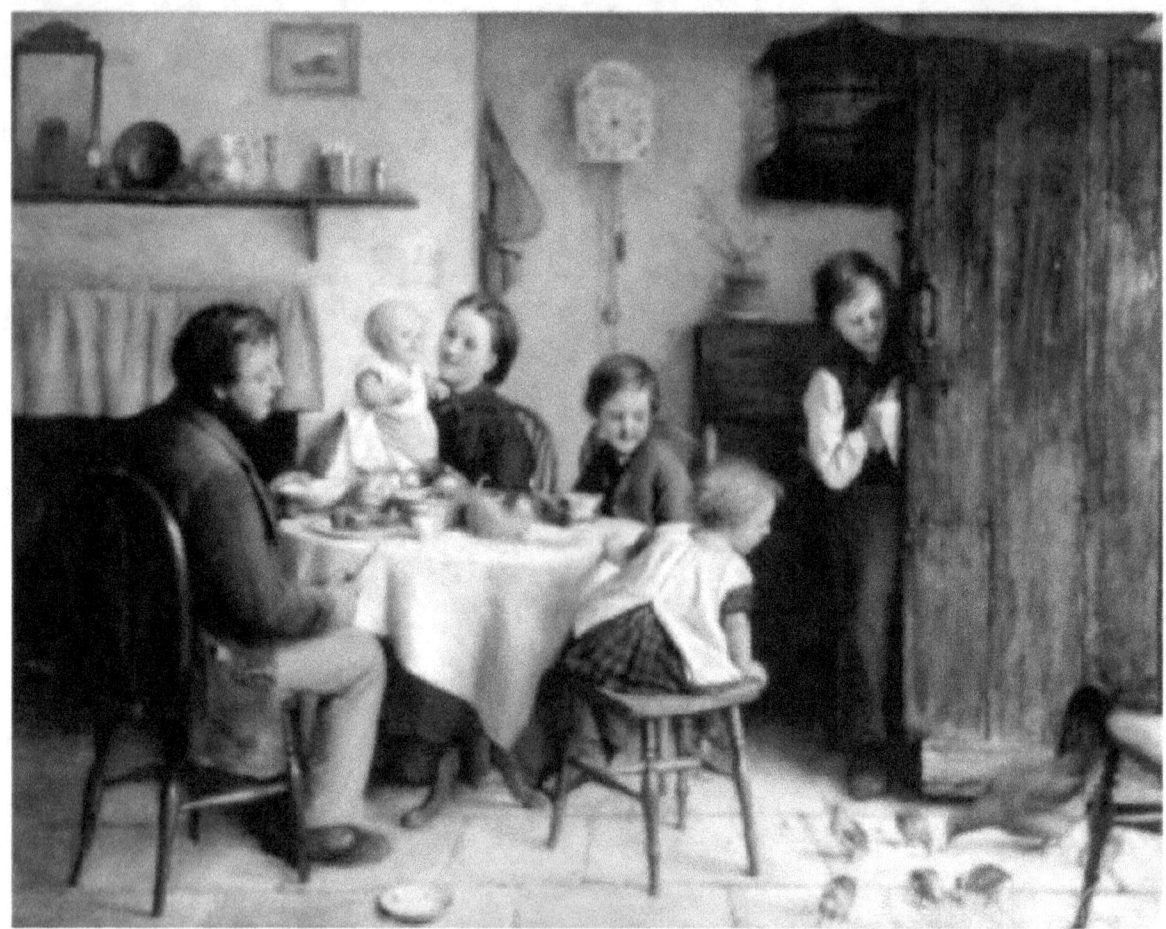

Plate 15. 'Crumbs from a poor man's table' (1869). (Source: Wikipedia)

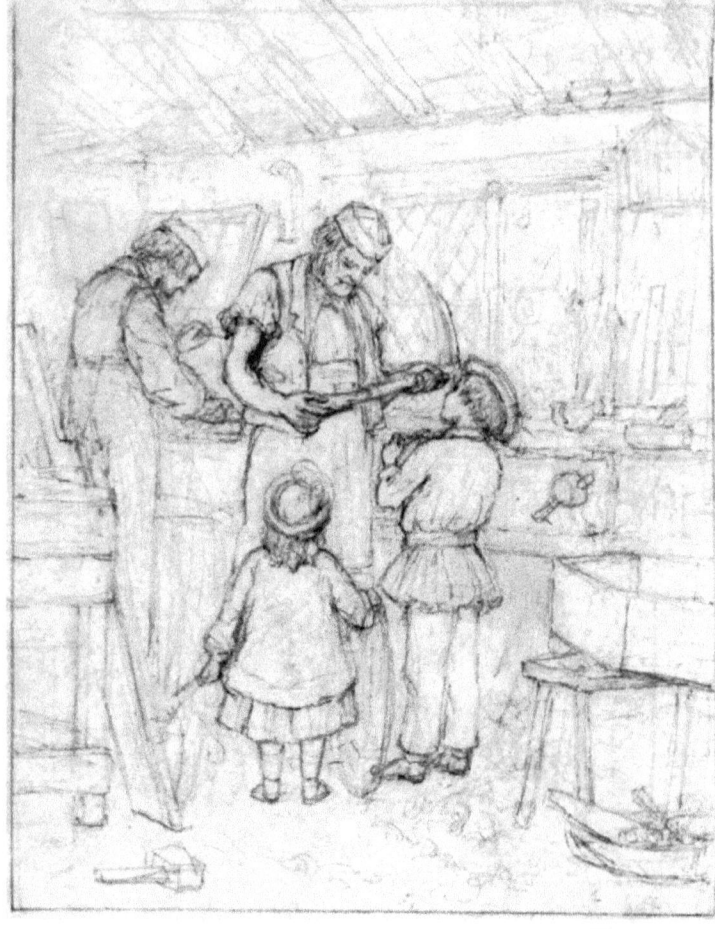

Plate 16. Drawing for 'Job for the carpenter' (1863). (Courtesy of the Victoria and Albert Museum)

SIX

A talented newcomer
(1856–1868)

As he began his career, Joseph had to make his paintings stand out from those of the 4,600 or so other professional artists working in London. During the twelve years covered by this chapter, he established his reputation as a highly skilled genre artist while experimenting with portraits, watercolours and a few religious works. He also deepened his understanding of the art market.

Family Life

In the second half of the 1850s, Joseph lived in Kentish Town with his mother and Jane Scard, their servant who remained with Joseph and his family until the early 1870s. His family life was largely undisturbed by his move from student to professional but major changes affected his family life during the eighteen sixties.

As well as the oil paintings exhibited at the RA and elsewhere, Joseph also produced watercolours. The Victoria and Albert Museum collections include an 1860 watercolour of a mother washing a young girl. Equally, at this stage of his career he produced family portraits such as that of Christina Mary Clark, his twelve-year-old niece. This was the first of several works depicting young people developing their artistic skills.

By the late eighteen fifties, middle class families begin to have studio photographs taken of themselves and their children. The Clarks were no exception. As a successful young painter, Joseph went to a fashionable photographer – Cornelius Jabez Hughes (1819–1884) – to have pictures of himself with his mother taken (picture 3, p. 42).

Hughes's studio was at 433 West Strand between 1855 and 1859; and the National Portrait Gallery holds a large collection of his works. His clientele included Queen Victoria, her close family, various European 'royals', Benjamin Disraeli, several leading actresses, and church and cultural leaders. Subsequently, he worked from a studio in Ryde on the Isle of Wight; wrote several widely read books on photography and was a leading member of the (Royal) Society of Photographers.

In 1860, Joseph, his mother and Jane Scard, moved to Belle Vue Villas on Seven Sisters Road in Holloway. This was an important step in Joseph's life as he was to live in Holloway until 1886 apart from five years in the mid-1860s. Belle View Villas were new when Joseph moved to Holloway, then a rapidly expanding largely middle class suburb. Joseph rented the accommodation from a private landlord, a pattern that lasted in the area until well into the 20th Century. Holloway had good public transport links to the City and West End using horse buses run by the General Omnibus Company.

1863 was a critical year for Joseph and his mother whose health had been in decline for some time. Seemingly, her doctor advised her to move close to the sea. The natural choice was the resort of Christchurch as several family members and friends lived there. Joseph's sister Mary Susan, her husband and their growing family had been there for about ten years. Joseph's brother, Edwin was

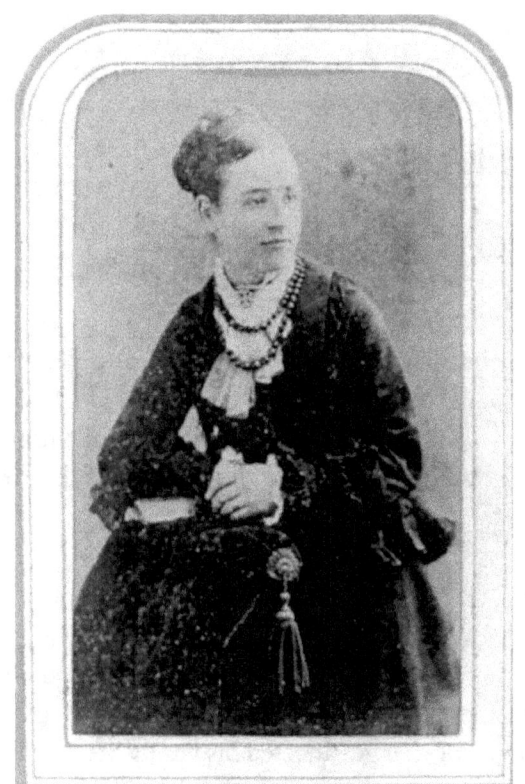
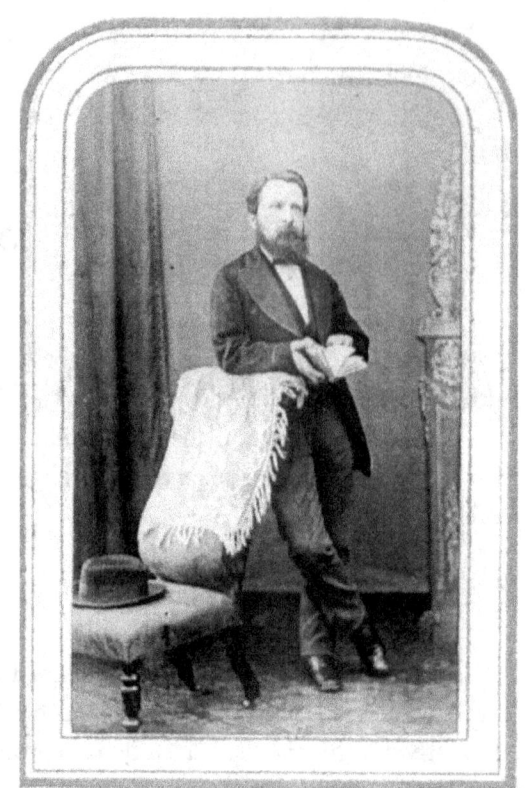

4. Joseph and Annie (1868). (Courtesy the artist's family)

running Yeatton Farm at Hordle, some eight miles east of Christchurch. William Ellisdon, the long-standing family friend and two of his children lived there. Joseph and his mother moved into Albert Villas in Purewell. Christchurch's rail links helped Joseph to maintain his contacts with London's art world.

Joseph's uncle, Robert Clark died in January 1864. Two years later Joseph's mother died and was buried in Cerne Abbas close to her husband and their children who had died in childhood. Susan's obituary in 'The Intellectual Repository' of April 1866 described her as an *excellent lady* and reported that her declining health induced her and her son *the highly respected painter* to leave London. It went on to say that, she had received the doctrines (of the New Church) early in life from her young husband and was for many years an attendant at Argyle Square. She had a *calm beauty and was beloved and respected by all who knew her*. The Intellectual Repository was a newspaper produced for the New Church.

On 14 June 1867, the Market House in Cerne Abbas was 'assigned' to Joseph under the terms of his father's will. There was a proviso that the reassignment of the property to William Henry Clark Jnr should occur on payment by him of £400 with interest to Joseph. In due course William Henry Clark Jnr paid the £400 – equivalent to £632,000.

It was apparent that his mother's death was a severe blow to Joseph and his career. It is possible that the insecurity he experienced in his teenage years resurfaced following her death. Certainly, the momentum of his career faded as he exhibited only one or two works a year between 1866 and 1869, none of which received much critical attention. Susan's death may also have unsettled Joseph's brother, Edwin, who returned to Cerne Abbas to run the 'New Inn'.

Two years after Susan's death, Joseph married Annie Jones of Eastgate Street, St Peter Colebrook, Winchester. She was the daughter of a wool-stapler, originally from Ospringe, near Faversham in Kent. The wedding notice read:

"On 30th ult, at the Wesleyan Chapel, Peter Street, Winchester, by the Rev. J. Taylor, Joseph Clark, Esq of 8 Upper Tollington Road, Holloway, London, to Annie, daughter of Mr J. Jones, Eastgate Street, Winchester"

Salisbury and Winchester Journal 3 October 1868

We do not know how they met or when. Annie was the second oldest of eleven children. Although there was a small New Church circle in Winchester, the number of worshipers declined during the 1860s and they no longer maintained a separate place of worship. There is no record of the Jones family as being members of the Swedenborg Society.

Annie was some sixteen years younger than Joseph. Such a disparity in ages was common in middle class Victorian marriages. Many men waited until they were well established in their careers (and in Joseph's case had inherited his share of his father's estate) and well able to support a family before marrying. After the wedding, Joseph and Annie settled in London; initially in Upper Tollington Road but moved shortly afterwards to Arthur Road. Both were in Holloway just a few streets from Belle Vue Villas where he had lived with his mother between 1860 and 1863.

Joseph and Annie maintained close contacts with the Jones family. In time, Annie's siblings married and had families of their own. These brothers and sisters in law gave Joseph a new range of insights into family life that doubtless offered inspiration for some of his works. Rosemary Chiles's (2010) book contains many pictures of Joseph and Annie at large family gatherings. We do not know if any of the Jones family acted as models for Joseph's works.

New Church Life

We know that Joseph and his mother worshiped at the New Church (Swedenborgian) in Argyle Square near Kings Cross Station. The church, designed by J.D. Hopkins in the Anglo-Norman style, opened in 1844. Jonathan Bayley was the minister and when he arrived the congregation, presumably including Joseph and his mother, was described as 'fashionable'. This term did not capture the true nature of the community in the immediate area of the church.

A better sense of the locality comes from:

"RAGGED CHURCH SERVICE – A Sunday evening service under this designation has been commenced at the national school room, Dutton street, Cromer-street, by the Rev. G.A. Rogers, incumbent of Regent-square Church St. Pancras, for the benefit of the poor of the district, who are prevented attending church from want of clothes', or who have children in arms, and who are invited to attend in their working dress. A considerable number of the poor residing in the neighbourhood have availed them of the opportunity thus afforded to them of public worship."

London Standard 8 August 1853

The New Church and Art

At least, three other artists attended the church in the eighteen fifties. They were Francis Oliver Finch, S. Hodson and Frances Black. Francis Finch (1802–1862) exhibited at the RA between 1817 and 1832 and showed 286 works at the Royal Watercolour Society of which he was an Associate (1822) and Member (1827). Rosemary Chiles donated one of Finch's works to the Glencairn Museum – part of the Academy of the New Church in Bryn Athyn in Pennsylvania. This has an inscription reading *To Joseph Clark in remembrance of his friend F.O. Finch, with E.F.'s best wishes, 1862.'* 'E.F.' was Elizabeth Finch.

Francis Finch and his wife moved in to Argyle Square in 1854. Elizabeth Finch (1865) wrote extensively about her husband.

> "And now the house in Charlotte Street being much too large for us, we removed, with our two aged friends, my godmother and her servant, into a more suitable residence in Argyll Square, Euston Road, where we remained for eight years. …
>
> … we became more and more attached to our quiet home, but our quietude was often cheered by friendly intercourse, my husband's old fellow-pupil being looked for at regular intervals, when the talk was of Art, and of bygone times, while other friends of more recent date, who used frequently to drop in were all men of superior intelligence, information and moral character …
>
> … Though my husband mixed little in the world, he continued in useful labours in connection with our church, which was very conveniently located on the opposite side of Argyll Square. Chief among the institutions set on foot by its intelligent and energetic minister, Rev Dr Bayley, was a society of junior members for mutual improvement. They held weekly meetings for the discussion of various subjects, at which my husband, with other senior members, always presided…"

It is not clear who the 'old fellow pupil' was, nor whether Joseph was part of the circle of 'friends of more recent date' or one of the 'society of junior members'. Towards the end of his life, Francis Finch appears to have suffered a stroke.

> "At length he ventured to pay a visit to the enlarged gallery of the Water Colour Society, where on the arm of a kind young friend, not unknown to fame, Mr Joseph Clark, he spent about two hours, most pleasantly. … [this seemed] to refresh his mind, but the brightness had passed away and although he responded to a degree to any ideas presented to him … and spoke but seldom. His affections however were active to the last."

In accompanying Francis Finch, it is unclear whether Joseph was acting as a deacon of the New Church, a role he undertook in the 1870s, or as friend in this act of kindness. There appears to have a close friendship between the Clark and Finch families.

Francis Finch spoke at a meeting of the 'mutual improvement' society on the purpose of art and its relationship with Emanuel Swedenborg's beliefs. Finch's notes for this lengthy lecture are included in Finch (1865) and it would be surprising if Joseph had been part of the audience. This extract may help to understand something of the influence of Joseph's faith on his approach to being a professional artist. Finch said:

> "Fine Arts, the subject before us is both wide and complex I must treat it in very general and cursory manner … and confine myself to one or two leading ideas or principles …
>
> What is art? Using this tem in its widest and most general signification, we may define Art as that Science by which some strong desire of the human mind endeavours to carry out its purpose. In more worldly and ordinary language, we may define it thus – Art is the best way of doing whatever we desire to do. …
>
> What are the true ends and purpose of the Fine Arts? I will do something towards the removal of a very general mistake … not confined to the ignorant. The ordinary notion about art is simply this. If a man takes a piece of paper, canvass, or anything that affords him a suitable surface, and can thereupon can arrange certain marks, touches of paint, and tints of colour, and do it in a skilful manner, that when the work is completed it shall resemble a man, or a tree, an animal, or a flower, in fact any given natural object, and if he can make his resemblance so perfect as almost

to deceive the eye, people think him an accomplished and skilful Artist. ... and they think the ends of painting and sculpture are in the practice of persons who can make these resemblances ...

I am happy to say that all inferior, collateral and subordinate functions of Fine Arts will, it seems probable, soon be much better achieved by machinery and the invention or rather discovery of Photography will emancipate the fine Arts from these more servile employments, and set them free for the performance of their higher, noble and important functions. ... The question therefore returns to us – what are these nobler higher, and more important functions of the Fine Arts? ...

... then the grand end of Art is to produce certain sensations and emotions in the human mind and that the true answer to the question – What is the end and purpose of the Fine Arts – would consist in a true description of these sensations and emotions. Doubtless, it would, but a sensation is not an easy thing to describe, whether of the body or the mind. ...

You can indicate a sensation only by naming it; call it by a name and those who have felt it and know the name mankind have assigned it, will know what you mean. ... But unfortunately for my endeavour, most of the best, the most delightful and the most elevating of the mental sensations, which the Fine Arts seek to adduce or produce, have either no accurate designation, or such as are only understood by the initiated.... But the most general purpose of the Fine Arts is to produce what we call impressions of the beautiful, or that delight which we derive from the forms and colours of object animate and inanimate, to which we give the general name beautiful.

... Great artists are only truly great in proportion, as they possess an organisation more keenly susceptible than that of other men to what are called artistic impressions. These they endeavour by means of ... the many dialects (painting, music, sculpture, drama etc] of the great language of thought and feeling, which all men, in one form or another, comprehend and use with more or less distinctness. Some people have no belief in beauty and justify their skepticism ... [by reference to different ideas of physical beauty in different countries].

I have a preference for [the term] Fine Arts – because, many things may draw from us the exclamation how fine that is, without being beautiful; and the Fine Arts produce mental impressions in great variety, and of great interest and importance also, which cannot be comprehended under the word beauty. Such, for example, as arise from the perception of character ... [and other examples] ...

In fact, the purposes of Art are as numerous as the impressions which the Artistic mind receives, and which it delights to render intelligible through the means that the Fine Arts provide to other minds. ...

The member of the New Church is lifted by his doctrine high above the entanglements in which human reason at the present day lies submerged and bewildered. Swedenborg has demonstrated to those who accept his testimony, not only that beauty exists, but it is intrinsically in the real ground or essence. He says that when the most exalted states of Love and Wisdom are presented in the Spiritual World to the eye in a personal form, as they are amongst the Angels, that form is always one of exquisite beauty. He says that the highest and most happy efforts of human art may sometimes have reached to a beauty equal to that of the lower heavens ... [but not of the two higher levels].

Beauty, then according to him is just this, it is the personal form of goodness and truth, and therein we may see why amongst all the living creatures God has made, man only is endowed with the perception of Beauty, for of what use would such a perception be to animals; they are never to know anything of that Goodness and Truth of which beauty is the form."

For our understanding of Joseph's art in the context of his faith, the key ideas are that art translates a strong desire to achieve particular ends through producing certain sensations and emotions sometimes called beautiful. In Joseph's case, we can surmise that his ends were about leading people in distress to appreciate the good things (or beauty) in their lives and for others in more fortunate circumstances to offer support and encouragement to others in difficulty to experience beauty through small acts of personal kindness.

As Joseph appears to have been a devout man, it is surprising he produced only two biblical scenes – in 1860 and 1868. Neither was a critical success. Indeed one critic castigated him for not producing a realistic view of the landscape in the Holy Land. He may have wanted to avoid similar negative comments. Another possibility is that he wanted to avoid engaging in the complex highly fraught debates in the art world and more widely about the position of religion in Victorian England. The increasingly bitter debates between the Anglican establishment and people holding a secular viewpoint intensified following the publication of Darwin's 'On the origin of the Species' (1859) and reinforced in 'The Descent of Man' (1871). The New Church stood to one side of this debate for many years, arguing that Darwin's work did not challenge Swedenborg's fundamental view set out in Arcana Caelestia (first published between 1749 and 1756) that the creation story in Genesis is symbolic of the spiritual progression (or evolution) of man rather than literal truth.

Somewhat earlier in the early eighteen forties, public interest in spiritualism grew generating much debate within the New Church. Spiritualism reflects the belief that spirits of the dead have both the ability and the inclination to communicate with the living. Emanuel Swedenborg's writings (2012) offered guidance for people seeking information about the afterlife. Although he warned against seeking out spirit contacts, Joseph writing in The Athenaeum magazine shortly before his death recalled that James Leigh was smitten by the craze for 'table turning' in 1853 as a way of communicating with the dead. Joseph and other students' participated in this activity – for a dare rather than for belief.

It was during this period, according to family recollections, that Joseph attended several readings by Charles Dickens, who like Joseph was a realist portraying life as it was lived by ordinary people. Apparently, Dickens had taken an interest in Swedenborg's teachings while writing 'A Christmas Carol' (1843). Certainly, other nineteenth century authors also show Swedenborg's influence through their subject matter, storylines or direct references. Among these are William Blake, Edgar Allan Poe, Honore de Balzac, The Brownings, and Samuel Taylor Coleridge.

The changing art world

Despite rapid changes in the art world during the early years of Joseph's career, he maintained his basic approach to art. However, these changes began to affect the reception of his works and the money he made towards the end of the 1860s.

The Royal Academy

Shortly after Joseph started exhibiting in 1857, a new Royal Commission into the Royal Academy began work and published its report in 1863. Its approach reflected the themes of the Northcote-Trevelyan Report (1854) into the civil service and subsequent reforms of the army. Broadly, the Commission was more favorable to the Academy than the 1836 Parliamentary Select Committee on Arts and Manufacturers. It recommended changes to the RAS including broader syllabus including chemistry; replacing The Keeper by a Director of Studies post filled by 'open recruitment'; and an annual exhibition of students' work. The maximum period of study at the RAS became seven years and Associates could become 'visitors' giving their students exposure to a wider range of contemporary styles and thinking. These changes resulted in an improvement in the quality of work produced by the next generation of RAS students and increased competition for Joseph's works.

Alongside these changes, there were other developments in art education. In 1871, the Slade School of Art led by Sir Edward Poynter opened as part of University College, London under the terms of Felix Slade's legacy. The legacy of £35,000 (about £3.3m) funded Chairs in Fine Art at Oxford, Cambridge and London; and six art scholarships of £50 a year (about £4,062) for students aged under nineteen. The Slade developed a distinctive syllabus and quickly established a reputation for excellence.

British Institution

The British Institution continued to hold the first exhibition of contemporary works at the start of each year until its dissolution when the lease on its galleries expired in 1867. Although it appeared to be flourishing, its exhibitions of contemporary works were less popular than previously. The Institution's residual funds went into scholarships for artists. Its closure meant 'new' artists lost a good platform for exhibiting and selling their works. Joseph exhibited at the Institution between 1857 and 1866.

London International Exhibition 1862

The Royal Society for the encouragement of Arts, Manufactures and Commerce (RSA) sponsored the 1862 London International Exhibition. Prince Albert, who died a few months before its opening, led the committee charged with planning the event. It featured over 28,000 exhibits from 36 countries, representing a wide range of industry, technology, and fine arts. It attracted 6.1 million visitors to South Kensington. Fine Arts were arranged by nationality; with each nation selecting a 'founding father' for its artistic traditions and traced their continuing influence. Britain selected William Hogarth, Joshua Reynolds and Thomas Gainsborough with exhibits tracing their impact on contemporary works.

This was the first time Joseph's works appeared at an international exhibition. Those shown were the 'Wanderer' and 'Restored' (RA 1861); the 'Draught players' (RA 1859) and 'The Sick Child' (RA 1857). Lewis Pocock who owned 'The Sick Child' lived near Lewes in Sussex and was a 'landed proprietor'. He had spent most of his life in the 'better parts' of North London, including Bloomsbury and Hampstead. He originally made his money as a coal merchant and was typical of the people buying Joseph's works throughout his career. W.J. Lancaster owned the 'The Draught Players' but he cannot be identified in census and other sources. Joseph remained the owner of 'The Wanderer' and 'Restored' as they had not sold at the RA.

Art Movements

Although the 'Pre-Raphaelite boom' began to wane in the late eighteen fifties, the sales of contemporary genre works remained strong. Two important nineteenth century art movements had their origins in the eighteen sixties. These were (with country of origin and rough dates) were Impressionism (1860–1890 France) and the Aesthetic Movement (1868–1901 United Kingdom). Neither had an immediate impact on Joseph's career in the period covered in this chapter but became significant factors in the decline in demand for genre works and in the growth of critical hostility to them that survives to the present day.

New technologies – photography

The Clark family photographs mentioned earlier in this chapter showed the inroads that photography was starting to make into the market for family portraits as predicted by Francis Oliver Finch.

At the time, there was a lively debate about whether photography was art. Brian Liddy (2006) suggests that as early as 1853, the amateur photographer William J. Newton proposed that 'a 'natural object', such as a tree, should be photographed in accordance with 'the acknowledged principles of fine art'. Other early photographers, including Henry Peach Robinson and Peter Henry Emerson, promoted the idea of photography as a new art form. The response of artists varied greatly. Some denied that there was any association between art and photography. They saw its value in capturing an image but refused to see its capacity to make a 'spiritual statement'. Some artists started to use photographs as a tool for capturing scenes that they could use as inspiration for their work – akin to the more traditional artists notebook.

As far as we are aware, Joseph did not embrace the new technology in his professional life despite commissioning photographs of family members and events. He continued to use drawings in preparing his paintings to capture poses, incidents, locations and objects. Photography's initial challenge to traditional art came in portraiture and contemporary genre, especially documentary works depicting the conditions under which the poor lived and worked. This contributed, to some extent, to the declining demand for contemporary genre in the later part of the eighteen sixties and the eighteen seventies.

Joseph Clark's career between 1857 and 1869

A key step in any ambitious artist's career was the acceptance of his works by a major exhibition society. Though the details varied, most societies shared similar criteria and processes. The best-documented system was that used by the RA.

Securing a place at the RA Summer Exhibition

The system used by the RA changed little during between the middle of the nineteenth century and the start of the First World War. This process became an important fixture in Joseph's professional life.

Any artist could submit up to eight works not previously exhibited elsewhere to the Royal Academy. All paintings submitted by RAs and ARAs were automatically accepted, but those by 'outsiders' had to go through a rigorous selection process. For these artists the judgments of the Selection and Hanging Committees meant the difference between success and failure. Each year paintings were submitted at the end of March or early in April. The Selection Committee, made up of the Academy's President and three eminent artists (five after 1871) identified works for display at the Summer Exhibition. This process was fast moving and relentless. Over four or five days, a team of porters, known as 'carpenters', placed each picture in front of the Committee for their scrutiny. Judgments were swift as the committee voted on each work; deciding whether to mark it with an A (accepted), a D (doubtful) or with a cross (rejected). Very few items achieved an 'A' at this stage. The 'doubtful' paintings proceeded to the hanging stage.

The Hanging Committee's job was to arrange the paintings in the exhibition rooms. This was an extremely sensitive and highly political task given the personal rivalries, commercial considerations and fundamental debates about the nature of art. All the members of the Committee were involved in identifying the outstanding works for the best locations that usually went to RAs and ARAs. William

Frith recalled in his autobiography that the principal room was the domain of the academicians' works. Paintings by ARAs seldom hung there and paintings by outsiders even more rarely.

At the time when Joseph began to submit his works, RAs were entitled to have all eight of their paintings hung 'on the line', while ARAs were lucky to have more than one of their paintings in such an honoured position. 'Being on the line' referred to paintings being at eye level, which was of great significance whilst the Academy was in Somerset House and before artificial lighting apart from candles. A ledge ran around the rooms at a height of eight feet from the floor, and a painting was 'on the line' if the top edge of its frame was level with the ledge. It was the best-lit position in the exhibitions rooms. The practical advantage of being 'on the line' diminished with later moves to Trafalgar Square and Burlington House, although it remained important to an artist's reputation. In practice, paintings at eye level were those best remembered by the public and mentioned most frequently by critics.

Once the principal paintings were in place 'on the line', the members of the Hanging Committee worked on their own in the various rooms, cramming every inch of wall space with paintings hung cheek by jowl right up to the ceiling. The fate of 'doubtful' paintings depended more on space considerations than their intrinsic artistic value. A few rejected works returned to fill specific gaps. Aesthetics played little or no part in the hanging process, leading many artists to complain that brighter and more striking works nearby overshadowed their more subtle paintings. Visitors could hardly see works hung well 'above the line' while artists and critics alike deplored the 'Octagon Room' in the National Gallery, where paintings almost disappeared into the dark shadows. This room was known by artists in the 1840s and 1850s as the 'condemned cell', and the reviewer of the 1849 Exhibition for the *Illustrated London News* (12 May 1849, p.350) missed out this room altogether, explaining *'it is unjust to artists for critics to condemn what they cannot see'*. A letter to the Editor of *The Times* the year before (6 Apr. 1848) he suggested that the room be turned into a refreshment room, as it *'was never built for showing pictures …* [This would be] *most thankfully received by all who know the fatigue of examining pictures in hot weather.'*

The move to Burlington House in 1869 was not accompanied by any change in the selection and hanging processes, except that a dado rail replaced the 'line' and the convention that the 'line' should not be broken by any pictures hung across it, disappeared gradually.

Though the selection process was complex, artists usually found out if their works had been accepted within a week of submission. In most years, the Selection Committee rejected ninety percent of the works submitted. Joseph's success in 1857 was noteworthy since, as far as we know, this was the first occasion on which he submitted works for exhibition at the RA. Equally significant was his success in having works accepted almost every year until his final retirement in 1916. This sustained success demonstrates the high regard for his work shown by successive generations of his fellow artists serving on these committees. We do not know whether the selection committee rejected any other works submitted by Joseph; but the odds must be that he submitted some pictures that did not make the grade.

Before the Exhibition opened to the public, and after it closed, several social occasions took place. In 1862, the previous practice of allowing artists to put final changes to their work on 'varnishing days' was restored after a ten-year gap. There were three days reserved for RAs and ARAs plus an 'outsiders' day for exhibitors who were not members of the Academy to put the finishing touches to their works. There they could also meet more established artists. George Dunlop Leslie, recalling his attendance at 'outsiders' Varnishing Days in the 1860s wrote:

> "of course … we outsiders were very much on our good behaviour, seldom indulging in hilarity or freedom of conversation, … 'the members kept up a certain amount of dignity and restraint in their manners towards us; but they were very pleasant days nevertheless."

After the 'varnishing days', the Exhibition opened to select groups (plate 3) before the general public came on the first Monday in May. The Royal Private View for Queen Victoria and her family signaled the start of the Royal Academy season – an important part of the London's society calendar. Admission was by ticket only, and those invited were the well-known members of the fashionable élite and members of the press. The final event in the run up to the exhibition, held on the Saturday before the general opening of the Exhibition, was the Royal Academy Banquet. The Banquet was strictly men-only, involving members of the Academy and personally selected guests from the very highest echelons of government, the Church, the armed forces, the universities and the worlds of literature, drama and music. The Times carried verbatim reports of the main speeches from the 1850s. It is unlikely that Joseph or other 'outsiders' ever attended either the banquet or the Royal Private Viewing.

In 1851 the Soirée, appeared in the social calendar for the first time. Originally, this came after the Exhibition had closed, but later moved to the first week in July. It was open to exhibitors and distinguished celebrity guests. 'Outsider' exhibitors only attended if a member of the Academy introduced them; and they paid one guinea (equivalent to about £80). Such restrictions were gradually relaxed during Joseph's career. Wallis (ed) (1957) records that William Frith said that the Soirée in the early years was an enjoyable event, at which the members 'seemed to lay aside a little of their dignity'. Reportedly, Edwin Landseer sang songs and told stories, and many senior Academicians made long speeches.

The Summer Exhibition was extraordinarily popular among the public in the mid-nineteenth century. In the peak year of 1879, over 390,000 visitors paid to their shilling to see the paintings at Burlington House. Its popularity meant that the exhibition was often so crowded that it was difficult to view the pictures. A shilling was equivalent to £4.44 in 2013; the price of an adult ticket in 2013 was £10. Around 159,000 paying visitors and 'friends of the RA' attended the 2013 Summer Exhibition – about 40% of the total in the nineteenth century.

Paintings exhibited by Joseph

1857

On 14 February 1857, the Illustrated London News gave its general verdict on that year's British Institution Exhibition:

> "… This being the first exhibition of the year is always, for us, fraught with pleasant anticipation. … The present collection requires, we confess, something adventurous to enhance its value and render us unmindful of its general mediocrity. …"
>
> **Illustrated London News** 14 February 1857

Clearly, the paper thought Joseph was one of the new arrivals on the exhibition circuit was above this general mediocrity. In the same week, the Oxford Journal carried an announcement that the Illustrated London News for 28th February 1857 would contain the following engravings '… *The Dead rabbit' painted by J Clark (from the exhibition of the British Institution)'.* This must have been a moment of great excitement for Joseph and his mother. The 'dead rabbit' sold for £20 (about £1,665).

The Illustrated London News for 28th February provided a full commentary on 'The Dead Rabbit' saying:

> "We have engraved this picture in order to more easily call attention to this promising little painting which, in the general distraction of the exhibition, might possibly be overlooked. It

contains indications of that simplicity of feelings and quiet sympathy with the joys and sorrows of boyhood which is so typical of Mulready. It bears some resemblance in its handling to the style of the great painter: that is to say the effect is gained by the amount of stippling which leaves a certain illusive in distraction – if you will.

The story is too simple and obvious to need description. The artist has so successfully rendered the expression of the boys' regret for the fate of their favorite that we can scarcely refrain from testifying our sympathy with their simple grief; especially their disappointment that 'poor bunny' will no more be able to nibble any of the fresh green fodder they have provided with such solicitude and so plentifully. There is a touch of humour in the way the bigger boy is holding up the rabbit. Indeed to ascertain whether their pet is really dead he holds it up by the ears in the most boy like manner possible. Indeed (as we have forgotten much of our boyish experience) we suspect that boys in general have a theory that rabbits are provided with long ears wholly and solely in order that they may be suspended by them … this reminds us that kindness to dumb animals – such as the pleasing specimen we have in this picture – is by no means a invariable trait in boys. Unhappily, they have established a capacity for cruelty just as much as for mischief. Some of this latent propensity will be invoked on the culprit when they discover him under the hutch with a very consciously criminal – and if I may be excused the solecism – 'hangdog' expression."

Illustrated London News 21 February 1857

Inspired by his reception at the British Institution, Joseph's next target was the RA Summer Exhibition. He steered his way successfully through the selection process and three months later created something of a stir with 'The Sick Child'. Margaret Drummond (1950), Joseph's youngest daughter, recalled that 'The Sick Child' was placed on 'the line' – a rare occurance for a 'first time' exhibitor.

The Times' art critic, although critical of much of the work selected for the exhibition, wrote:

"… But here and there on the wastes of wall, there are essays of raising ability and achievement of fresh talent which render the exhibition of this year interesting if not surprising."

The Times 2 May 1857

It's not clear whether this critic regarded Joseph as a fresh talent with rising ability. He was certainly seen in this light by the placing of the work by the hanging committee. Although The Times did not mention 'The Sick Child', three other papers did:

"'The sick child' by J Clark is well painted, low in tone but full of feeling. The bent body of a man as he fondles the little sick child on his lap, the anxious look of the mother, are all well rendered; the face of the child is perfect."

London Daily News 11 May 1857

"'The Sick Child' J. Clark. There is not on the walls of the academy a picture that surpasses; perhaps there is none that equals this unpretending little work in pathos. It is because it is very simple so very void of any pretense and effort to be effective, that it holds us with such strength – the strength of truth itself. The same story, such as it is, has been told hundreds of times before a father, a poor corduroy clad mechanic, holds on his knee a little wasted child, whose feeble limbs tell a tale (not an exaggerated clap-trap tale) of sickness and privation from fresh air and green fields. The gentleness with which the rough man bends over the poor little patient; the exquisite tenderness with which the uncouth mother holds towards it a basin of broth, her coarse features made sublime by love, are far beyond our powers of description; they are to be admired and reverenced – not talked about. We trust that this young artist may go on as he has begun if he only does that, he will be an honour to the school that has produced him."

Lloyd's Weekly Newspaper 31 May 1857

"Our readers will remember we engraved a little picture entitled 'The dead rabbit' exhibited at the British Institution; and we believe we were the first to call attention to its unpretending merit which was precisely the kind to be overlooked in the false gaze of an exhibition.

We are pleased to find that the promise by its previously unknown painter is more than redeemed in the present exhibition. 'The Sick Child' by Mr. J. Cark has excited general and well-merited admiration. Its simple story is told perfectly and yet in an unobtrusive manner, as to be like the poetry of Crabbe, almost painful in its literalness. Its execution furnishes an exact parallel to its leading spirit or sentiment. It is perfectly drawn and finished with great care, yet without any of the ostentation of dull clucking labour; but its colour is almost too quiet and subdued. We may remark that this is chiefly owing to the extreme blueness of the white draperies. They should be either less blue or as in Correggi, harmonised by a freer use of pearly tints in the receding parts of the other objects. The picture deserves the highest praise for its extreme naturalness and modesty."

Illustrated London News 25 May 1857

A Dorset paper referred to 'The Sick Child' later in the year:

"REVIEWS. The National Magazine. London: National Magazine Company, Fleet Street. This number is the first part for a new year, and we can only say, that as we have never been scanty in our praise of former numbers, neither can we withhold it from the one now before us. ... But we would at present draw attention to its numerous engravings, of which no periodical that we know of can justly make greater boast. 'The Sick Child' of Mr. Clarke, is an exquisite family group, made of a loving, tender father, pressing sick child to his bosom to which clings closely. The homely grace of the mother as she bends forward to share in the paternal anxiety together with the other adjuncts of the picture, are beautiful."

Sherborne Mercury 17 November 1857

Sadly, they did not mention Joseph's Dorset origins and misspelt his name. A similar story appeared in the Leeds Intelligencer. This lists seven other works selected for this edition of the illustrated periodical:

"The National Magazine. (London: Published at the Office, 73, Fleet-street.) – Part XIII. of this illustrated periodical equal, both a literary and artistic point of view, to any number yet issued. There are sixteen engravings in it – all first-class – chiefly by H. Linton. The subjects are extremely well chosen, and they appeal, through the eye, to the heart of everyone. Who can look at 'The Sick Child,' from a painting by J. Clark, – 'Time of War,' by J. Archer, – 'The Auld Style,' T. Feed, – 'Sportsmen Regaling,' by Louis Hague,– 'She has Two Byes, so Soft and Brown,' from a painting by C. Baxter, – 'The Land's End,' by Turner, 'The Italian Boy,' by W. Water-house, – or 'The Talking Oak,' by W.M. Egley, without feeling that they are works of great merit. Each tells its own story in silent but eloquent language, which language is further interpreted by the elegant writer who known in the National by the initials L.L."

Leeds Intelligencer 7 November 1857

However, these report show that at the very start of his career, Joseph had broken into the 'magazine market' taking his works, vision and message into thousands of readers across the country. Many of the later reviews of Joseph's later works referred back to the excellence of 'The Sick Child'; and the picture exhibited at several international exhibitions. There are no modern images of 'The Sick Child' in the public domain.

1858

Several critics reported positively on Joseph's next exhibited work, 'Grandma's Hope', seen at the British Institution's in 1858 and in doing so demonstrated the extent to which provincial papers, in this case the Birmingham Daily Post, copied material from the national press albeit with modest changes:

"… Mr J. Clark opened his career admirably by the 'Sick Child' in the academy exhibition. His 'Grandma's hope' is neither so delicately wrought nor so pathetic in subject as last year's picture. But it has merits of such admirable truth of conception in a narrow range, and in such a manly, broad, yet careful execution, that it lifts Mr Clark to the head of that long train of pinafore painters who are rapidly assuming the dimensions of a nuisance and, indeed lands him in the very narrow region within which a few painters justify their rights to find subjects in the nursery, the schoolroom, and the kitchen.

Webster has no pretensions of the power of painting shown in this little picture of Mr Clark which shows an old woman mending the garments of her grandson who is sitting in the window seat beside her – a bullet headed unkempt urchin, giving unmistakable promise of his vocation in the toy soldiers he is putting back in their box and the jolly Jack Tars whose pictures he has pasted on the walls. This little picture is not trivial for it tells a story of human hopes and aspirations, and tells that story skillfully, unaffectedly, and distinctly. Mr Clark in these two pictures has made his place and has only to go on applying his approved power towards the worthiest aims that are compatible with its range. How sympathetic is this kind of subject to British minds is evident from the terribly large proportion of artists who are taking to it. …"

The Times 8 February 1858

"Mr. J. Clark opened his career admirably last year by the 'Sick Child' in the Academy Exhibition. His 'Grandma's Hope' is neither so delicately wrought nor so pathetic in subject as last year's picture. But it has merits of such admirable truth of conception in its narrow range, and such manly, broad, yet careful execution, that it lifts Mr. Clark at once to the head of the long train of pinafore painters. Webster has no pretensions to the power of painting shown in this little picture of Mr. Clark, which represents an old woman mending one of the garments of her hopeful grandson, who sitting in the window seat beside her a bullet-headed, unkempt urchin, giving unmistakable promise of his vocation in the toy soldiers whom he is putting back into their box, and the fighting Jack Tars whose pictures he has pasted upon the walls. Mr. Clark in these two pictures has made his place, and has only to go on applying his approved power towards the worthiest aims that are compatible with its range".

Birmingham Daily Post 10 February 1858

"Among the little sketches of real life the best is Mr Hemsley's sketch of rustic immature coquetry, Hook my Frock. There are other pleasant pictures of this kind … Mr J. Clark's Grandma's Hope [and five others]."

The Examiner 27 March 1858

A few months later, the critic of the London Daily News reporting on the RA identified a theme that recurred in press reports of Joseph's works – a criticism of his choice of colours. He wrote:

"Mr. J. Clark, whose 'Sick Child' attracted considerable attention in last year's exhibition, has a kind of companion picture in 'The Doctor's visit', even less satisfactory in colour, but full of intelligence in the accessories in the room, the quiet sagacious look of the dog, the purring of the cat, who seem both to approve of the visit, and the higher merit of the truthful expression in the languor of the poor sick boy, and the anxious watchful hanging of the mother on the words as they drop from the doctor's lips."

London Daily News 6 May 1858

Other critics thought highly of the 1858 RA Exhibition and praised Joseph's contribution:

"The Royal Academy Exhibition. The preliminary notices we have published of the character of this year's exhibition have not been belied by the result. It is the most perfect collection of pictures which the Academy has contained for many years. Some idea of its excellence may be formed from the terse but comprehensive summary of the Times critic, which we quote almost entire. Recollecting the highly pitched tone of criticism which that writer has assumed this year, the praise he awards to the Academy gives assurance of no ordinary excellence. The unusually large number of pictures, many of them by unknown or undistinguished names, which testify to honest, hard, and in the main well-directed study of nature, is the most prominent and most satisfactory feature of the present exhibition. We can call to mind many exhibitions graced by single works of more attractive or striking qualities than belong to any particular picture of this year, but we remember none in which the element of decidedly bad work was so small, none which testified so unmistakably to the fact that the painters of England are as a class working so hard and so honestly that the results of this labour must eventually appear in a fair crop of excellent pictures. If it have as yet produced rather exquisite studies, marvels of patient finish and laborious imitation, than such consummate pictures as we hope for, it is because the best workers here are most of them still students of art rather than artists. Ten years ago, however, such an exhibition of the Royal Academy as the present would have been simply inconceivable? It is the very gradualness of the development of this will and capacity for hard and honest work which renders so many insensible to its good effects and impatient of its prominence. It is only when we commit the error of mistaking this labour for the end, instead of the means of art, that there is any ground for desponding at the present visible preponderance of such labour over the manifestations of triumphant mastery and mature imagination. ... J. Clark's 'The Doctor's Visit', (89) – intended, perhaps, as a contrast to 'The Sick Child' of last year – full of this young artist's merit of true expression, and consummately worked out."

Birmingham Daily Post 4 May 1858

Later in the week, the provincial press had noticed an article in the Illustrated London News saying:

"Though it is early in the day artists are beginning to complain, 'business is flat' and that bidders for their pictures are 'not numerous'. ... 'The Doctor's visit' a beautiful little picture by Mr Clark, who broke new ground so well last years with the 'Sick Child', has been painted as a commission by Mr Creswick RA."

Birmingham Daily Post 11 May 1858

Identical pieces appeared in the local papers in Manchester, Glasgow, Worcestershire and elsewhere. The purchaser, Thomas Creswick was a well-known landscape painter who became a Royal Academician in 1850 and died in 1869. This painting is known as 'The Sick Boy' in some auction catalogues, online and elsewhere.

A further positive notice appeared in early June:

> "… Such treatment of sacred and heroic subject gives a double zest for quiet little home pictures like Mr J Clark's 'Doctor's visit'. Here there is no grimace of art declaring itself absolute nature. We are shown simply the old doctor in the cottage, too familiar a guest there, kind as he is, for the cat chooses his leg as a rubbing post; the sick boy in his chair listlessly fingering a pictured spelling book, the homely woman is telling fifty times more than is needed, but yet a fiftieth of what is in her love to tell, and her loquacity and her just sense of her own medical attainments; the young sister looks up from her needlework, soberly watchful of her sick playfellow, and everybody's head is of the right size, everybody's arms are of the right proportion. The pre-Raphaelite is happiest, we half suspect, when he has put a pair of woman's legs on a little girl's body, coloured a rainbow upside down, made a man's arm as long as a baboon's, painted a horse with a whale's back, or a goat several times bigger than a mountain."
>
> **The Examiner** 5 June 1858

Clearly, the critic was in a positive frame of mind. It is interesting that he positioned Joseph's work as being distinctly different from that of the Pre-Raphaelite Brotherhood who had burst onto the art scene a decade earlier. In Joseph's choice of subject, we can see echoes of the sickness that afflicted Joseph's family, something not known by the critics at the time.

John Ruskin (1858) in 'Academy Notes 1858' was also in a positive frame of mind. He recognises that Joseph and similar artists had a serious somewhat evangelical purpose in their choice of subjects.

1859

In 1859, the Times's critic while largely dismissive of the British Institution's selection of paintings for its annual exhibition remained positive about Joseph's exhibit:

> "It is surprising to find how few of the 592 works exhibited have left any distinct impression on the mind after six hours conscientiously spent in examining them. Mediocrity must be the staple of all annual exhibitions … As a general rule all the best pictures are on or about the line and so far as we can judge the visitor may profitably be confined to this section of the walls. The principal pictures on which the critic would be justified in bestowing notice are Mr Joseph Clark's 'Cottage Door' [and about a dozen others]…
>
> Mr Joseph Clark is the young painter whose picture of 'the Sick Child' attracted much well merited praise in the Academy Exhibition of 1857. This year's picture is from the same class, and apparently from the same models. An artisan leaning against one of his doorposts is tickling with his empty pipe a baby which crows and chuckles in his mother's arms. The mother smiles placidly on her little one, while a toddler some years older swings on her apron. Perfect in its simple and homely expression of domestic love, satisfying technical requirements in drawing, colour and composition this picture is evidence that domestic subjects need not be either coarse or trivial. The love and peace that radiate from these common faces bring the work within that wide circle of the affections which includes the highest and lowest of us. Mr Clark is one of those among our

younger painters whose works may always be looked on with a confidence that they will repay examination."

The Times 9 February 1859

This piece gives some idea of the time pressures faced by critics at the time. Although the Times critic spent six hours at the exhibition, this represents around 30 seconds per work – and he reinforces the importance of positioning in being noticed by critics.

The Birmingham Daily Post was equally critical of the exhibition and largely positive about Joseph's entry:

"The British Institution. (From the Daily News.) The exhibition of the works of living artists at the Gallery of the British Institution … in Pall Mall, was opened to the public yesterday. This is usually called the spring exhibition, to distinguish it from the exhibition of 'Old Masters' in the summer. At the private view on Saturday, we were sorry to find the gloomy anticipations among the fraternity of St. Luke, caused by a dull December, realised in a very mediocre display. After the extraordinary gathering of last year, this exhibition has subsided even below its usual level. There are extremely few works of which any definite impression can be retained. Commonplace, to use a paradox, is everywhere paramount. At the head of the 'pinafore painters' are Messrs. Clark, A. Smith, T.F. Dicksee. and Mr. Hemsley. At Mr. Clark's 'Cottage Door' (S98), a countryman, in corduroys and crimson velvet 'vest', is, with intense glee, tickling his infant under the chin with the stock of his pipe. The figure holding the baby is of rather an ambiguous age – she is too old to be the eldest daughter of the man, and too young to be his wife. But the attitude of the 'child, clinging with a slight touch of jealousy, at the notice of baby to her apron strings, is admirable. The colouring is as usual heavy."

Birmingham Daily Post 9 February 1859

The reference to the fraternity of St: Luke is obscure for modern readers. It may refer obliquely to the early Christian tradition that St Luke the evangelist was the first icon painter or possibility to the Guilds of St Luke in the Middle Ages that gathered together and protected painters. It may also refer to the art movement in early nineteenth century Vienna mentioned earlier.

The Observer's critic (6th February 1859) was more succinct when he wrote that *'The Cottage Door by Mr Joseph Clark must be spoken of with high praise'*. The Examiner (12 February 1859) continued *'while Mr Joseph Clark, in his small, picture of the Cottage Door – a rustic tickling his child's neck with the end of his tobacco – pipe-adds to the credit he has won already'*.

As mentioned previously 1859 was a difficult year for William Barnes Hopefully he took comfort from a mention of 'The Cottage Door' in the Dorset County Chronicle recognising the growing fame of his pupil:

"It may not be generally known in our county that the fast-rising and already distinguished artist. Mr. Joseph Clark, the painter of the much-admired picture of this year exhibition of the Institution of British Artists, 'The Cottage Door' of which a print appears in the last number of the Illustrated London News, is a Dorsetshire man, a native of Cerne Abbas. He was formerly a pupil of the Rev. W. Barnes, of Dorchester, and under his roof, received his first lessons in art."

Dorset County Chronicle 31 March 1859

The Times' critic followed Joseph's success at the British Institution with a glowing review of his work – 'The Draughts Player' – at that year's RA Summer Exhibition:

"Unsurpassed not only by any work in its class here, but by any such work ever painted by an English Master is Mr J. Clark's 'Draughts players'. This is the same artist whose work 'The Sick Child' excited such admiration two seasons ago, and whose 'Cottage Door' in this year's exhibition of the British Institution, we called attention in our notice of that gallery. Mr Clark in the current picture has aimed at no excitement of the tenderer domestic sympathies. The interest is purely physiognomical and domestically dramatic. But, as it is, it is perfectly attained. Without the least trick of method, every part of the picture is presented with its proper strength, and holds its true relative prominence. We see no reason why Mr. Clark should not in due course rank with Wilkie, and above all who have followed in Wilkie's track. He has as keen a sense of physiognomical truth as Webster, with a far higher power of solid and effective painting …"

The Times 30 April 1859

Six days later the tone was much was less entustic about the 'Draught Players'. Presumably this came from a different Times critic who wrote:

"… J. Clark has been stronger in former years than he is in his 'Draught Players' though in this picture too we see enough of fine feeling for character and a power of feeling of seizing the paintable points of modern middle class life, without exaggeration, to entitle the work to the most respectful mention…"

The Times 5 May 1859

A hesitancy about the 'Draught Players' in the second review in The Times appears again in the London Daily News Review:

"Mr. Clark, whose 'Sick Boy' attracted notice last year, has in the 'Draught-players' (209) improved in colour. It is rather leathery still, but the colouring is not nearly so unpleasant as in former works. In other respects, this picture is very satisfactory. Cleverly, however, as the mere attitude of the boy perched up in the chair indicates his consciousness of having made the winning move, as he looks up in his grandfather's puzzled face, it was not necessary to conceal the boy's face altogether. Moreover, there is certainly no originality in the picture; the incident has been painted in every particular the same by innumerable small artists; and with all the evidence of improvement and with all the unaffected naturalness of this little work, we are not yet disposed to subscribe to the extravagant eulogiums which have been passed by a contemporary on this young artist."

London Daily News 5 May 1859

The Examiner's critic agreed and went further in his criticism:

"There is a little skill in Mr. J. Clark's Draught Players, where the grandfather is beaten by the boy, and the boy's triumph is cleverly shown, though his face is averted, and we see only his body and the outline of his cheek."

The Examiner 30 April 1859

The paper had clearly changed its assessment in its concluding remarks on the Exhibition three months later:

"One of the most popular of the domestic pictures this year is Mr Clark's Draught Players, to which we referred in our first notice. The love of a grandfather that, as Germans would say, joins with a kiss the two extremes of life, is not a hackneyed theme. The picture is full of it. The boy's kite is stuck behind the clock, his slate and sponge hang from a nail on the wall, — ornaments welcome there as any picture; his ship is on the mantelpiece: and while the old man is happy in the triumph of the boy over himself, he can make room between his knees for yet another child, to whom he has given up his watch for study. There are other signs that love of children is supreme within the room, but none of them are forced or conventional, Next to the admirable painting of the two draught players, the charm of Mr Clark's work lies especially in this."

The Examiner 9 July 1859

This critic is the first to draw attention to Joseph's particular skill in using minor details in works to reinforce the overall impression he wanted to convey.

The Art Journal record of the Summer Exhibition lists Joseph's work saying:

"'The Draught-players', J. Clark 'To teach his grandson draughts then His leisure he'd employ. Until, at last, the old man Was beaten by the boy' Such is the situation. A ragged urchin, whose feet do not reach the floor, as he sits on his rickerty chair, is chuckling over the draught-board whereon he beats his grandsire. The heads and extremities of the figures are less careful than in other works by the same hand; but is a perfect knowledge of the means of producing good effects: all the figures – (for besides the two mentioned there are others) – are well brought out."

The Art Journal 1859, p.165

The description from the exhibition catalogue quoted by the Art Journal may be an oblique reference an unattributed quotation in the preface in Frederick Milnes Edge's (1859) book about a tour of Europe in the late 1850s by Paul Morphy, the American teenaged chess champion.

By the end of the exhibition one critic was full of praise for Joseph:

"Literature, Science, and Art. Exhibition of the Royal Academy. (East room) The opening of the Exhibition of the Academy gives rise, usual, to an immense amount of criticism and invective, against the administration in general, and the hanging committee in particular. Sad accounts we hear of the labour of years being rejected for want of space, or worse, accepted and placed out of sight; of favouritism and extreme partiality the part of those gentlemen whose unenviable privilege it to be upon the hanging committee for 1859. ... We have neither space nor leisure to join in the discussion, for there are thirteen hundred and eighty-two works of art to be considered, and the most remarkable taken in review. It will be manifestly impossible, within the limits allotted to the Fine Arts to do much more than to point out the leading pictures: but we shall endeavour to this in such manner to give good general idea of the exhibition. ...

... come to one of the best works (in the style of Wilkie, Webster, and Mulready—surpassing the two latter it may be) to be found the collection and far advance of anything from Mr. J Clark's pencil before produced. The title is The Draught-players (209). Common-place incident described in the catalogue in four lines 'To teach his draughts then His leisure he'd employ. Until last the old man was beaten by the boy.' The subject is rendered unusually interesting by the admirable delineation of the whole group, the quiet humour, and excellent painting in all details. The grandfathers puzzled look, the attitude of the child between his knees, and of the boy play are all wonderfully truthful and forcible in expression."

Cambridge Chronicle and Journal 23 July 1859

Despite the wealth of contemporary comment about the 'Draught Players' there is a good deal of confusion about a sketch (or possibly two sketches) with this title. One is in the Victoria and Albert

Museum's drawings collection and the other sold in London on 19th November, 2008 and described as a study for 'Checkmate'. These images are similar if not identical but do not resemble either the 'Draught Players' or the 1860 work 'Chess Players'. The Victoria and Albert Museum's work has a penciled inscription 'chess players' without a date that may well be a later addition. 'Checkmate' exhibited in 1876 is similar in style and composition to the Victorian and Albert Museum's drawing.

It is clear that in just two and a half years after his first exhibition that Joseph was regarded as a rising star of the fine art world. In a piece complaining about a change in the rules for the Liverpool Academy's exhibition the Liverpool Mercury lists him as one of those who did not attend:

> "The names of Sir E. Landseer, Cooke, Lewis, D. Roberts Cope, Faed, J. Clark, Stanfield Lee, Oakes, and Mulcready, are suggestive only, so far as this exhibition is concerned, of what might have been there rather than what is. It remains to be seen whether long-impending consequences will be arrested and averted by the new self-protective rule which the Academy has thought fit to adopt."
>
> **Liverpool Mercury** 16 September 1859

1860

Early in 1860 Joseph exhibited the 'Dawn of Genius' sent from Kentish Town to the British Institution.

> "Fine Arts. British Institution. Private View. The picture season has not opened vary auspiciously. The private view which took place on Saturday, at this gallery, did not reveal to us any latent talent, and very little of established perfection. The plain fact is, that arts leading men have too much employment and too much inducement to earn money quickly, and the aspirants for fame have not enough skill and genius to alarm them with regard to the safety of their laurels, or, what would be ten times more exciting to their minds, sufficient standing with the public to endanger their profits. The consequence is, that all the works above 'the line' are crude in execution, and either far-fetched or common-place in subject, and those whose pictures are enjoying the best places are generally examples of considerable haste, or merely a new painting of an old subject to run on after its predecessors in the accustomed groove. ...
>
> Of the comic scenes, we prefer a little unpretending bit entitled 'Dawning of Genius'. A little girl is holding a dog to have his portrait taken by the dawning genius, her brother, perhaps, who is seated, fully prepared to do something fine, while other boys are looking on. There is much quiet humour in this subject, and it is judiciously painted in subdued colour, so as to draw the whole attention upon the figures and their occupation. It is by Mr. Joseph Clarke."
>
> **London Standard** 6 February 1860

On the 9th February, The Morning Post contained an advertisement saying that the Illustrated London News for the 11th February would containan engraving of pictures from the British Institution including the 'Dawning of Genius' by Mr J. Clark.

> "The Dawn of Genius Joseph Clark. 'Genius is here manifested by a boy, who makes a portrait of the fat household terrier, which he has pearched for that purpose on a table, and causes him to be held in pose by his sister. There is a great deal of point in the characters and situation; but the picture looks altogether slight, in comparason with former works."
>
> **Art Journal** p.50 1860

> "Mr Joseph Clark represents cleverly the Dawning of Genius by a boy sketching a dog."
>
> **The Examiner** 7 April 1860

This was the first occasion in which Joseph exhibited works dealing with young people beginning to draw and paint the world around them. Several others followwed.

Joseph exhibited two works at the RA's 1860 Exhibition from his new home – 25 Belle Vue Villas, Holloway, London.

The first was The Chess Players.

> "Mr. Clark has now painted Chess-players in polite lodgings by the sea. An old gentleman plays with a girl who refers for counsel to a brother or lover. There is admirable variety and consistency in the expression of the old gentleman's face, but as a whole the work does not satisfy the eye."
>
> **The Examiner** 5 May 1860

> "We confess we do not see any particular point of meaning or sentiment, or character especially worth painting in Mr. Clark's 'Chess Players' (456), nor is the colouring agreeable. We hope Mr. Clark will not prove one of those promising young artists who have been injured by injudicious praise."
>
> **London Daily News** 17 May 1860

This work is significant in that it was the first to place the characters in a middle class context and at a seaside location. It is tempting to speculate that the work's location was inspired by a visit to the seaside, perhaps to Joseph's sister in Christchurch.

The other work was not typical of Joseph's previously exhibited work. It was Hagar & Ishmael. In this choice of subject he was following in the brushstrokes of many others inspired by the emotional content of the story found in Genesis. This tells of Abraham, Sarah (his wife) and Hagar (her maidservant). In time both women had children fathered by Abraham – Ishmael and Issac. Sarah became angry and told Abraham to send Hagar and Ishmael away. He did this with a heavy heart. Hagar lost her way in the desert and the water they carried in a goat's skin ran out. In despair she prepared to abandon her child. At that moment she heard a voice from heaven and saw there was a spring close at hand. Joseph's picture depicts Hagar's despair in the desert giving rise to the work's subtitle 'And the water was spent in the bottle'.

This work attracted no attention from the critics and was the first of his exhibited works to be ignored. In 1863, The Art Journal issued an engraving of this work and introduced it with a lengthy piece on the distinction between sacred and historical art; which was viewed as a lower form than sacred art:

> "Repudiating the wish to put Mr Clark's touching and graceful work in the lower class than we would feel warranted in assigning to it, we cannot admit it to be within the canons of sacred art. Neither is it true to the description given in the Book of Genesis where we read that Hagar – when the bottle of water given to her by Abraham for herself and child when they were cast into the wilderness from Beersheba, was emptied – 'placed the child under one of the shrub, she went and sat her down over against him a good way off; for she said 'Let me not see the death of the child'. And she sat over against him, and lift up her voice and wept. The place too is very dissimilar to that which travellers and geographers assign to the locality where the event occurred. Beersheba – which means 'the well of the oath' from the treaty made there by Abraham with Abimelech – is not a rocky mountainous country, as it is here represented, but almost a flat desert with a few hilly elevations scattered about.
>
> We must therefore consider the picture as a kind of allegory; and a most pathetic and poetical rendering the artist has given the subject; the composition of the two figures is excellent, the drawing vigorous, yet careful and the expression or sentiment true and unconventional. The line

of cloud behind the head, and at right angles with the rock, should have been omitted; it is altogether in the way. The picture was exhibited at the Royal Academy in 1860; it was painted for Mrs Clark, mother of the artist."

Art Journal 1863, p.52

Joseph might have got the geography wrong, as this would have been less important for him than the underlying message of God's mercy for those in great distress. However, this work may also be evidence that Joseph had gained sufficient confidence to allow him to vary the style and subject matter of works submitted to major exhibitions. Perhaps the lack of a positive response from the media to this work discouraged him from going beyond contemporary genre in works submitted to exhibition societies.

Not all of Joseph's works at this time were successful in being exhibited and not all were oil paintings. The watercolour of a 'Mother washing a little girl' from about 1860 shows that Joseph was already producing work in varied styles and mediums.

1861

From time to time, newspapers recorded sales of Joseph's works for significant sums, though it is not clear whether these were sold by the artist themselves or by an original purchaser. In the first report of the kind mentioning Joseph in The Times (6th May 1861) said 'The Chess Players' had been sold for 110 guineas – about £7,700. This was despite the lukewarm response of the critics a year earlier.

In July 1861 his contributions to that year's RA Summer Exhibition received a positive reception from four critics:

"The 'wanderer' and 'restored' a double picture by J Clark of a lady and gentlemen finding a little girl who has strayed away into the woods, and of the child's restoration to its home. Sweet in colour and excellent in expression like all this young painter has done."

The Times 13 May 1861

"By Mr Clark there are two companion pictures, 'The Wanderer, a little child strayed with her kitten and 'Restored', the same little girl taken home to her family. Both pictures are too negative in colour. But no similar subjects in the exhibition are more charmingly naïve in treatment. The artist has certainly studied, and has not unsuccessfully rivalled the best efforts of a similar kind by the French painter, Mr Edouard Frère."

Daily News 21 May 1861

"… but Mr Clark has distinguished himself in two simple pictures, called The Wanderer [and] Restored. A child strayed away into a wood, is found, and bought back. That is the story, but Mr Clark has managed to infuse such expression and interest into his picture with very simple materials."

Leamington Spa Courier 25 May 1861

The Westmoreland Gazette contained a full description taken from The Athenaeum magazine:

"This exhibition contains few things to compare with Mr J Clark's two pictures for character, humour, and playful tenderness of the most genuine kind. Good in those qualities as this artist's works have hitherto been, he has gone beyond himself in these, and more than redeemed the temporary falling back of one or two recent examples. These paintings are entitled 'The Wanderer' and 'Restored'. In the first a young lady has been strolling through a wood with her father, and just at the margin of a meadow they come across a little girl of two years old, a chubby, toddling, shy thing that, following the gambols of a pet kitten, has strayed right away across a field from home, and never been missed, herself so absorbed with the kitten, and not yet hungry, missing nothing. Down knelt the lady by the child's side to coax from its half crying little self the news of where it lived and what was its name. The face of the child, as she puts her finger in her mouth's corner, and eyes the benevolent stranger half-askant, half-afraid, not without some suspicion of having taken offence at their intrusion on herself and the kitten, which she hold persistently by the leg is charming; up go the little shoulders and close the plump little feet. The lady herself has a charmingly natural action as she half kneels, half-stoops low to the sitting child; simple as this figure is it is very elegant. Behind stand the old man, leaning with grave and simple amusement on his umbrella. In the second picture they have led the little dumpling home and her mother almost before she knew the child was lost, gets her back again. Frightened by the unknown dander, and not a little so by the strangers, kind as they are, the little heroine trots to her mother, keeping fast hold of the kitten with one arm, while the other is unwillingly given to the strange lady's leading hand. The lady stoops to her charge with a conscious and pleased smile, natural and good; the old man fussily points to the place of capture with his umbrella and 'speaks of the deeds they have done'. The mother is glad and pitiful. There is good fun in the long necked and bodied black cat, who at the sight of her offspring comes forward, twice her natural length, topaz eyed all bright, mewing to her tabby child. Although very low in key, indeed almost grey in general colour, this picture has qualities of real and scientific colour."

Westmorland Gazette 18 May 1861

A more negative tone is taken by The Era:

"J Clark should beware of weakness in colour. His two little pictures – The Wanderer and restored – are as usual, very clever in expression, but look pale and chalky."

The Era 9 June 1861

The final comment is interesting for the light it throws on the way critics approached their task; and for being the first occasion on which the critic merely mentioned that Joseph had exhibited a work. This tendency grew over the years. Although some of this could be ascribed to the falling away of the critic's interest in contemporary genre there are hints in the review in the Aberdeen Journal that space (and thus cost) constraints were becoming more pressing. In the remainder of this book, such brief comments will not be recorded.

"We regret that, in passing through the West and Entrance Rooms, we have time to mention merely the names of Mr. Clark, whose 'Sick Child' made a sensation three years ago; of Messrs. Morris, Stone, Yeames; and of the Misses d Mutrie, so well known for their flower pieces. There are several other pictures throughout the rooms sufficiently noticeable, but we are not familiar enough with the styles of painters to detect their names without the aid of a catalogue, which, at the time we write, is not printed."

Aberdeen Journal 8 May 1861

The exhibition was not without incident:

"bow street. Baldueci, journeyman modeller, in the employ of Mr. Bruociani, of Russell Street, Covent-garden, was brought before Mr. Come, in custody of Sergeant Tanner, of the detective force, charged with stealing case, containing 7 cameos, 8 miniature brooches, a case containing silver impressions from rifle medal dies, and 7 oil paintings, the whole valued at [£200], from the Royal Academy, where had been employed in arranging the statuary."

London Evening Standard 4 June 1861

And:

"The seven pictures stolen early in May from the mass 'rejected' in the Royal Academy's [exhibition] have not yet been traced."

Leicester Journal 19 July 1861

1862

In February 1862, the critics praised Joseph's work but some questioned his use of colour and the handling of some aspects of composition in 'Return of the Runaway' exhibited at the British Institution. The model in this work is most likely Nathaniel Clark, Joseph's cousin, who had served in the Marines. There was extensive coverage:

"… This picture (The Jury by Mr J Morgan) and its near neighbour 'Return of the Runaway' (J Clark) are the best pictures of common life in the exhibition. Mr Clark is the painter of the 'Sick Child', which attracted much well deserved admiration at the Royal Academy Exhibition a few days (*sic*) ago. He has never since equaled either the interest or the workmanship of his first work.

The picture here represents a sailor coming back to his old father and mother after an absence long enough to make him a stranger to a nephew of three or four years, who stands wondering at the cool self-assured manner of the intruder. The old woman rises from her chair in the chimney corner and gazes with fixed tremulous earnestness at the stalwart sailor as he puts his hand on his father's shoulder, and scares him from his newspaper. The merit of the picture is well-conceived, quiet play of expression. It is free from the staginess which the subject rather provokes, and there is a happy selection of the moment of suspense to which Terbourg has resorted to give interest to his best pictures. Mr Clark's method of painting is dry and rather timid, but he shows a right feeling for air and graduation and the soundest judgment in his composition and in the arrangement of the quiet – many would say over quiet – colour. …

The picture strengthens our belief that Mr Clark is the best painter of expression in subjects of common life we have had since Wilkie, unless it be Webster. When Mr Clark has painted as many pictures as Webster the comparison between them may be made under fairer conditions. The only wish we would express in Mr Clark's case would be for a little more courage in colour and handling."

The Times 10 February 1862

The reference is to Gerard ter Borch (1617–1681), also known as Gerard Terburg, who was a Dutch genre painter of the Dutch Golden Age.

"The British Institution. There was a time when the annual exhibitions of this society were looked forward to by the lovers of art with something like feelings of pleasant anticipation, and when it was regarded, as its name implies, as 'an institution for promoting the Fine Arts in the United Kingdom.' Now, however, all this is changed; a constant repetition of displays, in which works of art in the true acceptation of the term – have been, as a rule, conspicuous by their absence; when the pictures which cover the walls have barely sustained the character of the exhibition up to the unsatisfactory standard of respectable mediocrity have told, year after year, of the waning glories of the British Institution. We are wholly, at a loss to understand why it is that an institution which boasts of Royal patronage … and at least a hundred names more or less influential in the world of art, has failed so egregiously in its mission. The hereditary principle, however it may apply to a House of Peers, certainly does not seem to work successfully with the 'Governors' of a British Institution that has to deal with matters of art. In former times the exhibitions of this association rivaled in their interest those of the Royal Academy itself, and. upon its walls were hung works by the most eminent artists of the day. Each year has, however, it seen a gradual falling off in the amount of talent displayed, while in the present year, with the exception of that of Mr. Frost, there is not the name of an artist of any great celebrity in the whole list of exhibitors. … Mr. J. Clark' sends 'The Return of a Runaway', a work pleasant to look at, and very meritorious in its execution."

Morning Chronicle 10 February 1862

"Mr. Clark, who first attracted notice in these rooms, but who is better known by his picture of the 'Sick Child', exhibited at the Royal Academy, is a painter of a very different stamp, yet of the highest merit. It would be difficult to define the nameless charm of perfect naturalness, or to over praise the modest reverence of the handling and the quiet silvery tone, in 'The Return of the Runaway' (28). The simple incident is already known from an excellent cut in a recent number of the Illustrated London News. A boy, whose early passion for the sea is indicated by the marine drawing, probably of his own performance, on the wall, has returned in his smart sailor dress, and with the honourable stripe on his arm, to the humble home from which he ran away long since. But be is so much grown and altered that he is not immediately recognised by his parents. His mother rises, with quickest instinctive apprehension in her pale yearning face, but the old gentleman, startled by the hand on his shoulder, looks up from his paper (which he has probably been searching for news of his boy) only in temporary bewilderment and helpless inquiry. The touching truth of expression in this unpretending picture we confidently commend to the reader's sympathy be he who he may, for here is the 'Touch of nature which makes the whole world kin'."

London Daily News 10 February 1862

These quotations show the way in which each viewer of a genre painting can develop their narrative contained within the work to focus on different issues and aspect of the work. The 'Return of the Runaway' sold for £189 (around £15,400). The Times reported in May 1867 that Christie, Manson and Woods sold this picture for £178 (around £13,780) following the death of Dominic Colnaghi. It became part of a collection formed by James Virtue, the publisher of The Art Journal and in turn was sold by Christie, Manson and Woods in March 1879.

Towards the end of the year, we see evidence of another early engraving of the 'Return of the Runaway:

"Literature. The Leisure Hour. Part CXXX, October. London; 6 at Paternoster-rows In the Leisure Hour we have read with interest and profit papers on lighthouses and lighthouse keepers. The life of these secluded beings is exceedingly well drawn, and both papers contain much that is new and interesting. The chief illustration is a really capital engraving of Mr. Clark's telling picture, 'The Return of the Runaway'."

Derby Mercury 12 November 1862

The Art Journal issued an engraving of the work in 1869 and the accompanying description read:

"The painter of this picture is one of our younger school of artists, who but in a comparatively few years since he worked his way into a favourable position as a delineator of genre subjects, and has succeeded in maintaining it. … [His works since 1863] all supply ample evidence of fidelity to his early faith. … Whatever of success may have attended an artist's labours in a particular department, it may be doubted if, as a rule, he does not in some degree compromise his independence and do injustice to himself by keeping so strictly within its limits. … We would kindly drop a hint to Mr. Clark to endeavour to get out of the labourer's cottage, and bid adieu, at least for a while to the family: we are sure he has within him good stuff that would justify a venture in some other field of action. … His 'Return of the Runaway' exhibited at the British Institution in 1862 is undoubtedly one of the best works he has painted. When English boys leave their homes, clandestinely it is generally to get to sea; and often one or two voyages curb their wandering spirits. But this runaway has evidently been absent for years, and has grown into manhood, so that when he again seek the parental roof he is a stranger to the old folk: the expression on the father's face, as the seaman declares his relationship, is capitally rendered, while the mother fixes her eyes on him with a kind of half recognition as if to trace out some line or mark that would set all uncertainty at rest. The picture, like all Mr Clark does, is very carefully painted in all its details."

Art Journal 1869 p.296

The press did not mention 'Preparing for Sunday' exhibited at the 1862 RA. William Frith, who exhibited 'The Railway Station' in 1862, records that 21,150 people visited over the seven weeks of the exhibition. Indeed Wallis (1957) mentioned that on three occasions, Frith's works needed protection from the crowd by rails and in one case, a police officer.

1863

Early in 1863, The Art Journal (1863) published a 'retrospective' assessment of Joseph's work in its series 'British Artists: their style and character' This offers a useful appreciation of his work after first five years as a professional artist.

"Seated on one of the benches provided by the Royal Academy … the thought has not infrequently induced us to ask ourselves – where are the men who are rising up to occupy the places of their elders, of those still sustaining the reputation of the British School. …

Pictures known as genre, or as they are commonly termed domestic subjects, seem to promise well for the future; certainly they are much in favour with those artists who aspire to be figure-painters, and are unquestionably the most popular with the public. The reason is obvious enough. We are emphatically a domestic people; other nations may equal us in their love of their country, but they have not the same regard for their homes. An Englishman, as a rule, fees pride in his home and household, whether he be wealthy or in humble circumstances; his sympathies are in harmony with everything that speaks of home-affections, home-influences, home pursuits. Art, which touches the slightest chord that harmonises with these feelings, he therefore welcomes; and because it does this, its spirit is intelligible to him, though he … might criticise the aesetic qualities of the work, or give any other reason for the interest he takes in it other than he likes it … When discussing this we must not loose sight of our immediate purpose which is to say a few words of a young artist who promises well as a genre painter. There are none of his standing from whom, by careful study and discriminating observation more might reasonably be expected. Joseph Clark… . His first exhibited picture 'The Dead Rabbit' evidenced at once the class of subject he had determned to adopt, while the excellent manner in which it was treated showed no less forceably his careful training. … In the same year he sent to the Royal Academy 'The Sick Child' which however represented – is undoubtedly a really clever picture – can never give unmixed pleasure. In truth, the more merit such a work exhibits in treatment, the less enjoyment it does offer to the spectator, and the artist producing it, therby limits, to a considerable extent, his chance of finding a purchaser. It is clear than such reasoning had no weight with Mr Clark … for in the folowing year he submitted to the Academy another work of a similar description, entitled 'the doctor's visit'. … whoever took the pains to give a little careful examination to the composition, could not fail to admire the vigour with which the figures are presented, their truthful individuality, and the skilful arrangemen tof light and shade. …

And out of the sick room …. We welcomed Mr Clark at the British Institution in 1859 with his 'Cottage Door'. In the same yeas the artist exhibited at the Academy 'The Draught Players' a picture which for humour Webster and for finish Meissonier might have painted. From a game of draughts in a rustic cottage to a game of chess in a well-furnished sitting-room appears ro be a very natural transposition; accordingly we find Mr Clark exhibiting at the Academy in 1860 'The Chess Players'. …

What we have to remark in this picture as a commendable point is the absence of any false sentimntality; there is no attempt at painting up to 'exhibition pitch'. The young lady and her lover … are not creations of some other world than our own, but are people moving in a good class of society, such a one ordinarily meet with. A subject of very diferent class to any of the proceeding was exhibited with 'the Chess Players'; this was 'Hagar and Ishmael' …

In 1861 he sent two pictures … entitled 'The Wanderer' and 'Restored'. Nothing in the world of art could be more unaffected and natural than these compositions; both are excellent. … We hold this to be a perfect specimen of genuine art – as perfect of its kind as could be placed on canvass.

The 'Return of the Runaway' was exhibited at the British Institution last year … Here again we have one of those unpretentious subjects treated with consumate skill and tact, which makes its own appeal to our achnowledgement of truth of Art. …

The only other picture exhibited by the artist is 'Preparing for Sunday' at the Academy last year. This is also a cottage scene … It is that this is not superior to his previous works, it is certainly not below them. Mr Clark in point of years, has scarcely got beyond the threshold of his profession, and yet is one whom picture buyers and the public look after. He has, if life be granted to him, a long and honourable career before him, if he does not rest satisfied with the laurels already won. Hitherto he has devoted himself, with one single exception, to one particular class of subject, and presented it only on a small scale. With the qualities he has shown in these minor productions – minor only in size – it is only right to expect from him more important works, even if he limits his practice to domestic compositions. We should however, like to see him take higher ground, and should have no fear for the result; but whether or not he pleases to do so, and without advocating an obtrusive style of colouring, his pictutes would ain immeasurably by a richer display of the pigments; it is only in colour that he shows any timidity." James Diaforne.

The Art Journal 1863

This itself became news for the Dorset County Chronicle:

"The Art Journal's superb engravings include Clark's Hagar and Ishmael, still in the possession of Mrs. Clark, the painter's mother, for whom it was painted. The Art Journal in fact presents also three spirited woodcut illustrations of Mr. Clark's genre pictures under the series in progress of 'British Artists, their style and character.' As our readers are immediately interested in him as a Dorset genius, we extract a portion of the memoir."

Dorset County Chronicle 5 March 1863

The Observer's critic commenting on the British Institution's exhibition in 1863 wrote:

"'Auld Lang Syne' by Mr Joseph Clark illustrates two lines of the favorite Scottish song:

'We twa hae run amang the braes
And pu'd the gowans fine'

It is treated with much of his usual discernment and feeling, but is very cold in tone and in the head of the boy a little forced in expression."

Observer 8 February 1863

The English translation of this phrase is 'We two have run about the slopes, and picked the daisies fine'.

The Illustrated London News review of the 1863 RA Summer Exhibition was dismissive of that year's work:

"The chief strength of this exhibition resides, unquestionably, in the work of 'outsiders'. As a whole this collection cannot be considered an advance; but the much larger proportion of what interest it has will be found in the numerious contributions, especially in figure subjects, by the many promising but comparitively little known men. We do not remember to have seen the academic body so poorly represented. Hardly half dozen of these gentlemen exhibit works of marked importance."

Ilustrated London News 9 May 1863

Was Joseph a 'promising but relatively unknown man' in the Illustrated London News? The Times' criticic returned to the question of Joseph's use of colour when he reviewed 'After Work':

"Near these pictures is one who should be our best painter of cottage life since Wilkie, if he would shake off his timidity of colour and handling, and give free play to his great power of true expression, and his quite unvulgar feeling for humble life. This year's picture is the best since his 'Sick Child'. It is called 'After work' and represents a cottage fireside – the father with a child on his knee looking at an illustrated paper, the old mother in the chimney corner, the wife pouring out the tea, and the baby with all the gravity of two upon the floor at the father's feet. Mr Clark should abate his propensity to scatter his accessories, appropriate and well painted as they are; and he might in time produce picture which should be for the English labouring life what Edward Frere's are for that of France. We don't know how we could give higher praise."

The Times 2 May 1863

A similar tone was adopted in the Guardian's review this exhibition:

"… Mr Clark whose 'The Sick Child' created so much admiration a few years ago, does not advance his art as rapidly as might have been anticipated. It is to be feared that he is restraining his hand to a style that is drier and colder than one might desire it to be. Many beautiful points of feeling and expression will, however be discovered in the picture he now exhibits entitled 'After work' in which a labouring man, seemingly a mechanic, is seen sitting before the cottage fire and amusing the youngest of his children with an illustrated paper while his wife prepares the tea and the grandmother and other members of the family look on or assist. The homeliness of the scene and the air of comfort and sentiment of affection which pervade the whole of it could hardly be expressed with greater graphic truth. All that the picture seems to want is a greater warmth and geniality of tone."

Guardian 17 May 1863

In the 1860s, Francis Turner Palgrave (1866) a civil servant in the Education Department, poet and critic wrote a series of annual reviews of the RA Summer Exhibitions. In his review of the 1863 exhibition he said:

"The experience of foreign art gained at the 'International Exhibition,' appears to have impressed English spectators in general with the knowledge that, in some highly important matters, we are unequal to our Continental contemporaries. We do not draw so well; we do not hit the point so dexterously; we are not so skilful in telling a tale without the aid of minor bits of humour or sentiment; we do not concentrate the interest of our landscapes with such frankness. ...

Mr. Clark reminds us too forcibly of his popular 'Sick Child' by a somewhat blurred and morbidly coloured repetition of very similar models and arrangement in his 'After Work ... In good scenes from everyday life this Exhibition is not peculiarly rich'."

Towards the end of 1863, Joseph extended his audience by exhibiting at a show of Cabinet pictures by British artists held at 120 Pall Mall. One critic said that:

"Other noticeable pictures are here, in figures, two of Joseph Clark's 'A job for the Carpenter' (two children bringing a cross bow to be repaired by a kindly old worker in timber), and 'Any crockery today Marm' (a vendor of earthenware at a cottage door, with the cottager's wife inspecting his wares surrounded by her little ones). In both Mr Clark has, in great measure, escaped from that besetting sin of avoidance of positive colour and abuse of grey, which seemed to be growing on him, and keep back a man who promised to be our best painter of humble life since Wilkie. Mr Clark's expression was always admirably true, and his way of treating his subjects, however humble, as they were, had never of any of that vulgarity or false prettiness which condemns to worthlessness so much English work of this kind. Why the French painters of similar kind with Frere at their head, (his followers and pupils Duverger and Thorn are well represented here) should delight us as unfailingly as the English painters repel and disenchant, is too large for discussion here. Even Clark's work, good as it is, suffers when compared – as respects pictorial effect – with the second hand cottage scenes of Duverger and Thorn, who have borrowed, with Fere's secrets of lighting and effect, something of his naive charm and sweet simplicity of conception."

The Times 30 November 1863

"Fine Arts. French Gallery, Pall-Mall. The eleventh 'Winter Exhibition' of Cabinet pictures by British artists will be opened to the public this day. There are to be two prizes given this year – one of £100, for the best figure picture, and another of £50, for the best landscape. These prizes are for the encouragement of rising artists, and will be decided by three established judges and as many members of the Royal Academy. The collection as a whole is fully up to the usual average. … 'A Job for the Carpenter is a most carefully elaborated subject by Mr. J. Clark, and the colouring displays refined taste on the part of the painter'."

London Standard 9 November 1863

Admission was 1s and the catalogue 6*d* (£4.17 and £2.08). The Victoria and Albert Museum has a preparatory drawing for this work.

1864

Joseph did not exhibit in the 1864 British Institution exhibition. Palgrave (1866) provides an impression the critics approach to assessing the RA exhibition:

"So the fine things of former Royal Academies have passed from our eyes, and are, perhaps, too often remembered through a mist of confusing and trivial criticisms, or the caricatures of wood-cuts and bad coloured copies in the popular illustrated papers. Meanwhile, the efforts which some three or four hundred hard-working men have been making, during a twelvemonth, to please and edify us, appeal for judgment rather on their own merits than by way of comparison with standards no longer in view. At the most, without trying to weigh the harvest of 1864 against that of years immediately preceding, it may be safe to point out what appear to be cases of improvement, and to say that this Exhibition gives fair grounds of confidence, and just cause for pleasure, to those who watch the progress of English art with affectionate interest."

He notes developments in contemporary genre and associated styles:

"We have now to consider, with the painters of domestic life, those noteworthy younger artists whose figure-subjects form the most interesting, and perhaps the most advancing, section of English art. These painters differ too much to be brought under one definition; but on the whole, besides the increased regard for drawing, colour, and brilliancy which they show, they may be said to have introduced a new series of incident-subjects which cannot be classified under the two ancient heads of common life or history – being more poetical, and of wider scope than the first, whilst they rarely answer, either in style or in the choice of incident, to the old conventional idea of the grand or historical school."

Joseph's entry in this year's RA Exhibition, 'The New Cap' did not result in any press comment. Nor did it find a purchaser either for we find later in the year:

Royal Institution. Exhibition Paintings. Entering the second room, we come to … No. 226, "The New Cap", J. Clark. Although very high-priced, there is nothing very striking in this picture. The incident itself, a mother buying some new head gear for a little boy, his admiring sister looking approvingly, common-place ; and although the mechanical parts the work are skillfully handled, we should readily pass it by without more than very cursory glance, so far interest is concerned.

Manchester Courier and Lancashire General Advertiser 25 November 1864

1865

At the start of the year he sent 'Going to School' to the British Institution. This was the last of his works to be exhibited there and it received no press coverage.

Almost two years after the move to Christchurch, Joseph attempted to widen his audience by displaying his first work at the Society of British Artists in Suffolk Street. The critic of the London Standard describes the role played by the Society in the careers of young painters and new collectors

"The forty second exhibition of this Society was opened to the public on Monday last. Over a thousand pictures in oil and water colours and sixteen pieces of sculpture form the collection. … Rising students meet with excellent treatment at the Suffolk Street gallery, and having acquired some degree of confidence they proceed thence to the Royal Academy. The young City merchant goes to Suffolk Street for his first bit of landscape, still life or rustic figure and when he has amassed a splendid fortune he follows the ungrateful art students to the saloons of the Royal Academy…

'The Fisherman's Home' by Mr J Clark is among the few true pictures of humble life of which the collection can boast. The little fellow looks up and contemplates so seriously the laying of the tabecloth for dinner and, indeed, all the various features of the design, are proofs that the artist not only understands, but, moreover entertains an affectionate regard for the people whose habits he so faithfully portrays."

London Standard 3 April 1865

Another critic was not impressed by the exhibition:

"The present exhibition of the Society of British Artists cannot be said to compare unfavourably with those of former seasons. For some years past the character of the gallery has been fixed, and the visitor knows well that he has to expect a mass of wholly uninteresting work, surrounding and overpowering a few pictures of real merit. Merely mentioned in these conditions, cannot be considered favourable either to the fame of the gallery or to the reputation of individual artists, we may pass on to notice a few examples that strive to redeem the collection from reproach."

The Examiner 24 April 1875

By this stage Joseph had begun to reflect his new seaside home in his works although the description places the work firmly within the contemporary genre school and displays the skills and content that had characterised the critics' earlier response to his work. The Society's records show Joseph's work sold for £105 (about £8,750).

The Guardian's critic remained unenthusiastic about Joseph's work in his review of the 1865 RA exhibition. His criticism covered both the general hanging arrangements at the Academy and Joseph's work

"One must at times stoop to look at a good picture even on the walls of the Royal Academy, it is worth while to do so for the sake of good character painting as……… and perhaps also for 'Good Bye Baby', only Mr Clark is so perseveringly uninteresting in colour …"

The Guardian 30 April 1865

This was the only press comment on this work.

1866

The Guardian's critic was terse in his comment on Joseph's RA entry saying '… *The* "Labourer's Reward" *is one of Mr Clark's unpretending bits of realism*'. (20th May 1866). In time this work also became known as 'A father's reward'. It shows an older woman, perhaps the grandmother with two boys. She has been cooking and the boys are tasting the contents of a large copper bowl. Nearby three ducks are taking an interest in what is happening.

The other work from 1866 in the public domain is 'An apple from grandmother' was only the second of Joseph's works in an outdoor setting; the first being the 'Wanderer' (1861). It shows a small child taking an apple from a large bowl held by her grandmother watched by her mother. They are on a garden path close to the gate leading onto a village street. Perhaps the child and her mother are taking their leave of the old lady.

1867

In 1867 the Times reported that Joseph's 'Return of the Runaway' dated 1862 and regarded by the paper's art critic as *'a very important work of this esteemed artist'* sold for 170 guineas (around £13,420). The press failed to comment on only work he exhibited in 1867. 'Sissy's Lesson Bricks' at the RA.

1868

In 1868 Joseph exhited two paintings at the RA. These were 'Goodnight Father' and 'Ruth and Naomi'. Both were submitted from 8 Upper Tollington Road, London N. and neither received much attention in the press. The Observer said:

> "The scene is set outside a cottage door where a father is kissing goodnight to his elder daughter holding a doll. He is watched by the mother standing in the cottage door holding a younger child in her arms. The father is sitting on a bench beside the door having been interrupted in his work making some form of pointed stake … 'Good Night, Father' by Mr J. Clark is pure and simple in sentiment and in treatment, and has a better tone of colour than some of the earlier works of the same artist."
>
> **Observer** 17 May 1868

There is some confusion over this work as another with the same title appeared at the RA in 1881.

Although not mentioned in the press at the time of the exhibition, the Art Journal (p.296) mentioned 'Ruth and Naomi' in 1869 saying:

> "Only in one instance, as far as we can remember, has Mr. Clark ventured on anything like new ground; and that is in a picture of Ruth and Naomi exhibited last year at the Academy; and even here the domestic characteristic of the subject assimulates so closely though borrowed from Scripture narrative, to scenes of everyday occurance among ourselves, that it scarcely stands apart from his other works; it is a domestic incident, and the feeling that traces such on canvass, however different are the costumes physiognomies, etc. is the same, whether the subject be of ancient Oriental or of modern English origins."

The first twelve years as an artist

Joseph's marriage and return to London is a good point at which to pause and consider the progress he had made in his career.

In these early years he established himself as a professional artist producing contemporary genre paintings displaying excellent technical skills and compositions with considerable empathy for his subjects and the situations they faced. In the first five years his works attracted a lot of critical attention, mostly favourable with some forecasting a bright furture with the potential to become an excellent painter in the genre tradition rivaling some to the most renowned artists of the past.

He also experimented with the works he exhibited including religious subjects and using middle class households. As neither attracted favourable critical responses, he returned to genre works in respectable rural settings. We know he was also producing but not exhibiting portraits and watercolours at this point in his career.

After 1863 and his move to Christchurch critical interest in his work waned. The end of the decade saw an upswing in Joseph's life with his marriage and the birth of his first daughter – Annie Susan.

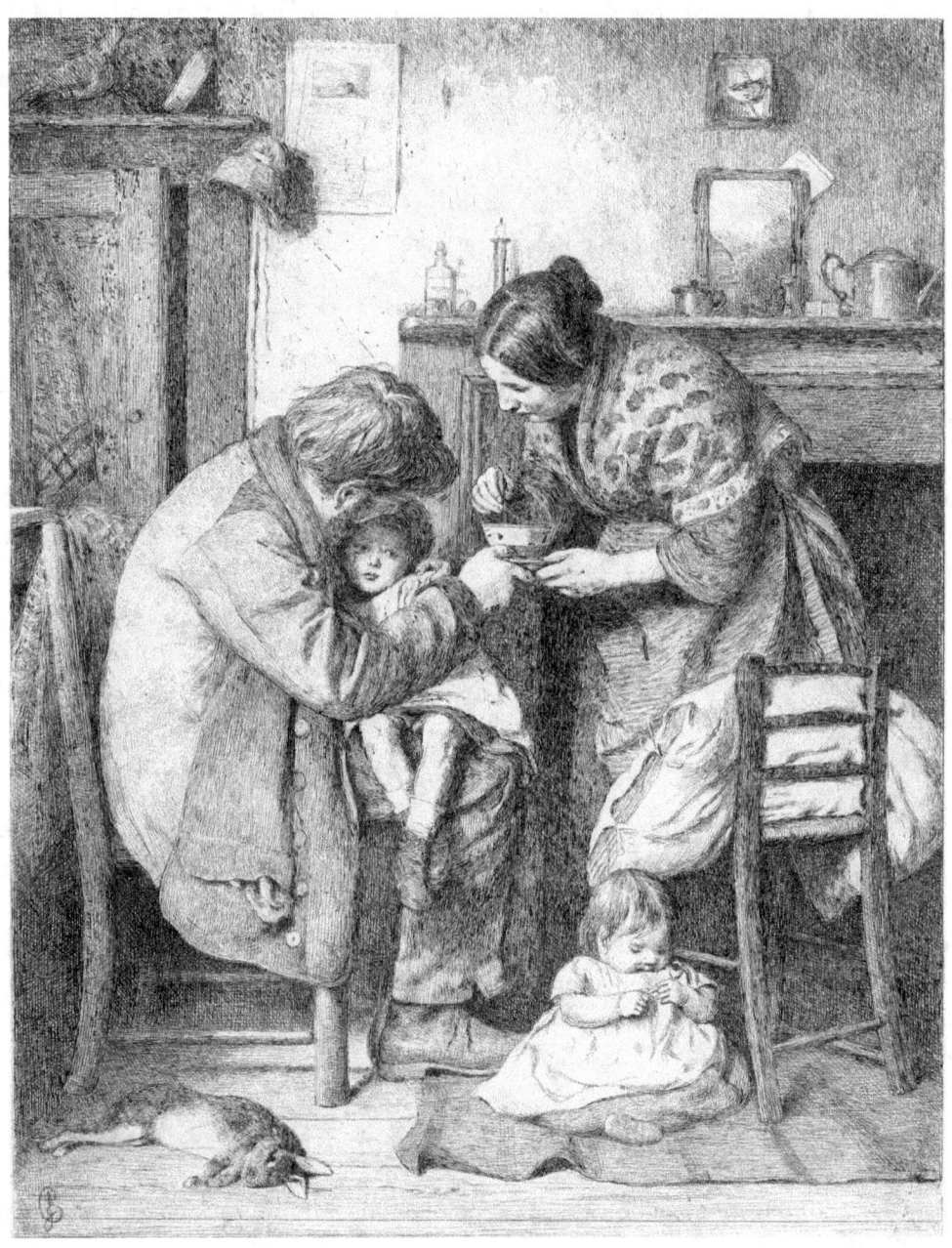

5. The Sick Child (1857). (Courtesy Victoria and Albert Museum)

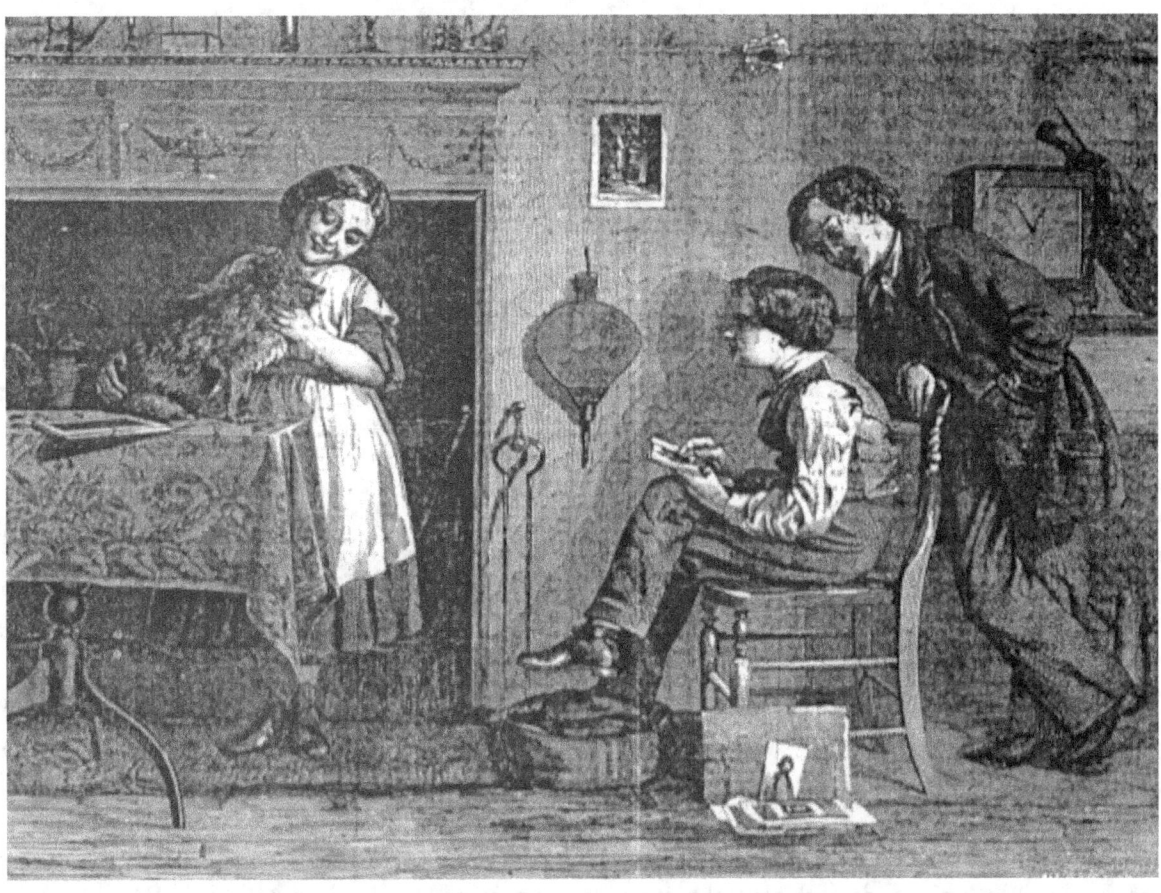

6. 'Dawning of Genius' (1860). Engraving by W. Thomas for The Art Journal 1860. (Courtesy the artist's family)

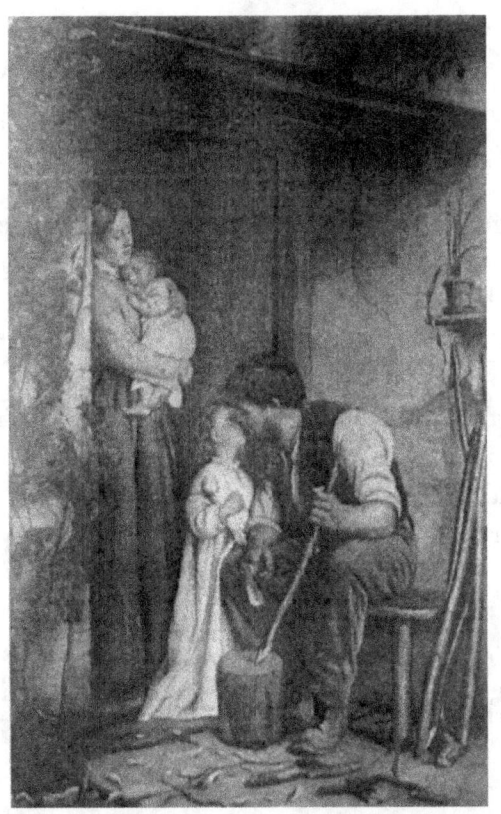

7. 'Goodnight Father' (1868). (Courtesy
Victoria and Albert Museum)

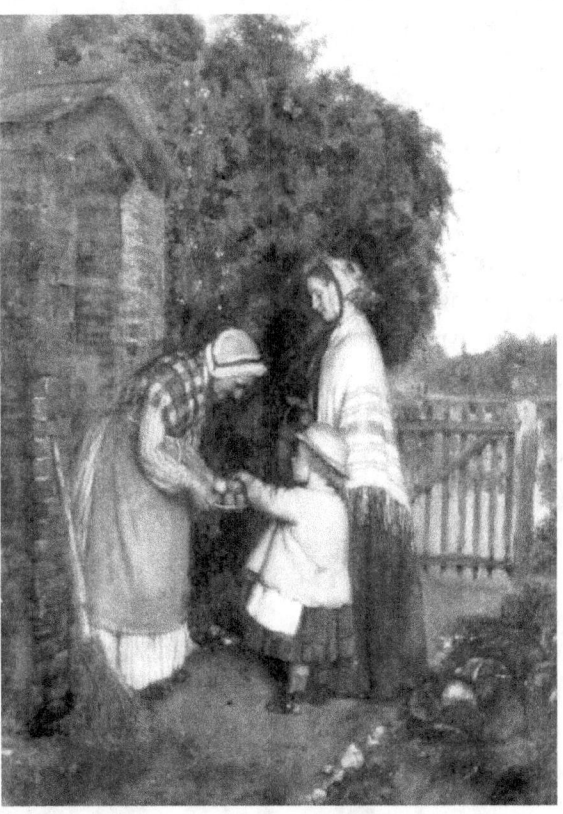

8. 'Apple from Grandmother' (1866).
(Courtesy Sothebys)

SEVEN

In the doldrums

(1869–1889)

At the end of the eighteen sixties Joseph was settling into a new phase in his life, domestically and professionally. He was an established professional artist who achieved early success but had somehow failed to realise the potential several critics identified in the eighteen fifties.

Family Life

Domestically Joseph was settling into married life at Arthur Road, Holloway, North London. Their first child, Annie Susan, known as 'Poppie', arrived in 1869 and by the time of the 1871 Census the household included both Jane Scard and Emma Mills, a fourteen years old general household servant. Annie sister, the eleven year old Alice Jones was also there on census night. Jane Scard died shortly after the census. Joseph registered her death from Holloway and entered her estate in the death duty register for 1871. At the time only estates worth more than £20 (around £13,800) had to be registered for Death Duty.

Married life and Joseph's return to London seems to have rejuvinated his career. By the early 1870s he was back into his stride with several pictures being accepted each year for the RA. But this phase in his career did not last long.

In 1873 the young Clark family moved to a larger house at 394 Camden Road where they lived until 1886. Prresumably this reflected his growing success and rising income. In time, Joseph and Annie had three further children; two of them while living at Camden Road. These were, Elsie in 1883 and Wilfrid in 1885. Margaret their youngest child arrived just after they left Camden Road.

The 1881 Census shows the household as Joseph, Annie, Annie Susan, Helen Jones (aged 16 – Annie's sister from Winchester), Kate Hampton (aged 22 – servant originally from Southampton) and Jane Brant (aged 72) and described as a 'monthly nurse'. A 'monthly nurse' cared for a mother and baby during the first few weeks of life. Why she was there is unknown although given the 14 year gap between Annie Susan and Elsie there is a possibility that Annie may have experienced one or more miscarrages.

As the young family grew and took an active part in community life, further sad events affected Joseph. His older brother, Edwin John, died suddenly in 1876 and his sister, Mary Susan in 1877. William Ellisdon, the long standing family friend and father-in-law to two of Joseph's brothers died in 1876. These made a deep impression on Joseph, perhaps reawakening some of the uncertainty and fears he experienced in his early life.

However, there were also happy moments too for the Clark family with the arrival of his son and two daughters and many new additions to the wider Clark and Jones's families. In total Joseph and Annie had well over 30 nieces and nephews providing many new opportunities for Joseph to observe and draw children.

One of these, Joseph Benwell Clark (b.1858), moved to London to study art and stayed at Camden Road from time to time. The middle name 'Benwell' being added to distinguish him from his uncle. In 1876 the Royal Society of British Artists' accepted Joseph Benwell Clark's 'Helping themselves'. He was just 19 at the time. In 1880 the RA accepted his portrait of 'Henry Scott Tuke'. Tuke was a fellow student at the Slade School of Art who specialised in male nudes. In the 1880s Henry Scott Tuke associated with Oscar Wilde and other prominent 'gay' poets and writers. Later, Tuke became a member of the Newlyn School in Cornwall.

Joseph Benwell Clark's recollections written in July 1920 mention having lived with 'Uncle Joe' for a time. In Joseph Benwell Clark's obituary written in February 1938, C.F. Fox FSA writes that:

> "His art developed early and it was through his uncle Joseph Clark that he began his serious work, I believe, firstly at Hetherleys and finally at the Slade School of Art, University College, under Professor Legros. ... Calderon, who, in after years ran the School of Animal Painting with Clark in Baker Street, and the Summer School at Headley ... Clark travelled much on the Continent and was well acquained with all the galleries abroad ... Samuel Butler told me that Joseph Benwell Clark was the most versitile man of art he had ever met ... confirmed since by many as a genius in all mediums. ... He was a frequent exhibitor at the now defunct Grosvenor Gallery and the RBA."

Joseph and Annie Clark seem to have kept 'open house' for relatives from Cerne Abbas, especially his nephews making their way in the world. In the early eighteen eighties, John Clark the son of Joseph's brother Edwin spent many Saturday evenings with Joseph and Annie. At the time John was an apprentice with the wholesale drapery firm of Pawson and Leif Ltd in St Paul's Churchyard. Family tradition is that during the week, John slept in the attic above the business sharing it with other apprentices and a colony of rats. John rose to become an Export Manager with the company but lost his job in the 1920s when the Government's decision to return to thje 'Gold Standard' caused a major downturn in Britain's exports. He was in his late fifties and never worked again.

Life in Holloway

We do not have much direct information about the lifestyle of the young Clark family in Holloway during these years.

Some idea of life in Holloway can be gained from Charles Booth's Poverty Map drawn up as part of his broader Inquiry into Life and Labour in London (1889) carried out between 1886 and 1903. Joseph's early homes in Holloway up to around 1874 were in locations classified by Booths inquiry as being *'Fairly comfortable. Good ordinary earnings'*. In detail the people in these areas had *'Regular standard earnings, 22s to 30s per week for regular work, fairly comfortable. As a rule the wives do not work, but the children do: the boys commonly following the father, the girls taking local trades or going out to service.'* These earnings were equivalent to between about £500 a week in 2013.

After 1873 the family moved to Camden Road, an area classified as 'Middle class. Well-to-do'. Specifically *'Lower middle class. Shopkeepers and small employers, clerks and subordinate professional men. A hardworking sober, energetic class.'* No average earnings figures are quoted for this group.

New Church Life

At this stage in their lives, Joseph and Annie were active members of the New Church in Argyle Square. John Presland replaced Jonathan Bayley as Minister. He was widely respected and an active minister with an interest in art. He had been a member of a large deputation from the National Sunday League who met the Marquis of Salisbury, the Lord President of the Council, to urge Sunday opening for the South Kenington Museum. The League was set up in 1855 to promote the opening of Museums, Art Galleries and libraries on Sunday afternoons. This would allow working families to learn from their collections. The League was still operating in the nineteen twenties with a mission to promote *'Sunday Excursions, Sunday Bands in the Parks and generally to promote intellectual and Elevating Recreation on that Day'.*

Although the church building was destroyed during the Second World War, we have a description from 1874 when Joseph and Annie worshiped there:

> "The sixty seventh general conference of 'The New Church' (Swedenborgian) opened its sittings for business yesterday, at nine a.m. in Argyll Square Chapel. The edifice selected for this annual gathering of the disciples of Emanuel Swedenborg has no exterior beauties. It is built of brick and the front facing the square consists of two short pyramid-tipped towers connected by a facade, in the centre of which is a large pointed Gothic doorway. The interior, which will probably accommodate about 600 worshippers, is cruciform. The vaulted roof of the nave is supported by clustered columns of light and airy proportions, and the transepts have semicircular ceilings. The chancel is very shallow and in place of an 'east window' is a Norman panel divided to represent the two tables of stone on which the law of Moses was inscribed. In the space above is a handsome rose window, and below the Decalogue is headed by the text, 'If ye love Me keep My commandments,' and after it is our Lord's summary of 'the law and the prophets' (Matt, xxii, 36–40). The communion table is covered with a rich crimson cloth, on the front of which is the sacred monogram 'IHS.' with a glory, and the Greek letters 'Alpha' and 'Omega'. On the table itself is placed in the centre a large Bible. On either side, and within the rails, are two pulpits of moderate and equal height, one occupied by the prayer reader and the other by the preacher. An excellent organ is placed over the entrance in a gallery, the front of which is ornamented with Norman tracing."
>
> **London Standard,** 12 August 1874

The 'Creed' recited at each service captures the fundamental beliefs of the New Church that Joseph and Annie would have shared:

> "I believe in One God, in whom is the Divine Trinity; who is a Being of infinite love, wisdom, and power; my Creator, Redeemer and Regenerator; and that this God is the Lord and Saviour Jesus Christ; who is Jehovah in a glorified human form.
>
> I believe in the Sacred Scriptures, as being the Word of God, or the Divine Truth itself; which is the fountain of wisdom to angels and men, and is able to make me wise unto salvation.
>
> I believe that if I would be saved, I must shun all evils as sins against God, and live according to the Ten Commandments.
>
> I believe that when I die as to my natural body, I shall rise again in a spiritual body, and shall be judged according to my works; and that if I am good, I shall go to heaven and become an angel, and be happy for ever; but if I am wicked, I shall go to hell, and become an infernal spirit, and be miserable for ever.
>
> I believe that Now is the time for the Second Coming of the LORD, and of the commencement of the New Church, called the New Jerusalem."

In time Joseph became a deacon, Sunday school teacher, and member of the committee of management of the Day School in Cromer Street (adjacent to Argyle Square); and Annie played a role in church life too. Joseph subscribed to the Swedenborg Society based in nearby Bloomsbury in 1861, 1868–73, 1877–80, 1882–3, 1885–6, 1891, and 1895.

While the church's congregation came from prosperous families living in Islington, Holloway, Hampstead and Camden Town, the immediate locality was mixed. Professional families lived next to 'common lodging houses' while the nearby streets were known for violent street robbery, houses of ill repute, forgery and several murders.

The church issued a monthly 'Argyle Square Calendar' giving 'parish notices' of forthcoming events. These give an idea of the activities involving Joseph and Annie.

As a deacon, Joseph supported the Minister and other parishioners by visiting the sick and bereaved. His experiences as a child in Cerne may have given him the understanding, compassion and empathy needed to undertake this demanding role. This role also refreshed and extended his understanding of the lives of ordinary people in the overcrowded areas of London close to Argyle Square.

As a Sunday School teacher Joseph attended the regular monthly meetings, often held in members houses, to plan the programme for the coming weeks. From time to time advertments appeared appealing for people to become Sunday School Teachers. New teachers received a preparatory programme lasting several weeks. In July 1868, Joseph presented the report of the Sunday School Committee to the Society's general meeting. This was about a year after he returned from Christchurch. Two years later the quarterly Sunday School collection raised £16 3s 10 (around £1,300).

Today we think of Sunday schools as being exclusively for the religious instruction of children. The Rev. E.C. Howe (1935) makes it clear that in Joseph's time their remit was much wider. Before the early eighteen seventies, Sunday Schools offered adults instruction in reading, writing and elementary arithmetic. He describes how shortly after the Elementary Education Act 1870, the New Church's National Sunday School Union decided to focus its energies on improving the quality of religious instruction for young people. The two main reforms introduced were a strong central control over the curriculum and teaching materials, and a national system of examinations for New Church Sunday School scholars awarded in partnership with the interdenominational National Sunday School Union.

The New Church Calendar also gives details of other activities for children that probably involved Joseph and Annie. These included an annual excursion for the children and their families to venues including Hatfield House, Petersham Park and Moor Park. These were made by train and usually cost 2s 6d (£10.68) for adults and 1s 6d for each child (£6.41). In 1873, 250 adults and children visited Croydon. Joseph, Annie and the four year-old Poppy probably went on this outing. Children also benefited from a Christmas party; took part in recitals for parents and friends; and attended a twice yearly special church service. Annie was one of about six ladies who collected donations each year to decorate the Church for Christmas and provide a Christmas dinner for poor children.

There is also an occasional mention of drawing classes, presumably for both adults and young people. This raises the interesting possibility that Joseph was invoved in running and teaching in these classes perhaps with his friend and fellow Swedborhgian Franci Oliver Finch. There was also occasional brief references to an 'Argyle Cricket Club' but without details. Again, given Joseph's long standing interest in the sport, he may have been involved in this team.

New Church School management committee

In the early 1850s, a Miss Adelaide Ford Lucombe ran the Cromer Street British School and it is possible that, in time, this became the Cromer Street Day School run by the New Church. In July 1871,

Joseph became a member of its committee of management and later its Secretary. A separate 'Ladies Committee' oversaw the education provided for girls. His work in the Sunday School and with the Cromer Street Day School reflected his commitment to education of all types.

In 1869 the school had a 'roll' of some 370 pupils; 225 boys and 145 girls. The average weekly attendance was 213 (60%); 58% for boys and 66% for girls. Mr and Mrs Collinge ran it until 1874 for a salary of £160 (around £13,300). A year earlier the School inspectors rated the school as 'very satisfactory'. At that time the school attendance was 217 – 98 boys, 59 girls and 60 infants. The annual grant was fixed at £192 1s 0d (£18,700) with an additional £6 4s 0d (£604) for candidates submitted for an examination in drawing.

At the end of the decade, Joseph was closely involved in the transfer of the school to the recently established London School Board. After June 1878, the School Board paid New Church an annual rent of £80 (about £7,000) for the use of the school building.

The London School Board was at the forefront of electorial and educational reform in nineteenth century Britain. From its frist elections in November 1870, women could vote and it used a proportional representation system. In 1870 Elizabeth Garrett, who five years previously became the first woman to qualify as a doctor in England, topped the poll for the Marylebone 'division' that included St Pancras. In 1871, the Board had passed a bylaw making school attendance compulsory btween the ages of 5 and 13 putting it in the forefront of educational reform in England. By 1880, there were seven women on the Board, including several who later became prominent in the womens' suffrage movement.

Religious education was one of the main issues in the debate in the local press before the 1870 elections to the London School Board. One letter to the editor of the Islington Gazette captured the emotions raised by the debate:

> "… This may include as much religious teaching they can usefully digest during the early years their school time, and may comprise the uncommentated reading of the Holy Scriptures as part of the regular school exercises, in the same way as practiced in many schools of the middle classes. By this means the children will be spared the burden of committing to memory obscure and cumbrous doctrinal formula, as well as the infliction of the wearisome theological discourses in which some schoolmasters are prone to indulge, to the certain creation of distaste for religion in early age. A right-minded Board will see that, in the schools under their control, the instruction imparted is of the elementary and practical character here described, and will steer clear of the fatal mistake attempting give a smattering all science and all knowledge, to the confusion the scholars' minds, and the utter waste of precious time."
>
> **Islington Gazette** 11 November 1870

This was signed 'A school manager'. Presumably this debate was setled to the satisfaction of the New Church leadership before Joseph and others signed the transfer documents for the Day school. Disquiet in St Pancras about the London School Board continued for many years. In 1883, the St Pancras Vestry called a meeting of 'vestrymen' from London parishes to protest at wasteful spending by the Board especially on teachers' salaries and senior postholders, and the behaviour of some middle class ratepayers who chose to educate their children in 'Board schools' rather than send them to fee paying private schools. Vestrymen were members of their local church's vestry; an ancient body that had responsibility for many local services. They were not members of the clergy.

Eighteen months after the transfer of the Cromer Street School the London School Board, they agreed plans to replace it:

"Mr. L. Stanley moved the adoption of a recommendation of the Statistical Committee, that application be made to the Education Department for authority to provide additional accommodation for 316 children in Sub-division C of Maryleborne, and that the Works Committee be instructed, as soon that the sanction shall have been obtained, to plan the Manchester Street school, which is to take the place of a transferred school in Cromer Street, for 800, instead of 484 children. After some opposition from Canon Money, the motion was carried."

London Standard 20 November 1879

Thus in 1880, the Cromer Street school moved into one of the 400 new schools, dubbed 'sermons in brick', built by the School Board. 70% of these were designed by Edward Robert Robson, the Board's chief architect whose work was heavily influenced by the Arts and Craft Movement. The new school was just two streets away in Tonbridge Street and is now known as the Argyle Primary School, still using the buildings constructed by the School Board in the 1880s.

Art still plays an important part in the curriculum in the twenty-first century. The Argyle Primary School prospectus (2014) says:

"Art and Design play an important part in the life of Argyle Primary School. We believe that art education provides opportunities for children to be imaginative, creative and inventive. It engages children and enables them to explore and express feelings in ways that are unique and particular to artistic activity.

Pupils' final outcome is artwork of a very high quality and is displayed in a school gallery as well as around the classrooms to illustrate a cross-curricular approach to learning. In November 2013 we were delighted to have our arts provision acknowledged through thr renewal of our Artsmark Gold Award."

It not clear exactly where the Cromer Street school was located but it seems likely that it backed onto the church. This site is now occupied by a public housing estate containing, amongst other things, the King's Cross Mosque where education continues today in a Children's weekend school.

At least one commissioned work came from his links with the Swedenborgian Society during this stage in Joseph's career. His portrait of Henry Butter (1797–1885) adorned the main meeting room at Swedenborg House for many years. Henry Butter became secretary of the Society in 1864 and served in that capacity for 8 years. He was a noted educationalist and author of numerous books on spelling, reading and arithmetic as well as helping to revise several English translations of Swedenborg's writings.

Changes in the art world

As we have seen in the previous chapters Joseph established himself as a well regarded painter of contemporary genre works during the eighteen sixties. But, several critics were already pointing to deficiencies in the narrowness of the subjects he chose and his handling of colours. We do not know how Joseph saw these criticisms or if indeed he read them; and whether he took a conscious decision to continue in the path he had adoped at the start of his career.

Perhaps sticking to a particular style and method was not an unusual pattern of behaviour for artists as seen in Palgrave's (1866) comment when describing the approach of Mr Poole:

"We suppose that a time comes in the career of many artists after which a deficiency, although often pointed out and observed, cannot or will not be amended. The carelessness of Mr. Poole's drawing, and the evidences of haste in his work, may perhaps fall within the scope of our remark;

and it is impossible not to regret that the artist thus does injustice to a poetical invention and a feeling for beauty, both in expression and in colour, in which English art is not very fruitful."

The Mr Poole is probably Paul Falconer Poole, RA (1807–1879) who was a genre painter elected as an ARA in 1846 and RA in 1861. Another example was Myles Burkett Foster (1825–1899) who as a member of the Royal Watercolour Society exhibited over 400 landscapes during his career.

By the end of the 1860's the art world Joseph entered fifteen years previously had changed markedly. The broad thrust of these changes was to maintain support for the traditional classical approach favoured by the more conservative parts of the arts establishment and their aristocratic patrons; and boost interest and access to avant garde work, much of it inspired by developments in France after the third republic started to overcome the disruption created by the seige and occupation of Paris by the Prussans in 1870–71; and the subsequent Paris Commune. During these years several prominet French artist moved to London including Claude Monet and Camille Pissarro.

When they returned to France they, together with others including August Renoir, Edgar Degas, Berthe Morisot and Mary Cassatt became highly influential members of the Impressionist movement. Unlike Joseph, they sought to captrure a single instant in time rather than depict a narrative flow of events. They concentrated on conveying the emotion they experienced in that instant rather than aiming to provoke a specific emotional response amongst people viewing their work.

The consequences for English art of these developments was to squeeze the middle ground of the art world occupied by Joseph and others working in the contemporary genre tradition. Despite this, genre remained attractive and popular amongst many people interested in fine arts throughout the period covered by this chapter.

Joseph's strong belief in the didactic purpose of his art led him to reject the growing emphasis on technique seen in many avant garde works. He maintained his attachment to realism, narrative and appeal to the emotions. He was far from alone in this attachment shared by many art patrons and and members of the RA's selection and hanging committees.

Towards the end of the period covered in this chapter, the impressionist movement in France moved in a new direction and much further away from Joseph's realist approach. This was 'Pointillism'; a technique of painting in which small, distinct dots of color are applied in patterns to form an image. Georges Seurat and Paul Signac developed the technique after 1886. Others, known as Divisionists used a similar technique where impressions were formed by much larger cube-like brushstrokes. None of this affected Joseph's style or approach, although it served to emphasise what some saw as his out dated approach.

Art Patrons

Charles E. Pascoe (1877) reported a major bequest from a well-known private patron of the arts and used the opportunity to sing the praises of the South Kensington Museum:

> "The South Kensington Museum, which we hold to be at once the most delightful and precious treasury of everything pertaining to the growth of English Art and Art-education, has recently received a valuable addition to its treasures in a collection of water-colour paintings, the bequest of the late William Smith, sometime deputy-chairman of the National Portrait Gallery. In addition to this acceptable contribution, to what is now, perhaps, the most complete historical collection of the works of British painters in water-colours in existence, the Library of the Department of Art has received from the same source a bequest of 1,000 books relating to the Fine Arts, some of which are exceedingly rare and valuable. The last valuable bequest of Mr. Smith, marking as it

does the progress of the art of painting in water-colour in England from the middle of the last century to the present time, is worthy evidence of the public-spirited munificence which tends so greatly to foster and encourage the love of Art in this country."

Also in 1877, a new source of art patronage emerged. When Sir Francis Chantrey (exhibited RA 1804; ARA 1815; RA 1818 and knighted 1835), the highly successful sculptor died in 1841 he left his personal estate, after the decease or second marriage of his wife, in trust for the President and trustees of the Royal Academy. The income from the estate had to be used to encourage British fine art in painting and sculpture by *'the purchase of works of fine art of the highest merit … that can be obtained.'* Purchases were restricted to works by British or foreign artists (dead or living) executed within Great Britain. The selection of works was to be solely on their intrinsic merit and the prices paid were to be 'liberal'. The RA could not to commission new works using the bequest as the intention was to establish a public collection of British fine art in painting and sculpture in the hope the government or the country would provide a suitable gallery for its display.

When Lady Chantrey died in 1875 capital sum available amounted to £105,000 (£8.7m) and this produced an annual income of between £2,100 and £2,500 a year (around £800,000). In 1877, the RA as the trustees of the Chantrey Bequest bought its first works in 1877 including Joseph's 'Early Promise' for £210 (£88,000). In 1885, bought 'Mother's Darling' for £89 3s 0d (£39,000) Both pictures remain in the keeping of Tate Britain – although neither is on show. To have two works purchased by the fund was a singular honour:

> "Professor Herkomer's 'Charterhouse Chapel' has been purchased by the President and Council of the Royal Academy under the terms of the Chantrey Bequest for £2,200. This is the second time the Professor has been thus honoured, the former occasion having been in 1885, when his 'Found' was added to the collection. The only other artist who has received the same distinction is Mr. Joseph Clark, in 1877 and 1885".
>
> **Pall Mall Gazette** 15 May 1889

The Graphic approved of the choice of works selected in 1877:

> "No one can complain of any indication of special bias in this year's purchase from this fund. Besides Mr. Leighton's 'Athlete' the purchases include Mr. Yeames's 'Amy Robsart', the painful, but powerfully-told story of that hapless lady's murder; Joseph Clark's 'Early Promise', a village clergyman and his pretty daughter looking over the drawings of a boy genius, amid the anxious expectations of his family; …"
>
> **The Graphic** 12 May 1877

Within a few years some people took exception to the Bequest's purchases. This critical pressure lasted well into the twentieth century. The coverage included:

> "Mr Joseph Clark's 'Mother's Darling, representing a mother bending over a sick child, has been purchased under the terms of the Chantry Bequest, but although a work of certain merit, it can scarcely be said to command this distinction."
>
> **Western Daily Press** 11 May 1885

> "The rest of this wall is practically monopolised by pictures from the Chantrey Collection. The first is Mr Joseph Clark's 'Mother's Darling' at which we would fancy Sir Francis Chantrey would shake a very doubtful head if asked if this were the kind of thing with which he meant to endow a grateful country"
>
> **The Manchester Guardian** 10 May 1887

Galleries in the South Kensington Museum were used to display the Chantrey collection.

In the early 1880s, another new art patron emerged. He was Thomas Holloway founder of the Royal Holloway College opened by Queen Victoria in 1886. In many ways, his art collection was an afterthought in the final years of his life seen as an adjunct to his interest in architecture. He bought 77 paintings between May 1881 and June 1883 for the college, mostly at auction for *'the decoration of the buildings and the benefit of the persons entitled to reside there'*.

Holloway's indiscriminate bidding and the scale of his spending spree disrupted the art market to the consternation of many. The huge prices he paid outraged the art establishment so that even in his obituary, the Art Journal (1884) could not forbear to criticise:

> "We believe he never purchased a picture direct from the artist. Those who were fortunate enough to send to auction pictures he fancied benefited no doubt largely from his princely mode of procedure . . . and those whose productions he acquired may possibly have to regret the inflated prices which for the moment their works assumed."

These works were of two kinds – the improving subject pictures and pastoral landscapes in the style of Constable and Gainsborough. His purchase of Edwin Long's 'Babylonian Marriage Market' set a new record for a living British painter at 6,300 guineas in 1882 (£565,000). Though he did not buy any works by Joseph, Holloway's impact spending spree produced a short-lived boom in prices for all contemporary works. Public access to this important collection has always been limited.

By the 1880s, new patrons emerged following the growth of the City of London. They differed from the earlier generation of wealthy middle class art patrons in that they had little empathy with the poorer classes and fewer close family links with rural communities. Thus, they lacked the instinctive feel for the subjects and situations portrayed by Joseph and others within the genre tradition.

Although the centre of gravity amongst the art buying public moved away from artists like Joseph, new sources of income were opening up. The arrival of 'The Graphic' created new opportunities for this group of artists. This specialised in works with sympathetic renderings of the conditions endured by the poor. Frank Holl focused on gloomier aspects of life to bring home the poverty and wretchedness of life in London's East End, and was often accused of sentimentality and forced pessimism. Luke Fildes produced realistic studies alongside decorative views of Venice and fashionable scenes. He was a key target for the Aesthetic Movement who confused his compassion and sentiment with over-sentimentality. James Tissot (in exile from Paris after the 1870/1 siege) painted idealized views of London Society joined this group of artists who had a profound impact on a young Vincent Van Gogh when he visited London in 1873.

Private galleries and auction houses

By the eighteen seventies, the French owned Goupil Company was publishing photographs alongside its main business of creating prints of original paintings. Its London branch became a leading global art house. By 1875, the London branch was second only to Amsterdam in importance and in 1883 moved to a new larger shop in more visible position in Bond Street. This boosted sales and moved London into pole position within the group. By this stage, the company had a close affiliation with artists in The Hague (e.g., Jacob Maris, Willem Maris, and Anton Mauve) and Barbizon (e.g. Jules Dupré, Constant Troyon, and Charles Daubigny) Schools. By 1894, its stock drew on a roster of artists working in London, including Whistler, Clausen, Steer, and Peppercorn, all of whom had strong ties to progressive French art through their training and subsequent career paths.

Exhibition Societies

The Grosvenor and New Galleries, and the New English Art Club established in the period covered by this chapter concentrated on works inspired by the Pre-Raphaelites, the Aesthetic Movement, and Impressionism. Joseph did not exhibit at these galleries, almost certainly because he was well aware that his subject matter and style did not fit with their aspirations and values. These factors also contributed to his decision to resign from the Society of British Artists following changes introduced by James Whistler, its President in the mid-eighteen seventies. James Laver (1930) describes these changes:

> "There was no more election of Painters for the sake of their subscriptions, no more overcrowding of the walls with mediocre paintings, no more willingness to accept the scourings of the Royal Academy. The rooms were redecorated, a velarium was introduced to temper the light and pictures were all spaced according to Whistlerian principles. To the horror of Sabbatarian members, the new President introduced Sunday tea parties, with charming girls in frocks to match the decorations, handing round bread and butter. Society, ever on alert for a new amusement flocked to Suffolk Street to show off its new gowns or to chat to Oscar Wilde or the President himself! Not only was the Royal Society of British Artists the talk of the town in London but under Whistler's conspicuous leadership, it began to be recognised abroad; with the result that both Monet and Alfred Stevens were persuaded to become honorary members. At a tempestuous final meeting in 1888, the society returned to 'respectability' once more. Whistler claimed that when he left, the Artists also left and only the Royal British remained!"

A valarium was a large awning, especially one suspended over a Roman theatre or amphitheatre.

Ruskin rejected the work of James Whistler that he considered epitomised a reductive mechanisation of art. When he visited the Grosvenor gallery, he famously compared one of Whistler's painting 'Nocturne in Black and Gold: The Falling Rocket', to *'flinging a pot of paint in the public's face'*. This became the subject of a well-publicised libel case in which Whistler won damages of one farthing – the lowest value coin in Victorian England worth one nine hundred and sixtieth of a pound (about 9 pence).

Joseph became a founder member of the Institute of Painters in Oil Colours in 1883. The Society went through an identity crisis with a series of name changes at the turn of the century. The Society's annual exhibition became a regular feature in Joseph's working life, as did its regular general meetings of members. The Society's minute books in the National Art Library's archives show that Joseph attended almost all of its general meetings until 1910 – between forty and fifty in total. He rarely spoke and did not hold office in the Society.

The Society's rules provided for up to 65 members plus 'honorary members'. Prospective members had to be professional artists and needed the support of two-thirds of the members present or submitting a proxy vote to the general meeting held each January. Works by prospective members were on display at the general meeting to allow members to assess their skills and the quality of their work. Artists with sufficient merit became associates for up to five years, during which time they could progress to full membership.

Each member was entitled to display three works in its annual exhibition, including one 'on the line', and there were strict rules about their size and a requirement that they should have gilt frames. Unlike the RA, the Society allowed artists to exhibit works previously shown elsewhere. Several of Joseph's unsold works exhibited at the RA were subsequently shown at the Society.

The Society's council had discretion to include additional works by members and works by non-members. The Society's accounts for 1891 show that 40% of its income came from commission on works sold at the annual exhibition, 33% from admission to the exhibition, 13% from profit on the sale of catalogues; and the balance from members subscriptions and fines for breaches of the long list of rules in of the Society's constitution. In 1891 Members paid a subscription of £3 3s od (£300) and paid a 10% commission on works sold – non-members paid 15% commission.

By the 1880s, the more formal ways of presenting new work had developed into an annual round of exhibitions open to all artists in various parts of the country. The main organisations involved in this cycle of exhibitions included Royal Academy, The Royal Scottish Academy, The West of England Academy, The Hibernian Academy, The Manchester Institute, Glasgow Fine Arts Institute and the Liverpool Autumn Exhibition. These gave people outside London a chance to see the latest artistic fashions and work by the great names of the day. Young artists wanting to demonstrate their distinctive styles and avoid conforming to the traditional values and perspectives of the older generation of artists avoided these regional venues. Established artists producing works appealing to middle class art patrons sent works to these exhibitions although Joseph did not do so regularly. One exception was:

> "Walker Art Gallery. The following is a return of the admissions to and sales at the autumn exhibition for 22 days ending Wednesday, 29th in September:– 10,384 admissions at 1s., £519 4s; 2373 season tickets, £447 9a. , 6771 catalogues, £169 5a. 6d. 134 pictures bare been sold, realising £3976 17s. 6d. as compared with 118 pictures sold a last year, £2671 2s. Amongst the recent sales are the following:– 'Tender Cares' (C.E. 11 Perugini), £400 'On the Hill' (Frank Walton), £36 15s. 'Sunrise from Waterloo Bridge' (J. O'Connor), £200; 'Ducks' (Joseph Clark), £73 10s. 'A Charge of Witchcraft' (H.G. Glindoni), £200 'Calais Fishing Boats' (H. Moore), £150; 'Weal and Woe' (C. Gregory), £200; 'Fisherman's Last Voyage' (T. IV. Wilson), £126; 'Bernese Alps' (W. Collingwood), £78 15s; 'Waiting for the Boat' (F. Brown), £47 5s. The evening exhibitions commence on Saturday next."
>
> **Liverpool Mercury** 1 October 1880

This is the only reference to Joseph's 'Ducks'.

International Exhibitions

A series of London International Exhibitions held in South Kensington between 1871 and 1874 offered a mix of trade, manufacturing and fine art displays. Its buildings became the home of the South Kensington Museum and parts of the British Museum's science and natural history collections.

In the two decades covered by this chapter the 'International Exhibition' movement built on the impetus generated by the Great Exhibition in 1851 and subsequent London and Paris exhibitions. There were over fifty recognised 'world fairs' between 1870 and 1889, although not all contained important displays of fine arts.

One of the largest and most prestigious was the 1876 Philadelphia Centennial Exhibition, where Joseph's works 'Sick Child' (1857) and 'The Birds Nest' (1874) received medals and a testimonial. These went to the painting's owner and not the artist, and have since disappeared from public view. The British press did not report the success of Joseph's works at the time. Henry James Turner Esq. of Stockleigh House, Regent's Park, London, loaned 'The Sick Child' and George Dibley 'The Bird's Nest'. George Dibley was probably born in 1829 and living in Streatham, South London in 1871 with his wife and six sons. He was a 'South Africa Merchant', possibly trading in diamonds discovered in the late 1860s. By 1881, he was in Russel Square, Bloomsbury. Unfortunately, the US National Archives in Washington and Philadelphia do not have copies of the texts of the testimonials presented for Joseph's works.

However, the well-documented arrangements for the Philadelphia exhibition illustrate the arrangements for selecting works for later major international exhibitions. The Visitors Guide to the exhibition described how these worked:

> "The visitor will find on exhibition … the works of all the leading artists of the world. Committees of selection – in most cases composed of the Presidents of the leading art societies – have been appointed by the Commissioners [*of the Centennial Exhibition*] – of the different nations taking part in the exhibition. They have selected from the numerous works of art submitted to them, those they considered as best representing the art culture of their country. From the works thus selected, and on exhibition, the best works of each country of the Old World have been taken and placed in the main gallery of Memorial Hall, opposite to and in close comparison with the best works of the most eminent artists of the United States, thus forming a most interesting exhibition. …
>
> An original system of awards … adopted by the United States Centennial Commission, which it is believed will yield most satisfactory results. Two hundred judges, one-half of whom will be foreigners and one-half citizens of the United States, will be selected for their known character and qualifications. Awards will be based on merit, and will be made by the United States Centennial Commission upon written reports submitted by the awarding Judges. The awards will consist of a diploma and bronze medal, accompanied by a special report of the judges. Exhibitors have the right to reproduce and publish the reports awarded to them."

The [American] Art Journal (1876) was appreciative of the British galleries. It commented in detail on works by the most famous artists exhibiting but did not mention Joseph specifically. These extracts capture the general flavour of its comments:

> "The exhibit of Great Britain is superior to that of any other country represented at the Centennial Exhibition. … These paintings fill some half-a-dozen rooms in all, and include about fifty by the old English masters …. This set of paintings gives this room the general character of one of the apartments of the National Gallery, … largely made up of paintings which for several years have appeared at the Exhibition of the Royal Academy, and a number of these are not a little distinguished. … Overall, this is the finest collection of English pictures that has ever been seen in America. Scarcely a poor one breaks the completeness of the Exhibition."

Though the Exhibition received some coverage in the British press, it failed to offer detailed descriptions of any of the works on display. This selection gives a flavour of the exhibition generally and issues that caught the somewhat jingoistic attention of the press:

> "Fine Art Treasures for the Centennial Exhibition – The steamer Pennsylvania has arrived at Philadelphia from Liverpool with the British fine art contributions to tile forthcoming Centennial Exhibition. Paintings valued at £50,000 have been sent by the Royal Academy, whilst those lent by private persons are valued at £55,000."
>
> **Preston Chronicle** 8 April 1876 – (£22.3m and £24.5m respectively)

> "Philadelphia Centennial Jottings. – The British Section is said to be the most advanced in the Art Gallery, the Industrial, and the Machinery Departments. The Women's Pavilion is more

remarkable for utility than ornament. ... The works of women as artists or artisans, mechanics or manufacturers, are exhibited, and neither dress nor needlework, except artistic embroideries, is to be seen, the committee declaring that the occupation of 'starvation sewing' is giving place to other employments. ... The Chinese contributions are worth over £32,000. (£41m) One Celestial sends six workmen with his goods to repair any damage done in the transit. New South Wales sends a fine selection of woods, the samples numbering 430. The collection in the Kew Museum forms part of the exhibits. The Paris Figaro has erected a small kiosque in the Exhibition, a miniature edition of the Timnro's establishment in the French capital, for the sale of that journal."

The Graphic Saturday 13 May 1876

"British Art at Philadelphia. Philadelphia, June 30. On the title page of a 'Special Catalogue of the Austrian Department in Memorial Hall' recently published here, there is the following note: – 'All the works of art exhibited in the Austrian Art Department are for sale.' ... The Austrian note ... representative as it is of the other leading European nations, offers us the strongest possible contrast between their exhibition of art and that sent from Great Britain. ... Whatever the critic may or may not think of the British collection as an illustration of contemporaneous British art, judging from the pictures actually before him, the manner in which this collection has been made shows a most liberal spirit on the part of British owners. It evinces throughout a desire to contribute to the dignity and value of the Exhibition by the display of works which are not 'in the market,' as well as by maintaining a fairly high standard for such as are offered for sale. The following facts concerning the British collection of pictures are interesting. Of 255 paintings – 199 in oil and fifty-six watercolours – no fewer than 75 have been lent by owners who are not the artists. Of these only sixteen are owned by English firms dealing in pictures. Her Majesty the Queen has sent five pictures, the Corporation of Liverpool one, the Society of Arts one, and the Royal Academy eighteen. The rest of the 175 have been sent by private owners of almost all ranks, from all parts of the country. ... Of the two hundred and fifty-five paintings, less than one hundred are in the market...

The natural result of this spirit is evident in every department, and the art gallery may be taken as a fair illustration of all. The British collection is the only one which an intelligent visitor can regard as a profitable or pleasant field of study. There are good pictures elsewhere, but the eye constantly rests upon pictures which could not pass any careful committee and claim a place upon the walls of a regular exhibition in Paris, Berlin, or Vienna. A critic in the British galleries may bring to his mind the names of many of the best English artists not represented. He may remember various 'loan exhibitions' in London, which were greater than this one; and the regular spring exhibitions of the Royal Academy are far more extensive, offering greater and more numerous works by contemporary artists. But what there is here is good; it is interesting and worthy of study; it does credit to British art.

Opinions as to the various pictures on the walls can be of little use, with the Atlantic Ocean between the writer and the reader. It will be an assurance of fair merit to the Englishman at home, however, to know that the standard of admission to this collection has been quite as high as that which the Royal Academy attempts to maintain at the present time. The oil paintings, for instance, 199 in all, have been painted by 129 artists. Of these artists thirty are now dead and are remembered by their works. Of the remaining ninety-nine names, eighty-seven appeared in the catalogues of the Royal Academy for the annual exhibition of 1875, the last held before the present collection was made. Thirty of these eighty-seven are the names of Royal Academicians or Associates. Of the eleven names which did not appear last year three are followed by the letters R.A. – Thomas Faed, Frederic Goodall, and J. Frederick Lewis. There are only eight more names to be accounted for; one is that of the President of the Society of British Artists, Alfred Clint, another is one of England's most celebrated painters, and a member of the Fine Art Committee under which the collection has been made, Holman Hunt. Every Englishman may rest assured, therefore, that the honour of his country is in the hands of men who have been declared competent artists. The recently deceased artists represented have all died – within the last quarter of a century. B. H."

Pall Mall Gazette Friday 14 July 1876

"The American Centennial Celebrations. The British Art Galleries in the Exhibition. One of the chief characteristics of our eminently Republican cousins across the Atlantic is their love to look on anything monarchical. Whenever a European Prince visits the United States, he is feted to his heart's content; while this year even the great Centennial celebrations were almost over-shadowed by the visit of the Emperor and Empress of Brazil. Queen Victoria in particular is intensely popular throughout the Union. She is everywhere spoken of in the most loving terms, and the greatest interest is ever manifested in the sayings and doings of the Royal Family. Thus, it is hardly surprising that the favourite painting in the British collection at the Exhibition is Mr. Firth's picture of the 'Prince of Wales's Marriage at the Chapel Royal, Windsor.' Before no other painting in the Exhibition is there so great a crowd; and it is curious to note that Benjamin West's picture of the 'Death of General Wolfe,' which hangs next door, hardly attracts a dozen spectators."

The Graphic Saturday 5 August 1876

In 1878 Paris again hosted an international exhibition. This was much larger than that in 1867 attracting thirteen million visitors, including half a million from other countries. The Prince of Wales chaired the British Commission of which Sir Francis Grant, President of the RA was a member. The ten members of the Fine Arts Committee chaired by the Duke of Westminster included Sir Richard Wallace and Frederick Leighton. Joseph's work 'Checkmate' was exhibited in Paris. It had been shown at the 1876 RA and was on loan from Mr Chas. Lucas; who also loaned a work entitled 'Autumn gold' by Vicat Cole ARA. The British Press did not mention the selection of Joseph's work for this exhibition.

Critics

Several of the leading mid-century critics died or retired during the two decades covered by this chapter and new faces became influential. Most of these newcomers had studied classics at university and moved between press criticism, academic writing and administration of the major public galleries; often holding down several posts at the same time. In their work administering national galleries, they often ignored contemporary genre works.

An exception to this pattern was Frederick Wedmore who wrote for The Spectator and London Standard; as well as publishing many well-regarded books. He frequently wrote about genre and other popular art forms. During the 1870s, many leading commentators became attracted to the approach of the aesthetic movement and their works. Reynolds's (1953) took the view that the growth of the Aesthetic Movement created an atmosphere of hostility towards genre works and its artists, and this can been seen in the reviews of Joseph's paintings later in this chapter. It also surfaced in the long running campaign about the RA's use of the Chantrey Bequest covered later.

One 'unprofessional critic' illustrates the huge task facing critics trying to report on the RA summer exhibition in 1888. Sadly, we do not know who the 'unprofessional critic' was:

"The tour of the Royal Academy personally conducted by an unprofessional critic. There are 2,077 exhibits at the Royal Academy this year. The critic is allowed one day in which to see them. Suppose that he has stamina enough to endure four hours' picture-seeing at a stretch. That gives him 500 works of art to do in an hour-or say one picture to see, and judge, every second. Now, the advantage of being an unconventional critic is his freedom to confess that he has not looked at the 2,000 pictures at the rate of one a second. Still less is he bound to pretend that, having done so, he has then contrasted this year's pictures with mental impressions of the 2,000 last year, and, weighing one lot with the other, found the present show decidedly better or even worse than the last. No; the unconventional critic does just what nine visitors out of every ten do. He first takes a general look round, and marks whatever strikes him for subsequent inspection; then he goes straight to what he knows by their position in the principal room are considered the pictures of the year; and then he makes his systematic tour of the rooms, finding time and strength to look perhaps at one picture in fifty. On this method, a visitor's first impression will certainly be that it is a very good Academy. The pictures of the year are all important and imposing, and most of them interesting also."

Pall Mall Gazette 5 May 1888

Art Journals

Two of the many new art journals launched in these decades took an interest in contemporary genre.

William Luson Thomas, a successful artist, wood engraver and social reformer, launched The Graphic in 1869. His principal motivation was his dislike of the unsympathetic treatment of artists by The Illustrated London News. Thomas's artists received a good fee for the use of their works. By 1882 the company employed over 1,000 people and its Christmas edition, printed in colour costing a shilling (about £4), sold over 500,000 copies in Britain and the USA. Improvements in production methods led to the launch of a Daily Graphic in 1889. At least two of Joseph's works appeared in The Graphic after exhibition at the RA. These were 'Private and confidential' (1875) and the 'Youthful Genius' (1888).

The Magazine of Art first appeared in 1878 as an illustrated monthly devoted to the visual arts containing reviews of exhibitions, articles about artists and some poetry. It presented itself as a 'lively cosmopolitan review of the arts influencing and shaping the public's perception of and taste in art'. Its lavish illustrations were by leading engravers of the period and contributors included John Ruskin, R.L. Stevenson, Richard Jefferies and J. Comyns Carr. After 1888, a supplement was introduced called 'Royal Academy Pictures' containing reproductions of the chief works from the year's exhibition. These appeared until 1916 and contained many references to Joseph's later works.

New styles and views on art

Joseph undertook his professional training when contemporary genre was increasing in popularity and the impact of the Pre-Raphaelite Brotherhood's success led critics and the public to seek out artists with similar high level technical drawing skills, the capacity to empathise with the subjects and tell a strong story. After the reforms of art education in the middle years of the century artists with high levels of technical drawng skills were becoming commonplace, increasing the competition between artists capable of such fine work.

By 1870 critical appreciation moved in new directions and many patrons and public taste followed. The eighteen seventies saw a significant move away from paintings with strong narratives of everyday life and a renewed emphasis on portraiture; in part reflecting the 'gentrification of the newly rich entrepreneurs' as they started to decorate their newly acquired grand houses. Many Academicians were accused of courting popularity (and boosting sales) by painting portraits, children, animals and historical scenes. Their response was that they spoke the language that the public understood and that art was to entertain not educate. By the end of this period many artists became specialists concentrating on a single style or subject.

Andrew Graham-Dixon (1996) outlined artistic developments in the final third of the nineteenth century. He believed that since William Turner's time British art had been afflicted by a lack of moral and emotional conviction without which great art rarely arises; accompanied by a chronic tendency for artists' careers to subside from a vigorous beginning to a tame and soft compliance with genteel taste. Certainly this period saw Joseph's career fall away from its early peak but without any suggestion that his works lacked moral or emotional conviction. Andrew Graham-Dixon saw art in this period as the '*aesthetics of genteel retreat*'. The ethical fervour of Ruskin and Morris came to be replaced by a move towards '*a complacent morally void cynicism*' in which much '*fin-de-siècle art was slick but emotionally and intellectually vacant*'. He suggests that the journey in this direction was led by two Americans trained in Paris – James Whistler and John Singer Sargent. He thought that Whistler had little to say about the world and that Sargent's art was '*beautiful but affectless, breathtakingly well-executed but entirely without moral or intellectual energy. His heartless virtuosity perfectly adapted to the sensibility of the turn of the century patrons of art in Britain*'.

Julian Treuherz (1999) refers to a 'classical revival' after the reaction in the 1860s against narrative, moral teaching and detail found in genre and early Pre-Raphalite works. Frederic Leighton and Edward Poynter led this with works depicting stories of heroism and tragedy. Leighton drew heavily on the bible and classical mythology while Poynter and George Watts believed that art should elevate the viewer. Watts invented allegories with the aim of creating a univerally accessible language independent of religion or creed. Others aimed to elevate the public by exposing them to beauty. Treuherz notes that other progressive artists emphasised formal values, colour, tone, line and pattern with the aim of getting below the surface to express inner truths.

Writing in the middle of Joseph's career Frederick Wedmore (1880), the art critic, offered a more extensive reflection on contemporary genre:

> "The act of Genre paintings has for its first and plainest characteristic that it deals with the actual and the common world and by its aspirations as well as its achievements belongs to the common world and to no other. … It records the struggles, the character, the happiness, the folly of men. It has in it the intelligent curiosity of common folk. And, like the intimate studies of our greatest fiction, it is itself history, and itself analysis. It records not the rare events which started history chronicles but the repeated incidents which we know to be events too. It quickens our senses to the spectacle, in actual life, not of a sensation scene, but of every-day drama.
>
> And the great Genre painters have been the ones to see that it is the every-day drama, after all, which must have our closest concern … Life itself … is a success or a failure according to the very closeness with which we hold on the incident or occasion of the hour … we grasp truly or falsely the relations of passing things. But to grasp justly, we must observe keenly. The great Genre painters and the artists of analytic fiction have done a part of our observing for us … Other gifted persons soared and dreamed; but these – their feet were very form on the actual world.
>
> Perhaps it might have been natural to reward with an equal fame those who in ways however different were working so much to a common end – the furtherance of knowledge of life and living character. But the honour which criticism has allowed so justly to such workers in the art of

literature, it has latterly in England been minded to deny such workers in the art of painting. ... few have grappled successfully with the unfolding of a narrative, and there are not many writers who in the vivid presentation of incident have had a painter's success. ... For both there are the accidents of human feeling, and the roll or serious chances of changing circumstances

The public voice is rarely heard in questions of painting, it has been able to dictate in questions of literature. And there too, in Art, where the preferences of influential men have counted for most, there have been the least perhaps, of critical shrewdness. ... And yet, whenever Genre painting of even moderate skill has been seen by those who have little prejudice because they have no predisposition, it has been liked and looked at, whether it has been of the order ... Perfected in a single generation among the artists of Holland ... or of the kind that the citizens of London found piquant in the designs of Hogarth ...

Genre painting has flourished most in compact and settled and highly civilized societies, not so large as to be very various, and at times when men's minds were little distracted by political movement or religious aspiration. For the Genre painter has needed, both in himself and in those for whom he has wrought, some sense of the immediate and ultimate importance of the themes he deals with. Other men, other generations, may be pleased to style him trivial; but he, to see clearly and to chronicle well, must believe in the value and the interest of his work. No overpowering thought of larger issues – of a future, of another world, of a different society – must overhang him as he records our moods and manners and gains his revelation into permanent character by the accidents of the passing moment. Somewhat conservative then, and on the whole content with itself, with its fortunes, with its daily ways must be the society that offers to the artist of character and comedy his most fovourable occasion ... the interest [in Genre's] history does not lie in the development of any one given system – the concern of the pedant, wherever they may be found – in the study of the minds of many men. How did these various men look at life and touch it? What struck them? What did they express?

Although Joseph may not have seen this reflection, it captures the context in which he worked despite challenges from three emerging art movements.

Aesthetic Movement

One of the most important new directions in art in the period covered by this chapter involved changes in subject matter and styles. It came to be called the 'Aesthetic Movement' and until recently was understood primarily as a feature of literature and the decorative arts at the end of the nineteenth century.

Elizabeth Prettejohn (2007) recognised that:

'The cohesion among the various art practices described does not involve 'a shared style, a shared range of subjects or a shared set of political and ideological concerns'. Rather it is a matter of exploring a shared artistic. For this reason I emphasise the motto 'art for art's sake', not as the name of an art theory, but rather as a statement of the problem... the problem of what art might be, if it is not for the sake of anything else. ... What was shared among all the art practices ... [of the Aesthetic Movement's leading figures] ... was a conviction that the problem could not be solved in a theoretical form, or indeed in any form that could be generalised sufficiently to be expressed in a verbal formula (hence the tautologous, or intentionally meaningless, phrase 'art for art's sake'). The problem could be addressed only by seeing what art might be in a singular case; that is, in a concrete work of art.'

The movement that started to emerge amongst painters in the late 1860s was a loosely framed set of ideas about art that had at its core the idea that life needed to be lived intensely following an ideal of beauty. The artists and writers of the aesthetic movement tended to hold that the arts should provide refined sensuous pleasure, rather than convey strong moral or sentimental messages coupled with a clear narrative. Proponents of the aesthetic movement stressed the role of emotion and imagination in depicting reality; and as in earlier generations, stylistic innovators wanted to reject the traditional approach of the art establishment embodied in the Royal Academy. They believed art should be judged in its own terms against an enduring notion of beauty rather than by reference to transient moral, religious or political standards. Thus they rejected the utilitarian view of art as something moral, didactic or useful advocated by Sir Charles Eastlake, John Ruskin and Matthew Arnold whose views had dominated the art world in the previous two decades. The artists covered in Prettejohn (2007) – Millais, Rossetti, Simeon Solomon, Albert Moore, Leighton, Whistler and Burne-Jones – did not have a collective public identity like the Pre-Raphaelites or the Impressionists. Rather they represented a something of a tendency or direction of movement in art.

James Whistler was one of the most controversial figures in the late nineteenth century art world. He was averse to sentimentality and moral allusion in painting; and became the leading proponent of the credo, 'art for art's sake'. He combined the subtle delicacy in his art with a highly combative public persona. He and Walter Sickert were pioneers of a modern sensibility in fine art in Britain. Whistler influenced the art world and the broader culture through his artistic theories and friendships with leading artists and writers. Writing shortly after Whistler's death, Frederick Wedmore (1906) said:

> "Even those who have had only a casual acquaintance with the life performance of Whistler must have been struck with the variety of the mediums used by him for its accomplishment. … he painted in Oils; he painted in Water Colour; Pastels he made so admirably that he may even be held responsible for 'prettily spurring on' some heavier-footed comrades to make them very badly; dainty was his touch with the Pencil; with Fantin-Latour he shares the honours of the happy revival of artistic Lithography; and in the art of Etching …
>
> What was the cause of Whistler's always enterprising, experimental employment of as many mediums as I have named each with its own special conditions, its technical difficulties? There were in effect two reasons that prompted Whistler to the exercise of mediums so numerous to the acquisition of the various technical skill those mediums demanded. One of them was his possession of an extraordinarily deep artistic sense of the appropriate and the fitting. So much an artist was he, that hardly once in his long career did he mistake, misuse, the medium in which was to be executed with delight his given, momentary task. Another reason was his enjoyment of change… He hated grooves. They were fatal to freshness; fatal to spontaneity. His principle that a pictorial work must before everything be decorative, he applied in different degrees."

Writing in a review of the 1912 RA Exhibition for The English Review, Walter Sickert (2002), Whistler's erstwhile collaborator' wrote:

> "It is odd that just as the 'up to date' critic has learned to cry 'Down with Poynter' with his eyes shut, and hail anything that he thinks distantly related to Whistler as reveleation, those of us who knew and understood Whister's work from the inside, when the said 'up to date' was in his perambulator, are coming to the very different conclusions. We have had time to see that the Whistlerian attitude has led to sterility while the 'classic' or 'academic' method remains … a durable framework."

Thus, the leading edge of the overall artistic endeavour moved rapidly away from Joseph. His attachment to contemporary narrative genre led the advocates of 'aesthetic movement' to regard him as a part of an art establishment increasingly out of touch with the spirit of the age. This fueled the initial attacks to the purchase of his works by the Chantrey Bequest.

Joseph was not alone in not responding to the aesthetic movement's approach. In 1883, William Frith exhibited a satirical work depicting a private viewing of the RA exhibition. Wikipedia (2015) (plate 3) describes the work in some detail including:

> "[This is] one of Frith's 'panoramas', depicting the art-world of his day at a private view, and satirising the influence of Oscar Wilde and the Aesthetic movement. Wilde is the main figure at the right, behind the boy wearing green. … Frith worked on the painting through much of 1881 and 1882. He later said in 'My Autobiography and Reminiscences', published in 1887, that 'Beyond the desire of recording for posterity the aesthetic craze as regards dress, I wished to hit the folly of listening to self-elected critics in matters of taste, whether in dress or art. I therefore planned a group, consisting of a well-known apostle of the beautiful, with a herd of eager worshippers surrounding him'."

We have no direct evidence of what Joseph thought of the aesthetic movement or its underpinning principles. The extent to which Joseph's work reflected his Swedenborgian faith would almost certainly place him at odds with the ideals of the Aesthetic Movement and in particular the new 'Cult of Beauty' adopted by some adherents from the late 1860s.

Simon Poe (2009) in his review of Prettejohn (2007) believes her major contribution lies in correcting the Francophile bias of much of twentieth century writing on the aesthetic movement and her recognition of the influence of German philosophers, particularly Kant and his 'Critique of Judgement'. The *Critique of Judgement* (*Kritik der Urteilskraft*, 1790), or in the new Cambridge translation *Critique of the Power of Judgment*, also known as the third critique, is a philosophical work by Immanuel Kant. He notes that she concedes that few of the painters would have been doing this sort of heavy reading themselves, but argues convincingly that ideas deriving from Kant would have achieved wide currency through conversation in the studios.

Arts and Crafts Movement

The other new direction, that began to make itself felt at this stage in Joseph's career, was the Arts and Crafts Movement. Two early engines in its development were Morris & Co from 1862 and the opening of Liberty's store in London in 1875.

William Morris entered Exeter College, Oxford, in 1852 where he met Edward Burne-Jones and Dante Gabriel Rossetti. John Ruskin's praise of the creative imagination expressed by medieval artisans; and his wider social criticism that sought to link the moral and social health of a nation to the qualities of its architecture and design influenced Morris and his friends. Ruskin thought mechanisation and factory life led to many social ills and that a healthy society depended on the availability of skilled and creative work.

Morris's thinking was, in part, a reaction against the style of many of the objects shown at the Great Exhibition of 1851 that he saw as too ornate, artificial, and lacking understanding of the qualities of the materials used in their manufacture. This viewpoint persisted well into the twentieth century when, for example, Nikolaus Pevsner (1936) described the exhibits at the 1851 exhibition as showing *'ignorance of that need in creating patterns, the integrity of the surface' and 'vulgarity in detail'*. The organisers of the 1851 exhibition including Richard Redgrave recognised this, and urged design reform when they emphasised that 'ornament should be secondary to the thing decorated' and that there should be 'fitness in the ornament to the thing ornamented'.

William Morris acted on these ideas when in 1861 he cofounded Morris, Marshall, Faulkner & Co. This became Morris & Co. who designed and made decorative objects for contemporary homes including wallpaper, textiles, furniture and stained glass. The company's production methods embodied John Ruskin's belief in the power of craftsman-designers. One of Morris's associates was the painter Walter Crane, a resident of Argyle Square. Although the Royal Academy accepted his 'The Lady of Shalott' in 1862, he met frequent refusals to exhibit his later works. After 1877 he exhibited regularly at the Grosvenor Gallery.

Liberty's opened in 1875 with the ambition to change the look of homewares and fashions. Arthur Liberty's intuitive vision and pioneering spirit led him to travel the world looking for individual pieces to inspire and excite his discerning clientele. The store quickly became the most fashionable place to shop in London and for both clothing and furnishings using the iconic Liberty fabrics. By the 1890s, Arthur Liberty had strong relationships with many leading English designers in the Arts and Crafts and Art Nouveau movements.

The Arts and Craft Movement that became critical in shaping public tastes towards the end of the nineteenth century. Again there is no indication that Joseph changed his approach in any significant way to accommodate the growing popularity of Arts and Crafts Movement amongst many of the people interested in his works. Some aspects of Joseph's subject matter echoed of the preoccupations and values of the Arts and Crafts Movement.

The Impressionists

During the period covered by this chapter, Édouard Manet and others developed a third challenge to Joseph's artistic perspective. Despite harsh opposition from the conventional art community in France, Monet, Renoir, Pissarro and Sisley organized the *Société Anonyme Coopérative des Artistes Peintres, Sculpteurs, Graveurs* ('Cooperative and Anonymous Association of Painters, Sculptors, and Engravers') towards the end of 1873 to exhibit their artworks independently. Some see them as the first Impressionists.

These 'Impressionists' found a new repertoire in daily urban life, especially middle class leisure pursuits, and adopted a distinctive aesthetic vocabulary with works reflecting, to some extent, the style of Turner's later works. They also drew on the nineteenth century realist and contemporary genre traditions within which Joseph worked. However, their main interest was in landscapes and outdoor scenes depicting contemporary middle class life rather than recreating the historical or mythological scenes favoured by the art establishment in France (and by the classical tradition in Britain).

The Impressionists sought to capture the movement, speed, and ephemeral quality of modern life by portraying overall visual effects without the fine detail. They relaxed the traditional well-defined boundary between subject and background their works. Their works tended to resemble a snapshot within a larger reality captured as if by chance. Photography was gaining popularity in this era and inspired Impressionists to represent momentary action, not only in the fleeting lights of a landscape, but also in the day-to-day lives of people. Generally their works did not have the narrative or educative elements found in many genre works. Impressionism was characterised by open composition, an emphasis on accurate depiction of light in its changing qualities and unusual visual angles.

Joseph's attachment to the slower pace of rural life and its embodiment of enduring spiritual values was fundamentally at odds with the perspective on life and art of the impressionists.

New technologies and sources of income for artists

Although in use from the eighteen forties, photography did not began to influence fine art until the decades covered by this chapter.

An important aspect of this came from its use in illustrating newspapers, journals and magazines. In 1878, the Czech painter, Karel Klíč, developed new photogravure techniques building on pioneering work by Henry Fox Talbot in the 1840s. This produced images by combining photography and etching. The gelatin in the photographic negative acted as an acid resist when etching the image. After further development, hard photogravure became commonplace late in the 19th century allowing the photographic transfer of images to a copper plate that was then hand-inked and printed. Many of the late nineteenth century prints of Joseph's work used this process.

Art critics did not always welcome these new technological developments, or at least the works selected for publication using these techniques. In 1884, the Times reported that:

> "…from Messrs. Goupil we have received three of the newest examples of that art of photogravure which they are carrying to such remarkable perfection. Two of these belong to the somewhat trivial class of subjects which find favour in our popular exhibitions 'Three little kittens' by Mr Joseph Clark and 'A feather in her cap' by Mr John Morgan …"
>
> **The Times** 27 Mar 1884

The Times' somewhat snobbish dismissal of 'Three Little Kittens' had little impact on the public's appetite for such works. Three years after its showing at the Royal Academy it was reported that:

> "The principal coloured plate to be issued with the forthcoming number of Yule Tide will be 'Three Little Kittens' from the original picture by Mr Joseph Clark, exhibited in the Royal Academy. Yule Tide will in future be published by Messrs. Cassell and Company."
>
> **Leeds Mercury** 14 August 1886

Any payment for the use of an artwork in photogravure or other plates usually went to the owner of the picture rather than to the artist. So the main way in which Joseph benefited from prints of his works was through his reputation and the possibilitry that art patrons may have been encouraged to buy works from an artist whose works had previously been copied.

As mentioned earlier, the decades covered by this chapter saw a vigorous debate about whether photography was art. Some argued the camera was too accurate and detailed in what it recorded to allow it to capture emotional responses to situations and scenes effectively. Others rejected this and adopted techniques emphasising composition, tonal values and atmospheric effects familiar to artists. They were more concerned with the aesthetics and the emotional impact of the image, rather than the reality of what was in front of their camera. They went on to develop new techniques including combination printing, the use of focus, the manipulation of the negative, and the use of gum dichromate to lessen the detail to produce a more 'artistic result'. The term 'Pictorialism' refers to their work. They drew inspiration from the amateur photographer William J. Newton who proposed in 1853 that 'a 'natural object', such as a tree, should be photographed in accordance 'the acknowledged principles of fine art'.

Art market trends

When Joseph launched his career at the end of the 1850s, the fine art world was still to some extent driven by the tastes of aristocratic patrons and those whose fortunes had come from mining, manufacturing and railways.

Robert Irwin (2013) reflects on the state of the art market in the 1880s and 1890s. He reports a general collapse in the art market exacerbated by Thomas Holloway's spending spree mentioned earlier. The demand for works by living artists fell significantly in the recession of 1884–7 as works by the Old Masters competed for investors' money. The growing hostility towards genre paintings and popularity of works by impressionists, the aesthetic movement and their supporters compounded the problem for Joseph's generation working in the realist tradition. Many artists' incomes fell and some galleries sold off unfashionable works.

Successive editions of the Year's Art complied bet ACR Carter (1898) allow the movements in art auction prices to be tracked. The number of paintings sold for more than £200 (around £17,000) gives a good idea of the extent of the 'boom' and the subsequent 'crash' at the top end of the art market. In 1880 just over 100 pictures were sold at auction for more than £200 but this fell sharply to an average of 25 a year between 1886 and 1889; before increasing to an average of 35 a year between 1890 and 1897.

Celebrity Artists

Despite variations in auction prices, the celebrity artists of the day became extremly wealthy. In 1866 Fredrick Leighton, who eventually became the President of the RA, had a house built in Holland Park – an emerging, highly fashionable and expensive area. By the 1870's, other artists fiollowed his lead having houses designed to their own specifications by up and coming architects, mostly in the Arts and Crafts fashion. They became known as the Holland Park Circle and most members became RAs or received state honours. The core members of the group were George Frederic Watts, Frederic Leighton, Valentine Prinsep, Luke Fildes, Hamo Thornycroft and William Burges. In time they organised 'Show Sundays' when the public visited their studios and saw the artists posing 'at home' for magazine photographers. These became a regular part of the 'London Season'.

Charles Eyre Pascoe (1887) 'London of To-day – an illustrated hamndbook for the season 1887' drescribes 'Show Sunday' in his chapter on art galleries saying:

> "'Show Sunday' is the day on which artists who exhibit, or hope to exhibit, at the Royal Academy or elsewhere, receive their friends and friends' friends at their studios. The artist-localities of London no longer centre in Fitzroy Square. Within the last ten years these have become extended to the remoter suburbs of London – to Hampstead and Highgate on the north, Kensington and Chelsea on the west, Chiswick and Putney in the south. It is a far cry, as some people know, from Chelsea Embankment to St John's Wood; and the picturesque settlements of Holland Park, at Kensington, are sufficently remote from the ancient art-regions of central London. Moreover, Highgate and Primrose Hill are not so nigh to Bedford Park, Chiswick, that a hansom cabman will accept with graceful courtesy, a half-crown as his legal fare. To compass all these outlying districts, and in the interevals of, driving and 'entraining' … to twist through folds of silks and satins, and to view a great variety of pictures, and listen to a lot of commonplace criticism concerning them – these are the ends of 'Show Sunday'. …
>
> A Londoner of fashion, who is in a position to say he has seen all the pictures of the year, worth seeing on 'Show Sunday' is a more important person in Mayfair dinner-tables than one who has

to wait till the 'Critics' Day' [*at the RA*]. And he who has entrée to the Academy on 'Critics' Day' is a greater person than he who has to wait to the 'Private view day'. And he who has the entrée then has to be preferred to one who has not. But the game is hardly worth the candle.

As, however, there may be some who might wish to indulge in it, we can but point the way. Invitations for 'Show Sunday' are to be procured through the introduction of any artist of position; though it may not be so easy to obtain admission to the studios of all the Academicians. This should be of no great disapointment, and the visitor might find compensation in seeking out the studios of the less illustrious artists.

To receive an invitation to the galleries of the Royal Academy on 'Critics day' one should, of course, be the accredited representative of some journal of recognised position and influence, though by the way, this is less necessary now than in years gone by. The entrée to the 'Private-view Day', a privillage eagerly sought in the fashionable world, is exclusively in the bestowal of the Royal Academicians. Influence in that direction would no doubt secure admission; but the galleries are generally so crowded that the chief delight is to be found, not in criticizing the pictures, but in ctriticizing the company."

This description suggests that 'Show Sunday' occurred in April before the opening of the RA's exhibition in early May. This extract highlights important aspects of the ways in which the Academy's leadership engaged with the social elite in Victorian Britain. It is highly unlikely that Joseph ever participated in 'Show Sundays'. Pascoe's annual guides published between 1885 and 1914 appeared in both London and New York.

Joseph Clark's professional reputation and response to criticism

The decades covered by this chapter include the time when Joseph should have been at the peak of his professional skills and standing; and thus considered as a potential academician. As most RAs were elected in their early forties, Joseph might have expected to be nominated as an ARA in the early to mid-1870s. He, like others born between 1834 and 1844, was part of a 'fallow' generation of artists in terms of election as Associates; only eight artists born in this decade succeeded compared with around twenty born in both the preceding and following decades. In fact, only three of Joseph's contemporaries at the RAS ever became RAs. The most interesting contemporary was Annie Swinnerton, the first woman to become an ARA – but she had to wait until 1922 when she was 78.

When Sir Frederic Leighton became the Academy's President in 1878, he lobbied successfully to promote the election of figures like Edward Burne-Jones and Albert Moore whose works differed sharply from those of many existing Academicians. He also ensured works by 'outsiders' received fair treatment and displayed prominently in annual exhibitions. This shift in the Royal Academy's priorities reduced the opportunities for artists in Joseph's generation whose works were in the mainstream of 1860s and 1870s art.

As we have seen the impact of sucessive economic downturns led some artists to focus their contemporary genre works on the miseries and misfortunes of urban working class families. The term 'social realism' was coined to refer to these themes. Joseph did not follow this trend so, even within contemporary genre circles, he occupied a specialist niche. This may have contributed to lessening of press attention for Joseph's works. This was despite the regularity of their appearance at the RA and competition from the growing numbers of professional artists at the time. It is unclear whether the critics of the major national papers no longer judged his work to be of sufficient merit as they embraced the views of the 'aesthetic movement; had simply run out of new things to say about his work; or were responding to the reduction in the space available in many newspapers devoted to detailed reports of fine art exhibitions com pared with earlier decades.

By the late 1870s, Joseph was dealing with the deaths of his brother and sister; reduced critical attention; and growing criticism of some aspects of his technical abilities, notably his use of colours. Alongside this, market for genre works shrunk reflecting, in part, the growing influence of new art journals promoting impressionism and the aesthetic movement.

Like all artists, Joseph had difficult choices to make about his response to these new fashions in the art world. Do they accept the perspective of the critics and adapt accordingly, or do they continue with their existing artistic vision? Should we see any failure to change as evidence of a strong self-belief often associated with an 'artistic temperment', a strong commitment to their particular artistic vision, or sheer stubboness? Certainly Joseph showed great tenacity in persevering with the subjects and style adopted at the start of his career, albeit with some modest developments as the years passed.

Towards the end of this phase of Joseph's career, John Heywood (1887) Professor of Painting in the Royal Academy, referred to him in his 'Fifty years of British Art as illustrated by the pictures and drawings in the Manchester Royal Jubilee exhibition' saying:

"There seems to be only one specimen of Joseph Clark in the collection, 'Mother's Darling,' lent by the Trustees of the Chantrey Bequest. It would have been interesting from an artistic point of view, and certainly conducive to our moral and spiritual welfare, to have had a larger and more representative selection. His history is altogether peculiar. During the last thirty years, there have been many reputations made and not a few lost; the trumpet tongue of fame has proclaimed with noisy clamour now one name and now another; at the dinner parties of each succeeding season this or that great Picture has been a theme of conversation; but it has only been amongst a few observers, who take more than usual heed of what is passing, that one has heard of the name.

Was Joseph Clark as an aspirant to fame? He has pursued the even tenor of his way, undisturbed by a notoriety which he apparently never courted; and this writer at least most sincerely hopes that retributive justice has not altogether failed in her mission, but has conveyed to him in the way of encouragement and consolation, some tidings from the inner world which have told him of the gratitude of many gentle hearts and the fellowship of many tender, loving souls. His pictures, could we see them grouped together, would merit the title of Die Erkentnisse einer schonen Zeele. ['Reminiscent of a nice Zeele'] A beautiful, tender, pious, and loving soul breathes through them all. He has altered little, and, cruel as it may sound, he has improved less; technically speaking, the aspect of his pictures has always been and still is forbidding at the first glance; but is it too much to ask of a busy world to pause one moment longer? And that is all that is needed. Joseph Clark is one of the most: consummate artists living in all that appertains to the construction of a picture; he knows as well or better than any man living how to concentrate the interest of his subject, and how to bring out its central point. There is no unnecessary detail, and yet nothing which helps the story is omitted. There is complete unity in his work; all the parts unite to form a perfect whole. His pictures are full of concentrated thought and feeling – sweet, tender, and loving creations. What ails them, then, that they are not more talked about? The reader may ask. Ah, gentle reader! What ails hundreds of glorious minds, full of knowledge and justice and reverence for all that is noble, of scorn for all that is base, of hearts full of tears for human woes, of rich, warm sympathy for its struggles and its sorrows – what ails them that the world does not kneel down, and throw honours and titles at their feet? A something, an infinitesimal quantity, which, perhaps, in the next world shall be as though it had never been."

Joseph Clark – experienced professional artist

1869

In 1869 two of Joseph's works appeared at the RA. These were 'The empty cradle' and 'Crumbs from a poor man's table'. Neither were reported in the press and we do not know what led him to return to his theme of childhood illness and death. The picture shows a cradle at the forefront of the work with grieving parents sitting nearby. This work prompts the viewer to conside what has gone before in the narrative. The death of a child, or perhaps he failure to have one, is centre stage. But what of the circumstances of the death; and what will happen to the young couple as the days and weeks pass? Despite the deep tragedy portrayed is there hope that the young couple will find some happiness with another child in the future? Does it also draw on the Swedeborgian belief in the afterlife with its expectation of their being reunited with the lost child?

The title of 'Crumbs from a poor man's table' refers to 'And she said, Truth, Lord: yet the dogs eat of the crumbs which fall from their masters' table.' Matthew 15:27 of the King James Bible.

This was the RA's first exhibition in its new home in Burlington House, Piccadilly. Some sense of the occasion comes from contemporary press coverage:

> "The Royal Academy has opened its new Temple of Fame in the fine building which Mr. Smirke, R.A., has designed. The new Royal Academy occupies part of the Burlington House site which fronts Burlington Gardens. Characterising the Exhibition in very general terms, the Daily News says, it is not distinguished by the works of the Academicians – except in those by Sir E. Landseer, Mr. Hook, and Mr. Leighton – so much as it is the variety and fresh energy that mark the works of artists who are yet candidates for the honours of the Academy."
>
> **Reading Mercury** 8 May 1869

An overview of the exhibition is offered by the Pall Mal Gazette:

> "This year's exhibition is noticeable for other merits besides the beauty of the new galleries. First, the pictures are all visible without kneeling on the floor to see those below the line, or using an opera-glass to distinguish those in the highest row. … we think that the Hanging Committee have done full justice to the interests of the artists whose works were committed to them … Secondly, it was wise in the Council not to admit a larger number of pictures than before. Twelve hundred works, fairly selected, will include everything of interest that is produced in this country during the year. … Thirdly, and here our praise must be qualified, the great plague of fashionable portraits is distinctly abated … The greatest buyers of pictures at the present day are of a class which the Academy does not delight to honour in this way [by allowing their portraits to be displayed], men whose guineas are scarcely purified from the taint of trade. … Turning to the pictures, we will notice first the most important figure subjects. The best places are, necessarily, very often occupied by the works of men who have outlived their reputation. The rapid change of views and practices in art during the last few years makes this class an unduly large one, but it will not be necessary to indicate the painters, of whom we think this might justly be said …"
>
> **Pall Mall Gazette** 10 May 1869

The opening of the new venue seems to have produced a marked increase in the numbers of visitors:

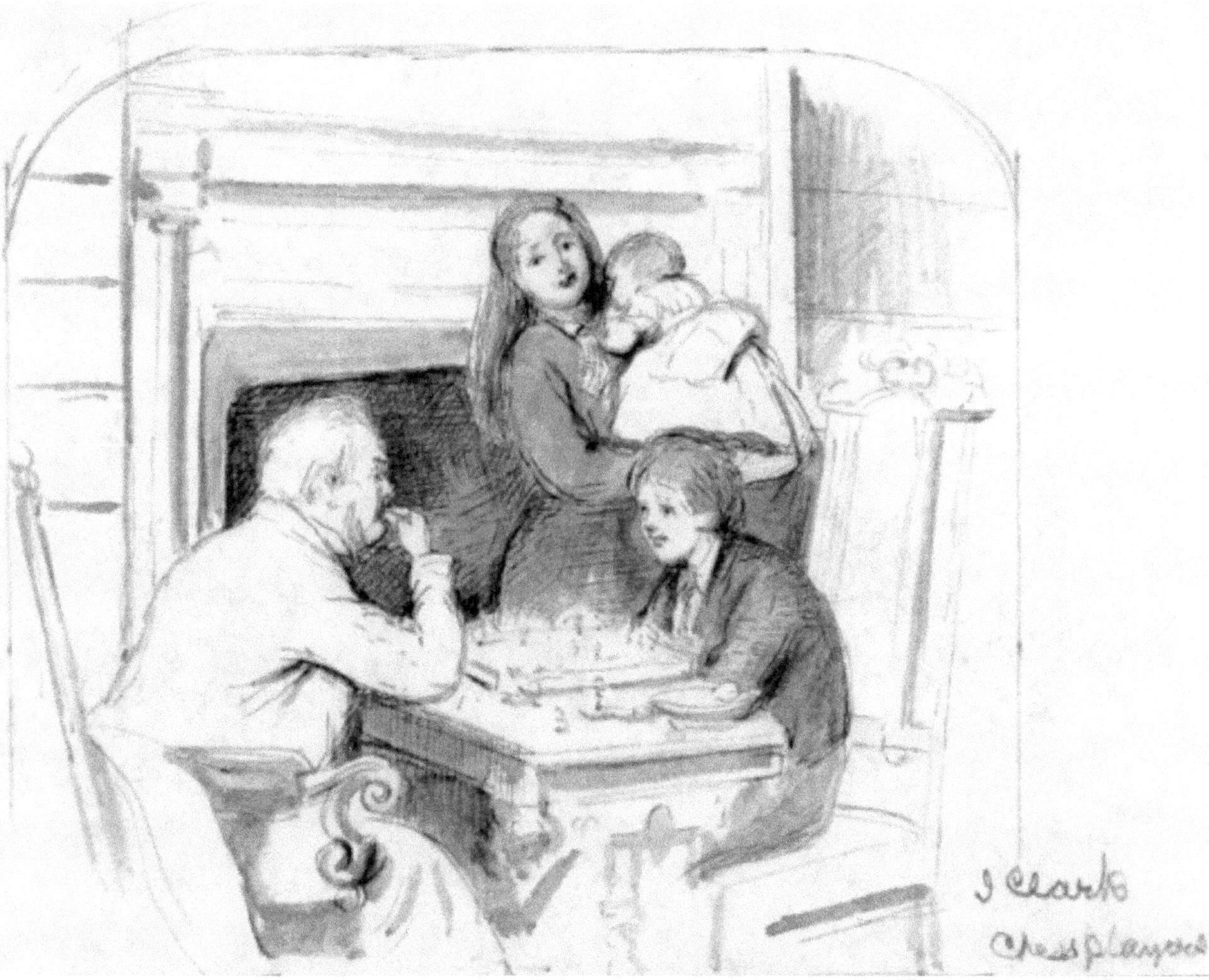

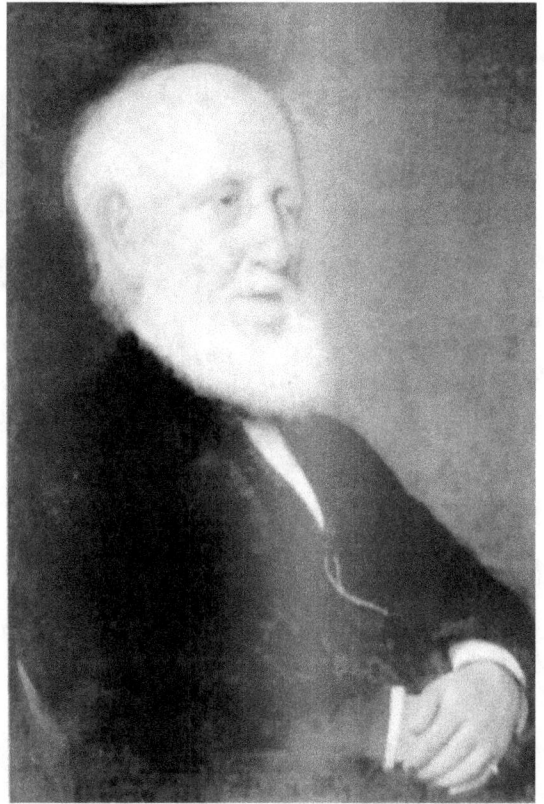

Plate 17. Drawing for 'Checkmate' (1876).
(Courtesy of the Victoria and Albert Museum)

Plate 18. Henry Butter (*c*.1870).
(Courtesy the artist's family)

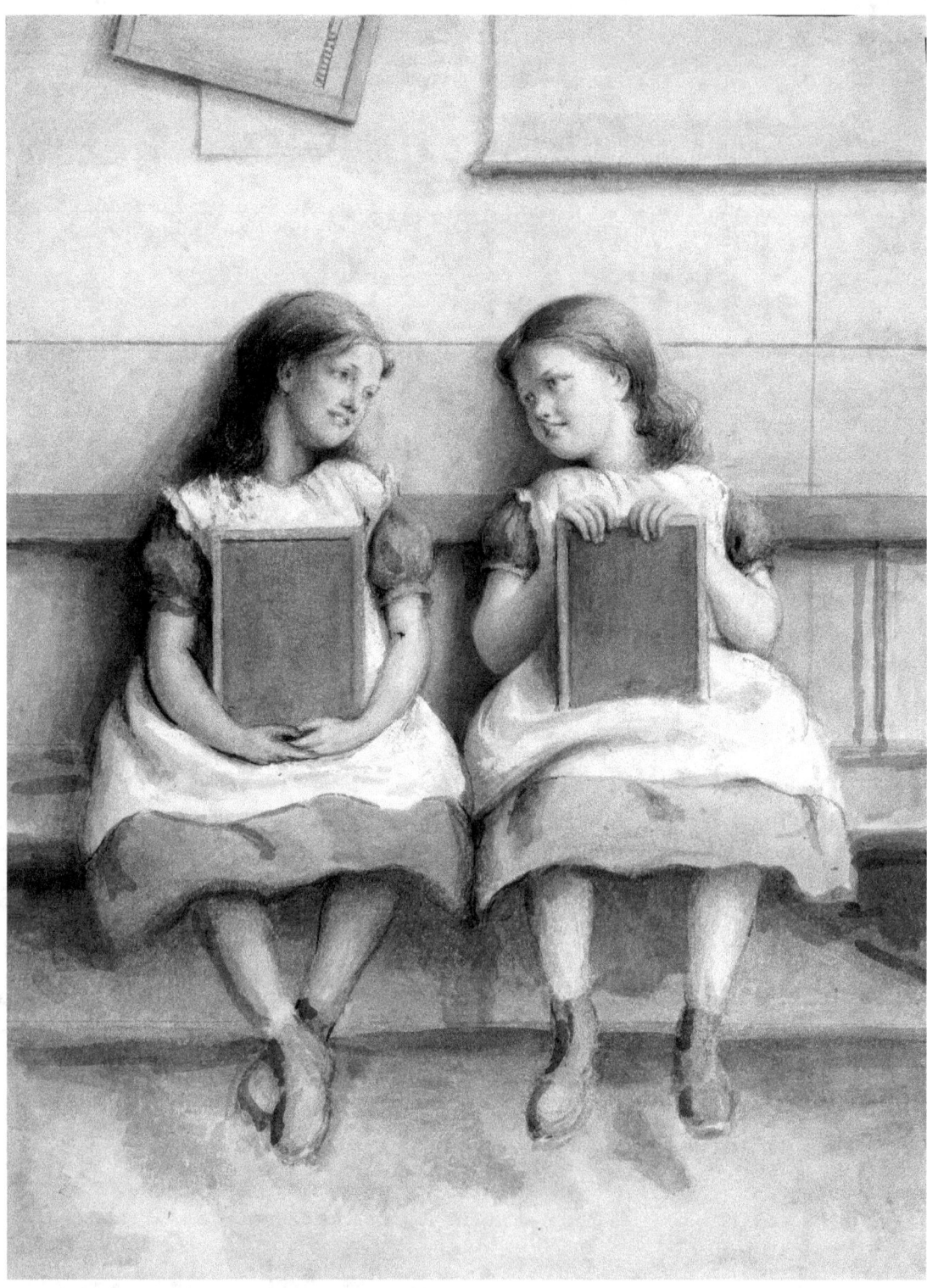

Plate 19. Sketch for 'Private and Confidential' (1875).
(Courtesy of the Victoria and Albert Museum)

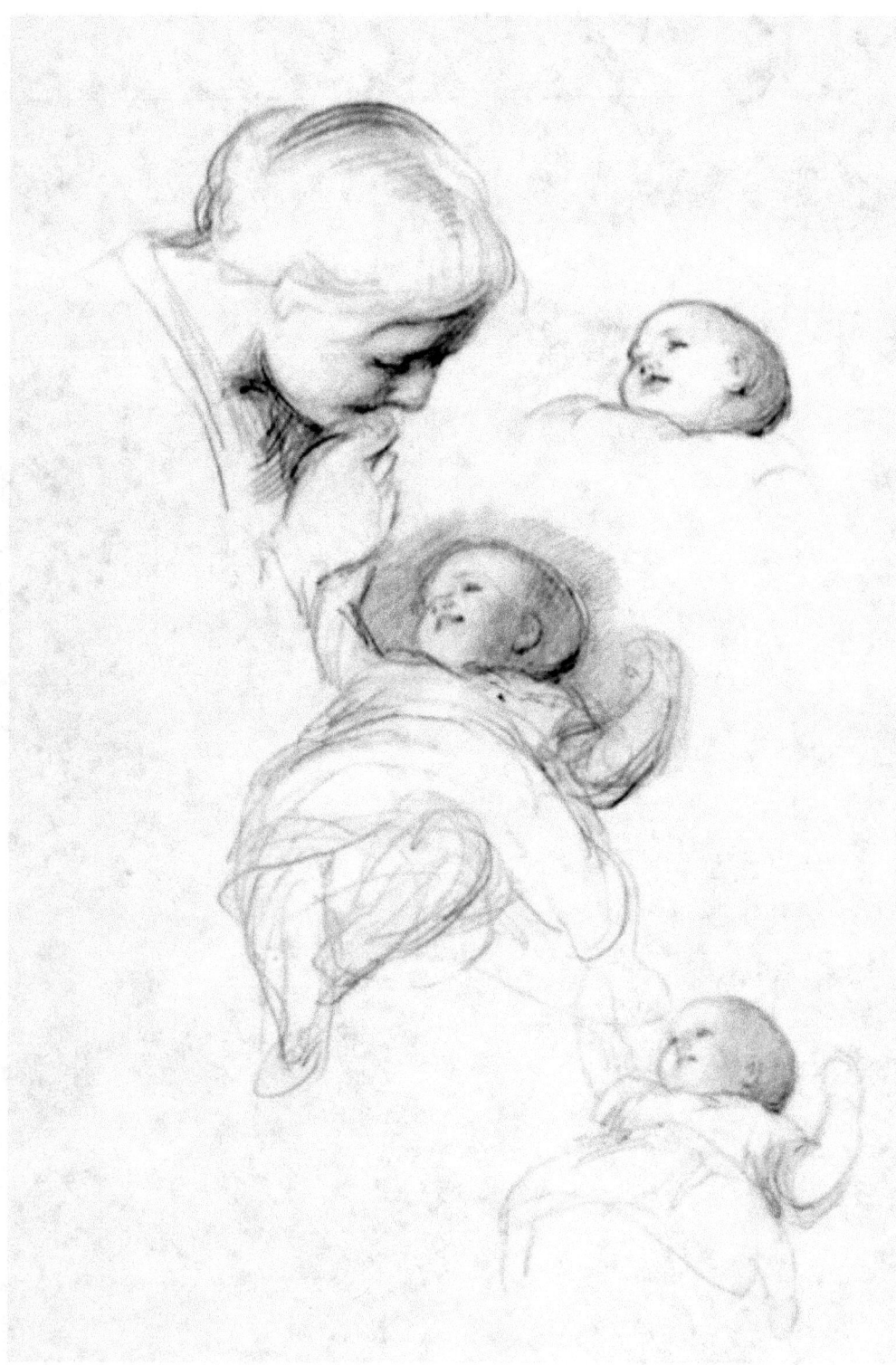

Plate 20. Drawing for 'Up to her lips the rosy palm she raises' (1878).
(Courtesy of Victoria and Albert Museum)

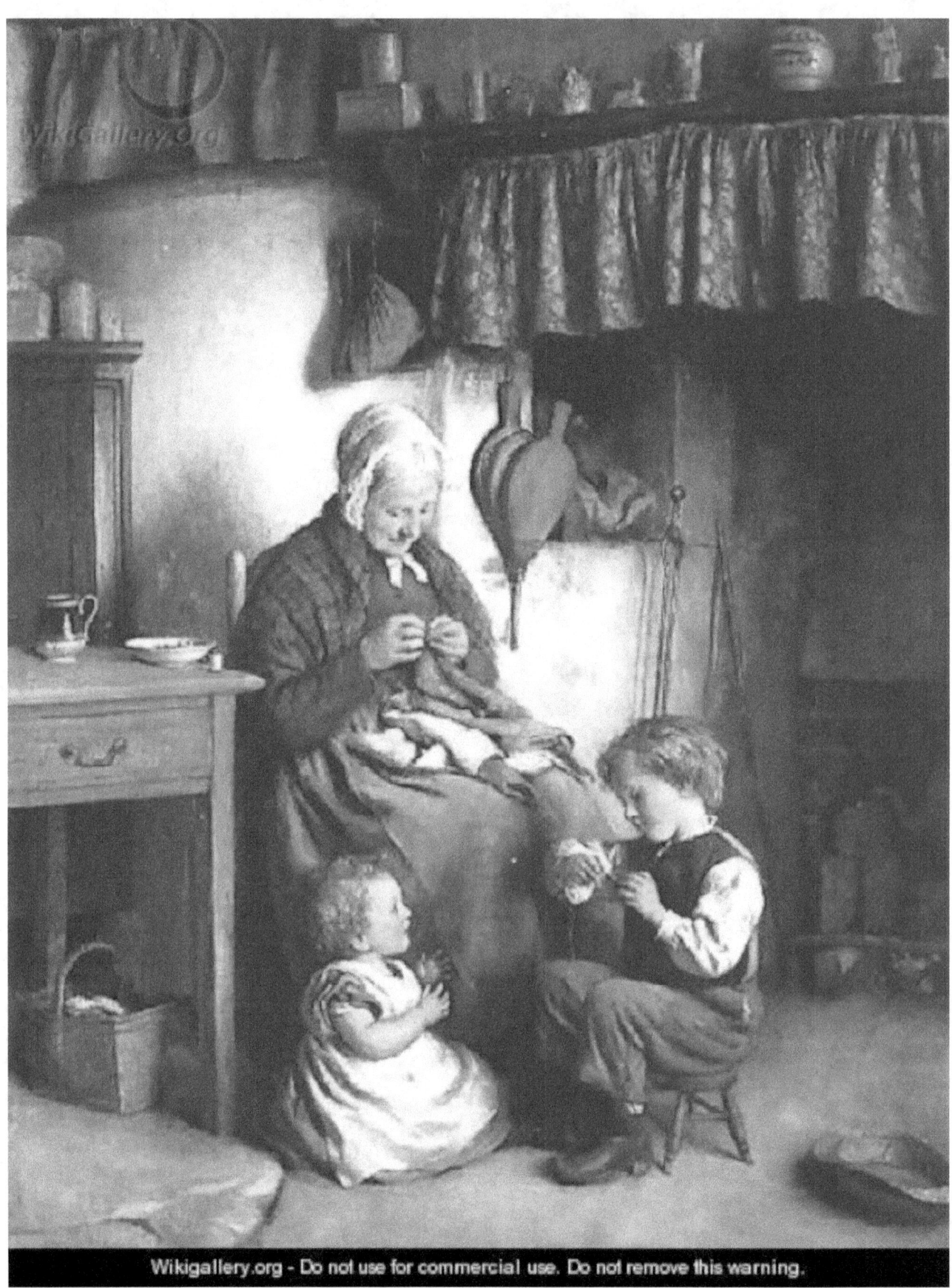

Plate 21. 'Chimney Corner' (1878). (Courtesy WikiGallery)

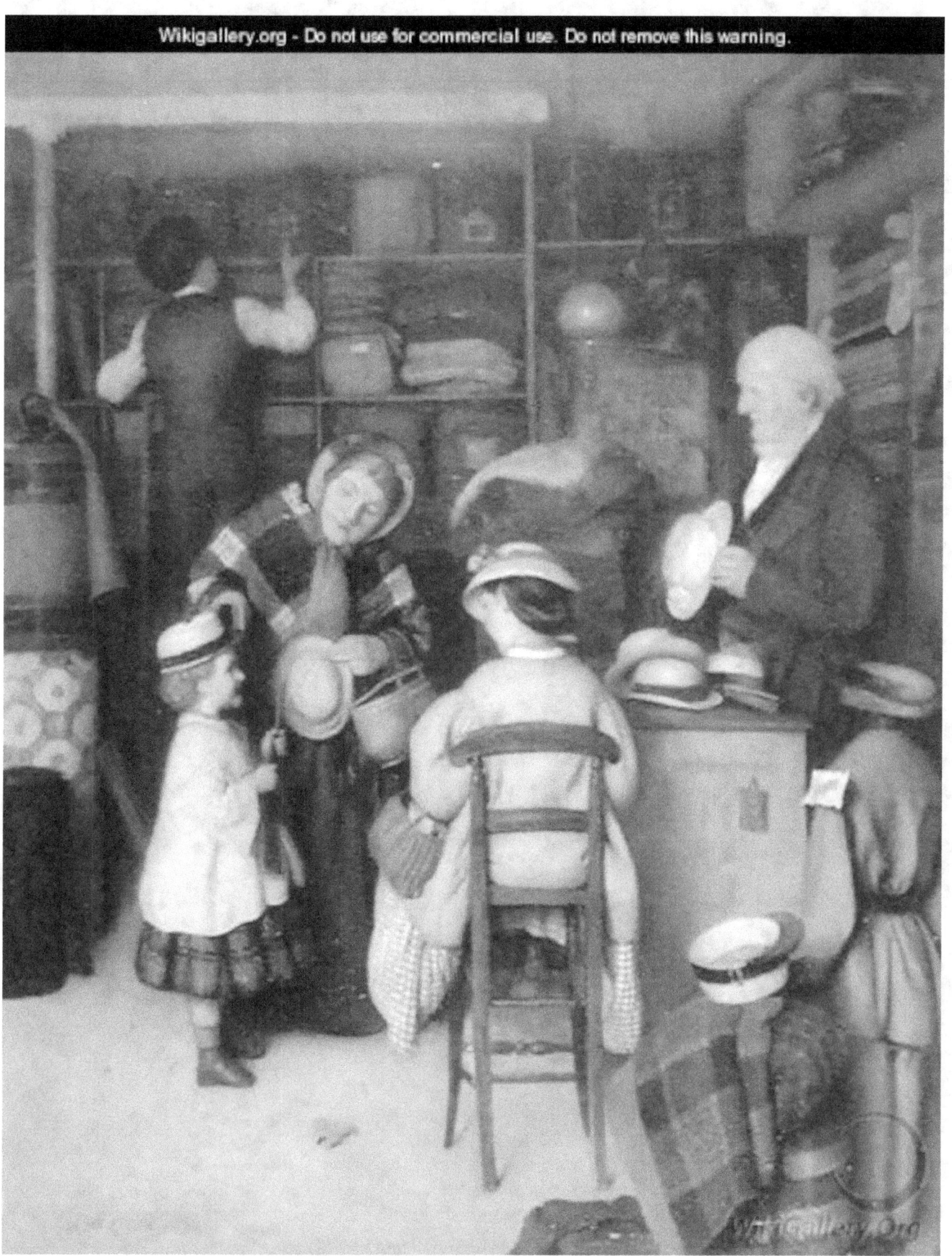

Plate 22. 'Buying a new hat' (1880). (Courtesy Wikigallery)

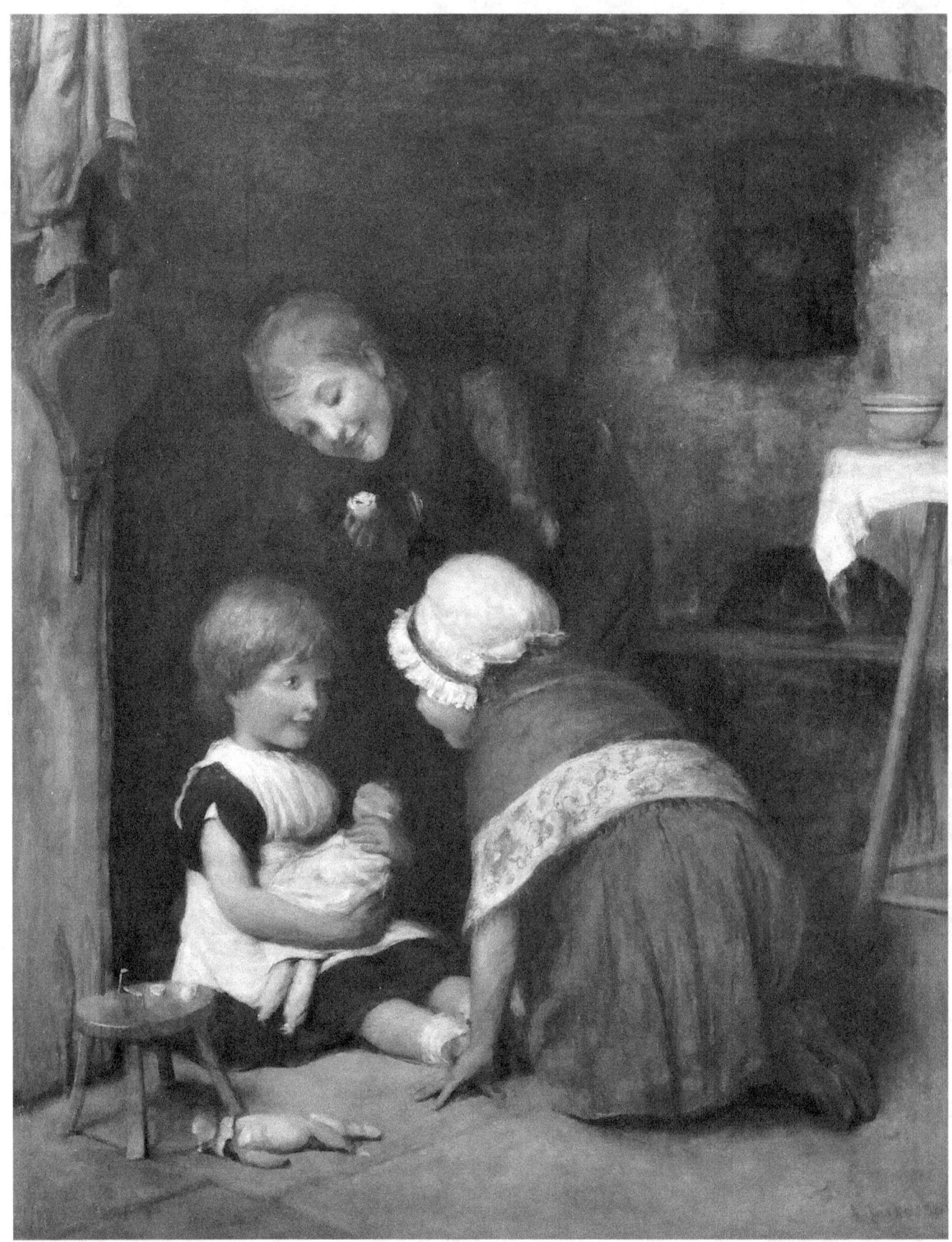

Plate 23. 'Children at Play' (1881).
(Courtesy Big Sky Fine Art, Nottingham, UK)

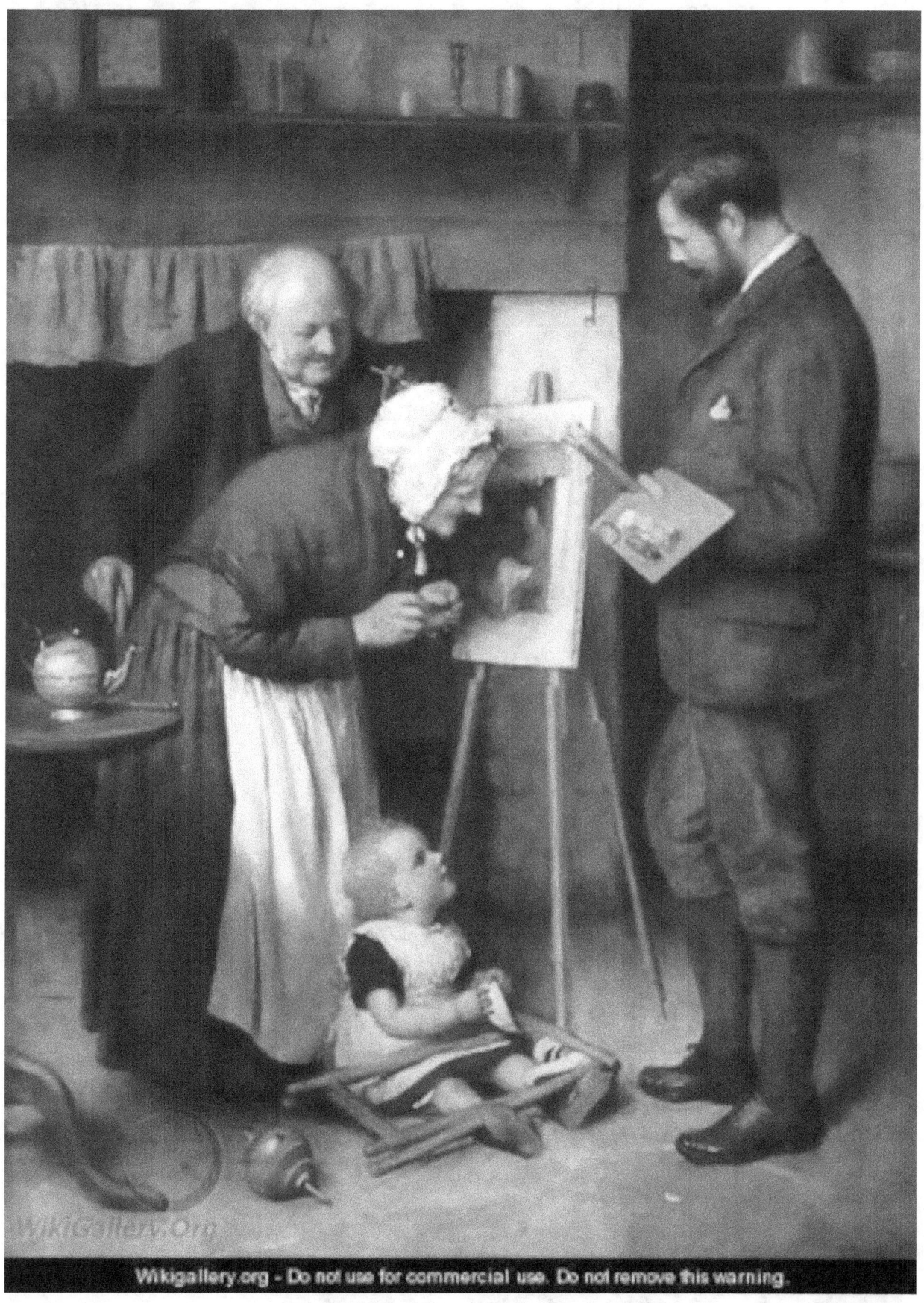

Plate 24. Facsimile of 'The Very Image' (1884).
(Courtesy WikiGallery)

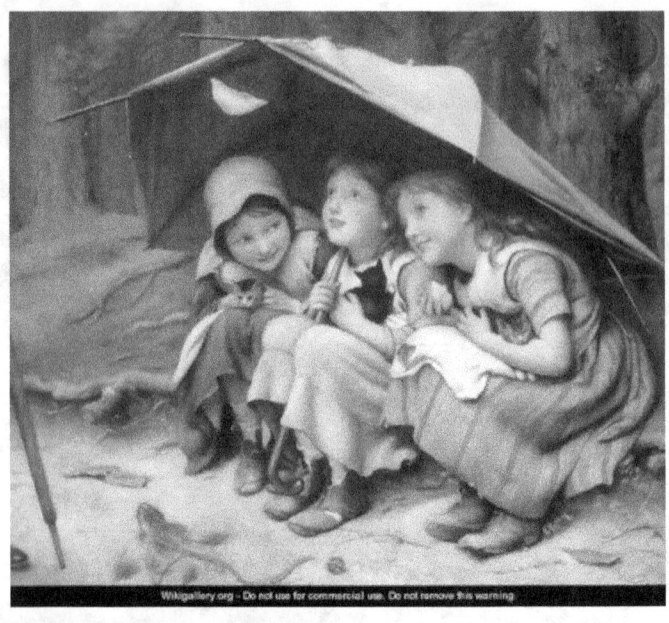

Plate 25. 'Three Little Kittens' (1883).
(Courtesy WikiGallery)

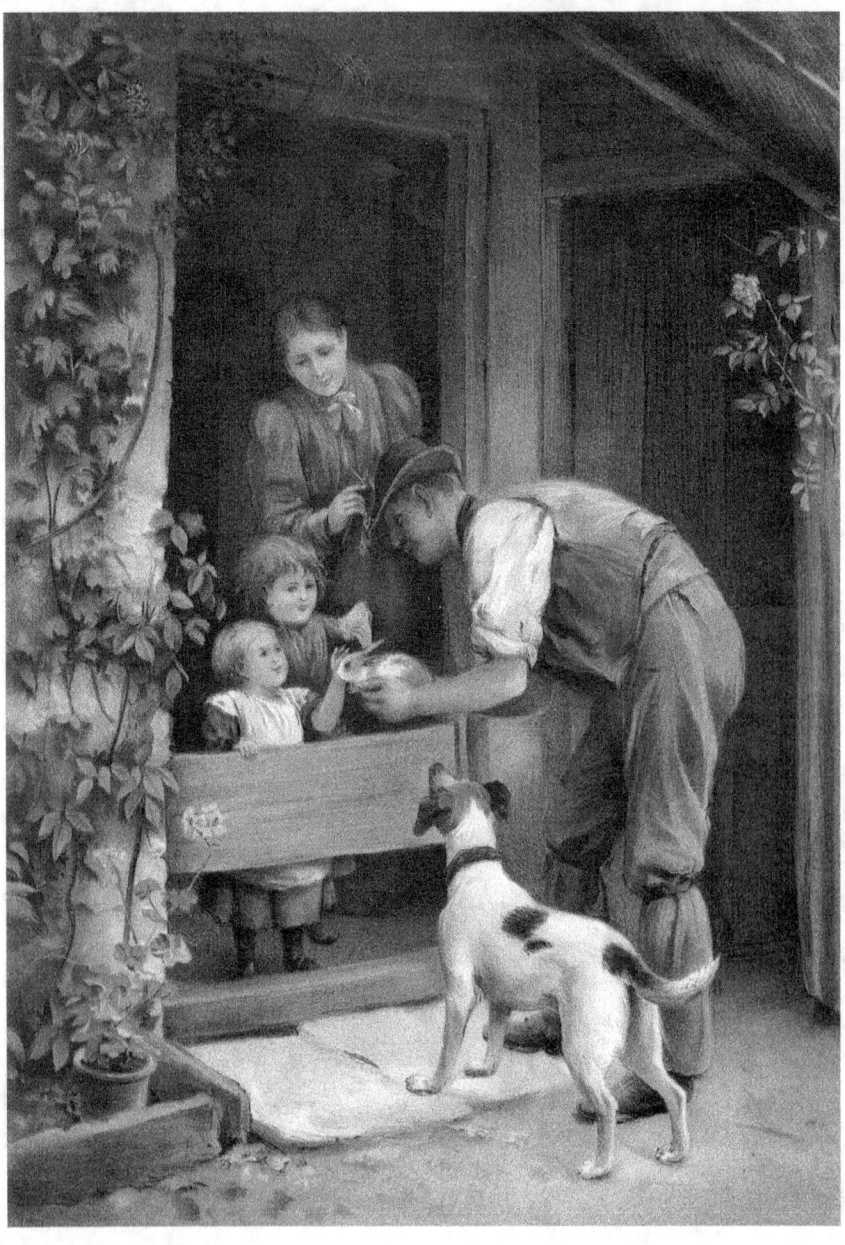

Plate 26. 'No Place like Home', *c*.1890.

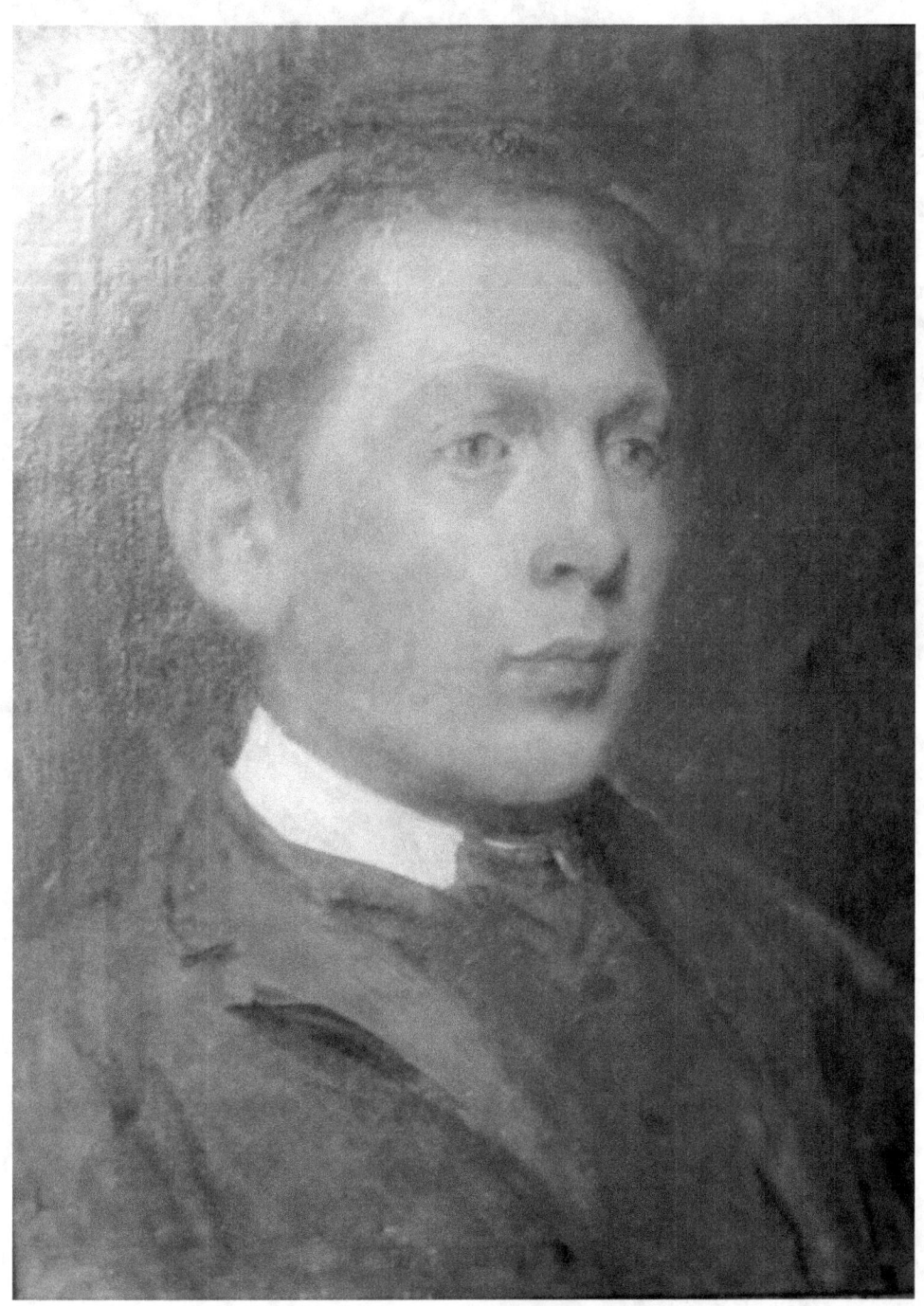

Plate 27. Portrait of John Clark (1885).
(Courtesy Sarah Galvin)

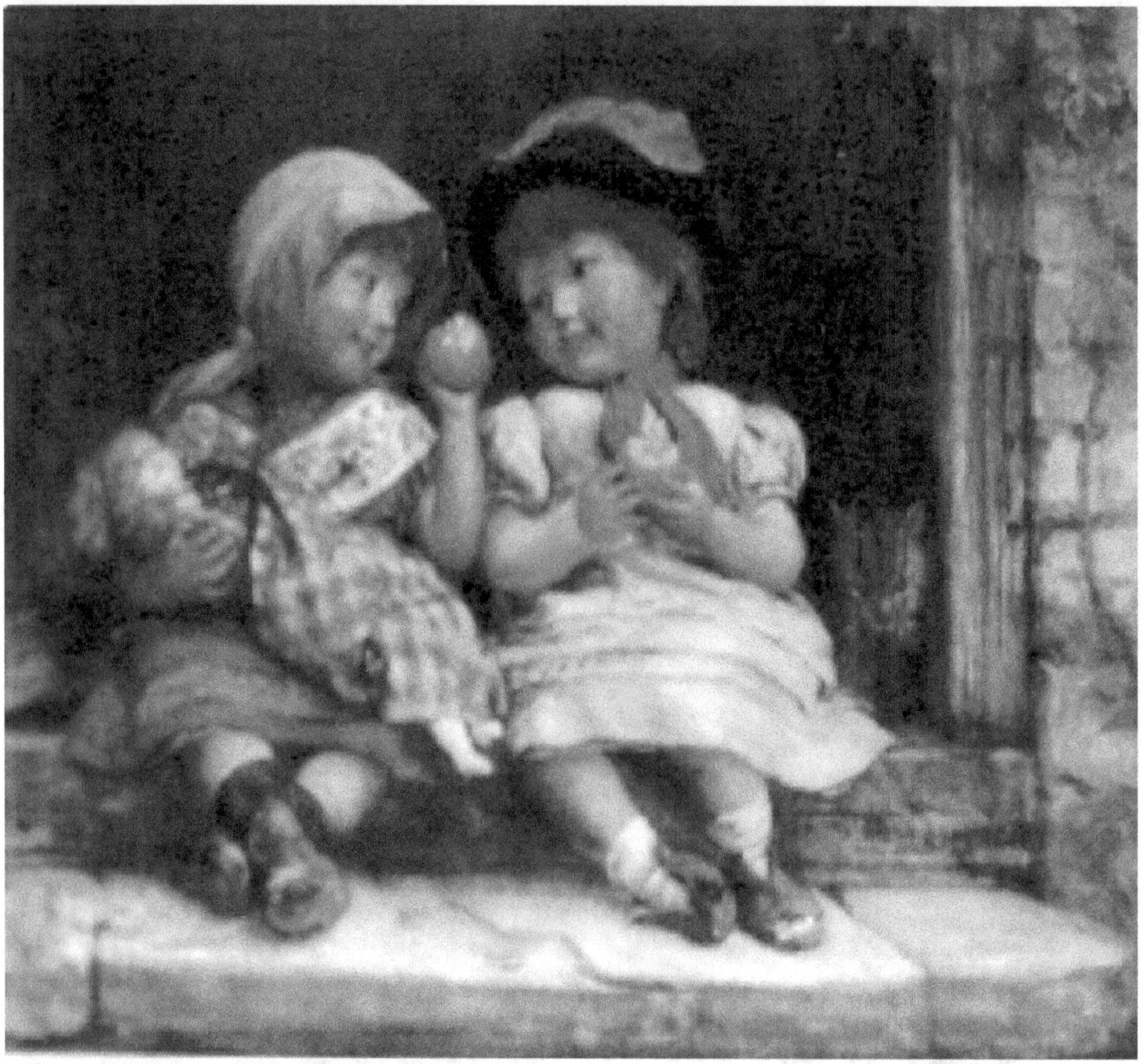

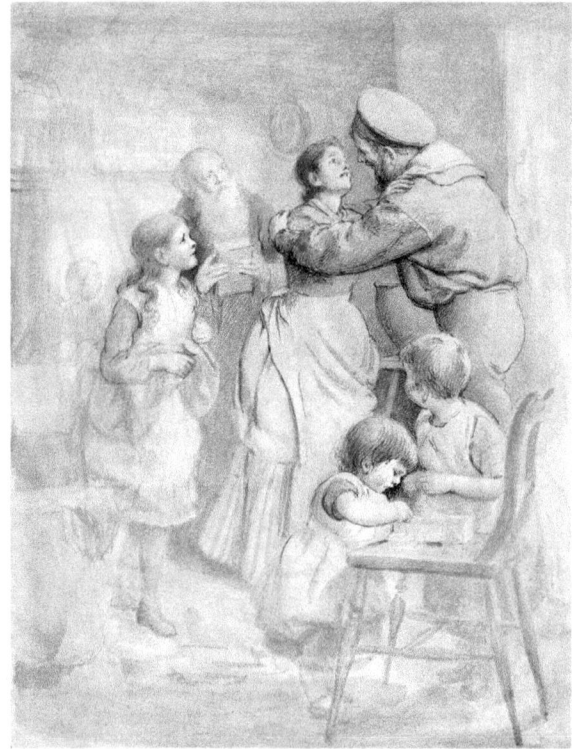

Plate 28. (*above*) 'Golden Days'
(1886). (Courtesy Christies)

Plate 29. Sketch for 'Home Again' (1885).
(Courtesy Victoria and Albert Museum)

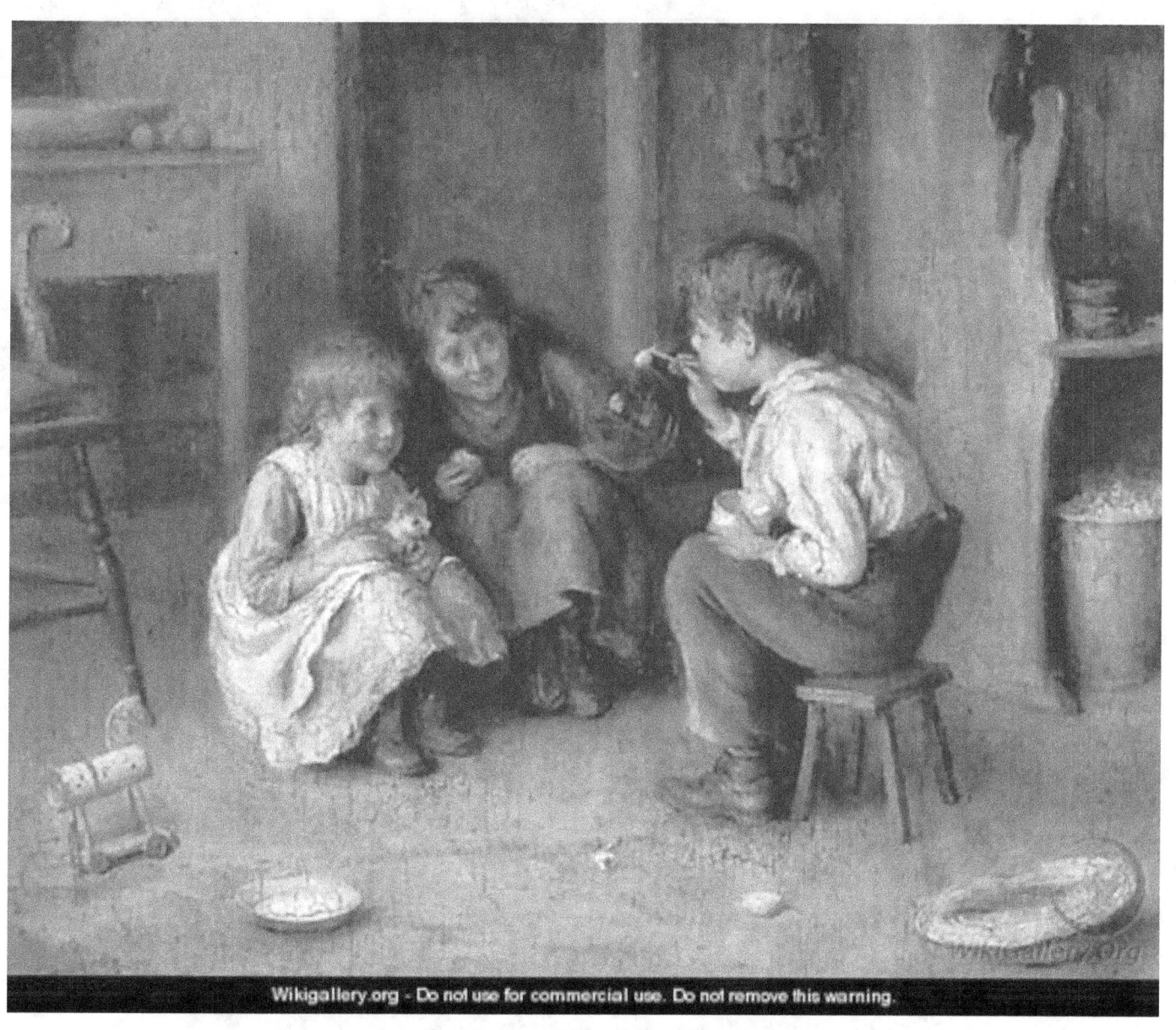

Plate 30. 'Blowing Bubbles' (1889).
(Courtesy WikiGallery)

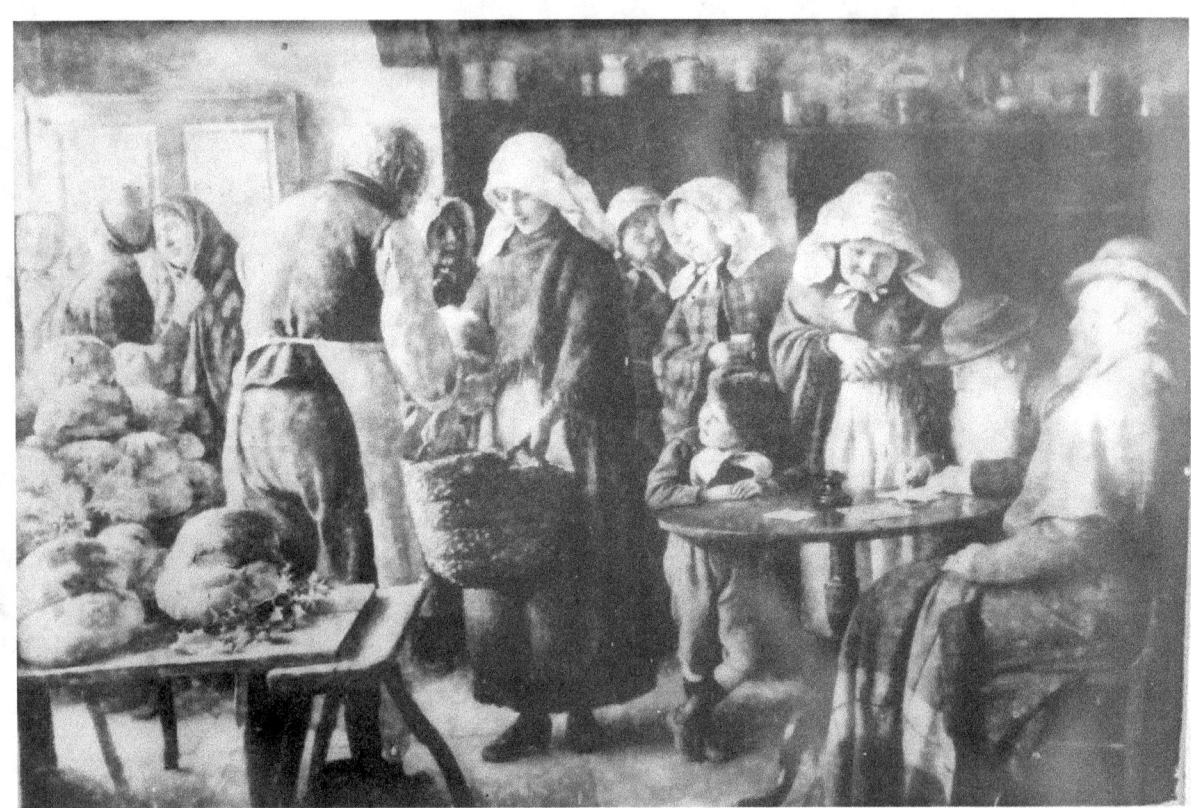

Plate 31. Photograph of 'Christmas Dole' in Hazelbury Plucknett Church.
(Courtesy Teresa Galvin)

"The Christmas Dole"

Painted by Joseph Clark. And exhibited at the Royal Academy in 1888.
A bequest from Mrs Mountford, who died in 1830, for bread to be distributed to the poor of Hazelbury Plucknett each year, on St Thomas's Day.
A Tablet in her memory is over the South Door.

"This has been one of the worst years ever known for artists, and yet it has been the best year ever known for the chief of our picture exhibitions. In 1868 the sum taken at the doors of the, Royal Academy was about £11,000. This year it was nearly £20,000. The receipts averaged nearly £260 a day"

Leeds Mercury 10 September 1869 (up from £836,000 to £1.6m).

Another interesting development in the year was mentioned by The Examiner:

"The extraordinary number of pictures excluded from the Royal Academy Exhibition this year, has induced a committee of gentlemen and artists to form a select supplementary exhibition. A spacious suite of rooms has already been secured in Bond Street, within two minutes' walk of the Academy."

The Examiner 8 May 1869

The newspapers did not say much about the 'overflow' gallery in Bond Street; or whether the experiment continued in later years.

1870

In its report on the RA exhibition in 1870, the Observer said:

"Mr J. Clark seems to be getting into a hard inexpressive (style) witness his 'School Time'."

The Observer 15 May 1870

Other papers did not mention this or his other two works exhibited that year. These were 'Visit from the Rectory' and 'The New Pet'. 'The New Pet' was a title that was recycled. Sothebys record that this work dates from 1876 and a second smaller work with the same title went to the Institute of Oil Painters in 1896.

1871

In the following year, the Observer reported on several exhibitions in Bond Street:

"The other new exhibition at the Old Bond Street Gallery contains upwards of 500 paintings and drawings, in oils and water colours, less remarkable than the above [*another Bond Street show*] for their originality, either of subject or treatment .... Messrs Morgan and Bauerle send pictures of child life, none so naturally rendered as Mr J Clark's capital group of a little boy and girl hard at work at a jam pot by a cupboard, which has incautiously been left open."

Observer 4 June 1871

The paper did not mention the name of this work by Joseph and none of the images in the public domain corresponds to the description. The Old Bond Street Gallery occupied the buildings previously used by the British Institution in a street long known as the centre of the fine art trade.

Later in the month, The Graphic's critic disliked some aspects of Joseph's work exhibited at the RA:

"'Wayfarers' is the title chosen for three pictures by Mr Charles Landseer, Mr J. Clark and Mr Rossiter respectively. … Mr Clark might be designated as an English Frere, but that his technical method is somewhat uncertain, and a particular timidity seems to attend his labour. There is much fidelity of expression in his picture, however, and homely sentiment of an unforced kind."

The Graphic 17 June 1871

Joseph also exhibited a work called 'The first letter' at the Society of British Artists without press comment – although it sold at the exhibition for £15 (about £1,250).

1872

Three new works appeared in the 1872 RA. These were 'All alone', 'Dumplings' and 'Mother's Darling'. Although none secured critical comment in the press, Joseph returned to these subjects in later years. The 'Mother's Darling' exhibited in 1872 was a different work from that exhibited in 1885.

1873

Joseph had three paintings accepted for the RA in 1873:

"Early Efforts' by Mr J. Clark (50 Arthur Road, Holloway), explains itself easily and pleasantly when we see the young shaver attempting a likeness of his grandfather. If he learns eventually to draw as well as Mr Clark his 'early efforts' will not be in vain."

The Era 8 June 1873

"… Among other painters of children, Mr J. Clark may be honourably mentioned. There is much homely pathos with delightful natural truth in his 'Farmer's Daughter' peeling apples with her baby brother beside her, and in his two other examples."

The Graphic 28 June 1873

The third painting exhibited was 'T'is good the fainting soul to cheer'. This title comes from 'Women' (1807) by George Crabbe, the early nineteenth century poet, surgeon and clergyman. His words inspired many over the years including Benjamin Britten whose opera 'Peter Grimes' was based on Crabbe's 'The Borough' (1810). Byron praised Crabbe as 'nature's sternest painter yet the best' and he was so much a favourite of Jane Austen that she jokingly declared her determination to marry him.

1874

Two works were exhibited at the RA in 1874 – 'Homely Hop' and 'The Bird's Nest'. Neither were reviewed by the press although the 'Birds Nest' was selected for the 1876 Philadelphia Centenial Exhibition.

Generally the critics seemed to be somewhat out of sorts and inclined to find fault with the Academy. Their initial focus was not on the art on display as seen in two early reviews:

"The opening of the grand saloons of the Royal Academy is an event, an art festival, not only for grave connoisseurs, but more so for the young world of fashion. Spring costumes vie with the colours on the walls, and the living beauty with the counterfeit presentment, not invariably, we may add, to the advantage of the work of art."

London Standard 2 May 1874

"There is one thing, however, in which the Royal Academy has made no progress … the unfortunate visitors burdened with that most unwieldy of all tomes, the Academy catalogue. … alas as years have rolled on the catalogue has become larger and larger, and this year it appears to be more bulky and unmanageable than ever. There is no reason why an elegant little volume, almost small enough to go in the waistcoat pocket, should not be substituted for the present cumbersome collection of leaves. As nearly double the number of works of art are annually exhibited at the Royal Academy to what there were in 1787, some alteration in the form of the catalogue would be especially acceptable. The present collection numbers 1,624 works of art; of these 947 are oil painting and 205 water-colours, 274 architectural drawings and prints, and 100 pieces of sculpture.

Though not abounding in many great pictures, it is an exhibition of great interest, and taken as a whole it gives evidence of correct thought and true artistic feeling, especially among the younger members of the English school. There are so many people who are so fully engaged in the height of the London season that their visits to the Royal Academy are naturally few and of short duration. It is impossible that they can give more than a passing glance at the 1,624 works of art that are on show at Burlington House, and it is just possible, in giving that passing glance, they may overlook the very pictures they ought to see, and pass over the most important paintings in the collection."

Morning Post 2 May 1874

The continuing critical concern about the integrity of the selection and hanging committees resurfaced in the Pall Mall gazette:

"The plea put forward for the members of the Academy that they conscientiously endeavour to do justice, will never become very convincing while there is so little modesty in displaying bad work of their own. A glance round the walls this year at the pictures contributed by the titled painters of the time is likely at least to put in peril any belief in the fitness of the body which governs the fortunes of English art, if not also to throw doubt upon its impartiality. For if we suppose a sincere faith in the merits of a large number of works that now disfigure 'the line,' then there is small chance of respect for critical powers employed to secure so curious a conclusion; and it would be most complimentary to the intelligence of those most nearly concerned if we were to interpret the presence of some of these pictures by Royal Academicians as being intended to assert a right rather than as implying any thought that they are worthy of their place. But in any case it is very easy to overrate the value of sincerity, and when it is put forward as a substitute for intelligence there is always a danger of very mischievous results. The general effect of the Exhibition of this year is seriously injured through the sincere belief of Royal Academicians in themselves, and valuable space upon the walls is in many cases occupied by works whose presence here not even the sincerity of their authors wholly excuses …"

Pall Mall Gazette 7 May 1874

1875

The Graphic offered a positive review of Joseph's work (plate 19):

"[In] 'Private and confidential' Mr Clark has given us a charming study of childhood life, two little girls seated on a bench holding mysterious converse behind their slates. It is school time, and the danger they are incurring by some lynx-eyed mistress evidently adds to the enjoyment with which the great secret is being discussed. The subject is being treated in an eminently amusing manner, and Mr Clark evidently intends to foreshadow that fondness for forbidden fruit with which the weaker sex has been credited from Eve upwards. The execution of the whole picture is excellent, the expression on each face is natural and lively without being exaggerated while the attitudes are simple and unstrained. In addition to this painting, Mr Clark exhibited two other pictures at this year's Exhibition of the Royal Academy 'A quiet Afternoon' and 'Don't touch'."

The Graphic 14 August 1875

In his Academy Notes for 1875, John Ruskin after criticizing the works of others says that Joseph's 'Private and Confidential' 'deserves a few moments more'.

Later in the year Joseph became a member of the Society of British Artists and exhibited 'Words of Comfort' at their 1875/6 winter exhibition; but the press did not notice it. A report of this exhibition was not enthusiastic about either the art or the newly installed gas lighting:

"I thought that peradventure I might view the paintings in Suffolk-street. Vain was the hope. I was hardly inside the doors before execrable gas had to turned on. It is impossible to judge shade and tone under such conditions. I must, therefore, speak with reserve. There may be exquisite paintings which looked ordinary in the glare of yellow flame, and I leave criticism generally to another time should it come. But I saw enough to prove that the new blood infused recently into the Society of British Artists is producing renewed energy. The present winter exhibition is the best they have had for years. There are bad pictures there – some wonderfully bad."

Liverpool Daily Post 10 December 1875

Writing at roughly the same time, Mrs. Julian Hawthorne, daughter-in-law of Nathaniel Hawthorne the American author, reported from London for the (American) Art Journal on the 1875 winter exhibitions saying

"There are no less than nine exhibitions of paintings now open to the public, and the total number of pictures exceeds twenty six hundred. It will be impossible, therefore to do more than notice the more prominent ones. Most of the Academicians are working for the spring exhibition, and are content to limit their winter show to a few small cabinet paintings and sketches."

(American) Art journal 1 January 1876

1876

As mentioned earlier, two of Joseph's works were shown at the US Centennial Exhibition in Philadelphia in 1876.

Joseph exhibited four works at the RA – 'Checkmate', 'The village chums'; 'A cheap entertainment'; and 'The ambulatory at St Cross, Winchester'. An ambulatory is place for walking, usually a covered passage around a cloister – or the processional way around the east end of a cathedral or large church and behind the high altar. This was the first of several pictures set at St Cross close to his parents-in-law's home. None of the 1876 works attracted much interest in the press.

The Illustrated London News for 3 June 1876 carried a front-page reproduction of 'A Cheap Entertainment' by Joseph. They described it as showing children teasing a kitten with a bobbin of thread with a grandmother looking on whilst darning something.

The only critical comment of 'Village Chums' was:

> "There is good little picture by J. Clark, called 'The Village Chums'. Two boys are seated on bench near rabbit hutch looking at a picture book."
>
> **Cheltenham Chronicle** 2 May 1876

As discussed earlier 'Checkmate' is sometimes confused with Joseph's 'Draught Players' (1859) and 'Chess Players' (1860).

He exhibited the 'Reading Lesson' at the Society of British Artists that sold for £73 10*s* (about £6,000). This was the last work he exhibited at the Society.

1877

In 1877, The Times' review mentioned all three painting exhibited by Joseph at the RA. These were 'Left in charge', 'The young mother' and 'Early promise'. The critic returned to the familiar theme of the dullness in Joseph's 'use of colour'; and used this as the starting point for an unfavorable comparison of British and French art:

> "Joseph Clark's 'Early Promise' is one of the pictures purchased by the Royal Academy out of the Chantry Fund. There is no painter of the humble domestic school, not Webster, not Wilkie himself, truer in expression and more blameless and often pathetic in feeling than the painter who first started into notice some years ago with 'The Sick Child'. That picture has ever since remained the high water mark of the painter's true and pathetic sentiment, as of his technical excellence. In all his pictures this year – the 'Left in Charge' a doting grandfather, left in charge of two happy babies, who have climbed on his knees, in that perfect companionship which unites the two extremes of life; the 'Young Mother' with the ineffable glow of a mother's love lighting her homely, but comely face, as she looks proudly and happily down on her baby, from her household work; and this 'Early promise', a shy boy artist whose works are being examined critically but approvingly by the good humoured parson of the parish and his pretty and sympathetic daughters, while the other members of the young genius's family stand around anxiously waiting for the verdict. Mr Clark shows the same qualities, rare truth of expression, clearness of conception and purity of sentiment in combination with an unpleasant mode of using his colours which does much to mar all the good there is in his pictures. He is a striking example of that defective technical instruction which keeps back our painters, though no longer to the extent it once did. Another drawback, it seems to us, to Mr Clark's work is his dull unpicturesqueness. It suggest the question of whether an English Edouard Frere be possible, Mr Clark has so much sentiment in common with that delightful French painter, yet such grievous lack of his pictorial charm. Of that which is most prosaic and commonplace in English humble lower middle life, in types of face, in dress, in surroundings he is the faithful and uncompromising recorder. His truth of expression, purity of feeling, and unswerving to fact in all he paints, are the rare qualities entitling him to the respect which the Academy has shown, and properly shown, in purchasing his picture."
>
> **The Times** 12 May 1877

The trustees of the Chantrey Bequest paid Joseph £210 (£17,250) for "Early Promise". A month later the Times mentions Joseph:

> "... Mr Joseph Clark's studies from children, in pencil highlighted with white on a yellowish ground, and his drawing in the same method for one of his picture's in this year's Academy 'Left in Charge' show the same mixture of true feeling for the subject and honest study, with a lack of pictorial feeling in the rendering, which puzzles the critics of this painter's pictures."
>
> **The Times** 12 June 1877

H.C. Richardson (1877), as editor of 'Academy Criticisms 1877' included extracts from the critical comments on all three works exhibited by Joseph. In addition to The Times article already mentioned, 'The 'Criticism' quoted:

LEFT IN CHARGE, – Joseph Clark.
> "... is a pleasing little domestic incident, which will gratify the not over-exacting tastes of the lady visitors. Grandpapa is fondling over two children, whom he has taken on his knees, the trio forming a very happy combination, truthfully realised, without undue elaboration."
>
> **Morning Advertiser**

> "We were delighted with it."
>
> **Athenaeum**

THE YOUNG MOTHER. – Joseph Clark.
> "... shows a kitchen interior, with a baby in a cradle, watched by a very young – too young – mother. The background and accessories are painted with more richness than usual."
>
> **Athenaeum**

EARLY PROMISE. – Joseph Clark.
> "Is a work of humble realism, pure, wholesome, and English in sentiment, irreproachable in expression, and conscientious in details, but with all-but entire absence of all sense of the pictorial elements in a picture, and a most disagreeable technical method, a work, in short, the purchase of which has been determined solely by appreciation of its quality of expression."
>
> **Graphic**

> "Not one of his best pictures, in expression, painting, or subject. A boy's drawing is being inspected by a benevolent parson, whose daughter – her hair plaited down her back – joins sympathisingly in the examination."
>
> **Athenaeum**

> "Clean, careful, but too smooth."
>
> **Daily Telegraph**

The art critic of the Examiner captured the overall critical view of the year's RA exhibition when he said:

> "There seems to be a general agreement that the present exhibition of the Academy is inferior to its predecessors, and notably inferior to that of last year; but this fact need not at all discourage the hopes of those among us who have faith in the future of English art. The influences which go to the making of a brilliant and effective display of contemporary work, are often independent of

the march of real progress. Last year, for instance, the galleries at Burlington House were more than usually interesting, chiefly because one or two men of established reputation were there to be seen at their best. But this can scarcely be expected to happen every year, and the absence from the present collection of any works corresponding to the 'Daphnephoria' of Mr. Leighton or the 'Atalanta' of Mr. Poynter unquestionably serves to give to the general appearance of the walls a sense of dullness and depression. Further, there is the fact that much must always depend in these matters upon the judicious arrangement of the material at the disposal of the hanging committee, and we cannot recall any occasion for many years past when the task entrusted to this body has been so imperfectly performed. Of course, it would be quite unfair to throw upon their shoulders the responsibility of all that is faulty in the relative positions of the pictures upon the walls. The hanging committee is not permitted to grant a charitable obscurity to the large mass of indifferent work produced by Academicians and Associates; and as the performances of many of these gentlemen are on the present occasion more than commonly bad, it is little wonder if the first glance at the exhibition yields more to deplore than to enjoy. We can offer no apology for returning again and again to this abuse, for the scandal steadily increases with the so-called liberal enlargement of the associate rank. It is not fair to the character of the Academy itself, it is still less fair to the great body of English artists whose interests the Academy professes to care for and control ..."

Pall Mall Gazette 5 May 1877

1878

The three works Joseph exhibited at the RA attracted little attention. They were 'A morning call', 'Up to her lips the rosy palm she raises' and 'Wandering Minstrels'.

The title of the first work comes is taken from 'The Quiver' – an illustrated magazine for Sunday published between 1821 and 1926 intended as 'A Witness for the Truth' addressed to a middle-class evangelical audience. During Joseph's lifetime, it became 'An Illustrated Magazine of Social, Intellectual, and Religious Progress' with bold illustrations in black and white appearing in weekly, monthly and half-yearly versions. It is unclear whether Joseph prepared any drawings for the magazine or whether it was part of the Clark family's regular reading at this time.

The Victoria and Albert Museum has a preparatory drawing for 'Up to her lips the rosy palm she raises' (plate 20).

Later in the year, Joseph sent two works to the Dudley Gallery. These were 'Chimney Corner' and 'In the Bath'. The Graphic starts its report with an attack on the British Institution that closed a decade earlier:

"The Dudley is the first of the societies Winter Exhibitions to open its doors. ... The Dudley takes the place of the old British Institution. It has not yet fallen into the abject pot-boiling ways which lowered the latter days of the venerable establishment in Pall Mall, begun in such high-reaching intentions for the advancement of British art, and ending in such an abject pandering to its lowest exigencies.

The Dudley Winter Exhibition does not reach high. The bulk of the four hundred and fifty pictures exhibited (out of more than a thousand set aside) keep within the margin of the safely saleable, but they do it with a certain grace. They are for the most part not bad pictures but simple studies, very faithful as a rule to the familiar nature they aim at reproducing, of good influence as far as they go, inasmuch as an honest rendering of the truth of nature must be so, and by their frank avowal of modest pretensions disarming attack because their aim is not higher. Better honest painting of common things and familiar scenes, such as we see here, than high aspiration after unattainable aims, ending in morbid affectation, or solemn, stupid pretentiousness. ... Joseph Clark's 'Chimney Corner' and 'In the Bath,' making allowance for his woolly texture and tame uniformity of execution... (Signed Tomm Taylor)".

The Graphic 30 November 1878

The Aberdeen journal includes a brief syndicated comment:

"Joseph Clark's 'Bath' recalls the 'tubby nights' of which we all as children used to have such an aversion."

Aberdeen Journal 30 November 1878

1879

Two works made the grade for the RA but neither attracted the critics. They were 'The bargain' and 'Jean's wedding day'. The second work is also known as 'Jeanes Wedden Day in Mornen' is taken from a dialect poem by William Barnes. It was the first painting taking its inspiration from a work by Joseph's teacher.

1880

The first RA Exhibition in the new decade did not impress the Art Journal when they wrote:

"The visitor to this year's Art Exhibition at Burlington House will at once be struck with the extreme dearth of any contributions of the prominent sensational kind. No example in the galleries will necessitate the London Policeman's courteously reiterated 'Move on, please' to a crowd of anxious gazers, and no title wearisome by constant repetition in drawing-rooms of the greater personages of London society. ... we search in vain for the one before which we linger in intensity of pleasure and leave with regret. Viewed as a whole this year's exhibition must be pronounced below the average of former years. ... In subject pictures of abiding interest, there is a very decided falling off. ... If an important picture is not sold before it is lent to the public for the summer months, it stands a weak chance of being sold afterwards."

Joseph exhibited two works drawing their inspiration from quotations but without comment from the press. 'Anger is the best sauce' appears to be a quotation, although its origin is obscure. It may be related to the old French quotation 'Hunger is the best sauce'. 'In as much as ye have done it unto one of the least' comes from Matthew 25:40 of the King James Bible. As mentioned earlier, he also exhibited 'Ducks' at the Walker Art Gallery in Liverpool.

1881–1883

In the second decade covered by this chapter, the press critics mentioned relatively few of Joseph's works despite his success in maintaining a steady flow of works to the RA, provincial exhibitions and, after 1883, to the Institute of Painters in Oil Colours. Works exhibited at the RA included 'Goodnight father' (1881), 'The expectant wee things' (1881) and 'The Word of life' (1881), 'A Dorset village' (1882),

'Waifs and strays' (1882), 'A tempting offer' (1882) and 'Home triumphant' (1882). 'Goodnight father' was a reworking of his successful better-known 1868 work with the same title. 'Expectant wee things' is another quotation from Robert Burns. The full text is:

> "At length his lonely cot appears in view,
> Beneath the shelter of an aged tree:
> Th' expectant wee things, toddling, stacher thro'
> To meet their Dad,
> With flitchtering noise and glee"

'Stacher' is translated as staggering or tottering; and 'flitchering' as fluttering lightly.

'The word of life' is another quotation, this time from Philippians 2:16 in the King James Bible that reads *Holding forth the word of life; that I may rejoice in the day of Christ, that I have not run in vain, neither laboured in vain*.

An unexhibited work from this period variously called 'Children at Play' or 'Playing Doctors' gives an impression of the style of work produced in this period. Curiously it is signed 'J Clarke'.

1883

'Three little kittens', 'Homely fowl' and 'Hampshire cottage' were exhibited at the RA in 1883. The press did not mention 'Homely fowl' or 'A Hampshire cottage'. The other work, 'Three Little Kittens' attracted an unusual coverage in the Nottinghamshire Guardian's piece aimed at children that said:

> "Without doubt, you and I, my pets, must pay a visit to the great exhibition of pictures, the one hundred and fifteenth exhibition of the Royal Academy of Arts; and on a June morning, too, when even smoky, dirty, noisy London is looking its best, snd the trees in the park are green and gay. …
>
> The prettiest pictures this year (I don't hesitate to say so) are those of children, and this proves what I said to you a few weeks sgo, that we grown up folks of the present century are all striving io see for ourselves, and make others see, the child-spirit in everything. 'A little child shall lead them' I said softly to myself as I passed through the crowded rooms, thinking of the men and women who had striven so hard with their brushes to put upon canvass ths grace, the sweetness, and the innocent tenderness of little children. …
>
> [In Joseph Clark's 'Three little kittens' we see that] there are three little village girls huddled together under an old umbrella, as snug and as merry as three little kittens, while the rain patters down upon their gingham roof. What fun it is to be out in the rain! At least, this is what their faces seem to say …
>
> AUNT MAGGIE. Address all communications to Aunt Maggie (Symington), Heacham, Norfolk'.
>
> **Nottingham Guardian** 8 June 1883

Notwithstanding the absence of critical interest when exhibited, 'Three little kittens' was sold in 1998 for £34,600 (about £53,00) and is one of the most frequently advertised prints on Internet sites.

Later in the same year Joseph exhibited three works at the first public exhibition of the newly formed Institute of Painters in Oil Colours. The works were 'There has never been such a baby', 'An interesting occupation', and 'The Humming Top'.

"The Institute of Painters in Oil Colours will open their first Annual Exhihition at the Galleries of the Princes' Hall, Piccadilly, on Monday December 17. The Illustrated Catalogue will be the same size as, and in other respects similar to, the highly successful catalogue of the last Spring Exhibition of the Institute of Painters in Water Colours."

Pall Mall Gazette 12 October 1883

Joseph like other artists exhibiting in the early years of the Society made woodcuts of his works for inclusion in the exhibition catalogues. In most cases, these are the only images of these works in the public domain.

1884

In 1884, Joseph contributed 'The Very Image' and 'Borrowed Plumes' to the RA Summer Exhibition. Neither was reported by in the press at the time but Henry Blackburn's (1895) review of English Art in 1884 said:

"The Very Image' is by Mr. Joseph Clark. The group here consists of a young artist standing, palette and brushes in hand, in some humble country cottage. He has just finished his picture standing upon the easel, which an old granddame is expressing high approval of, while her good man endorses her opinion, and their little chubby grandson sits upon the floor doing all the mischief, time will admit of, with the artist's camp-stool. The picture on the easel may be the interior of the cottage itself, with the admiring old couple introduced, and perhaps the child; but, at any rate, the picture is admired, and the painter has the satisfaction of having an approving critic. The contrast of stalwart manhood with trembling old age, and the charm of childhood, will also not be overlooked by the observant. For many years (without any special recognition from the Academy) has Mr. Joseph Clark had similar subjects on the walls, interiors painted with the precision and certainty of the old Dutch masters; and, like them, making every detail of household life an interesting part of the composition."

Later in the year, Joseph exhibited three works at the second exhibition of the Institute of Painters in Oil Colours in Piccadilly. These were 'Mother's Help', 'Hanging out the washing', and 'Appreciative Audience'. The press did not mention any of these works.

1885

'*Mother's Darling*' was exhibited at the Royal Academy in 1885. Joseph painted the 1885 version in his garden studio at Camden Road, the models were his wife Annie, and daughter Elsie, then aged two. The trustees of the Chantrey Bequest paid Joesph £89 3s od (£8,388) for 'Mother's Darling'.

The Academy accepted two other works. One, 'Kitty, Hygy and Doffy, children of James Davies Esq.' was a picture of Ellen (14), Edith (18) and Florence (11). This was the first of Joseph's named portraits exhibited at the RA. James Davies variously described as a wheelwright and joiner was a close neighbour of the Clarks when the painting was exhibited. In 1881, they were living in Minsterley, Shropshire with James' parents. By the time of the 1891 census the Davies family were living in Brewery Road, off the Caledonian Road. Emma Davies, James' wife, came from this part of London. Her father was an highly skilled foreman upholsterer working for the Gillow's. Family tradition has it that he carried out several commissions for the royal household at Windsor Castle. Florence, called Doffy in the painting's title, was later known in family correspondence as Dolly.

Joseph painted John Clark's (his nephew) portrait in about the same time (plate 27). A preparatory drawing for his portrait is dated 15 February 1885, John's eighteenth birthday. It is tempting to think that John and Florence first met in Joseph's studio as they married in 1891.

The third painting exhibited at the Royal Academy was 'Home Again', without press comment. It is possible that a sketch called 'Sailor's return' by the Victoria and Albert Museum is really one for 'Home Again'. Whilst this might be a sketch for one of two later works on the theme of a sailor returning home, from 1908 and 1910 respectively, this is unlikely as those finished works are quite different.

Two works were shown at the Institute of Painters in Oil Colours. They were 'Youth and Age' and 'The Village Postman'.

1886

In 1886, the RA accepted four pictures but only one, 'Golden Days' caught the eye of the critics.

"In each succeeding room, the supply of nursery subjects is well maintained. There are little children taking 'first bites' at oranges and at apples; babies listening to 'sea shells' at their ears (a flight of imagination twice attempted this year); little girls playing with lambs, puppies, kittens; and little boys saying 'take us, daddy' and 'do take me' Such pictures do not need further description. … 'Golden Days' by Mr. Joseph Clark (730) will also attract attention: there is just the proper touch for a Christmas 'Illustrated' in the two little children comparing bites in their golden oranges".

Pall Mall Gazette 1 May 1886

"Pictures of babies abound … should be studied as also Mr Joseph Clark's 'Golden Days'."

Bucks Herald 8 May 1886

"'Golden Days' by Joseph Clark, two bonnie happy children, seated on a doorstep, and rich as princesses in the possession of a sufficiency of apples."

Birmingham Daily Post 10 May 1886

The title of another of these works 'With smiles of Peace and Looks of Love' comes from the final verse of the hymn 'We Are But Little Children Weak' by Cecil Frances Alexander (1848) intended for the Feast of the Holy Innocents (28 December). It reads:

> "With smiles of peace and looks of love
> Light in our dwellings we may make,
> Bid kind good-humour brighten there,
> And do all still for Jesus' sake."

This hymn was included in her 'Hymns for Little Children' that reached its 69th edition before the close of the nineteenth century and is still in print today. She also composed the ever-popular hymns 'All Things Bright and Beautiful', 'There is a Green Hill Far Away' and 'Once in Royal David's City'. Seven of her hymns were included in the 1873 issue of the Church of Ireland Hymnal, and eighteen in a Supplement to Hymns Ancient and Modern (1889). Joseph almost certainly knew of her hymns while acting as a Sunday school teacher in the 1870s. It is possible the inspiration for this work came from his family as Joseph's son, Wilfrid, was born in 1885.

Joseph exhibited 'A Hampshire Dairyman – "Scalding out"' and 'Somersetshire Cottage' at the Institute of Painters in Oil Colours later in the year but the press noticed neither painting. These were the first works he submitted from Haselbury Plucknett in Somerset.

The Aberdeen Evening Express, like many other provincial papers, lifted material from the London papers. Their report threw light on the state of the art market at the time saying:

> "Eight hundred and seven paintings were included in the recent exhibition of the Institute of Painters in Oil-Colours. Of these, a hundred and fifty-six were sold, and the aggregate sum realised was exactly £7091."
>
> **Aberdeen Evening Express** 23 March 1887
> (£688,000 – an average of £4,010 for each work)

1887

The press did not mention the two works submitted to the RA exhibition. These were 'Orphans – The board is simply spread' and 'Unexpected visitors'. In the autumn, no works are listed as being sent to the Institute of Painters in Oil Colours. However, Graves' undated listing refers to two works 'In confidence' and 'Somersetshire cottage' that may have appeared there.

1888

Joseph submitted three works to the RA in 1888; two of which were reviewed in the press:

> "Mr Frith's admirers may be interested to have pointed out to them a good specimen of the master's style by a younger hand. This is 'Playmates' by Mr Joseph Clark."
>
> **Pall Mall Gazette** 5 May 1888

> "In a 'youthful genius' Mr Joseph Clark supplies one of those attractive domestic interiors which he has painted now for many years past."
>
> **The Graphic** 26 May 1888

'My clever brother' may have appeared at the Institute of Painters in Oil Colours.

1889

The Western Daily Press published a review of the three works accepted for the 1889 RA

> "Mr Joseph Clark of Crewkerne has some contributions in oils which excite considerable attention. They are figure subjects and all show considerable skill. In 'Children are the crown of old age', a veteran is seated in a humble though cosy apartment surrounded by little prattlers, whose mother, his comely daughter, is busied with a teapot. Two girls are standing at the grandfather's knee and he betrays pleasure at having them near while a baby seated contentedly on the floor is playing with the old man's hat. The scene is well finished and the textures are worked up with careful manipulation.
>
> A smaller production from the same hand 'Bless thy little lambs tonight' shows a mother listening to the prayer of one of her little girls, as the child kneels before her. Another girl curled up on a window seat looks steadfastly at her sister. The painting seems consistent throughout,

the good woman who superintends the devotion of her children having that serious and fixed expression that religious persons naturally evince when engaged in an occupation that excites devotional feeling. Like the other canvass of Mr Clark this exhibits excellent drawing and solid workmanship."

Western Daily Press 3 May 1889

'Bless thy little lambs tonight' comes from the hymn 'Jesus, tender shepherd, hear me' with words by Mary L. Duncan dated 1839. In 1841, her hymns, mostly for children, appeared posthumously and reissued in 1842 as 'Rhymes for My Children'. Again, Joseph's role as a Sunday School teacher may have inspired this work.

'Children are the crown of old age' is a shortened version of 'Children's children are the crown of old age' that comes from the Bible – Proverbs 7:16.

The third work mentioned by the Western Daily Press depicts the 'Christmas Dole' tradition in Hazelbury Plucknet. Roger Bucknell (2013) describes the origin of the tradition and its development. When Mary Mountford died in 1830, she left the annual rent from 2½ acres of land to pay for the upkeep of her tomb and ordered any surplus used to buy bread for distribution to the poor by the Minister and Churchwardens on St. Thomas' Day, 21st December. Originally this rent amounted to £6 (about £450). During the 'hungry forties' the mothers of families totalling 429 people, almost half the village collected the dole. The bread came for the four active bakeries in the village at the time. By 1880, a similar number collected the dole but this represented nearly three quarters of the village's declining population. They collected 324 loaves baked at the nearby Swan Hill Bakery.

Roger Bucknell (2013) continues:

"On the darkest day of the year, St Thomas's day in the old church calendar, the mothers of the needy village families would queue … for an allocation of free loaves … The ceremony was presided over by the vicar of the parish church of St M Michael and All Angels and his two church wardens."

The Western Mail's described Joseph's 'Christmas Dole':

"A third example which this painter furnishes will, to the majority of visitors, prove the most popular of his three contributions. The title is 'The Christmas Dole' and the scene depicted where in the vicar of the parish is seated at a table with a book, in which the value of the gift to each of a number of women assembled is recorded. By his side is a gentleman of a superior sort, mayhap the churchwarden, but if so his lofty expression evinces a soul above parochial charities. The presents bestowed take the form of loaves of bread, and a rotund factotum hands to the recipients their doles. Some of the countenances display keen observation and will repay close inspection. The vicar is gravely engaged in a task which, though to the superfine figure at his elbow may appear trivial is to the good man a duty to be carefully undertaken. As to the women who congregate to obtain from the charity as much as possible, their faces bespeak a keen outlook for the smallest favours. One who eyes the entry made by the pastor, will from her shrewish expression speak freely if the benefaction falls beneath her expectation, and the artist has succeeded admirably in this portrait, evidently a study from life. The simple story in this picture is well told, the gestures of the people in the picture being natural and appropriate."

Western Daily Press 3 May 1889

Roger Bucknell (2013) says:

> "The bearded book keeper is believed to represent the Reverend John Hancock at his last dole on
> 21st December 1880. He died in September 1881 aged 69, having been Curate and Vicar for more
> than 20 years. The central figure is Mary Dell, the village belle. … Mary Ann Dell was given 1 ½
> loaves at the 1880 distribution. She is portrayed by the artist as a young orphan girl; she was in
> fact a 36 year – old unmarried weaver who for several years had looked after two elderly female
> relatives."

If these identifications are right, this work has an unusually complicated history. Joseph may have
heard of the ceremony while visiting his cousin in Crewkerne and sketched the event almost a decade
before the finished work appeared at the RA. This would be consistent with his tendency to keep
sketches for a long time. However, in correspondence about another work Joseph makes the point
that his works are inspired by people, places or quotations rather than being documentary depictions
of specific incidents.

The distribution of bread continued until 1953 when the Mary Mountford Trust merged with
others locally and the charity commissioners agreed that the new trust need not maintain Mary
Mountford's grave nor confine its activities to the distribution of bread.

Most Internet searches lead to a painting that is not Joseph's 'Christmas Dole'. When that picture
came up for sale early in 2014 at Sotheby's, I drew their attention to the description from the Western
Mail and earlier advice from Rosemary Chiles to the seller, based on the 'brushwork', that this work
was not by her grandfather. After further investigation, Sothebys issued an amendment to their sale
catalogue saying that the work was a 1902 painting entitled 'Christmas' by James Clark, also a member
of the Institute of Painters in Oil Colours.

Later in 1889, Joseph exhibited 'Familiarity breeds contempt' at the Society of Painters in Oil
Colours. The press did not report it. This title refers to an ancient English proverb encountered in
translations of the Bible and Aesop's tales.

The middle years of Joseph's career

The two decades covered by this chapter was markedly less successful in critical terms than his first
decade, although Joseph maintained the quality of his work and the basic themes seen in his first
years as a professional artist. The loss of critical interest reflects the shift in the 'mood' of the times
from contemporary genre with its focus on fine detail and narrative content and towards works
demonstrating a concern with technique and the relationships between blocks of colour. Joseph also
suffered from the controversy surrounding the Chantrey Bequest and growing criticism of the RA in
the part of many critics, artists and patrons.

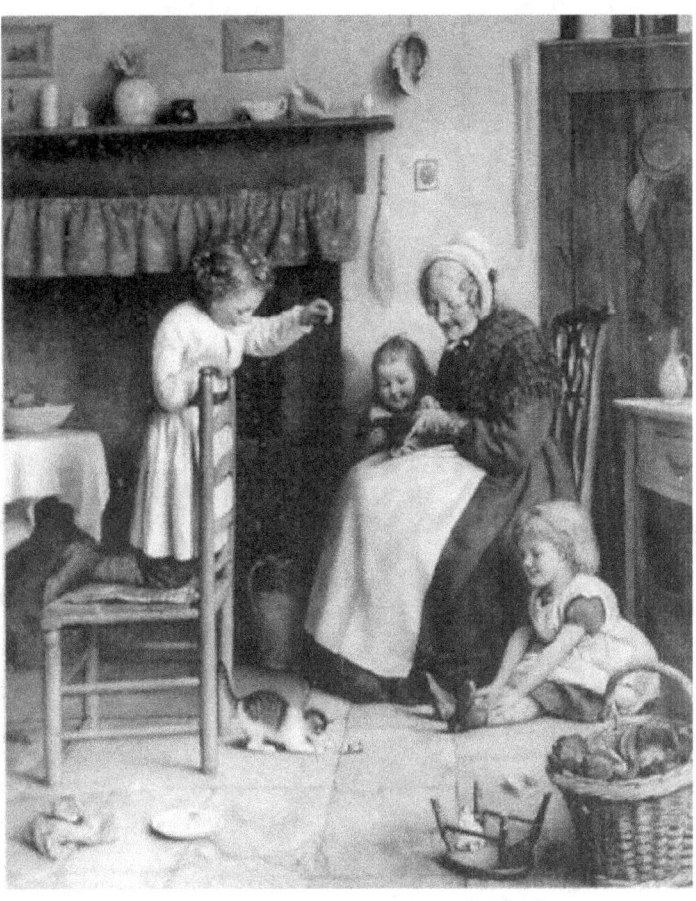

9. 'New Pet' (1876). (Courtesy Sothebys)

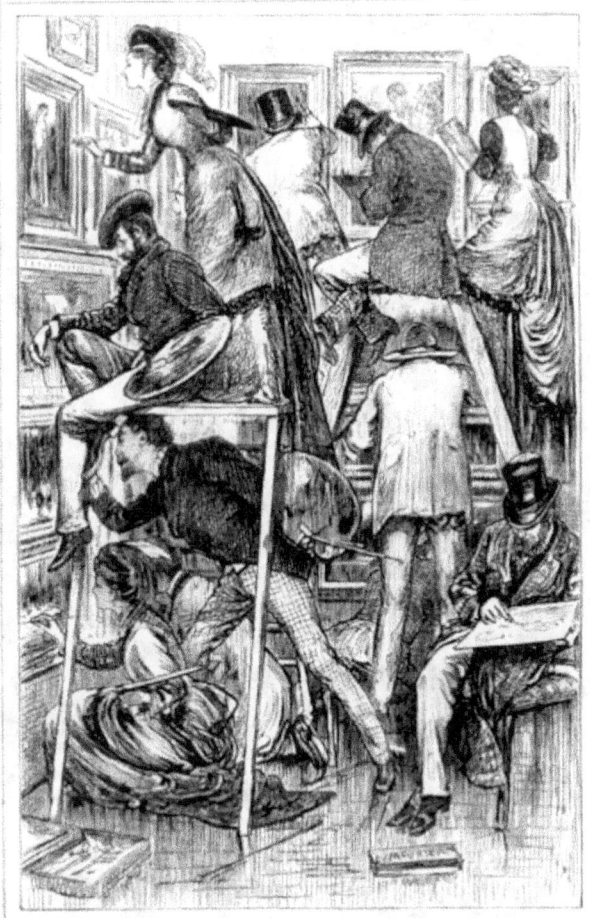

VARNISHING DAY AT THE ROYAL ACADEMY.

10. George du Maurier,
'Vanishing Day at the Royal Academy'.
From Punch 19 June 1877, p. 226.
(Courtesy Victorian Web)

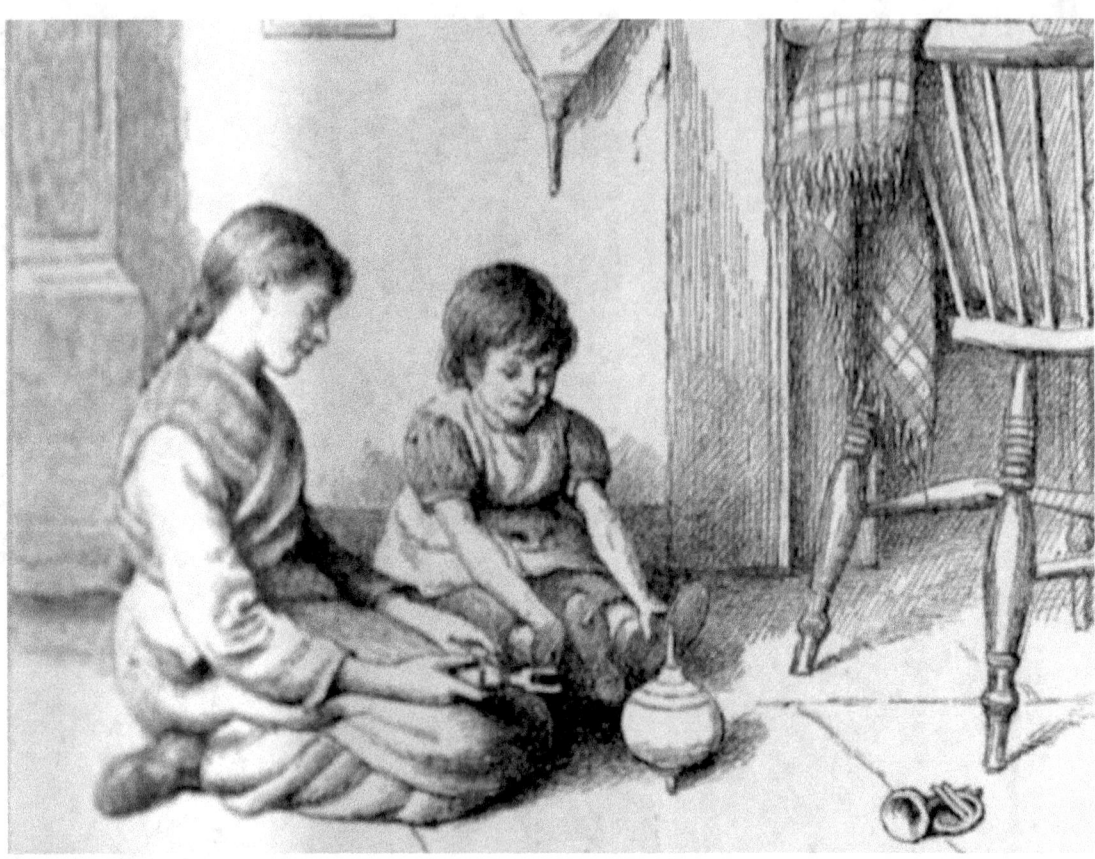

11. 'The Humming Top' (1883). (Source Society of Painters in Oil Colours)

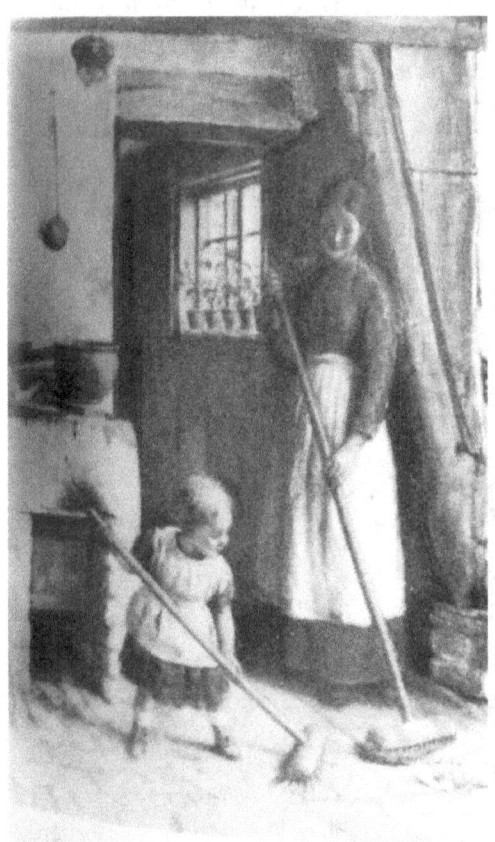

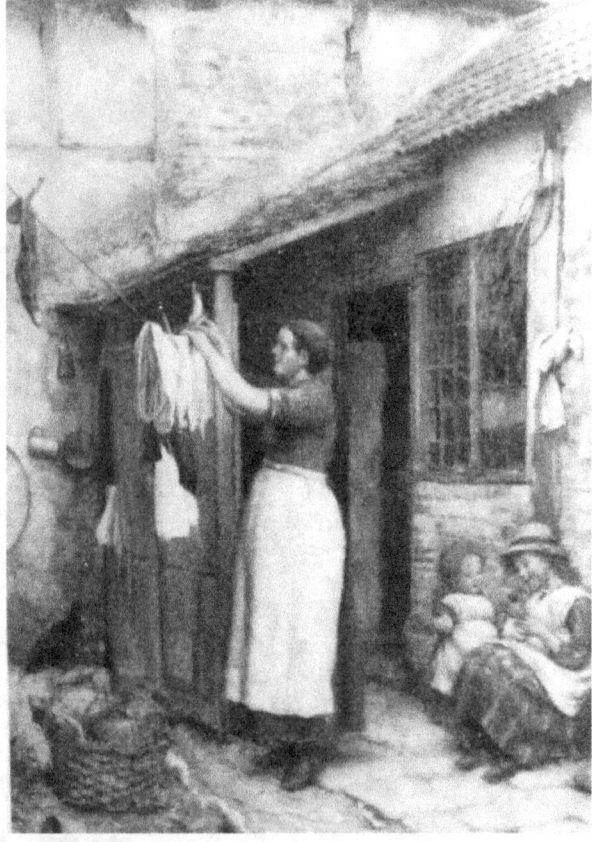

12. 'Mother's Help' (1884). (Courtesy Bearnes, Hampton & Littlewood Limited, Exeter)

13. 'Washing Day' (1884). (Courtesy Bearnes, Hampton & Littlewood Limited, Exeter)

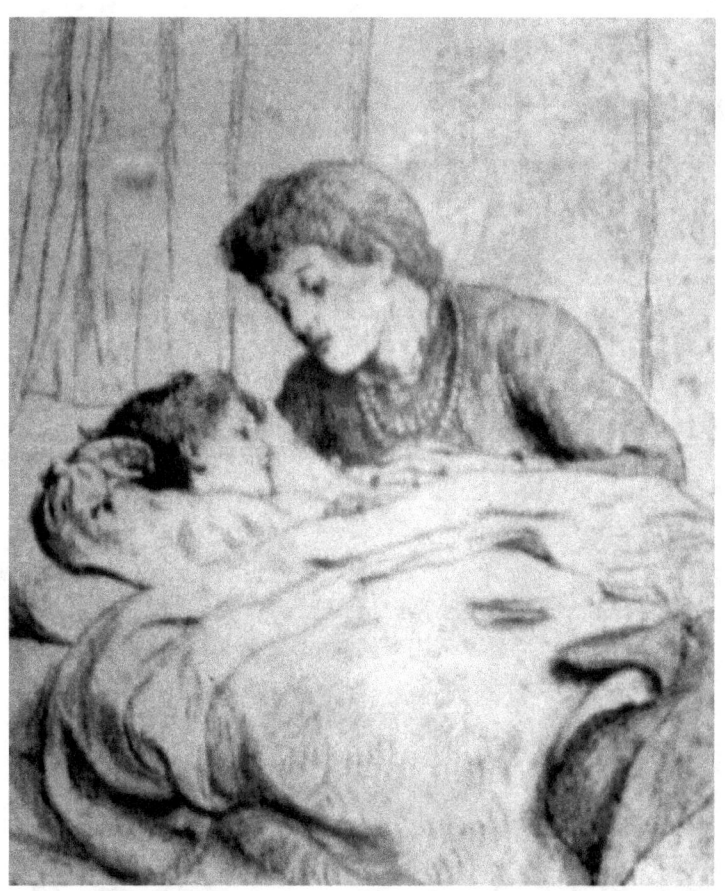

14. Monochrome etching of
'Mother's Darling' (1885).
(Courtesy the artist's family)

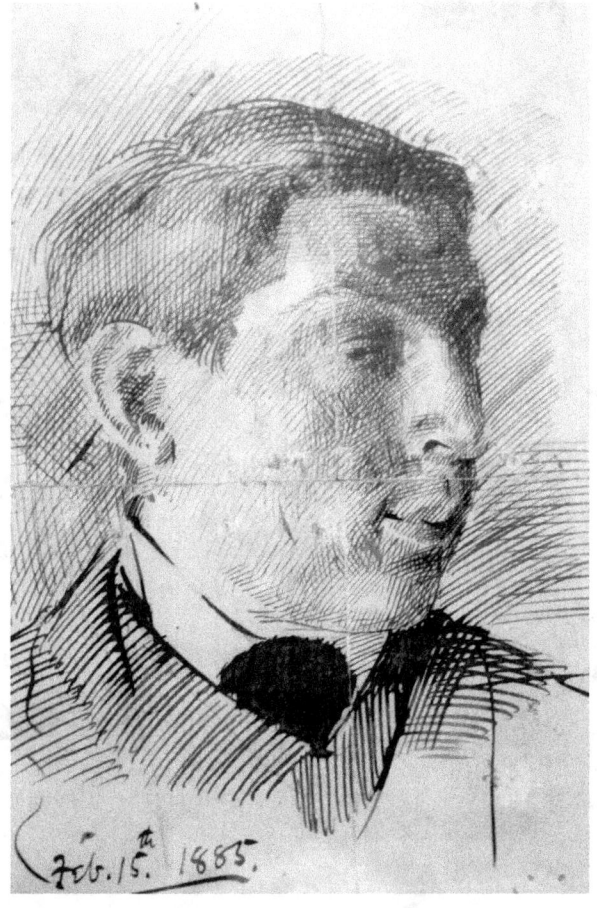

15. Pen and Ink drawing for portrait of John
Clark (1885). (Courtesy Sarah Galvin)

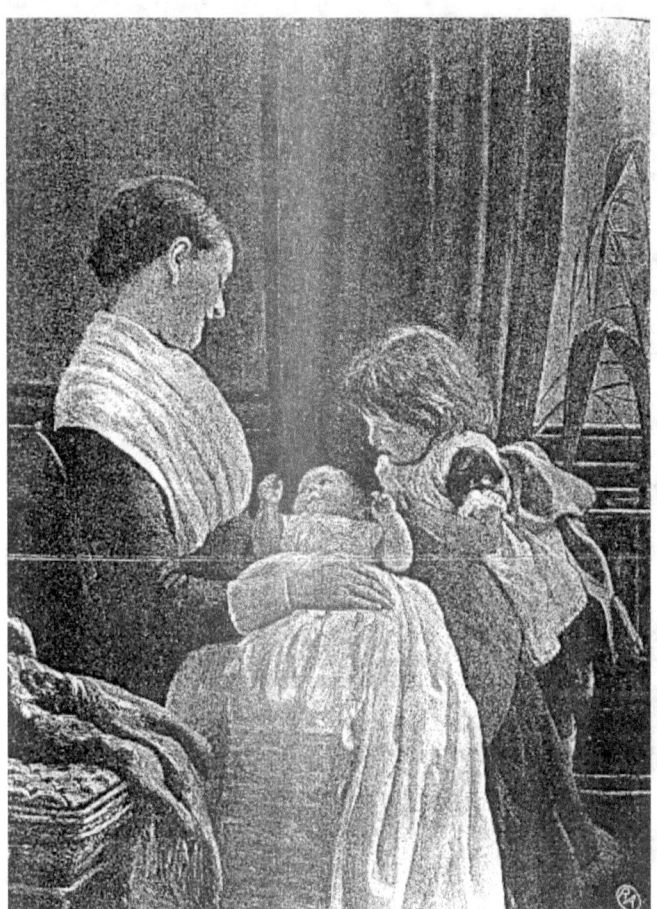

16. 'With smiles of Peace and Looks of Love'
(1886). (Courtesy the artist's family)

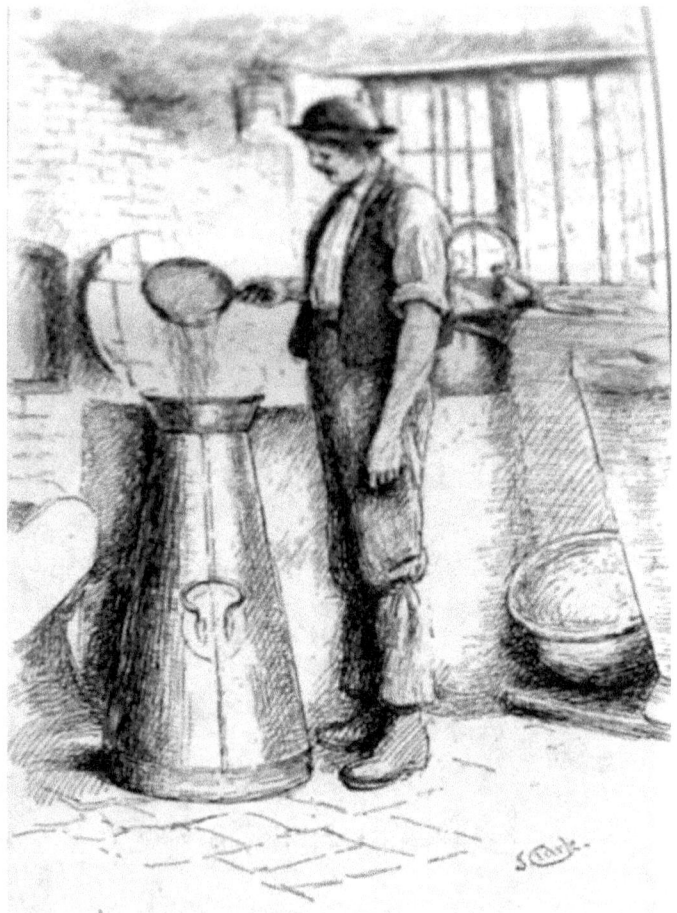

17. 'A Hampshire Dairyman –
"Scalding out"' (1886). (Source Royal
Institute of Oil Painters Catalogue)

EIGHT

The grand old man of English Art
(1890–1926)

This chapter shows how the tension between being the rising star of the art world and being in the doldrums as his works fell out of critical favour played out in the final years of Joseph's career.

Family life

Around 1890, Joseph and his family returned to London from Somerset. The sequence of moves constructed from the details of the addresses from which he sent works to the RA and the Institute of Oil Painters appears to be:

Table 4. Joseph's homes between 1889 and 1926.

Years	Address
1889–1892	23 Greencroft Gardens, South Hampstead, London NW
1893–1895	Northold, Chapter Road, Willesden, London NW
1895–1897	South Hall, Kingsgate Road, Winchester (Annie's parents home)
1897–1903	Wendaree, Pinner Road, Harrow, Middlesex
1903–1913	Hazelbury, 11 Stanley Gardens, Willesden, London NW
1913–1916	23 Hillingdon Road, Uxbridge, Middlesex
1917–1926	95 Hereson Road, Ramsgate, Kent

In 1890 and 1891, the RA records show works submitted from both Haselbury Plucknett and South Hampstead. He may have split his year between two homes in these years. Margaret Drummond (1950) suggests that the move to London was to be closer to the recently established New Church congregation in Willesden Green. Joseph and Annie Clark received adult baptism there on 28th December 1890. Adult baptism was common in the New Church at the time for both people previously baptized in other denominations and those who had worshiped in New Church congregations for many years. Their daughters were baptized as children – Anne Susan (13 August 1869), Elsie (23 May 1883) and Margaret (30 November 1887).

Between 1889 and 1917, Joseph and Annie had five homes, all in the rapidly expanding suburbs to the North West of London and close to recently opened stations on the Metropolitan Railway. Were they balancing a wish to combine easy access to central London with living close to the countryside? This wish may have first appeared when they set up home in Holloway in the 1860s, that at the time was an up-and-coming community close to the northern edge of London's urban development.

During the period covered in this chapter, the family shrunk as Elsie married in 1905, Wilfrid left home to train for the New Church ministry in 1909, and Margaret married in 1917.

Margaret Drummond (1950) recalled that Joseph enjoyed a regular unhurried lifestyle although she did not say when this started. Apparently, this involved reading a chapter from the Bible or from

Swedenborg's works, followed by a short morning walk. Only then did he go to his studio to begin work. She describes him as '*a great reader although had not a very wide choice of authors. Scott and Dickens were the chief favourites and his volume of Shakespeare was a constant companion.*' This may underestimate his breadth of reading judging by range of sources used as inspiration for the titles of his pictures.

During the mid-eighteen nineties, Joseph and his family spent time in Winchester with Annie's parents. This started in the autumn of 1895 just before her parents' golden wedding in April 1896. The photograph of the celebrations shows the size of the immediate family. Joseph is in the back row and Annie to the right of her parents in the second row.

Joseph also lost his remaining sibling, William Henry Clark Jnr, in 1896. By the turn of the century, there were only seven members of the Clark family left in Cerne living in three households. After William Henry Jnr's death, the drapery business passed to Joseph's nephew, William Clark and subsequently to his niece Christiana who shared a home at East Street corner. William Henry Jnr's widow shared a home in Abbey Street with Alice (her stepdaughter). Martha (Edwin Clark's widow) shared a house in Long Street with Martha Emma her daughter (a teacher at a private school) and her son Herbert Thomas Clark (assistant to the Relieving Officer with the Poor Law Union). Frank Clark, Joseph's nephew and Cerne Abbas's Relieving Officer spent the 1901 census night with Alfred Clark at South Stoneham, near Southampton.

By the 1911 Census there were only two Clarks remaining in Cerne Abbas – Christiana and Frank. Martha Emma was now a schoolmistress living in Salisbury and Herbert Thomas was the relieving Officer in Blandford. The other three family members died during the Edwardian period. Thus, although Joseph recalled the town with affection, it no longer held any great attraction for him.

Joseph and his family returned to London from Winchester in 1897 and moved again within North West London in 1903. Annie's father, John Jones, died at the end of April 1904. In July 1904 the probate records show his estate was valued at £5,466 18s 11d (£513,900). We assume the 'estate' was shared between his children for when Annie's mother died in 1915 her 'estate' was valued at £47 13s 9d (£3,334). A picture of Joseph's family taken later in the year shows his wife is clearly in mourning.

Elsie married married John Edward (Ted) Dixon-Spain in 1905. They first met in Haselbury Plucknet when he was about nine and she was five. At that time, Ted's father, the Rev Thomas Dixon-Spain, was Curate of St Oswald, Twerton (near Bath) about 45 miles from Haselbury Plucknett. The Reverend Dixon-Spain served in Somerset between 1885 and 1895 after which he moved to Lincolnshire. He was tireless in his social ministry taking a continuing interest in the temperance movement, campaigns for the early closing of shops, industrial schools and the work of the local 'poor law' guardians – all of which took him to communities across Somerset. The Clarks and Dixon-Spains became firm friends. The press report of the wedding read:

> "In the little church of Rand St. Oswald on Wednesday the marriage of John Edward Dixon Spain. A.R.I.B.A. the son of the Rector, the Rev. T. Dixon Spain, and Elsie Clark. second daughter of Mr Joseph Clark the well-known artist. The interior of the old building lost none of its sacred character by being adorned by white flowers and ferns and palms and a notable feature in the scheme of decorating was a specially erected floral screen running from the Rectory to the Church. The officiating clergy were the Rev. T. Dixon-Spain Rector of Rand and the Rev. H.C. Dixon-Spain of Heckington, brother of the bridegroom. The bride was escorted by her father who gave her away and in whose pictures she has appeared on the walls of the Royal Academy. She walked down the pathway the church, with charmingly attired village stewed flowers in her way. Her wedding gown was white silk with applique chiffon roses, her veil of Brussels lace lent by her grandmother, … her bouquet was a sheaf of white lilies which she held in her hand. The bridesmaids were Miss Clark and Miss Margery Clark, sisters of the bride, and Miss

Dixon-Spain and Miss Georgina Dixon-Spain, sisters of the bridegroom. They were attired in champagne muslin dresses ... and large white hats with strings and white roses, and carried bouquets of white carnations. They each wore a pearl brooch presented by the bridegroom. Mr H. Selwyn Dixon-Spain was best man. After, the service in Church, a reception was held at the Rectory when upwards of a hundred friends came together. The presents, over 300 hundred, included a handsome tea service of plate from the parishioners of Rand. After the reception the happy pair left for the East Coast where they are spending their honeymoon."

Lincolnshire Echo 24 August 1905

By 1905, John Edward was an established architect with a growing reputation. His later works included the New Church in Willesden Green, City Hall in Newcastle upon Tyne, Quasr el Aini State Hospital in Cairo, the Rock Hotel in Gibraltar, two London cinemas and a film studios. After 1945, he designed several Roman Catholic schools and the Churches of St Joan of Arc in Farnham and St Alphage in Hendon.

He saw military service in the Second Boer, Great and Second World Wars. He was a scout in South Africa. In the Great War he served in the Royal Artilary and Royal Flying Corps/Royal Air Force. While in France during the Great War, he stayed with a French family and converted to Roman Catholicism; and on his return to Britain, Elsie and their children followed suit.

In 1944, John Edward, aged 63, served under General Eisenhower as part of the small team from the Monuments, Fine Arts and Archives Division (MFA&A) landing in Normandy just after D-Day. Their role was to find and restore stolen art treasures to their rightful owners. The Division's work was celebrated as the 'Monuments Men' in the 2014 film. Monika Ginzkey Puloy (1998) summarised their achievements:

"About a fortnight after the Normandy landing, two MFA&A officers, Captain Bancel LaFarge and Lieutenant George Stout, and one Englishman, Squadron Leader J.E. Dixon-Spain, set out, without back-up or equipment, explaining and persuading their way into action in order to make a start on salvaging the art treasures of Europe. By the summer's end, three further Americans and two more British MFA&A officers had joined them. The amazing accomplishment of these eight men, who at first had to make their way by 'riding on anything from the regimental laundry trucks to liberated bicycles', ended in the fragmentary arrival of the Allies' full war-time art group, which, despite lofty ambitions, never reached more than about a dozen men up to the end of hostilities. None the less, they scoured France, Belgium, The Netherlands, Luxembourg and Germany 'with unbelievable efficacy and ubiquity and actually inspected 3,145 monuments and archives, or what was left of them."

Notwithstanding his advancing years and frequent moves, Joseph continued to produce works worthy of inclusion in the Royal Academy and the Institute of Painters in Oil Colours as it adopted a succession names. In 1910, he resigned from the Royal Institute of Oil Painters (ROI) and stopped exhibiting at the RA. However, in 1913 he exhibited 'Anxious Moments' as a 'retired member' at the ROI. The First World War seemed to inspire him to resume painting with 'News from the Front' (RA) and 'Loyal Citizens' (ROI) in 1915; and 'Tales from Flanders' (RA) in 1916. At least three of Joseph's relatives served in the Great War. As we saw previously, Edward Dixon-Spain served as an officer in the Royal Artillery, the Royal Flying Corps and the Royal Air Force; Wilfrid was a conscientious objector serving at the 49th Staiwwary Hospital in the Middle East; and Alfred Clark, served in the New Zealand Medical Corps. Towards the end of the war, Alfred published two books (1918 and 1919) telling in verse form the impact of the war on the emotional life of two 'friends'.

When Joseph and Annie retired to 95 Hereson Road, Ramsgate, probably towards the end of the Great War, Poppie remained in London and married in 1925.

Changes in the Art World

The eighteen nineties were characterised by a split between the elite world of the Royal Academy and its traditional interests in large scale works dealing with historical, religious and mythological subjects, and portraits; and the growing influence of innovative approaches discussed earlier. Queen Victoria's death in January 1901 ushered in the 'Edwardian age'. For people of Joseph's generation, her death although expected was a profound moment in their lives creating a sense of new beginnings.

Was Edwardian art different?

Dr. Ryan Linkof (2010) in his review of 'The Edwardian Sense: Art, Design, and Performance in Britain, 1901–1910' identifies several themes in defining what was distinctive about Edwardian art. In many ways, the Edwardian era was a buffer between the nineteenth century world and that of the twentieth. Some saw it as the last gasp of 'Old England' before the cataclysm of the Great War. Linkof (2010) suggests that Edwardian society underwent a bumpy transition driven by the agitation of trade unionists, feminists and Irish Home Rulers. One aspect of this transition was the interplay between aesthetic theory, artistic practice, popular entertainment and social contestation through politics, public debate, exhibitions, campaigning and publicity. Paradoxes abounded notably between private and public; spectacle and spectator; mass society and social hierarchies, art and decoration; motion and stasis; country and city; and the home nation and colonies.

Andrew Stephenson (2013) writing in an introduction to a special edition of 'Visual Culture in Britain' devoted to 'Edwardian Art and its Legacies' explores alternative interpretations of the term Edwardian Art. He echoes many of the themes in Linkof (2010) while emphasising other issues including the role the Bloomsbury Group in developing a radically modern domestic aesthetic infused by social ideals and political activism. Beyond that were Britain's rapid population growth (around 9%) between 1901 and 1911; the wave of overseas artists settling in London in search of its 'bohemianism' and the 'exceptional liberties of expression'; and London's continuing dominance in the English art world despite the emergence of regional art centres and rural artists' colonies. He also sees photojournalism and cinema leading to dramatically changed modes of visual perception.

Stephenson (2013) highlights important changes in art journalism and the response it produced.

> "The rapid expansion of the mass-market press and the specialist art press in the Edwardian era played a key role in disseminating the latest trends and in promoting modernist interests. By 1910, London had nineteen morning and ten evening newspapers accompanied by dozens of weeklies and monthlies. The press's energetic commodity advertising, driven by the emergence of the advertising agencies, shaped commercial culture and was staggering in its international scope and imperial reach. These developments even affected the intellectual press, leading to the generation of specialist titles dedicated to art and 'little magazines'. Established in 1909 with Frank Rutter as editor, Art News advertised itself as 'the only Art Newspaper in the United Kingdom' and its coverage extended throughout Western Europe and the British Empire. Roger Fry was a founder of the Burlington Magazine in 1903 with an international readership that complemented The Studio Magazine, founded in 1893. By 1899, the latter boasted it had 'the largest circulation in the World of any Magazine Devoted to the Arts', appealing to the army of art amateurs as

well as professionals. These specialist Journals circulated alongside a wave of mass-circulation newspapers that refashioned popular visual culture. The growth of the press, particularly the illustrated press, affected how knowledge of artistic developments was communicated at home and abroad: how questions about art and aesthetics were framed and specialist terminology developed. The popular press also directed the ways in which the public sphere was approached and understood by the art world."

Virtually every newspaper and journal carried some coverage of art exhibitions and art news. Stephenson (2013) also notes a significant shift in who was writing professionally about art. A.C.R. Carter (1898) writing in 'The Year's Art' identifies thirteen specialist art journals in publication at the start of the year. Many of the new journals lasted for only a few issues with small readerships. Others stayed the course lasting for several decades. The Studio Magazine, founded in 1893 appealed to amateur artists as well as professionals. The Burlington Magazine, established in 1903 by a group of art historians and connoisseurs including Roger Fry, Herbert Horne, Bernard Berenson, and Charles Holmes had an international readership that complemented 'The Studio'. By 1901, there were over thirty women art critics in Britain writing for newspapers and journals. They adopted new sets of conventions for looking at art and establishing its meaning for new groups of readers.

Therefore, the Edwardian age differentiated itself from nineteenth-century Victorianism while drawing on many of its elements. One of the defining features of its visual forms was a combination of the breathtakingly new and the reassuringly old. Linkof (2010) also highlights the importance of the international art market in which Britain played a key role.

Andrew Graham-Dixon (1996) wrote that the aesthetic movement led to a situation in which by the turn of the century the portrait was once again dominant. In the new century, the 'everyday life' tradition in art favoured by Joseph continued with painters like Bonnard and Vuillard in France, the Ashcan School in America, and to some extent by the Camden Town and Newlyn Groups in Britain, albeit with significant differences in their treatment when compared to Joseph's style. These changes continued the demise of narrative art.

The shifting pattern of new groups and movements in Britain and more widely in Europe, discussed later represented a growing challenge to the artistic elite during the final years of Joseph's career. Frank Rutter (1922) identifies another important source of the challenge when he wrote:

"Nothing has been more remarkable in our recent domestic art-history than the sterility of the Royal Academy Schools and the rich fertility of the Slade School. While paying lip service to the Old Masters, the Academy has constantly bolstered up the pretensions of British painters and made reference to their works. The Slade School is different; its tradition was founded by a Frenchman, Alphonse Legros, and its professors and pupils have always kept their eyes on what was being done at Paris. The Slade students studied Ingres while the Piccadilly people were still talking about Leighton."

A recurrent theme in the cultural debate in the early twentieth century was a negative view of contemporary genre. However, the artist and critic Water Sickert (2002) did not share these views of genre works. Writing in March 1918, in the preface to an 'Exhibition of Painting by Walter Bayes' he said:

"The branch of painting that is commonly classified as genre has the advantage that it is proper to narration, as a universal language, of things in which anyone may take an interest. It furnishes a bridge that renders no longer impassible the chasm between the producer and the customer

… 'Every picture tells a story' is by no means a device for a painter, and the best picture is after all a matter of no greater mystery than the 'best told story'! I commend this theory with my complements to the consideration of Mr Roger Fry."

Rutter (1922) in his 'Contemporary Artists' recognised Sickert's capacity to sustain a long career in contempory genre:

"You may say if you like that Sickert is a genre painter, but his genre, like that of the Little Masters of Holland, has been the common life of the community around him. Young or old, there has never been any question of vitality in a painting by Sickert; it is peculiarly his métier to present us with 'a slice of life,' and to present it in a fascinating form, quivering with light, atmosphere, and colour. He has never stopped still, never fallen into a groove, never merely repeated himself, but adhering to the main direction he chose in his youth he has kept his art fresh and allowed it to ripen into maturity."

Joseph, like Sickert, had a similar power to keep his art fresh and relevant to a large and changing audience. Joseph played no part in these debates, although they served to shape the art world in which many saw his works as hopelessly old fashioned despite their continued popularity with many art lovers.

Public Galleries

The South Kensington Museum continued to develop in the decades covered by this chapter. At the laying of the foundation stone of the museum's Aston Webb building on 17 May 1899, Queen Victoria in her last official public appearance, announced its change of name to the Victoria and Albert Museum and said *'I trust that it will remain for ages a Monument of discerning Liberality and a Source of Refinement and Progress.'*

During much of Joseph's career, there were several wealthy 'merchant' collectors active in the art market. For the most part their purchases did not include contemporary genre works. These collectors included John Sheepshanks, Robert Vernon, Lord Leverhulme (associated with Port Sunlight's Lady Leverhulme Gallery and Bolton Museum), Henry Tate (Tate Gallery), Sir Richard Wallace (London) and William Wills (Bristol). Their purchases alongside the buying policies of municipal art galleries, contributed to rising art prices, and increasing incomes and living standards for some middle ranking Victorian artists. Their taste also colours and to some extent distorts modern views of Edwardian culture.

Two of these private collections were at the heart of two new public collections in London opened to the public during this part of Joseph's career. Undoubtedly these new galleries helped to redefine what many people came to regard as 'good art' and contributed to the twentrieth century rejection of genre, including Joseph's work.

Henry Tate, the sugar refiner, built up a major collection of Victorian art. In 1889, he offered his collection to the nation together with the money needed to build a new gallery for British Art on condition that the Government provided the site and met the running costs. The idea of a National Gallery of British Art was first proposed in the 1820s by Sir John Leicester (Baron de Tabley) and came closer when Robert Vernon gave his collection to the National Gallery in the 1850s and John Sheepshanks donated his to the South Kensington Museum. Tate's donation finally convinced the Government of the need for a gallery dedicated to British Art. The new gallery built on the site of the former Millbank Penitentiary, remained part of the British Museum until 1954. It incorporated collections from the National Gallery and South Kensington Museum. The transfer from the National Gallery included the two works by Joseph purchased by the Chantrey Fund.

At the opening of the National Gallery of British Art in 1897, Arthur Balfour, the Prime Minister, captured the excitement and sentiment of the time in his vote of thanks to the Prince of Wales saying:

> "We have every reason to be most grateful to Mr. Tate for his munificent gift. We all know … about large collections of art … and the difficulty experienced in finding room for them. In this admirable building, so well-lit and so well arranged, we already have around us some most beautiful pictures, sixty-five he has presented himself and those purchased by the Chantrey Bequests, the very fine pictures that are the gift of Mr. Watts, and last, but not least, pictures from the National Gallery. As has been said, the site of the building has been well chosen, I am glad to think that in this place we have this beautiful Temple of Art instead of a building where unfortunate criminals were enduring punishment. (Hear, hear.) I am inclined to think that in this gift which Mr. Tate has made to the nation will assume the place of the gaoler by taking care of all these valuable pictures, which I hope will ever remain within these walls."
>
> **London Daily News** 22 July 1897

Mr Watts was George Frederic Watts (1817–1904) was a popular painter and sculptor associated with the Symbolist movement. He said 'I paint ideas, not things' and became famous in his lifetime for his allegorical works.

The National Gallery of British Art became the Tate Gallery in 1932 and Tate Britain in 2000. It now has offshoots in Liverpool, St Ives and Margate; and a home for modern works in a former power station at Tate Modern further down river.

The other major new gallery opened to the public in this era was the Wallace Collection. Between 1760 and 1880, the first four Marquises of Hertford and Sir Richard Wallace (the illegitimate son of and heir to the fourth Marquis) assembled the collection. Sir Richard's widow left his art works housed at Hertford House, London, to the nation on condition that no object should ever leave the collection, even for loan exhibitions. Her secretary, Sir John Murray Scott, sold the lease of Hertford House to the Government and became a Trustee of the Wallace Collection when it opened in 1900. It houses a world-famous range of fine and decorative arts from the fifteenth to the nineteenth centuries with large holdings of French 18th-century paintings, furniture, arms & armour, porcelain and Old Master paintings. As such, it has no works by Joseph.

There was continued interest in Joseph's work from municipal art galleries:

> "The committee of the Corporation Art Gallery have made an addition of six valuable pictures to the collections… Joseph Clark's 'Sick Boy' we see a lad seated in chair by the fire with pillows behind him, the doctor sits beside him eyeing him attentively, while at the back of the chair is an elderly woman, who is anxiously awaiting the verdict of the medical man, against whose legs a cat is rubbing herself."
>
> **Sunderland Daily Echo and Shipping Gazette** 24 November 1899

This is the picture first exhibited at the Royal Academy in 1858 under the title 'The Doctor's Visit' and is still in the collection at Sunderland.

The Chantrey Bequest

The debate about the way the Royal Academy administered the Chantrey Bequest mentioned earlier continued until the end of Joseph's career. These attacks often mentioned Joseph's works in the Tate Gallery.

"It is generally supposed that this bequest was for the encouragement of rising talent. But according to Sir Francis Chantrey's will nothing could be further from his intention, except in the general sense that when art is encouraged then it follows naturally that rising talent is encouraged. Works are to be bought for their intrinsic merits only, nor is a sympathetic feeling for any artist is to influence decisions of the president and council, who are to pay a liberal price left to their discretion. There is no arrangement that the pictures are to be bought from the annual exhibition of the Royal Academy, but there is a stipulation that no commissions are to be given, and also that the works of English or foreign artists may be bought so long as the works are executed in this country. ...

Whatever may now be thought of the work there can be little doubt that a few years hence, when impressionism has gone the way of asceticism, it will be found that it at least produced one fine work in 'Carnation Lily, Lily Rose'. Most people will remember Mr. Frank Dickese's 'Harmony' that was the forerunner of the ascetic craze, and the success it achieved on its first appearance 14 or 15 years ago. Even popular taste could not have fallen lower than when the pictures of 'Early promise' and 'Mother's Darling' both by Mr Joseph Clark were purchased which are of the kind styled facetiously by Mr Whistler as 'British'. Possibly, however this is what recommended them."

Liverpool Mercury 17 June 1891

"The fierce light that beats upon the Royal Academy is never so fierce as when turned upon its administration of the Chantrey Bequest. From the general public, that body usually has a little more, and from its enemies a little less, than justice; but the disposal of the Chantrey Fund almost invariably brings forth criticism that is both prejudiced and unfair. The Academy is compelled, under the terms of the bequest, to buy pictures and sculpture that have not come into dealers' hands, works which have neither been commissioned nor sold. The limitations restrict to an irksome degree the Council's field of selection; and if the Academy fixes its choice on those works which are, in its opinion, the truest works of Art, executed according to Academic tradition, and not less according to the presumable taste of Chantrey himself could he influence the trustees are they to be blamed? Mr. Langley's picture could not be acquired, as it had already passed into the hands of a purchaser who would not relinquish it, so the outsider's picture chosen was Mr. Tuke's 'August Blue.' On its merits, the picture deserved purchase, even though, like Professor Herkomer, Mr. Joseph Clark, and Sir Frederic Leighton, Mr. Tuke had on a former occasion been similarly honoured. Mr. Briton Riviere's admirable study of ice was another worthy selection, and Mr. Fehr's 'Perseus and Andromeda,' though a youthful and exuberant work, is perhaps a group of sufficient interest to justify its acquisition. The Academy has often done worse than this year's selection; it is unreasonable to have expected it to do better."

The Graphic 26 May 1894

The Chantrey Collection was displayed at the Victoria and Albert Museum until 1898 when it moved to the National Gallery of British Art. The Tate's trustees had no power over the selection or elimination in respect of the pictures and sculptures handed over to augment its collection.

A decade later, Dugald Sutherland MacColl (1904), a Scottish watercolour painter, art critic, lecturer and writer (and Keeper of the Tate Gallery between 1906 and 1911) returned to the dispute in his book on the Bequest. The principal thrust of the argument was that the trustees (i.e. the RA) had failed to consider the absolute merit of works (rather than the relative merit test used by the Academy) thereby excluding many artists. In his view, the merits of the excluded painters were greater than those of the 'included' artists including Joseph. He also pointed out that few of the paintings were by Scottish artists and most were by artists exhibited at the Royal Academy in the year of purchase. He believed that Academicians were treated 'in the most generous spirit'. He calculated that over £60,000 (£5.5m) of the money expended (to 1903), £30,000 went to Academicians (50%) and between £16,000 and £17,000 to those who shortly afterwards became members (28%). Up to 1905, the bequest purchased of 203 works. All but two were by living painters – 175 were oil paintings and 16 were sculptures.

He held that some recipients would probably deserve to be included in a national collection but the remainder represented some passing dubious fashion, a sensation of the year that time has discredited, the doubtful promise of a student not sustained or poor examples by men of popular reputation. He wondered if the trustees saw the bequest as refuge for unsalable works. He acknowledged that no criticism attached to the artists whose works he thought were inappropriate for purchase by the bequest. It was not their fault if the trustees acted inappropriately.

MacColl (1904), like the press, took particular exception to Joseph's work saying:

"… yet I think no one will be so bold as to say that Mr. Joseph Clark's 'Mother's Darling' or … scores of others were necessities of our national collection to be secured before we could indulge in works like 'Mother' by Mr. Whistler, secured by the Luxembourg at a price beggarly compared with the standard of the Chantrey Trustees."

MacColl's (1904) book was part of the growing discontent that led to the appointment of a House of Lords select committee in 1904. Its report made recommendations to improve certain administrative systems but dismissed other charges against the Academy.

The controversy rumbled on for several years. Walter Sickert (2002), the painter and critic, wrote:

"It is amusing to see that the poor little Chantrey Bequest takes the place for some writers on art that the Government and The Treasury fill in the mind of vague political thinkers. … that in clutching at the Treasury for solution of his ills he is like a man who would protect himself from falling out of a window by catching hold of his nose. … Painters being, on the whole, more childish than other men when they think the future of art in a country depends on the administration of a certain tiny fund which is able to buy – is it half a dozen pictures a year? … Since I first began to think for myself, it would not occur to me to waste paper and ink on the Chantrey Fund and its purchases."

The New Age 7 July 1910

In 1916 when Whistler's 'Nocturne' was seen in a loan exhibition at the Leeds Art Gallery in 1916 the story reappeared:

"MUSIC AND ART. The National Gallery to the Leeds Art Gallery Whistler's once notorious, now famous 'Nocturne, Old Battersea Bridge', was duly noticed in last Friday's Yorkshire Post. Seeing this most poetic; work again reminds us of the important part played in Whistler's career, and it is nearly forty years since it was first seen public, memories are short, it seems worthwhile to recall the circumstances of that infamous exhibition and its consequences. …

After his [Whistler's] death the picture was exhibited by its new owner at the Memorial Exhibition in the New Gallery 1903, and was then purchased by public subscription, through the National Art Collections fund, for £2,000 and hung in the National collection, where the authorities fixed on a label on which Whistler's name was misspelt. Whistler himself was described of the British school, and the title the picture was incorrectly given. Possibly the £2,000 was as high price as the £60 was inadequate, but the incident serves to illustrate the curious futility the administration of the Chantrey fund, which, having in paid £89 5s for a picture by a Mr. Joseph Clark, entitled 'Mother's Darling' but missed the chance of Nocturne by Whistler that in 1880 fetched just £60 as they missed the chance of buying Whistler's portrait his mother, which had actually been exhibited at the Royal Academy, was well known many artists, and might have been obtained for trifle tor years before it was, in 1891, bought for the French nation for 4,000 francs, a meagre price, but one which, together with the compliment of being made an officer of the Legion of Honour, satisfied the painter."

Yorkshire Post and Leeds Intelligencer 25 February 1916
(£2,000 in 1903 was about £187,500)

Until the 1920s, the Chantrey Bequest was the main source of funding for expanding the national collection in what is now Tate Britain. The fund remains active today but since 1949, the Tate Gallery and the Royal Academy have shared equally the task of identifying works for the Chantrey collection.

Exhibition societies

Position of the Royal Academy

In the last chapter, we saw the mounting challenge to the leading position of the RA with which Joseph was so closely associated in the minds of some critics and artists. The challenge continued well into the new century.

George Moore (1893) added a typically vitriolic attack on the Academicians, especially their focus on financial rewards when he wrote:

"That nearly all artists dislike and despise the Royal Academy is a matter of common knowledge. Whether with reason or without is a matter of opinion, but the existence of an immense fund of hate and contempt of the Academy is not denied. From Glasgow to Cornwall, wherever a group of artists collects, there hangs a gathering and a darkening sky of hate. True, the position of the Academy seems to be impregnable; and even if these clouds should break into storm the Academy would be as little affected as the rock of Gibraltar by squall or tempest. The Academy has successfully resisted a Royal Commission, and a crusade led by Mr. Holman Hunt in the columns of the Times did not succeed in obtaining the slightest measure of reform. …

Then the Academy has the handling of the Chantrey Bequest Funds, which it does not fail to turn to its own advantage by buying pictures of Academicians, which do not sell in the open market, at extravagant prices, or purchasing pictures by future Academicians, and so fostering, strengthening, and imposing on the public the standard of art which obtains in Academic circles. Such, in a few brief words, is the institution which controls and in a large measure directs the art of this country. …

The hatred of artistic England for the Academy proceeds from the knowledge that the Academy is no true centre of art, but a mere commercial enterprise protected and subventioned by Government. In recent years, every shred of disguise has been cast off, and it has become apparent to everyone that the Academy is conducted on as purely commercial principles as any shop in the Tottenham Court Road. For it is impossible to suppose that Mr. Orchardson and Mr. Watts do not know that Mr. Leader's landscapes are like tea-trays, that Mr. Dicksee's figures are like bon-bon boxes, and that Mr. Herkomer's portraits are like German cigars. But apparently the RAs are merely concerned to follow the market, and they elect the men whose pictures sell best in the City. City men buy the productions of Mr. Herkomer, Mr. Dicksee, Mr. Leader, and Mr. Goodall. Little harm would be done to art if the money thus expended meant no more than filling stockbrokers' drawing-rooms with bad pictures, but the uncontrolled exercise of the stockbroker's taste in art means the election of a vast number of painters to the Academy, and election to the Academy means certain affixes, R.A. and A.R.A., and these signs are meant to direct opinion. … for I repeat that the Academicians do not themselves deny the genius of the men they have chosen to ignore. So we find the Academy as a body working on exactly the same lines as the individual R.A., whose one ambition is to extend his connection, please his customers, and frustrate competition; and just as the capacity of the individual R.A. declines when the incentive is money, so does the corporate body lose its strength, and its hold on the art instincts of the nation relaxes when its aim becomes merely mercenary enterprise. …

The Academy is sinking steadily; never was it lower than this year; next year a few fine works may crop up, but they will be accidents, and will not affect the general tendency of the exhibitions nor the direction in which the Academy is striving to lead English art. Under the guardianship of the Academy, English art has lost all that charming naiveté and simplicity which was so long its distinguishing mark."

In this period, the RAS was not immune from attacks and its status declined as so many British students, including Joseph's nephew (Joseph Benwell Clark) went to study art in France or at the emerging network of art schools linked to universities such as the Slade mentioned earlier.

Institute of painters in Oil Colours

During this final stage in Joseph's career, the Institute remained an important part of Joseph's life. It suffered something of an identity crisis during the Edwardian period. Broadly, in 1899 it became the Society of Oil Painters; the Institute of Oil Painters in 1904; and the Royal Institute of Oil Painters in 1909. Joseph became a member of the Institute in 1896.

New Societies

Several new exhibition societies arrived on the scene during this phase of Joseph's career, although he does not seem to have exhibited works at any of their shows.

The Allied Artists Association formed in 1908 by the art critic Frank Rutter with the support of Walter Sickert, Spencer Gore, Lucien Pissarro, Walter Bayes and Wilson Steer. It was set up as a co-operative modeled on the Parisian Salon des Indépendants and known colloquially as the London Salon. The aim was to provide an independent venue where the progressives, mainly Sickert's associates, could show their work. Until 1916, its annual exhibitions took place at the Royal Albert Hall, London, after which they moved to the Grafton Galleries in Chelsea. Initially, its rules allowed fee-paying members to exhibit up to five works. After the opening exhibition that attracted over three thousand entries, this became three. The Association provided a forum for the development of new ideas at a time when the Modernist movement was emerging.

The Camden Town Group, founded in 1910 by English Post-Impressionist artists, was the most prominent of the new exhibiting societies. It like others took its name from a London district. Others included Fitzroy Street, St John's Wood, Cumberland Market and Grafton Street. These existed in an exhilarating, frenetic, highly competitive environment, where jealousy was rife and quarrels furiously erupted.

Frank Rutter (1930) describes the history of the Camden Town Group in the preface to an exhibition catalogue. He recalled:

> "In the winter of 1910–11 a number of us had formed the habit of dining on Saturday evenings at a now vanished hotel-restaurant in Golden Square. The most regular in attendance were Harold Gilman, Spencer Gore, Augustus John, J.B. Manson, Lucien Pissarro, Walter Sickert and myself. Soon after the habit started, we were joined by Charles Ginner, and afterwards by R.P. Bevan. ...
>
> For many Saturdays, the principal topic of conversation was the rejection by the New English Art Club of certain pictures which, the diners thought, ought to have been accepted. Gradually these weekly conversations grew into a debate when the question before the House was whether it was better to endeavour to reform the New English by capturing a majority on the Selection Committee, or whether it would be better to start an entirely new society.... Eventually ... It was decided to found a new society, which held its first exhibition at the Carfax Gallery in June 1911. Gore was elected President ... and I think it was Sickert, who already had some connection with that district, who suggested that the new society should be called 'The Camden Town Group'. In addition to the eight artists already mentioned, eight others contributed to the first exhibition."

Several of Joseph's contemporaries and possible friends were members of the St John's Wood group. Joseph was not. As noted earlier though a sociable man, he tended throughout his career to work on his own rather than in shared studios.

Temporary Exhibitions

The Guildhall Gallery selected Joseph to be one of one hundred and twenty eight artists whose works represented art through the first sixty years of Victoria's reign. A.G. Temple (1919), the Director of the Guildhall Gallery, wrote about the 1897 exhibition in his memoirs saying:

> "1897 brought the Diamond Jubilee of Queen Victoria, and the form the exhibition assumed that year was obviously that of the painters who had flourished, or come into prominence, during her reign. There was a wide and splendid field on which to work ... while landscape, animal painting, and domestic genre were ably dealt with by a variety of accomplished men. A fairly representative collection was brought together of the best examples obtainable of one hundred and twenty-eight artists. In many cases the chief work of the painter was secured ... which could not well have been brought together in one collection save under some special plea as that associated with the Jubilee. ... Queen Victoria allowed three of the Royal pictures to be shown in this exhibition ... The exhibition was very successful, and attracted 248,094 of the public during the three months it was open."

In the same year, Joseph's 'Playmates' and his portrait of 'Beatrice and Gladys Kell' appeared at the 'Victorian Era Exhibition' held at London's Earl's Court to mark the diamond jubilee.

International Exhibitions

The appetite for international exhibitions continued through this period with Joseph's work selected for major international exhibitions. These were Melbourne (1893), Glasgow (1901), Franco-British Exhibition (1908) and Japan-British Exhibition (1910). The Sick Child (1857) appeared at Glasgow and the Franco British Exhibition; 'Playmates' (1891) at Melbourne and the Franco-British Exhibition; and 'A Fount of Charity' at Japan-British Exhibition.

In 1908 'Playmates' belonged to R. Erskine. In all probability, he was Lestocq Robert Erskine, the son of a former Indian Civil Servant, born in Edinburgh. The 1901 and 1911 census records show that he was a stockbroker living in Epsom and Berkshire respectively. As such, he was very much the type of art patron that was the butt of George Moore's satire mentioned below. Joseph Clark owned 'A fount of Charity'.

The Duchess of Fife, the new King's daughter, opened the Glasgow exhibition that ran from 2nd May to 4th November 1901. Over eleven million people attended the exhibition that coincided with the opening of the new City Art Gallery. The press coverage appeared in the Scottish and some English provincial papers. Much of the critical coverage was restricted to generalities rather than to the specific artists or their works. Given the theme of the Glasgow fine art exhibition was the 'progress of art through the past hundred years', the inclusion of 'The Sick Child' recognised Joseph's impact in the nineteenth century.

The press coverage included:

> "… Here it may said that so successful was the last Exhibition held in Glasgow that a surplus of £55,000 was derived from it, and with that sum as the nucleus of the fund, it was decided to erect the new Fine Art Galleries on a portion the site. … It is enough [to] say that the Art Galleries beautifully illustrate British art in the nineteenth century."
>
> **Falkirk Herald** 27 April 1901 (about £5m)

> "The art section comprises the following divisions: Oil paintings of the nineteenth century, water-colour paintings and pastels, and miniatures of the same period, sculpture, and architecture, works in black and white, photography, art objects, Scottish archaeology and history. … Every photograph here exhibited has been taken direct from nature and from life. The photographic section is thoroughly international, the work of each country, whether Britain, France, America, Germany, or any other being hung in its separate group. Visitors will note how every country has developed its distinctive Style."
>
> **Western Daily Press** 20 July 1901

> "Of all the sections of the Exhibition, the art gallery and museum is perhaps the most advanced. Its loan collection pictures have been insured for a million sterling [about £95m]. It has been selected and arranged with a view to exhibit the progress of art during the last hundred years."
>
> **Sheffield Daily Telegraph** 18 July 1901

The venue for the 1908 Franco-British exhibition was London's White City, the home of that year's Olympic Games. It was the first co-sponsored international exhibition marking the 'entente cordiale' between Britain and France signed in 1904. Margaret Drummond (1950) recalls visiting the exhibition with her father to see 'The Sick Child' hanging next to William Frith's 'Derby Day'. She says that this prominence reflected its position 'on the line' when first exhibited at the RA in 1857.

The press focused on the ceremonial aspects of the event rather than the contents of the exhibition:

"The Prince and Princess of Wales on Thursday formally opened the Franco-British Exhibition at Shepherd's Bush. Weather conditions were most unfavorable, heavy rain fell throughout the ceremony; but, nevertheless, great crowds of visitors poured into the exhibition grounds from the time the gates were opened, and there were also large gatherings greeting the Prince and Princess on their route from Marlborough House. Arriving at the exhibition shortly after two p.m., their Royal Highnesses were received by the Duke of Argyll, the president, and Princess Louise, the French Ministers {of} Commerce and Agriculture, Lord Selby, and other distinguished personages, and were conducted to the Court of Honour, where, after renderings the National Anthem and the 'Marseillaise,' the Prince declared the exhibition open. The Royal procession was reformed and proceeded to the Palace of Music, where an ode written by the Duke of Argyll [with] music by Sir C. Villiers Stanford was performed. The Duke presented to the Prince, on behalf of the executive committee, an address to which his Royal Highness briefly replied. After another performance of the 'Marseillaise,' the Royal party passed through the Palace of the Fine Arts, the Royal Pavilion, the Garden Club, and the Imperial Sports Club to the Stadium, where a body of some 2000 athletes was drawn up in the arena. After the Prince had declared the Stadium open, a programme of athletic sports was begun. In the course of it the Prince and Princess concluded their visit to the exhibition and returned to Marlborough House."

Stamford Mercury 22 May 1908

The 1910 Japan – British Exhibition ran from 14 May to 29 October attracting eight million visitors. It was the largest exhibition of Japan's public image in Great Britain and followed the renewal of the Anglo-Japanese Alliance (1902–1923). In this era, fine art had clearly become a tool of Britain's international diplomacy. Major exhibitions continued to attract vast audiences.

The shifting focus of press reports of international exhibitions show how selection could support an artist's career. At the early exhibitions, many works were for sale to visitors. By the early twentieth century, the best an artist could expect was that his works would achieve greater recognition and recall by the visitors, especially prospective art patrons.

Art patrons

The decline of the Art Union of London continued until 1912, when it closed. Likewise the shift in the type and motivation of wealthy people buying art continued. Most new patrons entering the market were people who made their money in services, especially in banking and finance or as a merchant or entrepreneur rather than from heavy manufacturing and mining industries.

The impact of this shift was captured by George Moore (1893) in a satirical, polemic and rather jaundiced piece on art patrons:

"The general art patron in England is a brewer or distiller. Five and forty is the age at which he begins to make his taste felt in the art world and the course of his collection is the following. … After a heavy dinner … . Brown says to Smith… 'I know you don't care for pictures, so you wouldn't think that was worth fifteen hundred pounds; well I paid all that, and something more too, at the last Academy for it. … Smith [after looking at the genre scene when wine and food have stupfied his brain] determines to possess one by the same artist. … He had been doing pretty quite well lately. There's no reason why he shouldn't have one. Irredeemable damage has been done …; another five or six thousand a year will henceforth exert its mighty influence in the service of bad art.

Smith who has not looked attentively at a picture before ... does not see ...[it] is nothing but a magnifed christmas card. ... But of technical achievement how should Mr. Smith know anything? ... but Smith is a stupid man who has money grabbed for five and twenty years in the City. ...

Such is the genesis of Smith's collection, typical of a hundred now being formed in London. The popular RAs have appealed to popular sentiment, and popular sentiment has responded and the City has paid the price. But time is not a sentimental person: and when the collection is sold at auction twenty years hence, it will fetch about a fourth of that which was paid. Mr. Smith's artistic taste knows no change. The ordinary perception of artistic value does not rise above Mr. Smith's. It must be admited that the influence his money permits him to exercise in the art world is an evil influence, and exercise persistently to the great detriment of the real artist. ... Men should not be elected Academicians merely because their pictures are bought by City men, and this is just what is done.

The public can very readily – far better than it gets credit for – distinguish between bad literature and good; nor is the public deaf to good music, but the public seems quite powerless between good painting and bad."

This piece is prescient in that by the middle of the twentieth century the market for Victorian art had collapsed, especially that for genre work with scenes of domestic life.

The National Art Collections Fund

The National Art Collections Fund emerged in 1903 as a new art patronage organisation to help public galleries and museums acquire artworks for the nation. The original idea came from a lecture given by John Ruskin in 1857 when he called for the establishment of a 'great society' to save works of art for public collections and 'watch over' them'. At the start of the twentieth century, the immediate impetus for the Fund came from the perception that Government funding was inadequate. Christiana Herringham, daughter of Thomas Powel the wealthy patron of the Arts and Crafts Movement, provided the original money for the Fund. She was a talented artist, copyist of Old Masters, a leader of the revival of tempera painting and founder of the Society of Painters in Tempera in 1901. Other important founders of the Fund were D.S. MacColl (the severe critic of the administration of the Chantrey Bequest and of Joseph's paintings bought by the Bequest) and Roger Fry (art critic and close associate of the Bloomsbury group).

From the outset, the Fund came under savage attack from Frank Rutter who said it made him 'boil with rage' that the Fund had spent thousands of pounds on Old Master paintings but 'would not contribute one half penny' to his appeal in 1905 to buy the first Impressionist painting for the National Gallery. Much later, in 1933 he wrote that 'the Fund's inertia and snobbish ineptitude are entirely characteristic of the art-officialdom in England.'

Today, The Art Fund contributes to purchases by a wide range of galleries and museums across Britain and Northern Ireland.

Art Critics

Right at the end of Joseph's career, Arthur Clutton-Brock (1919) offered a collection of essays on art including one on the function of critics in which he took issue with Sir Thomas Jackson RA (1835–1924). Jackson was a leading architect, who said that critics told people what to think and made their living from their reputation. Like William Frith before him, Jackson believed artists only valued criticism from fellow artists, although it was often 'sharp and unsparing, but always salutary'. Therefore, for him, artists not critics should be 'the instructor of the public'.

In Clutton-Brock's view critics who told people what to think were of no use to artists and harmful to the public. Valuable critics should express their views in ways that stimulate the public's response to specific works. Although critics often offered their judgments, he saw their real value in revealing the thought processes leading to artistic judgements. In the best criticism, judgment is implied rather than expressed and reflects the critic's spontaneous expression of the intensity of their experience. The critic tells us what has happened to him and invites readers to share it. Few, if any of the reports of Joseph's work at any stage in his career came close to this model of 'critical excellence'.

Several new critics began to have an impact in the eighteen nineties as they promoted the values of the new art movements. They included Charles Holme (who commissioned a portrait of his young children from Joseph in 1890), D.S. MacColl, Frank Rutter, Henry Strachey and Robert Alan Mowbray Stevey. They had a profound and lasting impact on the way later generations assessed Victorian art; and on the reputation and legacy of many Victorian artists including Joseph.

In 1890, John Ruskin who had dominated art criticism up to this point in Joseph's career, died. In addition to his voluminous writings and teaching duties, he also produced many ideas that were to influence the art world until the present time.

Art dealers

George Moore (1893) also offered a typically challenging view of art dealers:

> "In the eighteenth century … artists were visited by their patrons who bought what the artist had to sell or commissioned him to paint what he was pleased to paint. But in our time the artists is visited by a showily-dressed man, who comes into his studio whistling, his hat on the back of his head. This is the West End dealer: he throws himself into an armchair, and if there is nothing on the easels that appeals to the uneducated eye, the dealer lectures the artist on his folly in not considering the exigencies of public taste. On public taste … the dealer is a very fine authority.
>
> His father was a dealer before him and the son was bought up on prices…. He cannot see the pictures for the prices…. he lies back … not listening to the timid struggling artist who is foolishly venturing an explanation. … If the public don't like – why they don't like it, and the sooner the artist comes round the better. … If the artist comes round … the dealer buys; and when he begins to feel the uneducated eye really hungers for the new man, he speaks about getting up a boom in the newspapers.
>
> The Press is in truth a great dupe; the unpaid jackal that goes into the highways and byways for the dealer. The stockbroker gets the new man … but the press get nothing but unreadable copy, and yet season after season the Press falls for the snare. … I am at a loss to understand why the Press abandons so large a part of its [potential] revenue. If the Press did not notice exhibitions, the dealers would be forced into the advertising columns.
>
> My quarrel is with … the press that foolishly, unwittingly; not knowing what it was doing threw much power into the hands of the dealers that our exhibitions are now little more than tributaries of the Bond Street shop. … It is true the dealer cannot be got rid of; … but if the press withdrew its subvention … and art would be recruited by new talent at present submerged. Art would gradually withdraw from the bluster and boom of an arrogant commercialism."

By the end of the nineteenth century, the 'higher end luxury' department stores, many of which began as retail drapers, stocked fine art works. This was the era of the rapid growth of businesses such as

Harrods and in the emergence of concentrations of luxury businesses in Saville Row, Bond Street, Piccadilly, St James's and Mayfair. There were so many galleries along Bond Street, that a critic for the American magazine Truth (1905) wrote 'Bond Street is getting more and more like one elongated picture gallery tempered by tea shops!'

Contemporary views of art

Cosmo Monkhouse (1893) in an updated version of Mrs. Charles Heaton's 1878 'Concise History of Painting' offers a somewhat negative view of British art at the time, saying:

"The Winter Exhibitions at the Royal Academy and the Grosvenor Gallery, and the local exhibitions at Liverpool, Manchester, Birmingham, and other places, sometimes devoted to the work of a single artist, have borne fruitful results.

Portrait painting as an art has latterly so much advanced in general estimation, and has been practised with such remarkable power by artists like Watts, Millais, Ouless, Holl, Herkomer, and other living painters, that the portraitists of the previous generation appear to us to compare unfavourably with both their predecessors and successors; but the names of H.W. Pickersgill (1782–1875), of A.E. Chalon (1781–1860), and of Sir William Boxail (1800–1879) at least deserve to be recorded here.

It is the pure landscape painters of England in whose favour time tells most clearly. It is now generally recognised that in this branch of art, at least, the English School may claim to lead the way in modem art, and to have founded a school purely native, and original. If the ranks of our historical painters are thin, those of painters of high spiritual imagination are still thinner, but more than a hundred and thirty years ago, the sacred fire of creative imagination of the purest kind fell upon the cradle of William Blake (1757–1827).

William Mulready (1786–1863), comes next after Wilkie in his natural expression of the scenes of familiar life, but he deals with the emotions of childhood rather than with the more complex passions of later life. His works have not the dramatic force of Wilkie's, but they are especially distinguished by their excellent drawing (a quality in which Wilkie by no means excelled) and harmonious colour. Leslie, Newton, Egg, and many other well-known artists, belong to a large class of genre painters, that chooses its subjects rather from the upper than the lower grades of social life, and especially delights to illustrate life as it is seen reflected in the pages of the novel or the poem. Even when dealing with history these painters still treat their subject in a genre-like manner, and care little for the classical dignity which the before mentioned class of history painters strove to infuse into their works. Like the Dutch Terburg, these artists delight in rich costume and splendid accessories; but, although not approaching the Dutchman in execution, their works are seldom so inane and trivial as his, and often possess a strong human interest, as is apparent, for instance, in Egg's 'Life and Death of the Duke of Buckingham', in his 'Past and Present', and in many of Leslie's pleasant illustrations from Shakespeare, Cervantes and Moliere.

Given the prevailing style of English painting at the present day, and it cannot much be wondered at, that foreign critics laugh and sneer at the enormous number of English artists, who draw their inspiration solely from the wells of home life, and represent sentimental lovers, pretty children and happy mothers in unending sameness? A more ideal style has, nevertheless, lately been manifest in some of our greatest painters, and whilst we still have such men as Holman Hunt, Frederick Leighton, John Everett Millais, Dante Gabriel Rossetti, Frederick Watts, Philip Calderon, E.A. Walker, and James Sant, working in their full strength amongst us, there is no need to fear that English painting is falling into decadence; on the contrary, we may justly hope from the fresh energy that it has recently put forth, that a nobler and fuller development awaits it in the future."

G.B. Rose (1900) writing a review of 'English Contemporary Art' by Robert de la Sizeranne, translated by H.M. Poynter in an American Journal offers a more optimistic and jingoistic view of British Art:

"There are now in Christian lands only two schools of painting, the English and the French. The former embraces the British Isles; the latter, the rest of the world. But when you go to the England of the last half of the nineteenth century you seem to be transported to another planet.

The stout little isle that yielded not one jot to the great Napoleon when all the world was crouching at his feet has remained in the domain of art equally independent of French influence. English pictures are rare in the galleries of the Continent, but when you do see one you have no difficulty in recognizing its origin at a glance. The difference is not easily defined, but it is most distinctly felt.

For a long time the French ignored English painting entirely, but the Paris Exposition of 1889 was a rude awakening. England was too important a nation to be ignored, and a generous allotment was made to her, with the expectation that she would fill it with dogs, cats, and crying babies, in her old-fashioned genre style; but to their amazement it was filled to overflowing with great masterpieces which were a revelation of grace and beauty and replete with deep significance. Then for the first time the great revolution that had taken place since 1850 burst upon them, and they saw that England not only had an art worthy to compete with their own, but one which in many respects was its superior. As we have said, you can distinguish the English pictures from all others at a glance, but it is not so easy to indicate the difference in words. There is a certain family resemblance in their style, but there is no school whose members differ more widely from one another. That marked individual independence so characteristic of the Englishman is apparent in his art.

In the first place, their pictures always mean something. They all have not the profound significance of those of Watts; their subjects are sometimes trivial; but they have a meaning. The mind enters into their production, not the eye alone. They all express some thought, some emotion. They are all imbued with that maxim of Pope that the proper study of mankind is man. They are all human. Even their landscapes are steeped in human sentiment

Then while French art has continually inclined toward a broader and broader treatment in which details are neglected, outlines blurred, and atmosphere insisted upon at the expense of concrete objects, the English school has conceded nothing to this Impressionist tendency, but insists strongly that every detail shall be clearly presented. And this is one source of their power and attractiveness. But pictures in which every detail is carefully worked out never tire us, for there is always something new to discover.

The fact is that the broad treatment is in large measure a device of the artists to make money with a little labour. When he left the pre-Raphaelite camp Millais gave as his reason that he could not live, painting like that – meaning simply that he could produce three times as many pictures and earn three times as much money by painting in a more facile method.

Another characteristic of the English school is their clear, gemlike color, put on almost dry. As Vibert, one of the most skillful technicians of the French school says, every medium with which paint is mixed will darken it in the end, and he who paints for posterity should use pigments that are as nearly dry as possible. Colors swimming in oil and bitumen have, when placed upon the canvas, great depth and lustre; but a few years suffice for their destruction. The abuse of oil and bitumen is the great fault of the continental artists, and their pictures painted twenty years ago are usually darker and more faded than the masterpieces of the Renaissance. That commercial integrity which characterizes the English makes them unwilling to sell a man a picture that will perish before his eyes. Then, too, they are not painting for the applause of their contemporaries alone. They hope to hand down to coming generations visions of beauty that will never fade and a fame that will never die.

Perhaps the most striking difference between the masters of the English school and their continental rivals is their high standard of general culture. The leading English painters have been the perfection of cultivated gentlemen, strangely different from the long-haired Bohemian of the Latin Quarter. Gentlemen themselves, they paint for gentlemen and ladies. They are immensely concerned with the welfare of the people, and seek to raise the populace to their level; but they will not themselves descend to meet it.

And who are the men that have wrought this mighty change in English art? First must be mentioned the truly grand patriarch G. F. Watts, whose length of days and prolonged capacity for production threaten to rival those of Titian himself. He is the painter of the soul. One of the greatest geniuses of modern art is Dante Gabriel Rossetti, in words a true poet and with his brush a poet of the highest order. It has been the fashion of late to speak slightingly of Lord Leighton because he did not paint peasants and clowns, as the style, now happily passing away, so long demanded, but principally because he was president of the Royal Academy, that noble institution which all smart critics deem it their foremost duty to attack, while they discover untold merits in all the impressionist daubs that it rejects. Though the English school is so strictly insular, the Italian Rossetti is not the only man of alien race that has contributed to its greatness. Alma-Tadema, while a Dutchman, is a true leader of the English school, though something of the Dutch nature clings to his art. They are just such snap shots as might have been taken with a Kodak had the ancients possessed that much-abused instrument. Just in the places and attitudes in which the Kodak would have caught them the figures are fixed upon the canvas. So haphazard an arrangement does not make a perfect picture, but it adds to the sense of realistic truth."

Martin Wood (1912) provides a reflection on the nature of 'interior genre' towards the end of Joseph's career:

"The desire to paint our surroundings springs from the fact that all our experiences are coloured by them, and they are involved in any communication of our feelings we would make. Even in the most immaterial mood, painting can communicate nothing to us except through a refinement of physical description. But in studying painting we must always remember that reality can never completely reveal itself to the consciousness through one sense alone, such as vision. If we remember this, we shall know in what esteem to hold the realism that seems based upon an idea that vision can respond to nature without involving the rest of the self.

Interior genre deals with every-day incident; with the unheroic and the accidental. Its task is always that of witnessing to a moment, rather than of framing an ideal. At any rate, it does not oppose ideals to nature, but accepts them from her – from the incidents which we expressively say give the poetry to a scene.

The very character of this kind of art is based upon the recognition that the Nature with which it deals is already partly human, and it tends to cling to sentiment. We are at the beginning of a period, I hope, when the quality of a picture will be weighed in its sentiment; not the sentiment of the narrative it perhaps happens to relate, but its own – the soul of its craftsmanship. Quite often craftsmanship has been written about as if it was something that could be separated from the subject of a picture, whereas the truth is we cannot know what the subject of a picture is until the craft has shown us; and then only of its worth so much as the craft can show. Thus the only measure in which to take the worth of craft is in the worth of that which it conveys.

Disgusted with false-sentiment, 'Pre Raphaelitism' threw the whole machinery of conventional, pictorial truths overboard. Thus it lost the control of 'effect,' the really emotional feature in a picture. But this was recovered again in a new shape in 'Impressionism.'

'Impressionism' had this in common with 'Pre-Raphaelitism'; a belief that by a close imitation of a scene in nature the artist could put the spectator of the picture through the very moods which he had himself experienced in the presence of the scene. We now admit that an artist at work is affected by a thousand influences that are not present to his vision, and that deeply intuitive, less obviously naturalistic art, brings us nearest to the truth.

As I have said, in Interior subjects the Nature that has to be dealt with is partly human, and all the accessories have their intensely human value."

At this point we can observe that although contemporary critics' views of genre shifted somewhat, Joseph persisted in the basic approach to his art developed at the start of his career.

Reaching new audiences

During the final phase in Joseph's career, the art market became less receptive to contemporary genre works as the emphasis moved from anecdotal painting towards pure technique. In effect, the grammar of a painting became more important than its narrative content. At the forefront of this trend was the new generation of critics including R.A.M. Stevenson and D.S. MacColl who appeared less inclined than mid Victorian critics to read the story incorporated into many of Joseph's works. Some of the changes in artistic taste were also responses to the influence of Newlyn and Glasgow schools, and the New English Art Club. As Reynolds (1953) noted, many of the popular Newlyn works combined social life with 'plein air' techniques; an approach used sparingly by Joseph.

In this period, the press offers evidence of further ways in which Joseph's works became available to wider audiences, especially through modestly priced reproductions in illustrated magazines. Newspapers carried advertisements listing the contents of magazines and periodicals:

"The Band of Hope Review is capitally illustrated by Robert Barnes, J. Clark, etc."

Shields Daily Gazette 20 May 1893

"We have received from the 'Leisure Hour' Office, 56, Paternoster-row, E.C., and 'The Boys' Own Paper' for the current month. ... From the same publishers come The Girls' Own Paper,' which contains a coloured frontispiece, entitled 'The Flower of the Flock,' from a painting by Joseph Clark, exhibited in the Boyd Academy"

Exeter and Plymouth Gazette 24 December 1895

"The Sunday at Home (50, Paternoster-row, London) ... The August number of this magazine contains many other interesting little sketches, besides a very pretty coloured frontispiece, entitled 'John Anderson, my Joe,' from the well-known picture of Joseph Clark."

Yorkshire Gazette 22 August 1896

"Sunday at Home had a coloured frontispiece, 'Mother's Darling' from the picture by Joseph Clark."

Leamington Spa Courier 27 October 1900

"The current number of 'Friendly Greetings,' published by the Religious Tract Society, contains many stories and sketches of interesting character, several of the articles being accompanied illustrations. A nicely coloured frontispiece entitled 'Mother's Darling' from the picture by Joseph Clark in the Tate Gallery."

Western Daily Press 10 April 1905

"Pleasanter reading than this will be found in Pearson's. I need only call attention the selection charming examples of story pictures of children from Mr Joseph Clark's work. Few artists have interpreted more felicitously than he characteristic phases and scenes from child-life, and these reproductions will be much prized. ... The letterpress descriptions are helped wonderfully by the admirable illustrations."

Arbroath Herald and Advertiser for the Montrose Burghs 18 January 1906

"The Sunday Magazine. The Easter number contains some delightful pictures of childhood, reproduced from the canvas of the well-known painter, Mr. Joseph Clark, who has exhibited in the Royal Academy for many years."

Cambridge Independent Press 30 March 1906

"LITERARY NOTICES. The Sunday Magazine (Amalgamated Press. Ltd. 1, Carmelite House, Carmelite-street. E.C.) for the month April is full of good reading and well illustrated articles There very interesting account of an interview with Mr. Joseph Clark, by Harold F.H. Wheeler, under the title of 'Painter Childhood'."

Lincolnshire Chronicle 3 April 1906

From this small selection of advertisements, it seems that Joseph had a good foothold in providing illustrations in the growing number of 'worthy' magazines for young people. Some used prints of works exhibited previously while some were original works commissioned to portray particular themes. Joseph's friend, Rev. T. Dixon-Spain, was active in his support for the Band of Hope and other 'temperance magazines' and may have been instrumental in securing commissions for Joseph.

Magazines were not the only vehicle bringing Joseph's works to a wider audience as demonstrated by this advertisement from 1897:

"The ever popular annual for the little ones. Chatterbox Christmas-Box 1897. – A Beautiful Coloured Picture (26 by 20), a reproduction from an original oil painting by Joseph Clark, is presented with CHATTERBOX CHRISTMAS-BOX; ... Price One Shilling in a coloured cover: post free 1s 3d".

London Standard 11 December 1897 (£4.80 and £6).

Another means by which Joseph's paintings reached a wider audience in this period was through advertising by commercial companies. One of the first was was the Bovril Company who used Joseph's 'Blowing Bubbles' (1889) to advertise its meat extract. Bovril licensed the reproduction of thirty-nine paintings between 1901 and 1914 from the leading print publisher C.W. Faulkner.

One the best known companies using art to promote their 'brand' was 'Pear's soap'. Between 1891 and 1925, Pear's issued a large format annual publication containing Christmas stories, advertisements and presentation prints of paintings. In some years, as many as four prints came with the annual. In total, the company issued over 100 prints. The most famous of them was 'Bubbles' by John Everett Millais given away with the 1897 annual. Joseph's *Welcome Home* was included in the 1910 annual and *Family Worship* in 1911.

Joseph Clark – the mature artist

1890

Joseph's work 'The Cup that Cheers' appeared at the RA but attracted little media interest. The title is taken From William Cowper's The Task (1785): '*... the bubbling and loud hissing urn / Throws up a steamy column, and the cups, / That cheer but not inebriate, wait on each ...*'.

Later in the year, three works appeared at the Royal Institute of Painters in Oil Colours. These were 'Familiarity Breeds Contempt', 'Far from the Madding Crowd' and 'Dora and Geoffrey, children of C.H. Holm Esq.' The portrait attracted press attention:

> "The eighth annual exhibition of the Institute of Painters in Oil Colours is about to open, and a private view will be held on Friday next of this collection of 631 pictures, contributed by about 500 exhibitors ... So large an exhibition, comprising work by so many painters, is every year looked forward to as one of the most important of the autumn shows. The handsome galleries of the society will be found this autumn to be well filled with judiciously hung work, the average of which is certainly not higher than that of last year... There are several portraits, among the most interesting of which are ... 'The two children of C.H. Holme, Esq.,' by Joseph Clark."
>
> **Glasgow Herald** 30 October 1890

> "The collection is not strong in portraiture, but there are in that department a few works of notable merit. Such, for example, are ... 'Dora and Godfrey,' by Mr. Joseph Clark."
>
> **Morning Post** 3 November 1890

The portrait was Charles H. Holme's family. He was a retired East India Merchant living in Bexleyheath, Kent at the time of the 1891 census. Dora was born in 1877 and Charles Geoffrey in 1888. Two years after Joseph painted the children, Charles Holme founded 'The Studio: an illustrated magazine of fine and applied art'. In 1895, he became its editor. In 1919, his thirty one year old son Charles Geoffrey Holme took over as editor.

The second work 'Far from the Madding Crowd' is the only painting by Joseph inspired by a novel by Thomas Hardy, the celebrated Dorset writer and friend of William Barnes. It is not clear why Joseph decided to produce this work some sixteen years after the novel first appeared in serial form. Sadly, no images of this work are available in the public domain.

The press did not mention the third work 'Familiarity Breeds Contempt', a title drawn from a saying attributed to Aesop.

However, the Pall Mall Gazette praises Joseph's exhibits and mentions a work 'Love's Language'.

> "The hanging committee of the Institute seem every year to be reducing the pictures selected to a more uniform cabinet size ... These are, moreover, packed so closely together that it is sometimes difficult to tell whether one does not like or dislike any given work, merely from the fortuitous surrounding in which it is found. There are some really good things to be seen ... Other noteworthy figure pictures which may be mentioned ... and some dexterous examples by Mr. Joseph Clark, notably 'Love's Language'. ..."
>
> **Pall Mall Gazette** 3 November 1890

It is possible that this was an unrecorded subtitle or misattribution by the journalist. Joseph exhibited a work called 'Love's Language' at the Society of Oil Painters in 1903. The title 'Love's Language' comes

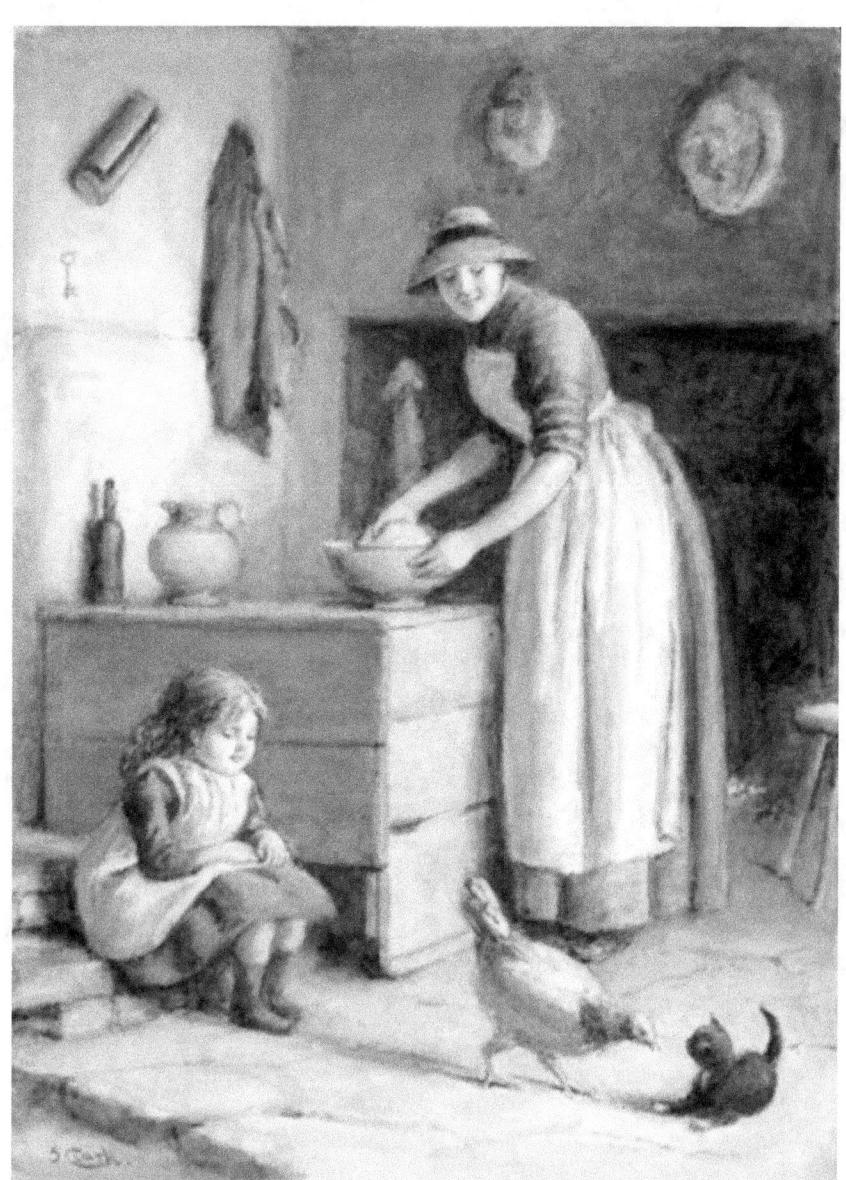

Plate 32. Sketch for 'Familiarity Breeds Contempt' (1890). (Courtesy Victoria and Albert Museum)

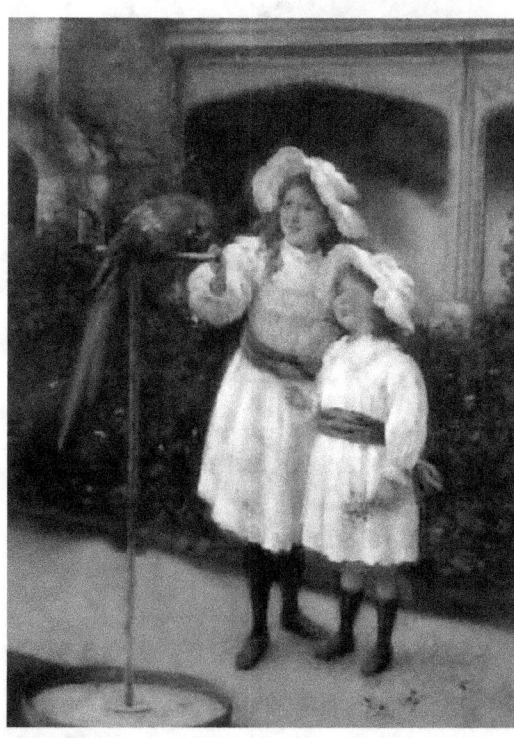

Plate 33. 'Scraping an Acquaintance' (1897). (Courtesy Sothebys)

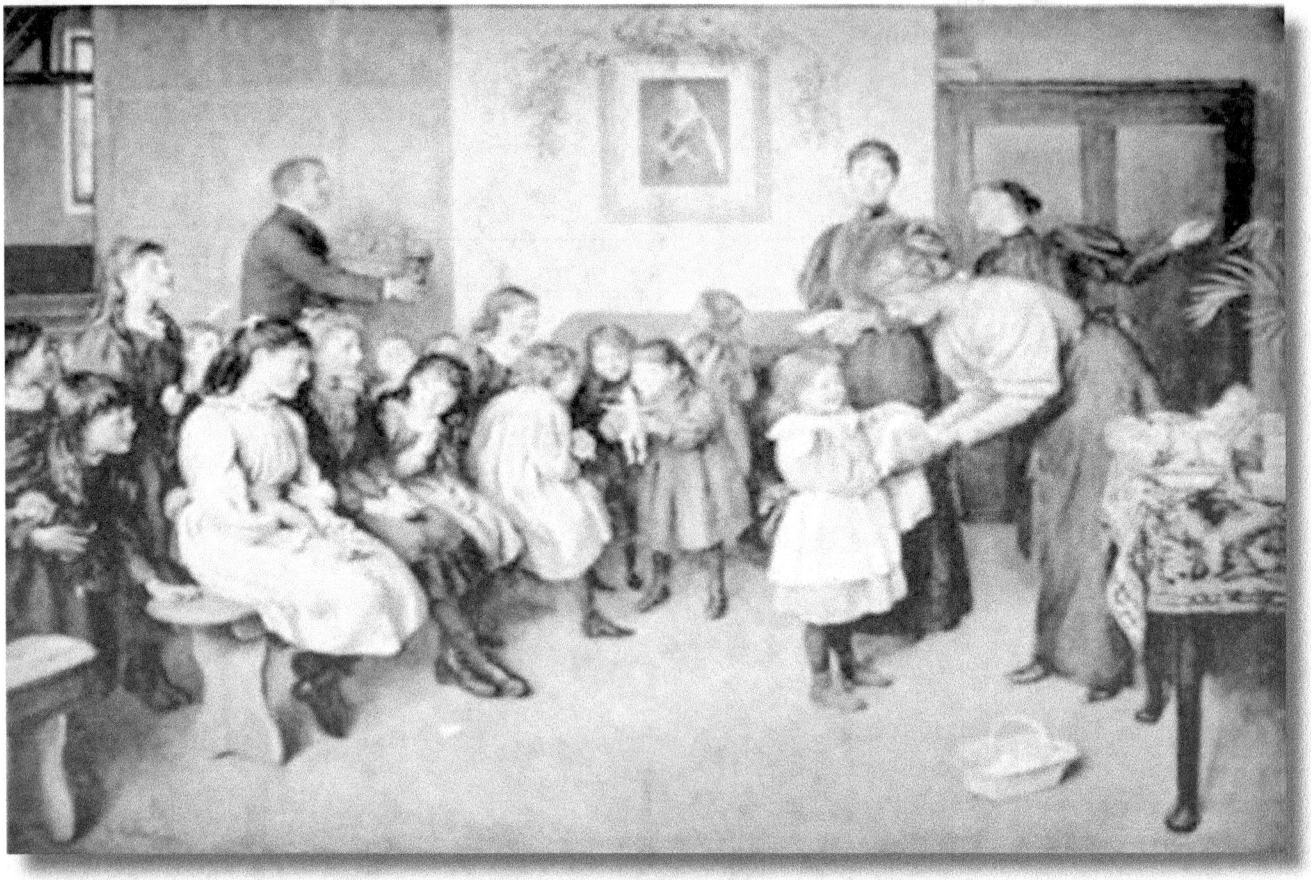

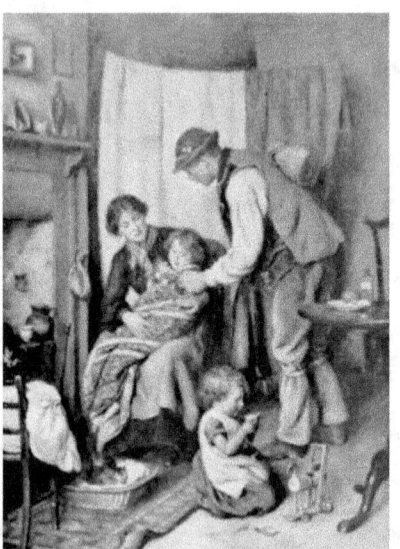

Plate 34. 'Jubilee Rejoicings' (1897).

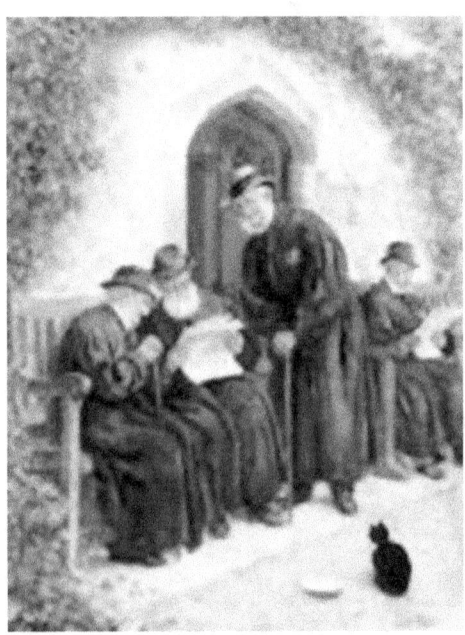

Plate 36. 'Daddy's Darling' (1904).
(Source: Cassel & Co)

Plate 35. 'War News at St Cross' (1899).
(Courtesy Christies)

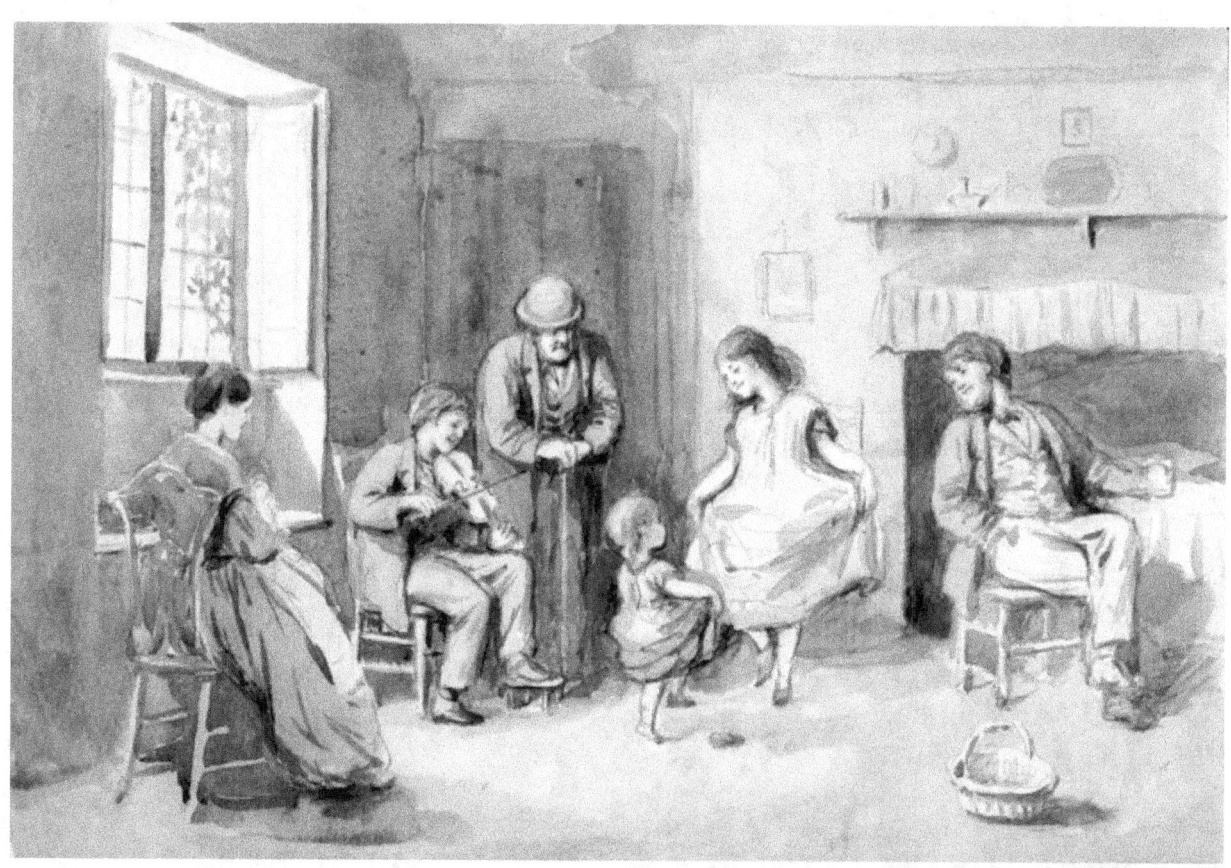

Plate 37. 'Dancing Children' (1900).
(Courtesy Victoria and Albert Museum)

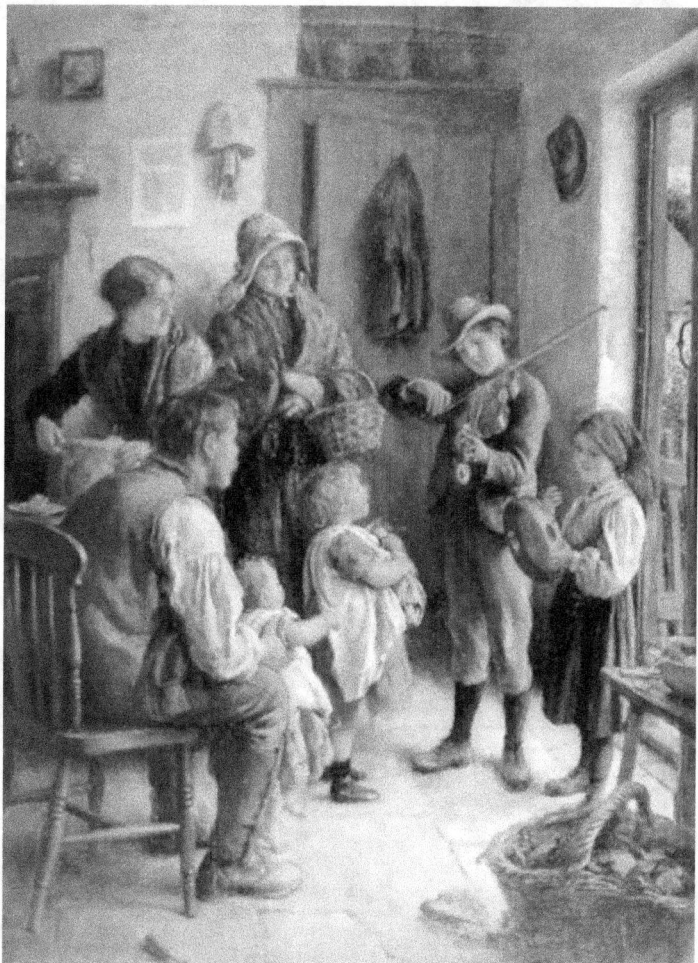

Plate 38. 'For Daily Bread' (1907).
(Source Pall mall Gazette)

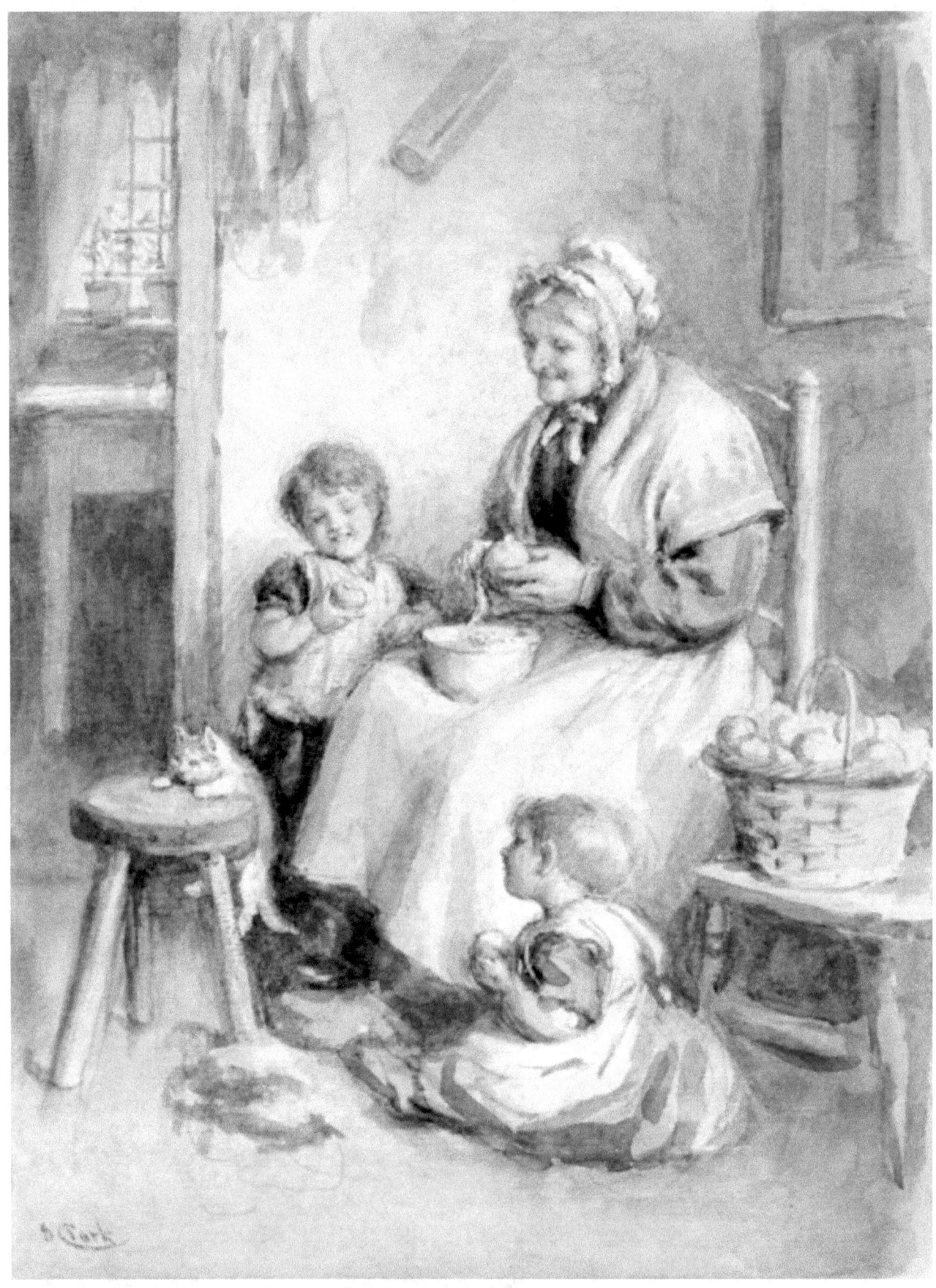

Plate 39. Sketch for the oil painting 'Vaulting Ambitions' (1901).
(Courtesy Victoria and Albert Museum)

from a poem by Ella Wheeler Wilcox published in 1883. The teachings of the Theosophical Society established by the spiritualist Madame Blavatsky in 1875 attracted Ella and her husband after the death of their only child. The society drew to some extent on the teachings of Emanuel Swedenborg. Without an image or contemporary description of 'Love's Language', it is impossible to say whether Wilcox's work influenced Joseph's artistic vision.

1891

The Birmingham Post gives full coverage to Joseph's work 'Playmates' shown at the 1891 RA Exhibition A painting with the same title appeared previously in 1888.

> "A capital little picture of the homely and semi-pathetic kind is Mr. Joseph Clark's 'Playmates,' … It is good for us to be acquainted with sickness, and pain, and sorrow, good for us at times to look even into the eyes of Death; but to have sickness at hanging before our eyes day after day the long year through is another matter. Here the sickness is not unto death, and has nothing ghastly or repulsive, or sickeningly sentimental about it. Of three little playmates one has had a bad illness, and has been very near the borderland, but the worst of it is over now, and little friends are allowed to drop in by ones and twos for a few minutes. The contrast between the pallid little fellow in bed, brightening at the approach of his friend, and the robustness of the lad who approached timidly and wonderingly is delicately and tenderly marked. The young mother is a graceful figure, and there is spontaneity in its action. The accessories are judiciously introduced – the lad's string of birds' eggs, his case of butterflies, the snowdrops on the table, denoting the season of the year – not too many and all significant."
>
> **Birmingham Daily Post** 30 May 1891

Later in the year, there was a brief mention of Joseph's work, 'Anticipation' exhibited at the Institute of Painters in Oil Colours autumn exhibition:

> "The Institute of Painters in Oil Colours opens its ninth exhibition to-day, the alteration from Monday having been made so as to give City men and others with a Saturday half-holiday an added opportunity of seeing the pictures while the show is still a novelty. The present exhibition contains work of about average merit, but it almost seems as if pictures were getting smaller and smaller. There are over six hundred and thirty paintings on the walls, which is a very large number indeed for the size of the galleries…. Some of the most noticeable of the remaining works will be found in … Joseph Clark's Anticipation."
>
> **Morning Post** 31 October 1891

1892

In the following year the Glasgow Herald comments less favourably on 'Playmates' then being exhibited at the Glasgow Fine Arts Institute:

> "In our last notice we had something to say regarding pictures in genre in the First Gallery … Joseph Clark's 'Playmates' is a picture in which much excellent brush-work is associated with what we cannot but regard as forced sentiment. A mother leans over the bed in which her sick boy lies, and whispering that his playmate has come to see him, the little, pale-faced invalid extends his hand to the newcomer with eager welcome in his eyes. Other children are in the

room, and all the details of the picture, even to the soft, white coverlet of the bed, are painted with the most painstaking skill."

Glasgow Herald 20 February 1892

1892 was one of the rare years in which Joseph did not exhibit works at the Royal Academy, the first since 1857. This may have been because of the family's move back to London or its impact on the quality of works submitted, if any. Towards the end of the year two pictures appeared at the Institute of Painters in Oil Colours. These were 'The Little Housewife' and 'Golden Wedding'. The Morning Post wrote:

> "Among the numerous pictures in the present exhibition but few are distinguished by such eminent merit as entitles them to exalted rank. But, on the other hand, there is 'an elegant sufficiency' – to use Thomson's phrase – of paintings well calculated to amuse or interest in various ways…Joseph Clark, who has deservedly won much popularity by his successful treatment of homely domestic incidents, bids fair for a renewal of favour with his picture of a hale, rosy old couple on the day of their 'Golden Wedding."

Morning Post 29 October 1892

1893

The critic, M.H. Spielmann, looked ahead to that summer's RA exhibition and mentions that '*Joseph Clark sends his 'An Unwelcome Guest'* (The Graphic 18 March 1893). The critic in the Lloyd's Weekly Newspaper mentions Joseph's other work exhibited that year:

> "Turning the corner of Gallery IV the eye falls upon Mr. Joseph Clark's 'Sweets of Life', the youngsters quietly enjoying dessert. How Missie enjoys her orange can be seen in her cheerful eye, and the little lads – are quite as much delighted with their queen as with the fruit."

Lloyd's Weekly Newspaper 30 April 1893

Before the 1893 Institute of Painters in Oil Colours autumn exhibition, the Clark family moved to Willesden. A press report of that exhibition foreshadows a tendency towards the end of Joseph's life for critics to mention his work by name but without elaborating on the scene presented or an opinion of its quality:

> "Rarely has a better collection of pictures been gathered together than that at present housed in the Institute of Painters in Oil Colours, Piccadilly. Taken seriatim or en bloc the result is the same – a feeling of satisfaction must ensue. The Hanging Committee have done their work admirably, and though one or two good pictures have not found a resting-place 'on the line' in the exact position which their merits seem to demand, yet one is scarcely inclined to regard it as a fault on the Committee's part, but rather as their misfortune at being restricted by want of space … 'Happy Days' by Joseph Clark."

Bath Chronicle and Weekly Gazette 16 November 1893

His other work 'A Bit of Fun' was not mentioned.

1894

Two works were exhibited at the 1894 RA exhibition; 'First Steps' and 'Beatrice and Gladys, daughters of F. Kell, Esq'. Frederick Knell was a lithographer living at West End, Hampstead with his wife Jessie. Beatrice was born in 1883 and Gladys in 1887. Frederick was evidently a prosperous man as the household included a cook, housemaid and coachman. Neither work was mentioned in the press. The Clarks and Kells were close neighbours for a time in 1892.

Two further works were exhibited at the Institute of Painters in Oil Colours in the autumn. The Morning Post enthused over one of them:

> "The well won reputation of this Institute is fairly sustained in the present exhibition ... Mr. Joseph Clark's 'John Anderson, My Jo,' ... [and 12 works by other artists]... are also to be classed among the attractions of the exhibition.".
>
> **Morning Post** 27 October 1894

The full title comes from Robert Burns' poem of 1790:

> "John Anderson, My Jo
> Now we maun totter down, John
> But hand in hand we go."

Joseph's other works were 'First Love' and 'The Woodman's 'Nunch-time'; neither was mentioned in the press. 'Nunch' is a Hampshire dialect word for lunch.

1895

He exhibited 'Flower of the Flock' at the RA. This title is possibly a reference to Pierce Egan's 'Flower of the Flock' issued in weekly parts by the London Journal between December 1857 and May 1858. The 'Flower of the Flock' is also a traditional Irish reel.

The addresses Joseph used for exhibitions between 1895 and 1897 suggest that he was splitting his time between Willesden and Winchester. By the time of the Institute of Painters in Oil Colours exhibition in the autumn 1895, he was using Annie's parents' address in Winchester.

He exhibited two works 'A Quiet Afternoon at St Cross' and 'A Fairy World' at the Institute of Painters in Oil Colours. The 'Hospital of St Cross and Almshouse of Noble Poverty' in Winchester is the oldest and largest medieval almshouse in Britain founded in the 1130s. It is also the oldest charitable institution in the United Kingdom. This was the first of several works by Joseph depicting scenes at St Cross over the following five years.

The Morning Post comment was succinct:

> "Nearly 500 pictures are shown in the present exhibition; of these many are marked by a high degree of technical worth, and not a few of them will be found interesting owing to the subjects or sentiments with which they deal ... Among other landscapes of interest will be found ... Mr. Joseph Clark, in 'A Fairy World' [and about 14 other works]."
>
> **Morning Post** 26 October 1895

The reference to 'landscapes of interest' is unusual but unfortunately, no images of this work are in the public domain. Around this time, Joseph was setting a larger proportion of his works in the open air than during earlier stages in his career. Most of these where we have images or descriptions were, in essence, 'outdoor genre' works with the focus on the people and situations depicted rather than on the qualities of the surrounding countryside.

1896

In February 1896, Joseph's work appeared in Sheffield although the local paper did not identify the work on display:

> "Mr. Willis Hudson's exhibition of masterpieces from the easels of the greatest brushes in oil and water colours grows in importance year by year. On the present occasion, Mr. Hudson has gathered for the exhibition, which opens at the Cutlers' Hall to-day, a collection of canvases which will well repay the attention of connoisseurs and of art lovers in general. ... There are among the oils also examples of the breezy work of Edwin Hayes, R.A., and specimens from the easels of B.W. Leader, A.R.A., Louis B. Hurt, Robert W. Allan, R.W.S., J. Clayton Adams, Thomas Blinks, James Webb, Joseph Clark ROI, E.J. Niemann, Sir Edwin Landseer."

> **Sheffield Daily Telegraph** 7 February 1896

The Art Journal was unimpressed by the works exhibited at the 1896 RA exhibition:

> "...the chief cause of lamentation is the lessening of the general inclination to make excursions into the realms of imagination. All round there is proof of timidity, of hesitation to give rein to fancy, or to try new departures in subject or matter. There are too many repetitions, too much harping on the one accustomed note, too great reliance on motives, which have become threadbare from frequent use. We feel in the galleries a lack of vitality and robust health; and in their place there is not the animation even of hysterical excitement; everything is too decorous and respectable to inspire more than merely perfunctory acceptance. However, to all rules there are, we may be thankful, exceptions enough to save us from the terror of absolute monotony. Despite the general failure to be either interesting or original, there are in the Academy exhibition enough pictures worthy of attention, to occupy us not unprofitably during the hours we may feel called upon to spend in Burlington House. Some of the least of men whose work hardly ever fail to be important have refused to give way to the prevailing fashion, and have done their best to uphold reputations that are based upon long years of wholesome work."

Joseph with his steadfast adherence to domestic genre in his work might have been one of the artists they had in mind for refusing to give way to the prevailing fashion. He submitted 'Red Letter Day' from Willesden.

The Morning Post remained succinct in its coverage of the 1896 Institute of Oil Painters including 'Feast in View' submitted from Winchester:

> "The Committee entrusted with the arrangement of the present Exhibition have hung less than five hundred pictures, and several of these are of modest dimensions. Hence it will be gathered that the walls are by no means inconveniently crowded, and that every contribution to the collection is so placed that it may be fairly seen ... while among other works of interest will be found [lists 4 works including] Mr. Joseph Clark's 'A Feast in View' ..."

> **Morning Post** 24 October 1896

No mention was made of Joseph's other work – 'A New Pet'.

1897

In 1897, Joseph was in touch with the national mood when he submitted his 'Jubilee Rejoicings' to the RA exhibition from Winchester. This was the first time he submitted a work inspired by a major national event. This depicts more figures than were common in his works set in an institution; a school or possibly orphanage. However, the critics did not mention it.

Three paintings submitted from Harrow went to the Society of Painters in Oil Colours. They were 'Patience is a Virtue', 'Brother Nobbs – A Study at St Cross, Winchester' – and 'Scraping an Acquaintance'. They represent three different strands in his work.

'Patience is a Virtue' refers to one of the seven heavenly virtues. These first appeared in the epic poem entitled Psychomachia, or Contest of the Soul written by Aurelius Clemens Prudentius, a Roman Christian poet and provincial governor, who died around 410 A.D. The poem depicts the battle between good and evil. The seven virtues are chastity, temperance, charity, diligence, patience, kindness, and humility. Practicing them protected one against temptation from the seven deadly sins. This thought would have appealed to Joseph but without an image or description, we cannot see how he treated the subject.

The second work 'Brother Nobbs – A Study at St Cross, Winchester' is the second painting in the series inspired by St Cross. Abraham Nobbs was born in 1826 in Hungerford, Berkshire and was, by the time of the 1841 Census, living at the Union Workhouse, Hungerford with his mother and five siblings. Ten years later in the 1851 census he appears in Winchester working as a Brewers' labourer. He was married to Rosella and they had a son, Charles. In 1901 he was living in St Cross with Prescilla, his grandaughter, the daughter of Charles. Abraham died in 1908 aged 83.

The final work, 'Scraping an Acquaintance' differs from many of Joseph's other works as the setting is clearly in a well to do household featuring a parrot and two children. Sotherby's dated the work as 1891.

1898

He did not exhibit at the Royal Academy in 1898 but three works went to the Institute of Painters in Oil Clours. These were 'Over the Garden Wall', 'A Questionable Character' and 'Nothing Venture, Nothing Have'. None were mentioned in the press.

'Over the Garden Wall' was a popular theme with artists at this time, for example in the later works by John Singer Sargent (1910), Helen Allingham and Frederick Morgan. 'Nothing Venture, Nothing Have' is a variant of the more familiar proverb of 'nothing ventured, nothing gained' first recorded in English in Chaucer's Reeve's Tale from the late fourteenth century. Without images of these works we cannot understand the treatment Joseph accorded them.

1899

This was an unusual year for Joseph. He became interested in issues of war and peace, or at least their impact on people at home in Britain. The RA exhibited his 'War News at St Cross' showing pensioners reading avidly the latest newspapers. It is sometimes known as 'After the Sunday service'.

It would be tempting to link this work to the outbreak of the Second Boer War in South Africa but the war did not start until the 11th October, well after the RA exhibition closed. Tensions had been rising for several years. There were some militrary encounters on India's North West frontier but these were relatively minor.

In the autumn, the Society of Oil Painters included 'Little Tommy Atkins'. Tommy Atkins was a long standing slang term for British soldiers in common use from at least the early nineteenth century, perhaps much earlier. Two other works appearing at the Society of Oil Painters were 'Elsie', a portrait of his daughter then aged sixteen and 'Mother's Birthday'.

1900

Joseph exhibited two works at the 1900 RA exhibition – 'Dumplings' and 'Goodnight Daddy' – neither was mentioned in press reports. In 'Goodnight Daddy' he returns to a theme appearing in works exhibited at the RA in 1868 and 1881 under the title 'Goodnight Father'. He did not exhibit at the Society of Oil Painters in that autumn at the start of what was a slack period in his career, at least in terms of the numbers of works exhibited in London.

In 1900 he also produced 'Dancing to Father's Fiddle'. This used similar models and poses to those seen in the drawing 'Dancing Children'.

1901

Joseph exhibited 'Golden Days' at the Royal Academy; and 'Wee Bairns' and 'Vaulting Ambition' at the Society of Oil Painters. 'Vaulting Ambition' is another work inspired by a quotation. The phrase can be traced at least as far back as William Shakespeare's Macbeth (Act I, sc. 7) 'I have no spur to prick the sides of my intent, but only vaulting Ambition, which o'leaps itself, and falls on the other'. This is a good example of a light hearted work using a widely used quotation.

1902

Joseph exhibited two works, 'A Grave Responsibility' and 'Many Happy Returns' at the RA. Neither was noticed by the critics. The general critical opinion was that this was a weak show:

> "It [is a] weak exhibition, especially when the importance of the coming season is borne in mind. But some excuse may be found for the members and associates and those other prominent painters who have not yet been favoured with admission to the inner circles of the Academy, in having withheld their best work for display in their own ateliers. It has been known for some time past that the coming Coronation festivities will bring to London hosts of wealthy Americans and many well-to-do Colonials. As these visitors are most likely to become extensive purchasers of pictures, painters have kept back their most notable work executed during the past year, preferring to sell outright and send their patrons home happy in the actual possession of their newly acquired objects of art. Last year the exhibition contained many works of unusual excellence; this year there nothing particularly striking, indeed, very low average has been struck."

Sheffield Daily Telegraph 5 May 1902

The 'importance of the coming season' refers to the coronation of Edward VII. Originally scheduled for 26th June, the ceremony had been postponed as the King had been taken ill with an abdominal abscess that required immediate surgery by Sir Frederic Theaves who like Joseph was a former pupil at William Barnes's school in Dorchester. The rearranged coronation took place on 9th August 1902.

Another aspect of the RA exhibition attracted a lot of press attention:

"POLICEMAN ARTIST 'HUNG'. On Saturday, police constable Edwin Thos. Jones, the artist, who is a member of the Leeds City Police Force received a communication from the authorities of the Royal Academy that his picture, 'Summer' had been accepted, and hung the walls of the exhibition. The painting is 3ft. by 2ft, a view of Shropshire Downs, near Church Stretton, with a flock of sheep browsing. This is the fourth occasion on which Mr. Jones has sent up pictures to the Academy, and three times they have been retained, although not hung."

Sheffield Daily Telegraph Monday 28 April 1902

Later in the year, Joseph exhibited two works at the Society of Oil Painters. These were 'From Sunny South' and 'Mrs. Jarvis'. Towards the end of the year, Joseph and his family moved to a house called 'Hazelbury' in Stanley Gardens, Willesden in North West London – presumably named after Haselbury Plucknet in Somerset.

1903

In January the Society of Oil Painters experimented with an exhibition early in the year. Joseph submitted two works – 'The Bird's Nest' and 'Gold Fish'.

"The twentieth exhibition the Society of Oil Painters at the spacious galleries is the first of the art shows of 1903, and hence questions of its merits or demerits have an interest as is invariably albeit not altogether warrantably, attached to new year ventures. Happily, of the 391 pictures a relatively large proportion possesses attraction some kind – and attraction more than momentary … There are pictures which if they be not actually epoch making – and that were to give too lofty a flight to ambition – at any rate possess qualities that arrest the attention, stir the spectator to thought and feeling unaccustomed kind … Pictures in which subjects are prominent include … Mr. Joseph Clark's 'Gold Fish'…"

Western Daily Press 3 January 1903

The only work selected by the RA's hanging committee in 1903 was 'Left in Charge'. The autumn exhibition of the Society of Oil Painters attracted three works from Joseph. These were 'The Cup that Cheers', 'Elsie, the Artist's Daughter' and 'Baby's Birthday'. Works with the same titles as the first two works appeared in exhibitions in 1890 and 1893. None attracted any critical attention.

1904

In 1904 one of Joseph's pictures exhibited at the RA, 'Daddy's Darling', was selected for the Cassel & Company's 'Royal Academy' pictures of 1904. This and two other works exhibited, 'Spring's Message' and 'Listen to a Little Child', were not mentioned in the press.

The press mentioned the Lincolnshire born architect, John Edward Dixon-Spain who married Joseph's daughter, Elsie, in August 1905.

"Local Honours. – We understand that the Hanging Committee of the Royal Academy have again accepted drawings for the Architectural Room by Mr. J.E. Dixon-Spain, A.R.I.B.A., son of the Rector of Rand St Oswald, and for some time articled to Mr. William Scorer, of Lincoln. It will be remembered that his first picture was hung in the Academy just previous to his sailing for the South African campaign, where he was engaged as a Lieutenant in the Scouts for eighteen months. His picture this year is the sanctuary of a church, and it is well hung upon the line. The same picture occupied prominent position at the Church Congress in Bristol last October."

Lincolnshire Chronicle Friday 6 May 1904

Joseph exhibited four works at the renamed Institute of Oil Painters in autumn 1904. These were 'A Wanderer', 'A Bracken Gatherer – near the New Forest', 'A Gipsy Strawberry Picker' and 'Fireside Reflections'.

1905

Joseph exhibited two works at the RA: 'Chip off the Old Block' and 'A Tempting Offer'; and three went to the Institute of Painters of Oil Painters': 'A Coming Storm', 'Suppertime' and 'Florence and Winifred, daughters of F.A. Gardner Esq.' It has not proved possible to identify the Gardener family concerned. None of these works were mentioned in the press.

In June, Joseph offered his resignation to the Institute which was 'accepted with regret' by its Council. Joseph withdrew his resignation in November but the Society's records do not give any reason for the resignation nor its withdrawal. It may have been connected to his move to Winchester and death of his father-in-law.

1906

Two works were exhibited at the RA. They were 'A White Wold' and 'The First Step in Life'. Four works went to the Institute of Oil Painters. They were '91 in the Shade', 'Sisters', 'Over the Garden Wall' and 'A Willing Helper'. It is not clear whether 'Over the Garden Wall' was the same picture as that exhibited at the RA in 1898 or a new work.

1907

His work 'For Daily Bread' exhibited at the RA was selected for the Pall Mall Gazette's publication 'Pictures of 1907'. This work was also known as 'For Daddy' reflecting a theme apparent in Joseph's works for several decades, that of children using their mucical and artistic talents to entertain their families.

Joseph exhibited two works at the Institute of Oil painters. They were 'My Turn Next' and 'His First Summer'.

1908

The RA selected two works – 'After Many Years' and 'The Farmers Woldest Dater' ('The Farmer's Oldest Daughter'). Both works looked back to themes from earlier parts of Joseph's career.

In 'After Many Years' Joseph returns to a theme first depicted in the 'Return of the Runaway' exhibited at the British Institution in 1862 and carried forward in 'Home Again' (1885). In both works, a sailor has just arrived home unexpectedly after a long absence to the surprise and delight of his family. The Daily Chronicle included a long piece on 'After Many Years':

"The picture reproduced above promises to be one of the most popular of the genres at this year's Royal Academy. 'After Many Years' is the work of that veteran artist, Mr. Joseph Clark. It depicts the unexpected homecoming of 'Jack' to his native village after many years absence in the service of his country in distant waters. It is a very characteristic example of the work of Mr. Clark, who throughout his long artistic career has employed his talents in recording with graphic strokes of his brush scenes and stories in the lives of the multitude. Few artists have achieved such success in the sympathetic delineation of episodes in the careers of the humbler classes as Mr. Clark. Born in a Dorsetshire village, he early conceived a fondness for giving pictorial expression to the rustic scenes amid which he dwelt, and many of his earlier canvasses set forth the pain and simple annals of the poor.

Coming to London at an early age, intent on pursuing art as a profession, he studied at Hetherley's and the Royal Academy Schools. Within three years of his admission to the latter, he was successful in getting his first picture accepted by the Royal Academy. This was as long ago as 1857, so that last year Mr. Clark celebrated his jubilee as a Royal Academy exhibitor.

An amusing story is told of Mr. Clark's first picture. It was called 'The Sick Child' and showed a young father and mother ministering to the petulant desires of a fretful first born, who appeared willfully insensible to the blandishments of parental affection. This picture, revealing a familiar domestic experience achieved a remarkable success. It was just one of those little touches of nature that made the whole conjugal world kin. How much attention it attracted may be judged by the fact that it earned for the artist the sobriquet of 'Sick Child Clark', a nickname that has stuck to him ever since.

The popularity of this picture clearly showed Mr. Clark his métier, but hardly a year has passed since in which the walls of Burlington house have not been graced by one or more of his canvasses depicting similar scenes of domestic life. Through the medium of the engraver, a great number of Mr. Clark's pictures have been made familiar throughout the country. Perhaps the most popular and widely known is that entitled 'Baby's First Tooth'. Equal success has attended Mr. Clark in his paintings of the poor and friendless waifs of London, for whom he has always shown so much tender sympathy."

Daily Chronicle May 1908

The reference to the popularity of 'Baby's First Tooth' is noteworthy as this is the only reference to a work bearing this title. It is possible that this was a 'popular' name for a work exhibited under a different name, perhaps 'His first summer' exhibited in 1907. It is unclear whether the reference to 'poor and friendless' waifs recalls the 1882 work exhibited at the RA – 'Waifs and Strays' or to later works – especially those using the same models.

The press reported that Joseph's work 'After Many Years' had attracted a buyer in a year when sales elsewhere went slowly:

"The attendance the Royal Academy since the opening day has been excellent, but as yet the sales are not encouraging. About seventy works have been disposed of, and apart from the Chantrey purchases, few prices have reached three figures. The President, Sir E.J. Poynter, has sold his two water-colour drawings, Glencalvie Falls, Ross-shire,' and 'The River Car-Ton, Ross-shire,' and among others fortunate in attracting buyers are … Mr. Joseph Clark. 'After Many Years' …"

Manchester Courier and Lancashire General Advertiser 19 May 1908

The destination of 'After Many Years' became clear early in 1909 albeit with considerable marketing puff:

"A notable offer is being made by 'Answers' which will enable its readers to obtain a fine gravure production twenty-three inches by twenty eight inches of Mr. Joseph Clark's Royal Academy picture 'After many years' at a price which even a schoolboy could easily afford. 'After Many Years' was acclaimed as one of the most popular successes of the Academy last year and Mr. Clark was inundated with offers for his painting, but the proprietors of 'Answers' outbid them all, and they are now offering copies to their readers for almost nothing. It is stated that this picture took Mr. Clark no less than forty-five years to accomplish."

Manchester Courier and Lancashire General Advertiser 5 February 1909

This report suggest 'After Many Years' took forty five years to complete. This is unlikely and the reporter may have confused this work with 'Return of the Runaway' (1862).

'The Farmers Woldest Dater' takes its inspiration from a line in a poem by William Barnes shows a young woman hard at work baking watched by several children.

He submitted four works to that year's exhibition at the Instiute of Oil Painters – 'Motherless', 'Monica', 'A Rest by the Way' and 'Bosom Friends'. 'Monica' was a portrait of Monica Dixon-Spain; Joseph and Annie's first grandchild born 15 March 1908.

1909

Joseph exhibited just one picture at the 1909 RA exhibition. It was called 'Our Heart's Delight'; possibly another work inspired by Monica.

In 1909, King Edward VII awarded the Instiution of Oil Painters permission to use the designation 'Royal'. Joseph exhibited three works at its frist exhibition. They were 'The Beacon Trees, New Forest', 'Pleasant Thoughts' and 'Gipsy Hollow, New Forest'. Joseph may have received renewed inspiration from the Hampshire countryside as he had in the eighteen nineties. Even at this late stage in his career he seemed to have been experimenting with new styles. 'Gipsy Hollow' is more of a landscape work albeit with two main figures in the middle ground.

1910

The introduction to the review of the 'Royal Academy 1910' said:

"We English people dearly love an institution, and in spite of the fact that we are popularly supposed to be an inartistic nation, which is, by the way, one of many popular absurdities, we hail the opening of our great pictorial institution, the Royal Academy Exhibition at Burlington House, with no small enthusiasm. The R.A. is our annual Feast of Pictures and we flock there in our thousands in the high days of the London Season full certain that we shall come away with a good general idea of what is going on in the Art world of Britain. And we are never disappointed. Of course no one looks upon the R.A. as representative of the whole of British Art; Burlington House stands for the average. It aims, in our time at least, at the happy medium. And, although the extremists among painters are not encouraged, the Royal Academy of to-day does not by any means turn its back upon the newer and more adventurous spirits.

The raising of the average modern tendency of the pictures, which has been so conspicuous a feature of the R.A. Exhibitions for the past few years, is still maintained; and the present show is well up to the new standard. Not so much, however, in the presence of a few canvases which are obviously more or less independent of the classical and academic traditions, but, what is far better, in the general tone of the whole Exhibition. The purely 'academic' picture looks as much out of place to-day as, say, the purely 'impressionist' picture did a few years ago. A compromise has been arranged, and our artists are more independent and individual than they were a decade ago. The presence amongst RA's. and A.R.A's. of such free and independent spirits as George Clausen, J.J. Shannon, Frank Brangvvyn, George Henry, Charles Sims, Stanhope Forbes, and Arnesby Brown has had its good effects, and the Royal Academy is no longer the old fogey of picture exhibitions."

However, Joseph's only exhibited work in 1910 was 'Tales of the deep' at the RA. It was the fourth and final work in the 'homecoming sailor' series including the 'Return of the Runaway' (1862), 'Home Again' (1885) and 'After Many Years' (1908).

This attracted the attention of Bovril in 1911:

"PICTURES FOR THE HOME. Fine art and advertising hand-in-hand a good deal nowadays, and the combination often enables the public to secure good specimens of art easy way. Perhaps one of the best-known picture schemes that Bovril (Limited), who hare published three excellent pictures by well-known artists. One is artist's proof 'Blind Man's Buff' by Arthur J., which was exhibited at the Royal Academy this year, and the others are entitled 'Babes in the Wood.' Fred. Morgan, and 'Tales of the Deep' by Joseph Clark. All three pictures are full of 'joy and happy faces' – those features which Sir Alma Tadema stated only a day or two ago he contrives to introduce into his own work. Each 'picture can obtained under the coupon system, which Bovril (Limited) have introduced."

Yorkshire Evening Post Thursday 12 January 1911

Towards the end of 1910, Joseph resigned from his membership of the Royal Institute of Oil Painters. He may have intended this to be his retirement as a professional artist.

Two letters held in the Getty Archive show that Joseph retained a close interest in the use of his works at this stage in his career. In 1910 Alfred Benjamin Cooper, a well-known writer of story books for young people, mainly from a Christian perspective, wrote asking Joseph's permission to use 'Early Promise' (a work first exhibited at the Royal Academy in 1877) in an unnamed book. His reply to Alfred Cooper of 24 October 1910 said '*In reply to your enquiry regarding my picture 'Early promise' I had no particular person in mind. I simply thought the subject a good one.*' By extension, this may be seen as saying that as a rule Joseph did not intend his works to record actual events but rather to narrate an interesting thought provoking story.

Seven years later, Joseph was writing:

"Dear Sirs
Please supply Mr A D Cooper with a photo of my picture 'Tales from Flanders' at his own expense.
                    Yours truly
                    Joseph Clark"

It is not possible to identify who Mr A.D. Cooper was but the most likely candidate, from census records, trade directories and trade union records, suggest that the recipient was a young lithographer.

1911–14

He did not exhibit again until 1913 by which time, Joseph and Annie (and possibly Margaret) had moved to Uxbridge. By then Elsie was married and Wilfrid was working as an 'Ordained Leader' at the New Church in Horncastle, Lincolnshire. This was close to Elsie's father-in-law, the rector of Rand St Oswald.

The work shown at that year's Royal Society of Oil Painters was 'Anxious Moments'. His work continued to sell at auction as in this example from Derbyshire:

> "SIR HENRY BEMROSE'S COLLECTION. THREE DAYS' SALE AT LONSDALE HILL. The late Sir Henry Bemrose's collection of oil paintings, water colours, and engravings, and Continental china, Wedgwood medallions, miniatures and enamels, rare old glass, jewellery, and bric-a-brac, is at present being dispersed. The sale, which will occupy three days, opened at Lonsdale Hill. Utoxeter Road, Derby, … Other prices of 10 guineas and upwards were … 'Dressing Dolly' (Joseph Clark), guineas."
>
> **Derby Daily Telegraph** 19 February 1912

This is the only reference to this work and the price paid is the equivalent to £2,268. Sir Henry Bemrose was a partner in a large printing and publishing house, mayor of Derby and the local MP.

1915

The start of The Great War in August 1914 inspired Joseph to exhibit three final pictures. 'News from the Front' appeared at the 1915 RA Exhibition; the first to be held during the war. 'Loyal Citizens' appeared at the Royal Society of Oil Painters later in the year.

1916

In 1916, he exhibited 'Tales from Flanders' at the RA. This was his one hundred and fourth work accepted by the hanging committee over the fifty-nine years since his debut with 'The Sick Child' in 1857.

It received some press comment notably in terms of its inclusion in 'The Royal Academy Illustrated':

> "The 'Royal Academy Illustrated' is the first book of its kind issued with official authority by the Royal Academy, and no such Publication has yet been entirely produced in photogravure. It contains reproductions of considerably over 200 pictures, including works of R.A.s and A.R.A.'s. Included in the illustrations are 'A Devonshire stream' Frank Brangwyn A.R.A.; 'Tales from Flanders' Joseph Clark, who formerly lived near Crewkerne … Sir Harry Veitch (bronze bust), by Alfred Drury, R.A.; 'A West-Country Farm' Stanhope Forbes, RA. The book published by Walter Judd. Ltd. 6 Queen Victoria Street, London. E.C. It is an excellent production."
>
> **Exeter and Plymouth Gazette** 9 May 1916

The Journalist showed his eagerness to comment on 'West Country' works but a limited knowledge of Joseph's career or West Country roots. The journalist of a small piece in the Portsmouth Evening News was somewhat better informed:

"At the age of 82, Mr. Joseph Clark, the artist, who has had picture the Royal Academy each year for the past fifty years, has sold 'Tales from Flanders' his latest picture exhibited this year."

Portsmouth Evening News 4 July 1916

Retirement

Sometime after 1916, Joseph and Annie moved to Ramsgate. Some reports say he lived in a 'colony for retired artists, part of the Sebag Montefiore estate' but it has not proved possible to verify the existence of such a 'colony'.

From time to time his works received coverage in the press:

"On the wall opposite is Joseph Clark's 'Early Promise' interesting specimen the anecdote pictures which once well within living memory, enjoyed great vogue. Joseph Clark a West-Countryman, having been born Cerne Abbas, Dorsetshire and educated by the Rev William Barnes 'The Dorset Poet'. At 18, he came to London and his first picture at the Royal Academy remained always one of the most popular. 'The Sick Child' exhibited in 1857. He was only 23 when he painted 'The Sick Child'. For many years afterwards, he was almost an invariable exhibitor at the Academy and a popular one too. The work which called forth an immediate popular applause remained typical of all his subsequent output, and 'Early Promise', done twenty years later, showed how he continued to concern himself with the construction of pictures, that conveyed a simple domestic, story with a dominating npote of tender feeling. A good many of his works on same lines, as this 'Early Promise' exhibited in 1877 having been engraved. ... P.E.B."

Western Times 7 May 1918

"FOLKESTONE EXHIBITION OF PICTURES AT THE MUSEUM To the Editor, Sir, – No doubt your readers will be interested to know that the F.J. Dickins's collection of pictures in the Art Gallery of the Museum and Free Library has been replaced by an important loan from the National Gallery, Millbank, (formerly known as the 'Tate Gallery'). The examples are fifteen in number, and taking them consecutively, from the left on entrance, and following on, comprise 'King Charles' Spaniels', by Sir Edwin Landseer; 'A Disciple', Sir John Everett Millais; 'The Last In', William Mulready; ... 'Early Promise' by Joseph Clark; 'Study of a Lion', by Sir Edwin Landseer ... two pictures by Sir Edwin Landseer, 'Uncle Tom and his Wife for Sale', ... And two others presented by Sir Philip Sassoon , and painted by Mrs. Sassoon from the nuclei of what, when some more donors appear, will be a permanent gallery worthy of the town. Will those who can spare a fine picture or so, remember Folkestone's need in this direction? Penny handbook of the National Gallery pictures, now exhibited, will be on sale shortly. A.M. BROWNE-ANDERSON, The Director, Art Gallery and Museum. Folkestone."

Folkestone, Hythe, Sandgate & Cheriton Herald 2 September 1922

Death

Joseph spent his last years in Ramsgate and died on 4 July 1926 – his 92nd birthday. Annie died in 1928.

The New Church Magazine in its October-December 1926 edition reported that Joseph had been been induced to write some of his reminiscences for The Athenaeum magazine shortly before his death and reprinted extracts. These included:

"It is, I think, the experience of most persons who are advanced in life to remember vividly the events of childhood than those of recent times; and to those who, like myself, have been blessed with the loving influence of a dear mother, this experience is especially the case. ... I was the youngest of a large family, several of whom died in infancy. My father died when I was quite young, and my remembrance of him is very slight. ... I afterwards went to Dorchester to a school conducted by William Barnes, the well-known author of poems in the Dorset dialect, many of them very beautiful and dear to all lovers of Dorset. ...

After the death of my father, my eldest brother continued the business, to which he added that of tailor. For this purpose, it was necessary to engage the services of a cutter from London, named David, who came and settled in the village. His residence in London had made him acquainted with picture exhibitions and art generally, and happening to see some of my drawings and to think favourably of them, he strongly advised my mother to give me the advantage of an art education in London. To this end it was, of course, necessary that I should reside in London. As I was the youngest and only unmarried son, my dear mother decided to accompany me there. ...

I can well remember my first introduction to the school [*J M Leigh's*] We were shown into a dark hall, at the end of which were green baize curtains, and immediately in front of these came steps leading down to the gallery. It was a novel sight to me to see the students at work drawing from casts that lined each side of the gallery and among which were the Fighting and Dying Gladiators. ...

During the time of my studentship at Leigh's gallery' the craze for table turning broke out and Mr Leigh was deeply smitten by it. ... I was careful to refrain from any conscious pressure and have every reason to believe that my companions were no less so. After waiting a short time, a slight movement would be felt in the table and this would increase in speed until we had to run. ...

Mr. Clark's genre was essentially and characteristically domestic; his love was the love of home. He pictured the scenes of home; the sanctities of home-life; its joys, its tenderness, its pathos. He shows us the pure family affections; brooding motherhood; fatherly pride; childhood's appealing ways. And all his thoughts are 'good thoughts'; you can see it plainly in our work. He is 'right by nature' and the free children of God are with him all the time ...

It is distinctly as a painter of domestic scenes that Mr. Clark has made himself famous; and through the simple incidents of the common life, portrayed with rarest sympathy and skill, he has succeeded in reaching the hearts of the people. His pictures awaken gentle feelings and tender memories in us all. They show us familiar things, and deal with themes that present no difficulty to the understanding. We seem to know the people he depicts. ... Here are works of art, emotional rather than intellectual."

New Church Magazine Oct–Dec 1926

This assessment is important in confirming the spiritual framework within which Joseph worked.

The Times printed a lengthy obituary in August 1926:

"Mr. Joseph Clark who died recently on his 92nd birthday, was formerly a very well known and popular painter. For many years he produced subject pictures, scenes of the homely rural life of his native Dorset, which when exhibited, and also when multiplied in reproductions moved and delighted great numbers of people in each generation of his long working career. Mr. Clark was born in Cerne Abbas, Dorset, where his father was a draper, and was taught by William Barnes, the Dorset poet. He early showed a great fondness for drawing and expressed an earnest wish to be an artist, but his mother who had been left a widow, apprenticed him in Huntingdonshire.

When he was 18 his mother, yielding to his entreaties, settled with him in London that he might study painting regularly. For two years he attended Mr. J.M. Leigh's studio in Newman Street, and then passed on to the Royal Academy schools, which were then in the National Gallery building in Trafalgar Square. In 1857, when he was 23, he made a reputation with his first picture 'The Sick Child' at the Royal Academy, and another 'the Dead Rabbit' at the British Institution, proved hardly less popular. Two of his pictures were bought for the Chantrey Bequest and are now in the Tate Gallery – 'Early Promise' (1877) and 'Mother's Darling' (1885). For 60 years from 1857 to 1916 his work was rarely absent from each Royal Academy exhibition. The titles alone are almost enough to indicate both the character and the limitations of his art, such as 'The Doctor's visit', 'The draught players', 'The Wanderer', 'Restored', 'The Return of the Runaway', 'The Empty Cradle', 'Private and Confidential', 'Wandering Minstrels' and 'Three Little Kittens'. Many of his works have been engraved and in that form have found a large sale. His last picture at the Academy 'Tales from Flanders' was painted when he was 82. Mr. Clark was a member of the New Church (Swedenborgian) He was married and leaves a son and three daughters."

The Times 19 August 1926

The Dorset County Chronicle and Somersetshire Gazette also published an obituary reading:

"But few of our readers probably remember a very distinguished son of Dorset, Joseph Clark, the painter, who, as recorded last week died at Ramsgate where he had lived for some years. He was educated by William Barnes, the Dorset poet, at his school at No. 40 South Street, Dorchester. He went, as a young man, to London to study art at Leigh's School in Newman Street, Oxford Street, from whence he passed into the schools of the Royal Academy, which were then in Trafalgar Square before Burlington House days. Leslie, Storey, Marks and Calderon, whose names are famous in British art, were Clark's fellow students. He exhibited at the Royal Academy for half a century, and through all these years, though he continued to live in London, he carried with him impressions of the beauty of Dorset rustic life, painting the people and them. Two of his paintings bought by the Chantrey Fund may be seen in the Tate Gallery. Joseph Clark bought honour to his native county, and his passing at the venerable age of 92 will be sincerely regretted. The simple unaffected beauty of his art and the homeliness of their themes have by popular reproductions made his works familiar in thousands of homes."

Other papers did not report his passing. The exception was:

"News in brief – Mr. Joseph Clark, who died recently on his 92nd birthday, was formerly a very well known and popular painter. For many years produced subject pictures, scenes of the homely rural life of his native Dorset, which when exhibited and also when multiplied in reproductions moved and delighted great numbers of people in each generation of his long working career."

Gloucester Citizen 19 August 1926 and **Gloucester Journal** 21 August 1926

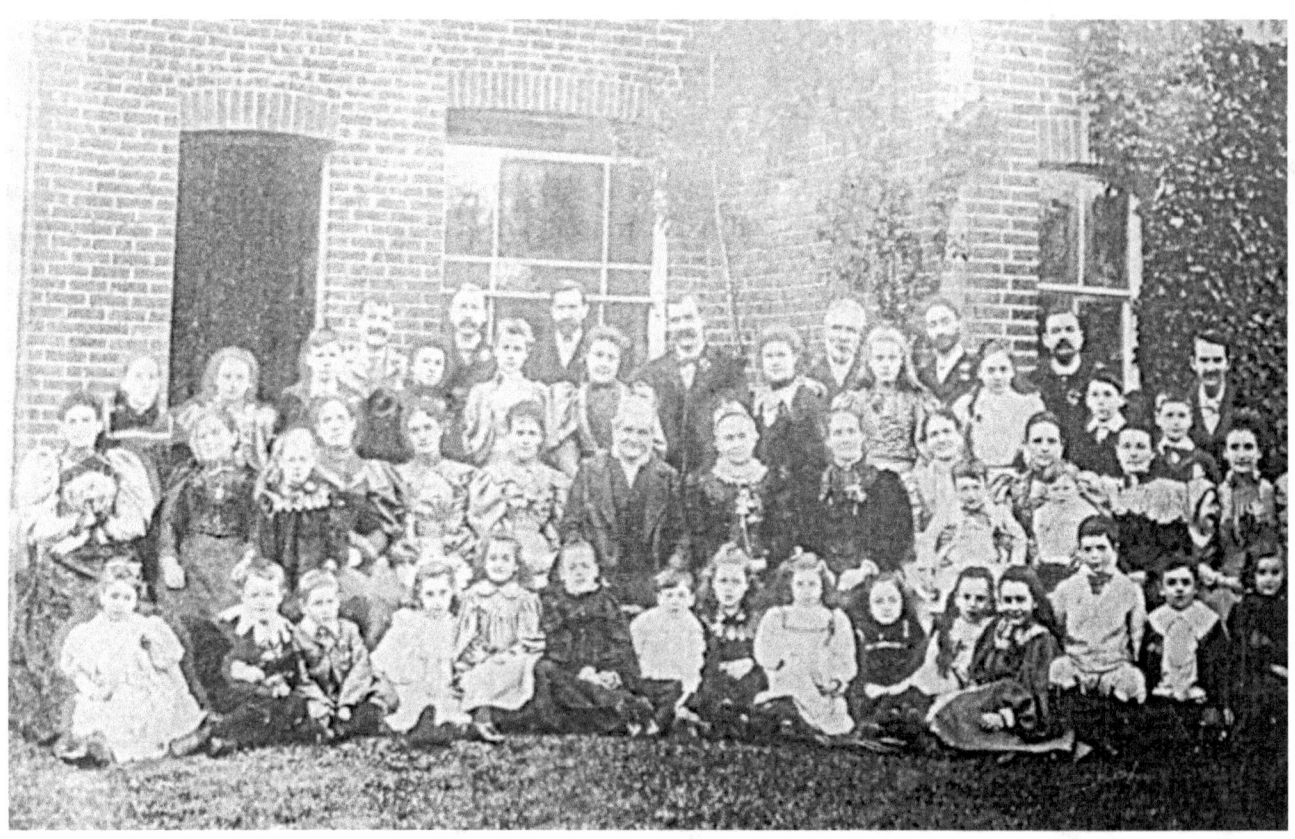

18. Golden wedding of John and Anne Jones, 22 April 1896. (Courtesy the artist's family)

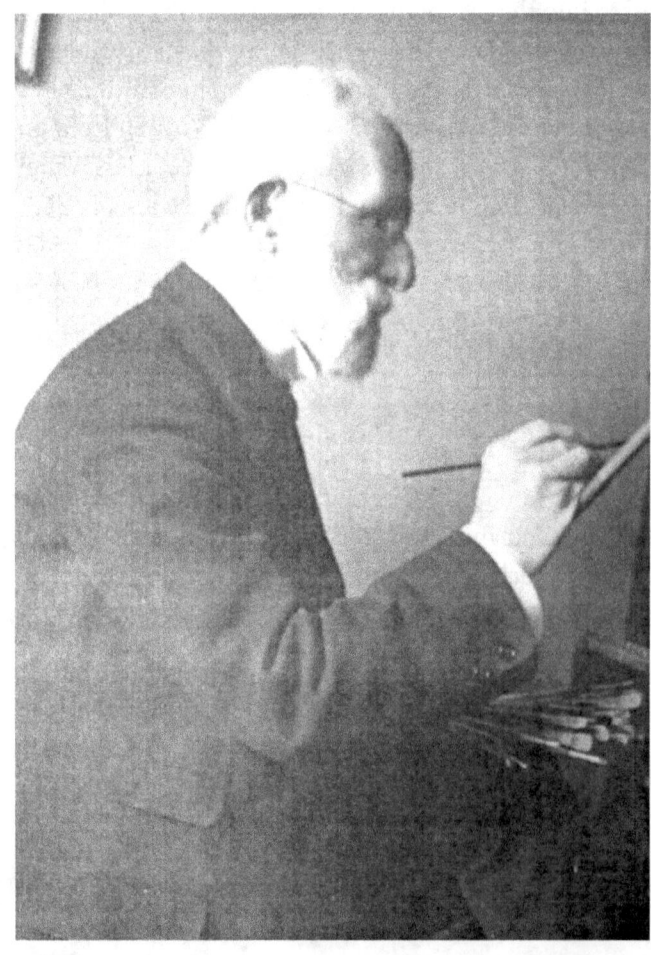

19. Joseph Clark at work (*c.*1900).
(Courtesy the artist's family)

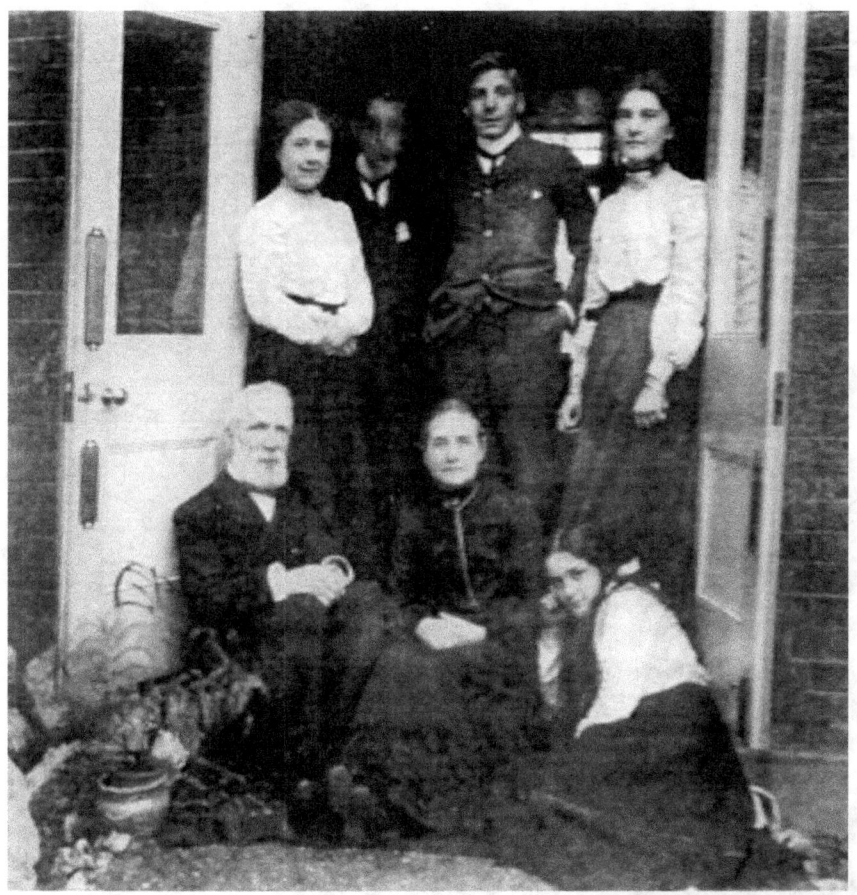

20. Joseph Clark and his family (1904). *Back left to right* – Annie Susan, Wilfrid, an unknown friend and Elsie. *Front left to right* – Joseph, Annie and Margaret. (Courtesy the artist's family)

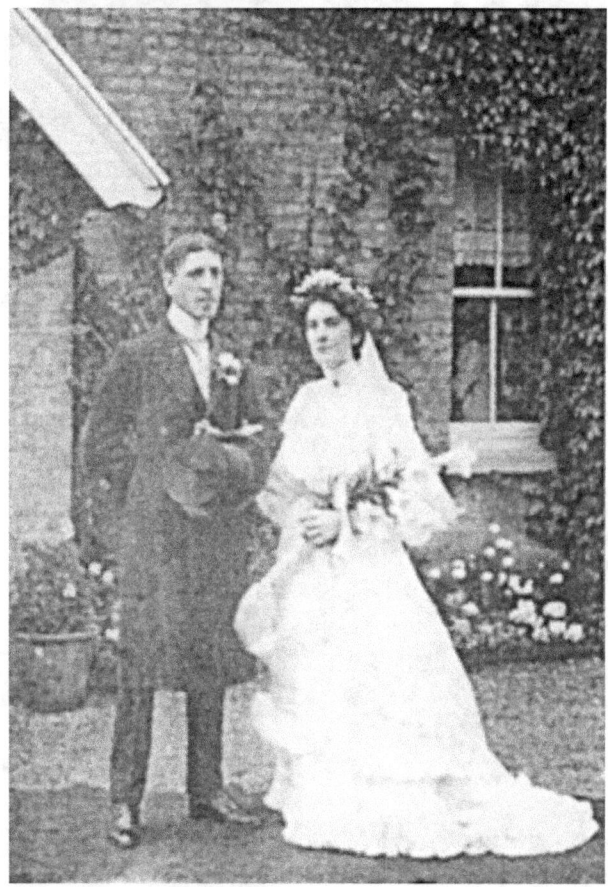

21. Elsie and John Edward Dixon-Spain on their wedding day 23 August 1905. (Courtesy the artist's family)

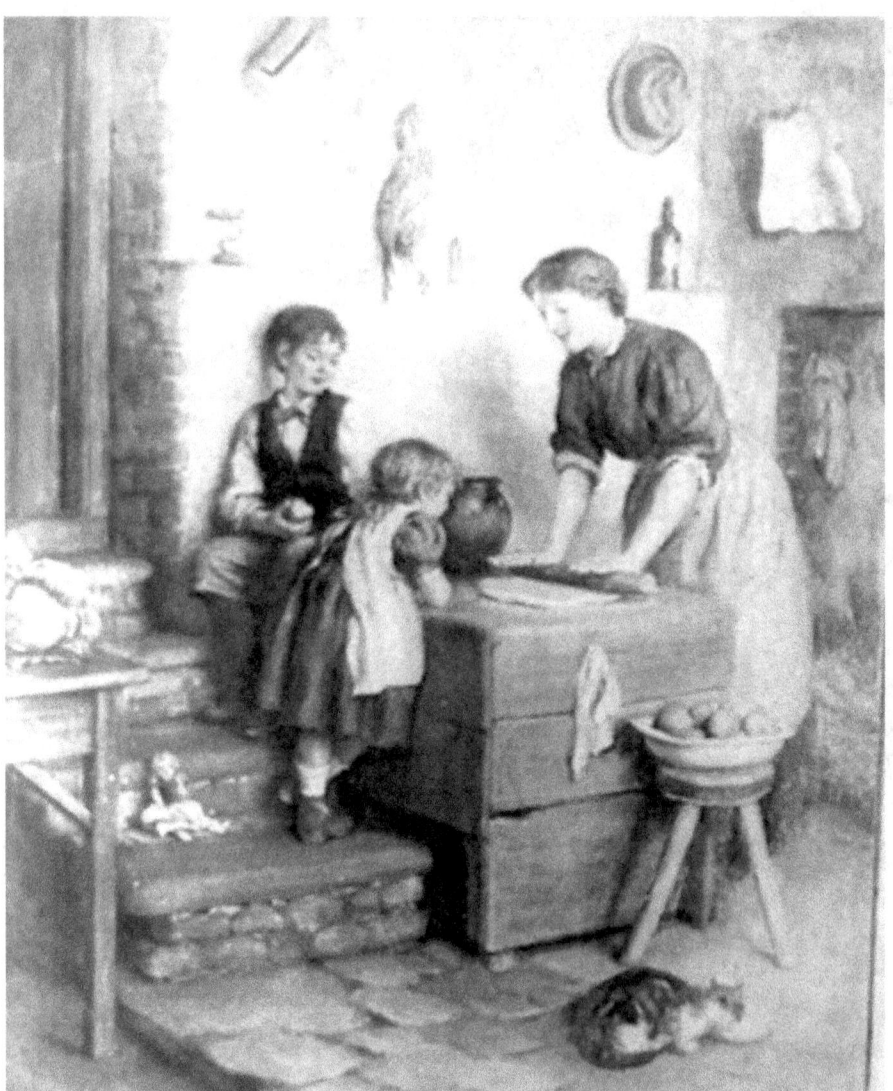

22. 'The Farmers Woldest Dater' (1908). (Courtesy Sothebys)

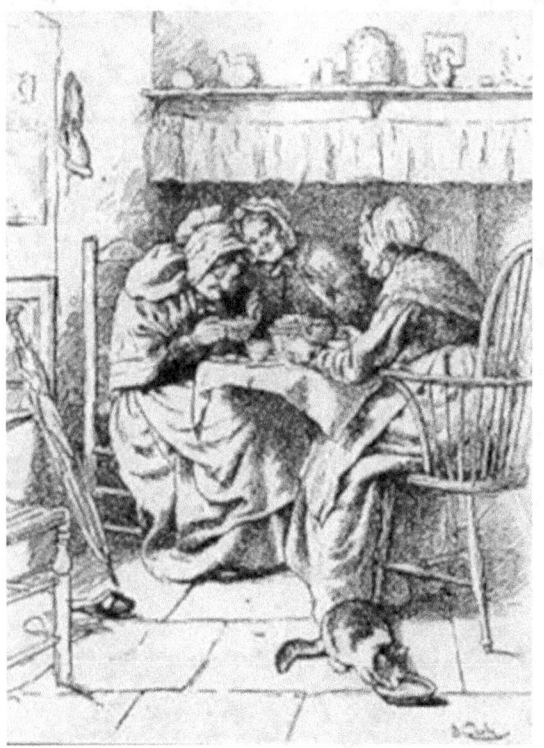

23. Drawing for 'The Cup that Cheers' (1890). (Courtesy Victoria and Albert Museum)

24. After Many Years used in an advertisement.
Source: Derby Daily Telegraph, 2 February 1909.
(Courtesy British Newspaper Archive)

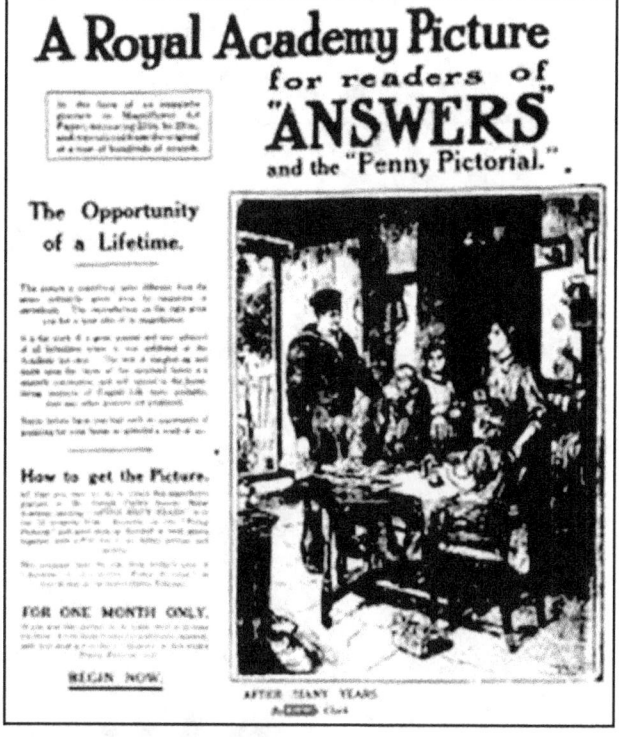

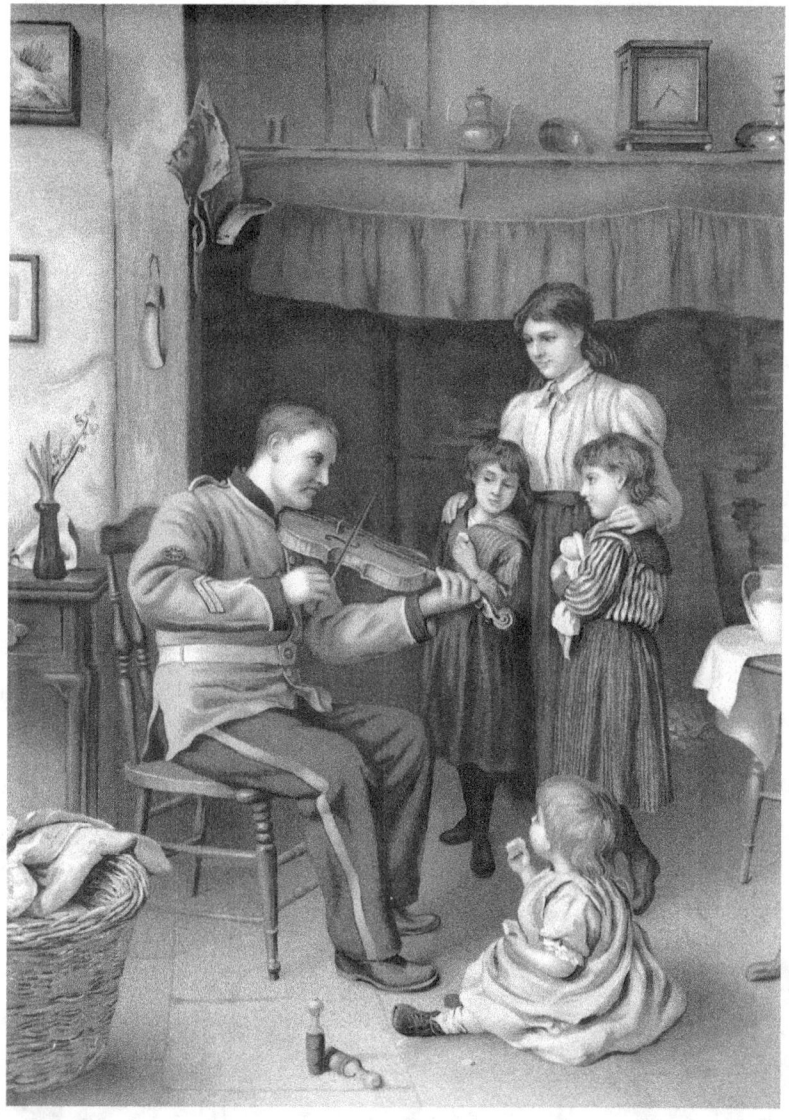

25. 'Soldier of the Queen' (1890s).

PART III

Appreciating Joseph's Total Output

NINE

Joseph Clark's works

The previous chapters have charted the course of Joseph Clark's life and career with comments on individual works. This chapter looks at the whole body of his work.

As far as we know Joseph did not articulate in any detail or subscribe to a specific set of artistic ideals that shaped the way he selected and developed his subjects, equivalent – for example – to the PRB manifesto. He gave the two interviews to journalists. This does not mean that we cannot develop an impression of how his works fit together to facilitate an assessment of whether he was successful in artistic, financial or other terms.

We have seen in earlier chapters that Joseph was a hard working artist who maintained a steady flow of paintings worthy of exhibition in the major exhibition societies. We do not know how many works he produced in total nor what happened to many of them over the century and a half since he began exhibiting.

What do we know about his overall output?

Table 5. Joseph's exhibited works.

Venue	Year	No. of works
Royal Academy	1857–1916	104
Royal Society of Oil Painters (and its forerunners)	1883–1915	71
Royal Society of British Artists	1865–1876	4
The Dudley	1878	2
International Exhibitions – 10 pictures – 7 previously exhibited in Britain	1862–1910	7
Liverpool Autumn Exhibition	1880	1
Manchester Royal Jubilee Exhibition, Victirian Era' exhibition (Earl's Court) and Guildhall Jubilee exhibition – all pictures previously exhibited elsewhere	1887	3

We know that he showed at least 190 works at major exhibitions, he also exhibited elsewhere including, for example, an unknown work in an exhibition while living in Winchester towards the end of the nineteenth century. He also made numerous drawings and some water-colours.

Beyond the exhibited works, we know the titles of about 220 others attributed to him. Some of these, perhaps 10%, are almost certainly misattributions. This means that in total we know the titles of about four hundred of his works giving an annual average of six works a year. Joseph was by no means the most prolific painter in the nineteenth and early twentieth centuries. Reynolds (1987) says that a detailed catalogue of William Maw Egley's works contain over one thousand historical and contemporary genre works between 1840 and 1910.

Looking at the 400 works attributed to Joseph, an important question is whether they provide a balanced view of his total output. We know that most of Joseph's works went to private buyers, whether direct from exhibitions, at auction or as a result of commissions. Portraits present a particular problem in this respect. Many stayed within the sitter's family passing from generation to generation thereby never having been in the public domain. These will often be treasured possessions but some owners may have little interest in the artist. Works of all types may have been lost, stolen or destroyed since they were sold, especially during the two world wars. Some were lost by accident and others destroyed by people who failed to appreciate their financial or artistic value. So the simple answer is that we do not know how representative the 'known works' are of his entire output.

We have images of about eighty five of Joseph's works (about 20%) compiled from the internet, auction and gallery listings and from contemporary books, magazines or newspapers. More previously unknown works attributed to Joseph appear in auctions each year. Thirteen original oils are in UK public galleries; only one of which is on pemanent display; and there are between thirty and forty drawings, water colours and sketches in the Victoria and Albert Museum.

Compiling a full list of Joseph's works

Inevitably, any listing of an artist's work however carefully compiled will be incomplete and contain some inaccuracies. This arises from the inherent difficulty of making correct attributions of works long after their creation, the loss of some works over the period since the artist was active and similar factors. This section explores the impact of this in assessing Joseph's work.

What counts as a separate work of Art?

The first difficulty in compiling a full list of Joseph's work is about what should count as a separate work of art. We know Joseph achieved his mastery of fine detail in his works by using numerous detailed drawings of the main characters, their gestures and the background details. He also used watercolour sketches of complete works. Rosemary Chiles (2011) includes several of these that are now on the Victoria and Albert Museum's website. Are these separate works or simply experimental tools?

We have images of a fifth of Joseph's known paintings, that can help identify misattributions and resolve problems where several works have similar names. Likewise, contemporary descriptions in press articles, art journals and contemporary books can help with attribution of works. For experts the colours used, brushstrokes and other technical detail provide additional material to aid attribution.

A second difficulty is that Joseph, like others in his generation, used some preparatory sketches and detailed drawings to create several works. For example, the front row of boys in 'Waifs and Strays' exhibited in 1882 reappear at from slightly different angle in 'Red Letter Day' shown in 1896. In this case, these are clearly two distinct works albeit with a similar theme using the same models. Again, like other artists he had 'favoured' models captured in different works. Sometime the use of particular models helps support a tentative attribution. The elderly man in 'Feeding time' (1903) and 'Treat for Puppy' (1897) seem to be from the same model.

Thirdly, like many in his generation, Joseph 'recycled' his creative ideas, sometimes with different names but also as a new 'take' on an idea or title used previously. He also occasionally made copies of his own works for sale. One good source of images for works where we have only a name, especially in the second half of his career, are the woodcuts he prepared for exhibition catalogues, especially those of the Institute of Painters in Oil Colours. The 1883 catalogue includes woodcuts of 'The Humming Top' and 'Hampshire Dairyman'.

Fourthly, several advertising campaigns mentioned earlier presented Joseph's work to a wider public. Again, the question arises of whether such advertisements are separate works or simply alternative media through which Joseph's original artistic conception reached a wider audience. Some advertisers 'enhanced' works to improve the fit with their 'brand images'.

One critical element in deciding whether a print, woodcut or advertisement is a separate work is the degree of any involvement by the original artist in its preparation. In the nineteenth century, the sale of an artwork transferred the rights from the artist to the purchaser. This means that an artist might not have been aware of or approved the use of his work in these ways; let alone receive any financial reward.

Attributing a work to Joseph

The second major difficulty in compiling a comprehensive list of an artist's work is that of attribution. One element in this is that many artists were inconsistent in signing or dating their works, although in this respect Joseph was more consistant than many others but even his signatures vary over time – though the underlining flowing from the capital 'C' occurs frequently (see plate 5).

A second element in attribuition arises when several artists in the same generation have similar names and work on similar subjects using similar styles. There were at least five other artists working in the nineteenth century in the contemporary genre field called Clark or Clarke. Some of Joseph's contemporaries, critics and modern commentators tend to be inconsistent, even within a short piece, in spelling the surname 'Clark' often adding an 'e'. This confuses auction houses, galleries, online print dealers and elsewhere where paintings are catalogued or sold. Anyone searching for images of works by Joseph needs to be mindful of this potential confusion and treat all attributions with great caution.

The most important of these other 'Clark(e)' painters were:

- James Clark was a fellow member of the Royal Institute of Oil Painters. He also exhibited occasionally at the RA and the New English Art Club. There is a degree of confusion between their works, most significantly in relation to 'Christmas Dole' (1889) mentioned earlier.
- Joseph Clayton Clarke (1856–1937) worked under the pseudonym 'Kyd' and is best known for his illustrations of characters from the novels of Charles Dickens. His other work includes cigarette cards, postcards and a range of paintings (mainly water colours). His works are distinctive in subject and style and therefore rarely confused with Joseph's but it happens from time to time, especially when using Internet search engines.
- Joseph Dixon Clark (1849–1944) who worked in oils produced landscapes with cattle or depicting rural activities. He lived and worked in Blaydon and Durham for some time and five of his works were selected for RA exhibitions between 1890 and 1902, and at the New English Art Club (1893). Again, his subject matter and palette are distinctive and should not be confused with Joseph's.
- Samuel Joseph Clark (1834–1912) concentrated on pictures of horses, animals and farmyard scenes. He used a variety of signatures, including S. Clark, S.J. Clark (often with the J running down through the S), Saml. J. Clark and S. Jas. Clark; adding to the scope for confusion. Samuel exhibited eight works at the British Institution between 1856 and 1864 but did not exhibit at other major art societies. Again their works ought not to be confused but they are from time to time.
- Joseph Benwell Clark (1857–1938), Joseph's nephew produced some genre works similar in style and subject matter to those of his uncle. His finest paintings, done between the mid 1890s and 1920 were landscapes, many with horses and other animals. In 1894, he helped to found the school of Animal Painting. He also worked as a book illustrator and did humorous drawings for Judy before it amalgamated with Punch. Their works and names are often confused in listings of various kinds. Joseph Benwell Clark adopted the name 'Benwell', drawn from earlier generations in the family, to avoid confusion – and may have experimented with adding an 'e' to Clark.

Even where works are unsigned, an artist can often be identified by a distinctive technique, style and subject or by reference to contemporary descriptions of their works. This is more straightforward when working with originals than with photographic images of variable quality; although unfortunately this is the main media we have to study Joseph's paintings and drawings today.

A useful further step in considering the attribution of any painting to Joseph is whether the subject matter and treatment is typical of Joseph. He is best known of these 'Clark' artists, in terms of domestic genre works, inclusion in major exhibitions and the prices reached at auction. This creates an incentive for some to attribute works to our Joseph or to accept earlier attributions without sufficient critical attention.

The third element in creating confusion in attributing works arises as some paintings suffer from an 'identity crisis'. By this, I mean owners forget, misremember or change the names of works over time. This is common where works pass between distant relatives from different generations over a century or more. When works come up for sale, they sometimes acquire a descriptive title, perhaps one with greater appeal to modern art buyers. One example may be the work known variously as 'Children at Play' or 'Playing Doctors'. There is the possibility that some works attributed to Joseph, especially on websites, without a title or date that may turn out to be works where we have only a title. This book uses original titles drawn from contemporary exhibition catalogues or press accounts but adds a note of widely used alternative titles.

Internet sources

The information in this chapter about websites was correct in early 2015. The content and range of websites with art images changes frequently and rapidly. A general search for Joseph's paintings using the major internet search engines will bring up many images that have nothing to do with Joseph. Most 'hits' have a 'click through' facility to an original website holding the image that often has information about the artist, a brief description of the work, its history, location, copyright status or sale prices. Some images of varying quality appear on several web sites. Broadly there are four main groups of websites where Joseph's work can be found.

The first group are from museums and galleries including the eight UK galleries holding works by Joseph. The Victoria and Albert Museum's website is particularly useful as it has images of numerous drawings and sketches by Joseph donated by Rosemary Chiles. The 'Your Paintings' website, covers the UK's national collection of paintings, the stories behind them and where to see them. In late 2014 it included seven images of works by Joseph and three by Joseph Benwell Clark. Its coverage depends critically on the collecting policies of the national institutions during Joseph's lifetime and their subsequent disposal policies.

The second group are art valuation sites. These give details of works of art sold at auction in recent years; some with listings going back twenty five years. Many limit access to images and other data to fee-paying subscribers, although most have 'taster' rates for short term use. 'Art Price' and 'Artvalue.com' have several works attributed to Joseph. Many auction houses have websites with copies of online catalogues with images and descriptions of works handled over the past decade or so. Isolating works by specific artists can be time consuming and subject to errors made at the time of sale.

The third group come from companies offering modern prints or hand painted copies of works by Joseph. 'All Posters', that claims to offer the best selection of posters and art prints in the world, has nine works by Joseph. 'Art.com' offers a selection of art and décor items including prints, posters, photography, fine art reproductions and limited edition prints. It too has nine works attributed to Joseph.

The final group includes an eclectic range of sites. Several aim to help people seeking information about specific artists and their works. 'Art Net' offers facilities for buying, selling and researching art online. The 'Art Net Galleries' provide information from 2,200 galleries in over 250 cities dealing with 166,000 works by over 39,000 artists. 'Artchive Web Gallery' has information on more than 10,000 artists and images of 150,000 paintings. It includes eleven works attributed to Joseph, two of which are almost certainly by other artists. 'Mutual Art.com', an online art information service, has details of 200,000 arts related articles from over 250 magazines, newspapers and journals. 'Wikigallery' has 14 Images but 6 of these are doubtful or by Samuel Joseph Clark. 'E-Bay' often has images of works attributed to Joseph, mainly prints. Then there are various 'art blogs' with images of Joseph's works. For example, the 'I am a Child' Art Blog has has good quality images on the theme of children in art history includes twenty works by Joseph. 'Golden Age Paintings' has three works by Joseph. Facebook has several groups dealing with art interests, some of which feature Joseph's works from time to time.

Galleries

While images on web sites are a useful way of building an appreciation of works attributed to Joseph, nothing compares with seeing original works. Sadly few original works by Joseph can be seen in public art galleries. Chiles (2010) lists twelve oil paintings or sketches held in eight British gallery collections.

Table 6. Joseph's works in Public galleries.

Gallery	Works
Graves Art Gallery, Sheffield	'Labourer's Reward' (1866)
Newport, Gwent	'The Draughts Players' (1859)
Sunderland Art Gallery	'Doctor's Visit' (1858)
Lang Art Gallery, Newcastle	'Return of the Runaway' (1862)
Tate Britain, London	'Early Promise' (1877) 'Mother's Darling' (1885)
Bentlif Gallery, Maidstone	'Home from the War' (1901) 'Chip of the Old Block' (1905) 'The Pianist' (1912) 'A birthday party' (1913)
Mercer Gallery, Harrogate	Print of etching of 'Sick Child' (1857) 'Still life with Marrow, caulifliower and red cabbage (ukn) Young Girl at easel (ukn) – oil sketch
Victoria and Albert Museum, London	Collection of sketches, drawings and water colours donated by Rosemary Chiles and other family members.

The distribution of works around the country reflects the artistic tastes of influential local people towards the end of the nineteenth century. At the end of 2014, only the 'Doctor's Visit' (1858) was on general view to the public but most galleries offer access to works not on display by prior application to the gallery concerned. Contact details are on each gallery's website. It is disappointing that the National Trust's large art collection does not contain any works by Joseph, probably reflecting the preferences of the nineteenth century owners of the properties the Trust manages.

Occasionally private galleries offer Joseph's works for sale. They need contacting before visiting as the works are often in store. The Society of London Art dealers' website has details of 160 private galleries across the country – with a useful facility to search for gallery by specialism. At the end of 2014, none of these listed works was by Joseph Clark.

Books and Journals

Over the past hundred and fifty years, various books, newspapers and journals included illustrations of works by Joseph. Copies are available in some universities, specialist art libraries and archives. Almost all of these collections have online catalogues for public use. 'Internet Archive' is a valuable source for full electronic versions of books by Joseph's contemporaries and later authors. Some of these have contemporary engravings or early photographs of Joseph's works. However locating them is difficult as the Internet Archive's search focuses on the author's name, journal and title of the work.

In Britain, the National Art Library (NAL) based in the Victoria and Albert Museum is invaluable and has a large collection of original art auction catalogues; many of which have images of the works sold. The Library and associated archves have long runs of exhibition catalogues stretching back into the nineteenth century, some with engravings or photographs of the paintings displayed. The NAL catalogue is online and its staff are extremely knowledgeable and helpful. For visitors to the NAL, up to date technology allows readers to take good quality copies of images in books and magazines for private study by downloading to data sticks or emailing to their home computers.

The Royal Academy and Tate Britain have extensive archives containing original documents; some of which contain contemporary images or references to Joseph's work. Both are in London and need advance notice of visitors and the materials required. The British Library and the Westminster Art Library have good well indexed collections. All the libraries and archives have websites explaining procedures for ordering books and other materials.

What did Joseph paint?

In assessing whether a particular picture is by Joseph, irrespective of any earlier attributions, an important factor is considering whether it is consistent with his known works, although this can lead to missing experimental and uncharacteristic works that would add depth to our understanding of his overall output.

Art reference books tend to describe Joseph Clark as a painter of the domestic genre. They elaborate by reference to rural indoor settings, many with children, capturing the spirit of family and rural life in nineteenth century England. They also refer to his use of playful titles. Some follow Richard Redgrave (1866) in highlighting the moral worth of genre paintings through their capacity to 'stimulate compassion for social injustice'. Redgrave's conception of genre art went well beyond that espoused by Wedmore (1880) quoted earlier. Some later critics following the lead given by the proponents of aesthetic and later movements confuse Joseph's capacity for stimulating empathy for the people depicted with excessive sentimentality.

These shorthand descriptions of Victorian genre fail to capture the volume or complexity of Joseph's total output. They omit any reference to works such as privately commissioned portraits or outdoor scenes that rarely reached exhibitions or came to critical attention. Conversely they over emphasise works exhibited at the RA and the Royal Institute of Oil Painters that caught the contemporary public's imagination. In Joseph's case, works featuring children remained in the public consciousness for up to a century and a half, whilst others those inspired by national events, proverbs and poetry have not.

A broad assessment of Joseph's known works identifies at least seven distinct subject areas. The rough percentages shown against each category draw on an analysis of the eighty or so images available in 2014.

Table 7. Subjects painted by Joseph Clark.

Subject area	%
Pictures of everyday and special family events, usually joyful occasions such as Christmas, homecomings, shopping or visits from grandparents. Many of these works show the interaction between three generations – children, parents and grandparents and several show people in work settings	50%
Studies of children in routine settings but without adults reflecting Joseph's statement that 'I am always much interested in children and their pathetic expression when they are ill appeals very strongly to me.'	25%
Groups of figures in communal settings such as schoolrooms, orphanages or almshouses	5%
Works inspired by special events such as Queen Victoria's Jubilee in 1897, and the impact of the Boer and Great Wars on families 'at home'	5%
Portraits, some of family members and others commissioned by reasonably affluent middle class families or neighbours	5%
Scenes inspired by well-known proverbs, quotations from major poets and Bible stories	5%
Miscellaneous works	5%

The broad proportion of works in different categories remained constant throughout his career. Of the fifty or so images featuring family events, eighteen feature the interaction between children and grandparents; seven depict childhood illness; and six household chores such as washing or cleaning.

Any inferences drawn from this brief analysis must be highly speculative as we have so few images of Joseph's works. When the full list of titles attributed to Joseph is taken into account, his output is more complex than suggested by the images in the public domain. This complexity would be consistent with what we know from Drummond (1950) about Joseph's education and the place of reading within his daily routine.

Many of Joseph's works came from his reflections on his life experiences, literary works and broad themes used by other artists or writers. Examples of these themes include 'The Doctor's Visit' (Royal Academy – 1858) following in the brush strokes of Jan Steen, Jan Havicksz, Frans van Mieris the Elder and Egbert Van Heemskerk III; and 'Hagar & Ishmael' (Royal Academy – 1860) in those of Guercino, Gioacchino Assereto, Barent Fabritius and Benjamin West. Later his career, his interpretations of subjects used by his contemporaries. A good example is 'Blowing Bubbles' (1889). Well over forty artists produced works entitled 'Blowing Bubbles' during Joseph's lifetime. These included Mary Allingham, Claude Monet, Théophile-Emmanuel Duverger and John Everett Millais. Another example is 'Over the Garden Wall' exhibited by Joseph at he Society of Oil Painters in 1898 and 1906.

What was Joseph trying to achieve through his works?

In thinking about Joseph's works, we need to recall that he was less interested in demonstrating his artistic virtuosity and creativity than in communicating his ideas about society and personal behaviour to a wide audience.

A crucial theme for Joseph was that of people in distress through illness, old age or separation from loved ones. Numerous Victorian painters and writers attempted to demonstrate their empathy with ordinary people at a time when the awareness of the harsh conditions experienced during successive economic downturns was growing. Joseph's exceptional sensitivity to the impact of these conditions came from his experience of living in the declining rural area around Cerne Abbas and close to overcrowded parts of London. His friendship with Francis Oliver Finch and time as a New Church deacon stimulated the emphasis he gave to positive aspects of life for people even in the poorest settings. Thus, he avoided both the overly sentimental or brutal styles adopted by some contemporaries. His works reminded people of their good fortune in having a caring loving family or living in a strong local community at a time when so many people lived isolated lives distant from family and friends. His aims were to raise awareness that too many people did not appreciate or enjoy these benefits and had to endure hardships alone.

Linked to this was the distress caused by separation from loved ones. His works highlighted the extent to which such isolation was not always permanent. Some partings in his works are short lived. Examples include the couplet 'The wanderer' and 'Restored' (1861) while others depict long awaited reunions, including 'Return of the Runaway' (1862). Sadly, some separations depicted were permanent for example in 'The empty cradle' (1869).

Another theme was the possibilities for improving the situation of those in distress by small changes in personal behaviour especially by the more fortunate. Joseph hoped those in better circumstances would reflect on how they could make a difference to the lives of those in distress. His aim was to help others recognise that combinations of individual and collective actions would make the world a better and more humane place. This approach had its roots in the positive outlook at the heart of his Swedenborgian faith. The strong desire to communicate these ideas helps explain his sustained output, consistency of subject matter and efforts to widen his audience. It also suggests that he was far more interested in this wider audience than the close-knit rather inward-looking world of the artistic community, especially that of wealthy connoisseurs, fashionable critics and celebrity artists.

Joseph was not afraid of tackling the aspects of nineteenth century life that created acute distress for many people most notably through rural poverty, old age, the illness and death of children or the personal implications of rapid industrialisation and urbanisation. These implications including the growth of large-scale and impersonal businesses, the adoption of new 'deskilling' technologies and the inability of over stretched public services to keep pace with population growth. Many of his contemporaries or later critics did not understand the roots or motivations for his work. Without a good grasp of Joseph's family background and faith, it might be easy to see why some who thought his work overly sentimental and ignorant of the impact of the economic and social consequences of the rapid change in nineteenth century Britain. They thought his work lacked a proper appreciation of the pain and extreme difficulties these changes produced for hard working families. They also failed to understand his belief in individual action working alongside collective action. For Joseph art was simply a medium for communicating his values to produce a 'healing' response from his audience.

Although there was a serious intent behind much of Joseph's work, he often used humour to reinforce his messages. The guilty dog hiding under the hutch in the 'Dead Rabbit' (1857) is a good early example of this as are the titles of many of his works that suggest humorous or at least unexpected interpretations. This suggests that while Joseph took his work seriously this did not always lead him to great solemnity in his works.

Narrative and story telling in Joseph's works

Like many other genre artists, Joseph made extensive use of story telling in his works to stimulate the imagination of his audience and encourage them to think about the implications of the 'storyline' for their behaviour and attitudes.

One aspect of this was Joseph's narrative abilities was to create a moment of suspense in the scene presented. For example, in the 'Return of the Runaway' (1862) (plate 11), the viewer is left wondering what was happening before the runaway entered – something known today as the 'backstory' and the emotions of the characters. Joseph also asks the viewer to speculate on what might might be about to happen next. How will the family react at the sudden arrival of the long separated relative, if indeed he is a relative? Will he be accepted back into the family? Had he returned for good or was he paying a flying visit between voyages? Joseph like many mid-Victorian critics thought the public needed to be told the story to illustrate, understand and assimilate the artist's central argument. The Times critic reviewing the 'Return of the Runaway' devoted some 850 words to just one of the hundreds of pictures in the 1862 British Institution exhibition. In reading such reviews, we are left wondering if the critic is reporting verbatum what the artist said to them or if it the critic's imagination talking to us.

Another aspect of story telling was the intense effort he put into using clothes, artifacts, ornaments and other domestic items to enrich the narrative by communicating a wide range of information about the characters and their interests, relationships and lifestyles. These add emotional depth and spiritual dimension to our interpretation to what is happening. The ornaments in 'Return of the Runaway' (1862) tell us much about the household's interest in the sea – maps, shells and pictures on the walls and mantelshelf. That said, some contemporary critics thought that Joseph's works were too detailed and crowded with one writing disparagingly of his propensity' to scatter props around his works'. He felt these reduced the impact of the main themes of his works on the viewer. It is not clear whether these comments represent a shortage of time, lack of imagination on the part of the critic or a patronising understanding of his readers' capacity to look critically at paintings – perhaps all three.

Such critics were in the minority as seen in the extracts from newspaper reviews in earlier chapters. One unnamed reviewer writing in 1913 said:

> "Since that time (his first entry at the Royal Academy) he has produced pictures which have called forth not only popular applause, but have gained him the reputation of being a master of his craft in all that concerns the construction of a picture, especially in the skill with which he conveys his story and concentrates the interest upon its central figures. This effect is gained not merely by clever construction, but by a wise discrimination which, while it omits nothing vital, rejects superfluous details in favour of essentials. Above all, his pictures are noteworthy for the gentle thought and feeling which reveal the creations of his mind in a mood that is at once sweet and tender".

The following year, George Dunlop Leslie (1914) one of Joseph's contemporaries at the RAS, defined genre art in its broadest historical, literary and moral sense as:

> "… those [pictures that] represent scenes from domestic or moral life, humorous pictures of various sorts, those in which strong dramatic situations or scenes of sentiment or love are depicted and pictures with subjects taken from the greatest dramatists or novelists. In such pictures great care was usually taken in representing the backgrounds, costumes and accessories with archaeological accuracy; the canvasses were of modest dimensions, and the figures introduced into them were always smaller than life."

A closer look at Joseph's work 'Buying a New Hat' (1880) (plate 22) helps to illustrate some aspects of interpreting narrative works. The face of the young girl shows her feelings of happiness at the prospect of a new hat, perhaps one bought to mark an important milestone in her young life. The expression of the younger woman with her back to the viewer is harder to discern, but the glimpse we have suggests both pride and happiness. The older woman, maybe the grandmother, suggests some concern that the hat is right for the occasion. Both may be recalling similar happy events in their lives. The shopkeeper looks on with apprehension to see whether the hat he suggests is finding favour with all three involved in the decision. One has already been tried and set to one side. He is ready to suggest a different style of hat should the need arise. One senses that the shopkeeper knows the family well and he has participated similar transactions with the family in the past – and indeed for many other families. The young shop assistant, although not involved, with his studied attention to the task in hand suggests that he knows the family too. Perhaps the young lady has an older brother who is his friend. The fittings in the well-stocked shop are basic and functional.

Joseph asks his viewers to experience again their feelings when reaching important milestones in their own progress towards adulthood. Can they recall similar treasured moments? Can they draw on the feelings evoked to support younger family members making similar steps in life? Do the retailers want to understand better the varying emotions of their customers to reach a sale acceptable to all?

The composition of the picture also asks viewers to build for themselves a narrative flow, perhaps, from the family's decision to visit the shop, the excited anticipation of the event, their arrival and subsequent to the purchase, their concern to make just the right purchase for a special occasion and the impact it has on her future life. It also asks the viewer to consider the varied contribution of each of the 'actors', including the 'shop boy' and the shopkeeper to the event. This work draws on Joseph's experience of his father's business. As already mentioned the only first-hand description of his father's business we have is Catherine Davies' diary for 1820, records that she visited it to look at the millinery. Given the date of the picture, Joseph's oldest daughter, Poppy, was about ten. Perhaps an important purchase by Annie and Poppy inspired this work. Clearly, Joseph was dealing with a scene and situation with which he was thoroughly familiar. We can also see how Joseph produces the opportunity to engage all elements of a person's being – their feelings, intellect, morals, knowledge, memory, and every other human capacity.

Working methods and models

Another dimension of attributing a work to Joseph is about his working methods. As an artist trained in the classical approach, he used detailed drawings to achieve the skilled draughtsmanship praised by many critics, even those who disliked contemporary genre. The catalogue records for the Victoria and Albert Museum's collection of Joseph's drawings, says that *'Before he started his oil paintings, he normally made a series of precise drawings and expressive watercolours of the chosen subject. He frequently used members of his own family as models.'* While this comment refers to a preparatory drawing for 'Boy Reading' from the early 1890s, it is equally true for a large part of his known works.

Relatively little detailed information is available about the models Joseph used in his paintings. In addition to portraits of family members, his family modelled for other works. As identified by Rosemary Chiles (2010) identified works in which family members acted as models (see Table 8).

One wonders how many of the faces and scenes in other works feature members of the Clark, Jones and associated families; or their acquaintances in Cerne, Christchurch, Winchester or London. Rosemary Chiles (2010) recalls that her father – Joseph's son Wilfrid – mentioned several family visits to Cerne Abbas during his childhood. Thus, it is reasonable to think that he sketched people there and used these drawings in developing his artistic ideas, perhaps some years later.

Some models appeared in more than one work. The elderly balding man with a prominent nose appears as the shopkeeper in 'Buying a New Hat' (1880), the elderly man in 'The Very Image' (1884) (plate 24) and the old man sitting outside the cottage door in 'A Treat for Puppy' (1897). If we had a more complete set of images of Joseph's works, it would be possible to chart the appearance of individual models, the dates they worked for him' and where the drawings were completed.

Table 8. Family members who modelled for Joseph Clark (courtesy Rosemary Chiles).

Figure and Work	Name of Model'	Relationship to Joseph Clark	Year painted
Mother in 'The Sick Child'	Mary Clark	Sister	1857
Woman in 'Draughts Player'	Mary Clark	Sister	1859
Sailor in 'Return of the Runaway'	Nat Clark	Cousin	1863
Mother and child in 'Mother's Darling'	Annie Clark and 'Poppie'	Wife and Daughter	1885
The young artist in 'the very image'	Joseph Benwell Clark	Nephew	1884
The boy in 'The Boy Reading'	Wilfrid Clark	Son	1890s
One of the boys in 'Sweets of Life' (also called 'Favourite fruits' in some sources)	Wilfrid Clark	Son	1893
'Weddin' Morn'	Elsie (Bride) Wilfrid (Groom)	Daughter Son	1909
The young lady in 'The Pianist' Young man listening	Poppie Wilfrid	Daughter Son	1912
'The artist's family' – 'Girl at an easel' Girl watching Boy watching	Margaret Elsie Wilfrid	Daughter Daughter Son	[ukn]

Influences

In a similar vein we might be able to look for signs of the main influences that shaped Joseph's works when attributing works to him. We have a reasonable understanding of where he found inspiration for his works although we do not know if he had difficulty in identifying stimulating subjects. Neville Wallis (1957) records that William Frith had great problems in finding suitable subjects and offered large rewards to people suggesting worthy subjects.

Joseph's choice of career, its development and the subjects depicted in his works responded to important influences in his personal life. As we saw earlier these included his personal experience of family life as a son, husband, father, grandfather and uncle in a large middle class family; his strong religious belief; changes in the art market; the communities where he lived; wider changes in society, its beliefs and aspirations; and significant national events.

Family life and background

As is apparent from earlier chapters family life was a powerful and continuing influence on Joseph's professional life, especially in relation to the subjects depicted. As we have seen, he spent his early years in a household that was no stranger to ill health and death. By his mid-teens his father and two older sisters had died. In middle age, two of his three surviving siblings died within a year. It is hard to see how these events could not have affected him deeply. This sadness was balanced by his evident delight in family events including weddings, arrival of children (his own and numerous nieces and nephews) and significant anniversaries. Thus, family life became a major source of inspiration for his work.

There is strong evidence that the Clarks were a close-knit family offering mutual support in times of need and distress. This gave him a positive view of families and help steer him towards optimistic situations and events. Graham Clark's (2013) unpublished analysis of the homes occupied by the Clarks in Cerne Abbas during the nineteenth century showed the extent to which the property rented from the Pitt-Rivers estate was in some respects 'held in common' by the family. As family units grew, they moved to larger homes and, later as children left home, they moved into smaller accommodation. By the middle of the nineteenth century, the town's economic decline caused this pattern to break down as younger Clarks migrated to London, other large cities and Britain's empire for professional training or employment. Joseph was one of the first to do so. Amongst the few Clarks to return to Cerne were his brother (Edwin) and nephew (Joseph Benwell Clark).

Joseph's marriage to Annie Jones, the second eldest of ten children in a large, prosperous and community minded family from Winchester, reinforced his positive view of family life. This opened up a completely new range of personal experience as he came to know his wife's younger brothers and sisters as they grew to adulthood and in time added to his already large array of nieces and nephews. Naturally, the arrival of his own children gave him the unique experience of fatherhood. The intensity of his experience of fatherhood shows through in the many drawings of his children, and in time, of his grandchildren in the Victoria and Albert Museum's collection. As mentioned earlier, Joseph and Annie in turn played their part in supporting younger Clark and Jones relatives when they came to London. They also spent more than a year with Annie's mother in Winchester around the time of her father's death.

As well as the direct experience of the Clark and Jones families, Joseph also saw many other aspects of contemporary life at first hand. This may have contributed to his use of 'folk wisdom' in the titles of some paintings. Equally he drew on his education as a 'young gentleman' in William Barnes' school for works inspired by telling phrases from major poets including William Barnes himself. The treatment, sometimes humourous, he gave these topics appealed to the emotion as well as to the intellect. Together his works offer a compassionate and tender response towards people of all ages in distress as in the words of Alain de Botton (2012) they 'wrestle with the dilemmas of childhood, education, family, work, love, ageing and death'.

Joseph's religious faith

Gillett (1990) highlights the number of deeply religious English artists in the nineteenth century. As we have seen already, Joseph was one of these as was his close friend Francis Oliver Finch. This manifested itself in his choice of subjects stimulated by Swedenborg's vision of the ideal (spiritually speaking) society as being formed of small communities with the family unit as their essential foundation. Swedenborg also praised innocence and equated it (again spiritually) with wisdom. One of his famous sayings is 'to grow old in heaven is to grow young'. He believed that in the afterlife people, or at least the good ones, appear younger as they mature spiritually. Joseph's deep attachment to family life may have come in part from Swedenborg's view that 'nations and families represent heavenly communities, and so the things of love and charity' – Arcana Caelestia, §2943 in Swedenborg (2012) edition. Similarly, the positive portrayal of simple homely family life in Joseph's pictures reflects New Church's ideas of love and respect as evidence of the spiritual aspects of ordinary people's lives. His works also embody Swedenborg's view that in each human being can be seen an element of the divine.

The New Church's UK web site (accessed in 2012) captures this when it says:

> "In common with most other churches we believe that people are basically spiritual. We live for a time in the physical world, but we are essentially spiritual beings. We can rise above our physical limitations, above the seeming demands of the moment. We can think rationally: we can see and respond to ideas – ideas that are timeless and beyond where we are now. Our spirits are free to

choose new thoughts and feelings over old ones, higher ones over lower ones. We can learn new things every day. We can change! We can do these things because we are spiritual and eternal beings."

This openness to new ideas may have stimulated Joseph's interest in education and the didactic role of art. The Swedenborg tradition places particular emphasis on an individual's actions in their daily life as central to their continuing life after death. In summary, Joseph's spiritual life found expression in his art that was neither academic nor sentimental, but rather a practical down to earth one in which spirituality can be seen at the heart of the individuals and family settings he depicted. Despite the influence of religion on his work, Joseph did not produce 'religious art' as such. He rarely produced images of biblical scenes and did not produce 'devotional works'.

The changing art market

Earlier chapters trace the major changes affecting the art market and Joseph's career. Generally, the picture emerges of an art world where the continually changing views of artists, critics and patrons created an iterative cycle driving modifications in the nature of art, the subjects tackled and their treatment. Like many established artists of his generation, Joseph was not a slavish follower of artistic trends or fashions.

Frequently changes in the art world are presented as a sequence of movements, each dominating the art market in turn over the sixty years of Joseph's professional career. The market did not work like this. In reality, each successive movement was a step in the evolution in art that created a good deal of interest, shifted the critical view of what constituted 'good art' and motivated some fervent practitioners. These fervent practitioners worked alongside numerous other artists producing works in earlier styles and fashions. The overall result was a complex ever shifting web of styles competing for patronage, critical acclaim, public attention and sales. Within this milieu, Joseph remained a 'realist' attached firmly to the contemporary genre style that continued to be popular with many 'ordinary' art patrons, readers of the illustrated press and visitors to galleries.

As seen in earlier chapters, the genre art boom in the middle of the nineteenth century involving many of Joseph's teachers at the RAS emphasised the technical drawing skills displayed in his works. Joseph was well aware of the emerging art movements and probably knew many of their practitioners personally; but this did not lead him to modify significantly his style, subject matter or techniques. A significant slump in the art market followed Thomas Holloway's spending spree in the mid-eighteen eighties. While the prices paid for Joseph's works in auction rooms fell, the prices paid for his works at major exhibitions were stable.

Most of the new art market movements during Joseph's career travelled around the world in what became an increasingly international art market. This arose from frequent International Exhibitions, significant improvements in technologies including electric telegraph (called the 'Victorian Internet' by Tom Standage (1998)), telephones and cinema newsreels; and the ease with which artists and their works could move between countries in the absence of border controls and improving road, rail and sea networks. Britain did not introduce border controls, apart from checks on contraband taxable products, until the Aliens Act 1905. Joseph seems never to have left Britain, as he did not have a passport. We know his nephew; Joseph Benwell Clark visited Paris frequently and studied there for a time.

Among the most important art movements, with country of origin and rough dates, during Joseph's career were the Pre Raphaelite Movement (1848–1860 United Kingdom); Impressionism (1860–1890 France); Aesthetic Movement (1868–1901 United Kingdom); Arts and Crafts movement (1880–1910

United Kingdom); Post-impressionism and Neo-Impressionism (1886–1905 France) and Art Nouveau (1890–1914 France). Apart from the positive effect of the PRB and the hostility engendered by the Aesthetic movement's philosophy towards genre works, these did not affect significantly the course of Joseph's work.

Perhaps Joseph warmed to Frith's views of fashions in art Wallis (1957) when he wrote:

> "… the caterers for public amusement have to deal with an amalgam of ignorance, prejudice, fickleness, and vulgarity to a degree altogether out of proportion to the critical faculty which is the outcome of enlightenment, and by which the truth of public judgment can be tested. The goddess fashion [in ladies clothing] reigns supreme. Where, I wonder, is the realm of the deity whence issues decrees so readily and universally obeyed? …
>
> The rushing from one extreme to another, so characteristic of Fashion's freaks was pursued for a time. … Fashion in art, though, is not so immediately palpable in its results, is no less serious a factor in the history of painting. There are instances of great artists who have retained public favour to the ends of their lives, and there are some admirable painters who have never been fashionable at all. Vandyke died at the age of forty-two, but he lived long enough to outlive the fashion for his portraits …
>
> Are there signs of real knowledge of art arising amongst the purchasers of art? I fear not I think I see proofs of the influence of fashion in all exhibitions of the present day – glaring mistakes of eccentricity for genius, a hunger after novelty, and a 'casting of bread upon the waters' … in the form on purchases of works by young aspirants in whom the purchaser sees signs of power to be fully developed in the near future."

We have no way of knowing but in giving priority to the 'healing mission' of his art he rejected both the somewhat elitist, patronising and snobbish tone of Frith's comments and the increasingly 'fashion driven aspects' of the art world.

Earlier chapters highlighted the impact of changes in the art market, especially the continuing decline in the dependence of professional artists on commissions from wealthy patrons, the growing influence of middle class patrons, the opening of many new public galleries and the increasing numbers of people with high level drawing skills coming from the new publicly funded art colleges. Middle class art patrons tended to admire both a meticulous finish and humorous characterisation displayed in genre works placing their continuing support at the heart of Joseph's career. We need to distinguish between different groups within the middle class audience. The core of Joseph's support came from 'middling' folk akin to the Clark, Jones and Ellisdon families living in communities of the type where Joseph lived for much of his life.

At the start of Joseph's career, several celebrity artists working in the genre tradition were his teachers in the RAS. Richard Redgrave pioneered the shift towards portraying 'middle class' life while continuing to use his paintings for social and moral purposes. Likewise, William Frith shared the PRB's talents in observation, acumen in subject selection, patience with models, good use of accessories and a painterly capacity for putting visual interest into his canvasses. While using these talents for commercial gains, he remained at heart a 'pictorial journalist' showing contemporary life with great integrity.

As the nineteenth century progressed, the attempt to depict reality became increasingly important in critical debates about art. These debates focused on what sort of reality and how best to capture it. At the risk of over simplification the succession of art movements through Joseph's career can be seen as attempts to resolve the key tension between the role of the eyes and the hand in depicting the subject and of the mind and emotions in capturing the essence of reality to produce a response in the audience. Joseph, as a well-educated and well-connected artist, understood the implications of this debate for his work. He reconciled these tensions by combining his acute observation of the external perspective while using the viewer's imagination to construct a narrative that enlists and shapes the emotions and moral sensibilities of his audience.

Creativity in Joseph's works

A further tension between realist works such as Joseph's and those of artists in later art movements was about the role of creativity and innovation in fine art. His works are not highly creative in the sense of setting new directions, adopting new techniques or following new trends in the art world. Many of the more famous artists of the day, at least in terms of those readily recalled a century or more later, introduced novel ways of looking at the world and expressing their inner vision. Their works occasionally produced the paradigm shifts that lie at the core of modern views of nineteenth and early twentieth century art. It appeared to many of Joseph's contempories that the pursuit of novelty and technical innovation alongside growing commercialism had replaced the deeper moral and spiritual aspirations of earlier generations of artists. Joseph probably shared this perspective.

Joseph's creativity lay in finding images and narratives that expressed his social and religious values. He was confident that his narrative and technical skills were sufficient to secure the impact he wanted to make on his audience and their ethical values. In this, his work exemplifies the 'therapeutic' role of art in society and artistic ambitions expressed by Alain de Botton and John Armstrong (2012). Joseph embraced many of the ideas that inspired artists through the ages to exemplify their concept of what it means to live a 'good life' and what must be avoided. Instead of trying to be innovative for its own sake, Joseph used titles and themes that had been presented many times before but gave them his distinctive treatment geared to capture the interest of contemporary middle class patrons and readers of the popular illustrated press. Therein lay his creativity – finding up to date triggers to engage the emotions and moral sensibilities of his generation with the issues that moved him. This can make his works difficult for many art critics in the twentieth century operating with the benefit of a century or more of artistic innovation and from a wholly different philosophical outlook on art and its purpose.

The wider social context

After a lull in the popularity of Joseph's works, including those by Joseph in the 1870s and 1880s, they started to attract more attention towards the end of the century. Whilst reflecting broader changes in Victorian Society, genre works captured something of the growing liberal trend in the public's mood. Increasingly people rejected the 'laissez faire' view of social and economic life with the result that the public became increasingly receptive to the subjects Joseph chose to emphasise than they had been during the middle years of his career.

Other manifestations of this shift in the public's mood were seen in the social and economic legislation in the later decades of the nineteenth century and the formation from the 1880s of organisations prefiguring the emergence of the 'welfare state' in the twentieth century. These included the Fabian Society, general trades unions, the Social Democratic League, the Socialist League, and somewhat later the Independent Labour Party. Although fellow artists including William Morris and Walter Crane were actively involved with these organisations, there is no evidence that Joseph participated in their work. However, as we have seen, he allowed his works to be used in social campaigning, especially on the temperance issues espoused by his friend Rev. Thomas Dixon-Spain.

One particularly English aspect of this shift was the weakening of the 'stiff upper lip' philosophy emphasised in many aspects of communal, educational, family, professional and public life in the middle years of Victoria's reign. The consequent softening of public attitudes towards displays of emotion in public was helpful in boosting the reception of Joseph's works towards the end of his career.

How does Joseph's work compare to that of his contemporaries?

Compared to his contemporaries there were some subjects that featured rarely in Joseph's work. There were hardly any landscapes and not many where the action takes place out of doors. Most of the works with outdoor settings have names suggesting that Joseph drew inspiration from his regular visits to the West Country (Somerset, Dorset or Hampshire). As we do not have images of many these works, it is impossible to identify the balance he struck between the people and landscape generally. Early in Joseph's career, critics tended to the view that his two religious works were really genre works set in the Biblical past, so this might be equally true of his outdoor scenes.

Likewise, animals do not feature much except as props for family scenes set in cottages. Cats predominate. In the works with publicly available images, there are twelve cats, two dogs, one parrot, one goldfish and four rabbits – three of which are dead. There are sundry chicks and other small birds. Cats have no specific symbolic meaning in art but critics refer to them as graceful, gentle, affectionate, aloof, independent, self-sufficient and dignified. Joseph did not use classical themes, depict well-known people or portray models in historical dress or in the nude.

There was an active debate about temperance and the abuse of alcohol in Victorian Britain, including within the Swedenborgian Church. Joseph does not seem to have been an active participant in these debates although none of his works depicts bottles or glasses or bottles of alcohol in creating the narrative flow. Perhaps, he omitted alcohol, as it did not enter into his conception of the 'good life'. In the 1890s he allowed his works to be used in temperance journals. *'The Band of Hope Review is capitally illustrated by Robert Barnes, J. Clark, etc.'* (Shields Daily Gazette 20 May 1893). The Band of Hope Review was an 'improving' magazine for the children of the poor and working classes. It also had a wider purpose of supplementing Sunday school instruction by offering temperance advice to the young while 'serving as a resource for religious and moral teaching in the home'.

Was Joseph a successful artist?

Critics and others use many criteria to assess the success of an artist. Four of the more important criteria in the nineteenth century were the artist's ability to gain access to the major exhibitions, the attitude of the critics, the income they generated and the award of Public and Professional Honours.

As we have seen, Joseph was extremely successful in having his paintings accepted by the leading exhibition societies, especially the RA and the Royal Society of Oil Painters. Few artists who were neither RA Associates nor Academicians, exhibited anything like the number of works over such a long period.

Another way of assessing Joseph's success in artistic terms is to see how Joseph's contempories at the RAS progressed as artists. Christopher Wood's (1995) Dictionary of British Art – Victorian Painters mentions seven of the class of July 1854, including Joseph. Alexander Glasgow and Thomas Brown were the only two who had sustained success in terms of exhibiting at the RA and other major exhibition societies. Like Joseph, Alexander Glasgow produced genre and portraits; while Thomas Brown specialised in landscapes. The others had occasional success in terms of exhibiting and some made their way in allied fields of engraving and print making.

Critical responses varied. At the start of his career, Joseph received 'rave reviews' for his work and received many predictions of a stellar career. Later on critics, especially those highly committed to the values of the Aesthetic Movement, became hostile while others with less time and space available tended to ignore contemporary genre works or only mentioned them in passing. Later in his career, there is a sense of an unfulfilled potential coupled with considerable respect for his technical skills.

Earnings

We do not have much information enabling us to estimate Joseph's income during much of his career. Earlier chapters have mentioned occasional income from sales at exhibitions. Graves (1918) provides a somewhat patchy list of sales at auctions including:

Table 9. Prices raised at auction for Joseph's works.

Date	Title	Year	Price at time	Price at 2013 values
11/3/1865	Any crockery today, Marm	1863	£46 4s 0d	£3,850
4/12/1875	Strayed from Home (i.e. Wanderer)	1861	£110 5s 0d	£9,050
	Wanderer Restored	1861	£105 0s 0d	£8,600
18/5/1878	Little Wanderer (i.e. Wanderer)	1861	£99 15s 0d	£8,470
	Restored	1861	£94 10s 0d	£8,000
4/3/1903	Sick Child	1857	£168 0s 0d	£15,750

Although substantial these sums were a good deal less than the amounts paid for works by 'celebrity artists', it is worth noting the significant loss made on the two pictures from 1861 between 1875 and 1878. Auction prices affected the amounts people would pay for a new works exhibited by the artist. In April 1925, The Times reported that 'The Sick Child' was sold by Christies for 100 guineas (about £5,225) – a fall of 70% in just over twenty years.

A better guide to Joseph's income from the middle years of his career comes from Graves's (undated) handwritten manuscript held at the National Art Library. This shows Joseph's sales at exhibitions, mostly those of the Society of Painters in Oil Colours between 1883 and 1892:

Table 10. Prices paid for selected exhibited works 1883–1893.

Year	Title	Income at 'year of exhibition' prices	Income at 2013 values
1883	An interesting occupation	252	22,150
	A humming top	375	32,950
1884	Mothers help	58	5,275
	Washing day	353	32,110
	Appreciative Audience	504	45,840
1885	Youth and Age	294	27,710
	The Village Postman	283	26,670
1886	Hampshire Dairyman (also at RA 1886 but unsold there)	580	55,013
	Somersetshire Cottage	751	71,380
1887	In confidence (unknown exhibition)	486	47,150
	A Somersetshire weaver (unknown exhibition)	710	68,890
1888	My clever brother (unknown exhibition)	590	57,340
	Preparing for a Constitutional	453	44,030

Table 10. Prices paid for selected exhibited works 1883–1893 (continued)

Year	Title	Income at 'year of exhibition' prices	Income at 2013 values
1889	The basket maker	277	26,710
	Blissful moments	462	46,480
1890	Dora and Geoffrey Holme	197	18,920
	Familiarity breeds contempt	387	37,160
	Far from The Madding Crowd	462	44,360
1891	Anticipation	527	50,220
1892	Golden Wedding	80	7,591
	The Little Housewife	352	33,400
1893	A bit of fun	311	30,100
	Happy Days	380	36,770
	Total	9124	868,219

So from exhibiting at the Society of Painters in Oil Colours over the 11 years from 1883 he earned an average of £789 a year (£76,690). On average his works earned £377 each (£37,640). In estimating his income from exhibition sales, account has to be taken of the commission charged by the Society of Painters in Oil Colours. These amounted to 10% of the sale price. So in the average year Joseph paid £79 in commission leaving him £710 (£69,010). The comparison of these sales with works exibited suggests that over the eleven years only three works exhibited were not sold at the exhibition – 'There never was such a baby' (1883), 'In confidence' (1887) and 'A Somersetshire weaver' (1887).

During the same period he exhibited 25 works at the RA. Assuming that prices and commission rates at the RA were similar, his total exhibition income from these years was around £1481 a year (£144,020). Beyond that he also has some private commissions.

Honours

Joseph did not seek honours or professional acolades and this may have contributed to his lack of progression within the RA. That said his works were recognised by the extent to which they found homes in public collections and displayed at international exhibitions. There is an uncorroborated recollection in the family that he turned down a 'state honour' on the grounds that he could not see how it would help him.

Seemingly honours and awards did not reflect his view of what constituted success in his professional life. For him success lay in attrracting a large audience for his beliefs and values directly through his paintings and indirectly through prints, illustrations and press coverage. Certainly very large numbers of people saw his works. It is far more difficult, if not impossible to assess whether in viewing them they were, in fact, stimulated to strengthen their approach when facing difficulties in their own lives or in doing more to help others in trouble.

The next chapter presents an appraisal of Joseph's works drawing on critical frameworks current during his working life and from the late twentieth and early twenty-first century.

An appreciation of Joseph Clark's works

This chapter presents an overall appraisal of Joseph's works. It goes beyond comments on individual works to consider his output against six critical frameworks developed over the past century and a half.

Critical Assressments – Joseph's contemporaries

This section provides a contemporary assessment of Joseph's works. After summarising themes occuring in press reports it draws on the critical frameworks offered by the PRB, John Ruskin and Frank Rutter.

Press Critics assessment summarised

Earlier chapters focused on press coverage of individual works in the context of others shown at specific exhibitions. Occasionally these critics set their comments in the context of Joseph's previously exhibited works. Several consistent themes emerge. It is unclear how far these were independent judgements or hurredly prepared reflctions incorporating 'received wisdom' about Joseph's works. Inevitably, critics were not in full agreement about the merits of his work.

At the start of his career, Joseph did well in terms of the frequency with which the newspapers reported his works. These reports typically contained one or more of three key elements – a brief description of the visual elements of the painting under review, the critic's understanding of the story being conveyed by the work and their assessment of its artistic merit. Several of Joseph's works received extensive coverage of this type, usually as part of much longer reports of major exhibitions. As the years went by the press coverage of the fine arts shrank markedly so references to specific works became rarer and more succinct.

There are some themes that occur throughout his career. The first was that he showed an exceptional quality of draughtsmanship in capturing details of characters and the background. Equally apparant to the most critics was Joseph's high level skills in composition which gave his work a 'graphic truth' that was much admired. So too was the agreement that his works showed an unusual clarity of conception founded on his capacity for discriminating wisely between the people and props essential to convey the message and those which would distract the viewer. They also saw that his works displayed a clarity of anecdote and simplicity of moral appeal that stimulated the viewer's emotions. As a result Joseph was seen as achieving excellence in expressing the narrative ideas and values that motivated him at different points in his professional life. It is also apparent that critics varied greatly in their understanding of Joseph's artistic ambitions discussed in previous chapters.

In the middle years of the nineteenth century a fierce critical debate raged about the respective virtues of contemporary realism and classical fine art. As the balance in the critical debate shifted so too did the reception of Joseph's works. His choice of genre as the vehicle for communicating his ideas, values and thoughts drove many aspects of critical comment later in his career. His focus on works dealing with family scenes in rural settings made him something of a puzzle for critics.

While recognising his technical strengths, his depiction of the commonplace experiences of ordinary people excited the more liberal minded reviewers but caused great nervousness amongst their more conservative colleagues. He was praised for demonstrating the underlying character of the people in his pictures with regular references to his capacity for capturing a naturalness in the poses aopted and an absence of pretentiousness in his work; something critics deplored in the work of other artists.

One one aspect of his work that attracted sustained negative comments, especially in the late 1860s and 1870s, was his use of colour. Some saw this as timidity in developing his palette making his work uninteresting and at times cold, hard and dry.

Some saw him as a good example of a naturally talented artist whose potential was limited by deficiencies in English art education when compared with French realists. As the years passed, there was a growing sense of an under developed talent and unrealised potential. Some critics with a strong interest in the technical and 'political' aspects of art dismissed his works as being both over sentimental and highly provincial, then terms of abuse in intellectual circles. Towards the end of his career Joseph was seen as an almost permanent fixture in the art world; one with considerable popularity amongst successive generations of exhibition visitors and others from outside the 'charmed' circle of critics, celebrity artists and art educators.

Many critics in the second half of his career, and subsequently, took Joseph's works at face value. In doing so they were missing his underlying message of 'look how much better society could be if we as individuals were to change our attitudes, behaviour, values and sensitivity to other's situations'. Several critics wrote about the enormous time pressures facing them given deadlines and the large number of works at major exhibitions. Some may have lacked the inclination, patience or skills to look below the surface to find the underlying meaning of Joseph's and other genre works.

Assessment against contemporary critical frameworks

Going beyond press comments on specific works meant for general consumption means using more structured critical frameworks. Then, as now, there was never a dominant framework for assessing an artist's work. This results from the dynamic nature of critical standards as they respond to changes in artistic practices, emerging philosophical thinking about aesthetics and the fundamental purpose of art in rapidly changing societies.

Consequently the choice of three specific frameworks used here is arbitrary. All come from the pens of well educated men at different stages in Joseph's career. They lived in a world that saw the purpose of art through the lens of well over a thousand years of Christian philosophical study tempered since the Age of Enlightenment by intensive study of Classical writers, strong challenges from new scientific and philosophical thinking, and an increasingly secular view of the world. While Joseph understood both the classics and the scientific approach, he remained a committed Christian. The three frameworks used here are those proposed by the Pre-Raphaelite Brotherhood (1840s), John Ruskin (1850–1890) and Frank Rutter (1926).

The Pre-Raphaelite Brotherhood (PRB)

The PRB manifesto issued at the end of the 1840s identifies the four key themes they believed should underpin an artist's work.

The first was that an artist should have genuine ideas to express. The previous chapters illustrate that Joseph had a clear and consistent vision of the ideas he wanted to express and the impact he wanted to achieve. His vision combined his Christian beliefs with mainstream thinking about art in the middle of the nineteenth century. The dominant idea in Joseph's works was that each individual had a personal responsibility for supporting those in difficulty. Joseph communicated this through a narrative expresed through 'realist' images of the lives of hard working contemporary families of modest means. This gave his work a contemporary feel distinct from the medieval settings and styles found in many PRB works.

The second PRB theme was the importance of the attentive study of Nature. In Joseph's works this translates itself into presenting the essence of the whole environment in which ordinary families lived rather than the 'natural world' seen in many PRB works. This coupled with his strong drafting skills, captures the fine detail of domestic settings to reinforce the storyline and moral significance of each work. In later works with outdoor settings Joseph demonstrates his mastery of plant life especially flowers, fruit and vegetables growing in cottage gardens, and of domestic pets.

The third PRB theme is one of sympathising with what is direct, serious and heartfelt in previous art to the exclusion of the merely conventional, self-parodying or learned by rote. Right from the start of his career Joseph showed his mastery of the principles developed by Dutch, French and earlier British artists in the genre tradition.

The final PRB theme was one of producing thoroughly good pictures. Many critics, even those who were hostile to genre, acknowledged Joseph's great skills, workmanship and ability to express abstract ideas in a concrete form while sustaining the interest and commitment of several generations of middle class art lovers.

John Ruskin

John Ruskin, the foremost academic art critic and writer in the second half of the nineteenth century, dominated the critical world in which Joseph built his reputation. Kenneth Clark (1964) in an introduction to Ruskin's writings on art and architecture concluded:

> "Ruskin's views on art cannot be made to form a logical system, and perhaps owe to this fact a part of their value. Ruskin's accounts of art are descriptions of a superior type that conjure images vividly in the mind's eye."

Notwithstanding this, Kenneth Clark (1964) summarised seven key themes that underpinned Ruskin's voluminous writings.

He describes the first of Ruskin's themes in terms of:

> "Art is not a matter of taste, but involves the whole man. Whether in making or perceiving a work of art, we bring to bear on it feeling, intellect, morals, knowledge, memory, and every other human capacity, all focused in a flash on a single point. Aesthetic man is a concept as false and dehumanizing as economic man."

As we have seen, Joseph's works exemplify many of these aspects of human existence. His contemporaries highlighted his capacity to express his deep feelings for the people depicted and the situations in which they found themselves. Many of his works embody a strong moral sense of the value of family life, the innocence of children, and care for and by the older generation drawn from his understanding of a large, caring supportive family and his Swedenborgian faith. For many, Joseph's works evoked memories of their upbringing and family life. These were frequently memories of a childhood in villages and small towns prior to their family's move to large industrial and commercial centres.

As a narrative painter he captured an instant but with sufficient clues to enable the audience to understand the social and economic context in which the action takes place; and imagine what went immediately before and what might be about to happen. He forced them to draw on their knowledge of society and make inferences using the objects included in many of his works, something that eludes many people in the twenty first century. Although Joseph's works were of contemporary scenes, the fundamental values and situations depicted can speak to modern audiences. Thus, Joseph showed an unusual capacity to engage viewers over the decades on many of the levels suggested by Ruskin.

Ruskin's second theme was:

> "Even the most superior mind and the most powerful imagination must found itself on facts, which must be recognised for what they are. The imagination will often reshape them in a way, which the prosaic mind cannot understand; but this recreation will be based on facts, not on formulas or illusions"

The routine minor facts of daily life underpin many of Joseph's works. These demonstrate his capacity to use day-to-day objects to stimulate the viewers' imagination to create a deep understanding of the circumstances and relationships facing the main characters depicted. This adds greatly to the power of his work while giving the modern viewer an accurate view of daily life for many people in Victorian Britain. Joseph was not a documentary artist. Although the physical objects depicted were real, most of the situations shown were imaginary and used to communicate deeper ideas about life and its potential.

Progressing from this, Ruskin's third theme about the nature of the facts the viewer uses to create the impact of the artwork. Thus, *'these facts must be perceived by the senses, or felt; not learnt.'* By restricting the bulk of his works to contemporary genre, Joseph avoided the tendency amongst some of his peers to create somewhat superficial visual impressions rather than displaying a deep understanding of their subjects. This reflected Joseph's desire to influence how people related to each other in an increasingly pressured and isolated urban world. Joseph's was the first generation to live in a society where the majority of British people lived in crowded, dirty, insanitary towns, often without access to clean water or open spaces. Joseph's aim was to help people understand how best to respond to the stresses this engendered.

The fourth theme in Ruskin's writings was that:

> "… the greatest artists and schools of art have believed it their duty to impart vital truths, not only about the facts of vision, but about religion and the conduct of life."

As we have seen already, Joseph's strong Swedenborgian faith and acute observation of the world around him provided the stimulus for his work. As a cultured educated man, he also drew inspiration from literature to help formulate insights to help people lead a well-conducted life.

Ruskin also believed that:

> "Good art is done with enjoyment. The artist must feel that, within certain reasonable limits, he is free, that he is wanted by society, and that the ideas he is asked to express are true and important".

Taking Joseph's works as a whole there is a sense that they depict a world with which he was comfortable and free to respond to contemporary behaviour and beliefs. He understood the rural and middle class society in which he lived and believed their values offered a good basis for society and individuals, especially those in distress. His contemporaries recognised the value of his work both financially through sales and commissions; and through his continued success in having his pictures accepted by the RA, his position in the Royal Society of Oil Painters, the production of popular prints and, from time to time, in favourable press comments. The financial independence he enjoyed allowed him to create works that were true in sentiment to his values and beliefs. They also meant that he was free from undue pressure from patrons commissioning works.

As part of his conception of the 'good society', Ruskin also perceived that:

> "Great art is the expression of epochs where people are united by a common faith and a common purpose, accept their laws, believe in their leaders, and take a serious view of human destiny".

Unlike some other contemporary genre artists working explicitly on problems flowing from industrialisation, urbanization and Britain's imperial role, Joseph chose a more subtle approach. He emphasised the common solidarity of humanity rather concentrating on the things that divided people. During his lifetime, he witnessed a significant decline in the religious and other beliefs that had united English people in earlier generations. Towards the end of his professional life, he showed interest in expressing the collective experiences of the nation in works such as 'Jubilee Rejoicings' (1897), 'War News at St Cross' (1899), 'Home from the war' (1901), 'Letter from the Front' (1915) and his last exhibited work 'Tales from Flanders' (1916).

This does not mean Joseph was blind to the tensions and great inequality between individuals within society during his lifetime. In old age, he witnessed the cataclysm of the Great War, the break down in solidarity in many European societies and the 'General strike' in Britain.

The Western Mail's coverage of his 'Christmas Dole' (1889) (plate 31) quoted earlier highlights Joseph's skill in capturing and displaying the differing viewpoints of the participants from different parts of society in his works:

> "There is a gentleman of a superior sort, mayhap the churchwarden, but if so his lofty expression evinces a soul above parochial charities … The vicar is gravely engaged in a task which … is to the good man a duty to be carefully undertaken. … One who from her shrewish expression will speak freely if the benefaction falls beneath her expectation … the women who congregate to obtain from the charity as much as possible, their faces bespeak a keen outlook for the smallest favours."
>
> **Western Daily Press** 31 May 1889

The 'Christmas Dole' deals with the balance a rural community achieved when all parts of society fulfill their expected roles. If we think of society as an organism, we can see that many of Joseph's works reflect Ruskin's view that:

> "This fulfillment of function depends on all parts of an organism cohering and cooperating. This … he called the 'Law of Help', one of Ruskin's fundamental beliefs, extending from nature and art to society."

Another much earlier example occurs in 'The wanderer' and 'Restored' (RA 1861) that demonstrate the 'Law of Help' in action when a young couple comes across a child and her kitten who have wandered from home. By returning the child to her mother and the kitten to the cat, the couple restores balance to the world.

Joseph's works resonate with Ruskin's final theme that:

> "Beauty of form is revealed in organisms which have developed perfectly according to their laws of growth, and so give, in his own words, 'the appearance of felicitous fulfillment of function.'"

Perhaps Joseph's awareness of imperfections in individuals and society came through most clearly in his works dealing with childhood illness, death and old age. In many works dealing with elderly people, he showed the beauty and contentment appropriate to their age and situation in life.

Later critical frameworks

This section examines Joseph's output in terms of frameworks put forward by Frank Rutter, Graham Reynolds and Alain de Botton with John Armstrong.

Frank Rutter's Propositions

Frank Rutter (1926) sets out nine propositions reflecting his long experience as a critic, curator and political activist. After education at Merchant Taylors' School and Queen's College, Cambridge, he became an early and passionate champion of 'modern art'.

The first of Rutter's propositions was that '*can be no Art without Life*'. As we have seen Joseph's life was typical of many well to do middle class men of his generation. Like them, he spent his early years a small country town, was educated to become a cultured gentleman, undertook a good professional training; settled in London, had a strong religious faith and partook fully in family and community life. As we have seen, Joseph bought his varied experience of life into his pictures thereby speaking to large audiences from similar backgrounds.

His life also illustrated Rutter's second theme that '*can be no Life without Growth*'. Joseph shows a steady growth in the professional, spiritual and personal aspects of his life. He selected the subjects he presented after careful thought and experimentation while avoiding the twists and turns of fashion in the fine arts.

Joseph's history illustrates his capacity to deal with, initiate and manage change to make the best of the opportunities open to him and his family at each stage in life. In this, he typified Rutter's third proposition that '*There can be no Growth without Change*'. Many of his works were a call for change in behaviours and attitudes couched in terms that spoke to middle class patrons.

The long lasting debate about the Royal Academy's custodianship of the Chantrey Bequest and the particular venom attracted by its purchase of two works by Joseph exemplifies Rutter's proposition that '*There can be no Change without Controversy*'. Although the controversy was not of Joseph's making, the main protagonists were advocating change in the RA. Though the controversy involved two of his works, we do not know what Joseph thought about the long lasting debate.

Joseph's career also speaks, albeit to a far more limited extent, to Rutter's propositions that '*Vital art work is controversial and displeasing to the Majority*' and '*Uninformed opinion is hostile to the Unknown*'. By the time the Chantrey Bequest controversy erupted Joseph's works no longer attracted the attention of fashionable critics whose tastes had moved towards accepting the thrust of the arguments of the aesthetic and other later movements.

As Joseph kept well within the familiar bounds of the Victorian genre tradition, he did not test Rutter's point about the hostility of the uninformed to the unknown. However in the Chantrey Bequest debate, some participants showed extreme hostility and others seemed not to appreciate the how to get the most from good quality genre works. Nor did he test Rutter's views that '*Of any given subject the number of persons possessing knowledge is smaller than the number of the uninformed*' ... and '*Ignorance triumphs at a General Election*'.

Rutter's final proposition that '*a Minority is not always right; but right opinions can only originate in a Minority*' speaks to a fundamental truth about the evolution of creative ideas and concepts. I argued in my unpublished Master's dissertation on 'Leading for creativity in the public sector' (2003), that really creative ideas arise from the bringing together of two previously unrelated thoughts to produce something novel and of value; and this starts in the mind of a single individual. Many highly creative people acknowledge the oft-repeated idea traced to John of Salisbury's (1159) 'Metalogicon' that says:

> "Bernard of Chartres used to compare us to [puny] dwarfs perched on the shoulders of giants. He pointed out that we see more and farther than our predecessors do, not because we have keener vision or greater height, but because we are lifted up and borne aloft on their gigantic stature."

Only slowly do new ideas gain followers who test the validity of the originator's thinking in the light of their experience. If successful, the new idea becomes a 'right opinion' subject to later revision in the light of experience. In this sense, Joseph's works were not highly creative as he worked in a style that has its roots several hundred years earlier. His originality lay in the specifics of the situations and narratives he used to communicate ideas that appealed to him.

Twentieth Century

For much of the 20th century, Victorian Art was deeply unfashionable and seen as devoid of interest or value. Many art critics were bleakly negative. The Pre-Raphaelites were dismissed as being of *'utter insignificance in the history of European culture'* and *'but a shallow interlude in Victorian philistinism'*. Their paintings were but *'a bonnet shop!'*. Kenneth Clark (1964) who made these comments, writing more in sorrow than anger, considered Victorian Art as not very good, producing in a slack period in the history of art. The 'bonnet shop' reference is interesting as Joseph produced two successful and popular works involving new headware – 'Buying a new hat' (1880) and 'The new cap' (1864).

A good example of this mindset comes from the story that in the early 1960s, Andrew Lloyd Webber asked his grandmother for a loan of £50 (around £1,000) to buy Lord Leighton's painting 'Flaming June'. Her response was 'No, I will not have Victorian Junk in my flat!'. By the turn of the Millennium, Victorian Art had been rehabilitated to the point where in 2000 a wealthy Lord Lloyd-Webber paid £6 million (about £8.8m) for another Victorian painting; 'St Cecilia' by John Waterhouse.

The critical aversion to works in realist genre like styles survives until our time. Frank Whitford (2013) took a hostile position in his review of the 'Lowry and The Painting of Modern Life' exhibition at Tate Britain:

> "It is a sobering thought: L.S. Lowry may rival Rolf Harris as Britain's most popular painter. But popular does not necessarily mean outstandingly gifted or even particularly good. Just look at Lowry's paintings and pencil drawings in this curious exhibition. Most of the drawings are dreadful. The paintings are better; though they are repetitive … It's not just the uniform subject matter that makes Lowry seem repetitive. Almost every factory, chimney, terrace house or wall in a Lowry painting is enclosed by a straight black line. His pictorial language is formulaic … and, of course, people, masses of people, trudging to work, Sunday service, or celebrating beneath the bunting … his figures, especially in motion, look Chaplinesque: they have slapstick qualities inappropriate in paintings as serious, as we are repeatedly told by the curators, as these … It looks as though Lowry found it difficult to draw characters fully in the round and therefore showed most of his people from the side or from the front … From painting to painting the mood is similar. The weather almost never changes, nor does the mood. It never rains, not even in Manchester. Though some paintings show 'Cripples' or 'The Fever Van', no emotion intrudes,

and there is about as much anxiety and impatience in the 'Ancoats Hospital Outpatients Hall' (1952) as in a Kneipp bath on a health farm…

Lowry's many admirers, including this year's Reith Lecturer, Grayson Perry, claim that their idol has been shamefully ignored and under-appreciated … So what's all the fuss about now? Accusations persist that the Tate, by willfully ignoring Lowry for years, was being snobbish and overbearing, but the Tate must now be sensitive to an art public different from the one to which it formerly catered, and it has reconsidered …

The key phrase [Painting of Modern Life] comes from Baudelaire who, in the Salon of 1845, first demanded that artists address their own experience and their own times. Baudelaire's ideal, it turned out, was a jobbing illustrator for the Illustrated London News called Constantin Guys who was an 'observer, philosopher, flâneur' and 'the painter of the passing moment' … I prefer something Lowry said in that marvelous BBC television film directed by John Read and first transmitted in 1957. 'No, I'm not a social reformer … I don't have any propaganda in my work – I just paint the scenes that I see and like … other people paint landscapes or flowers or anything else'."

In its tone, contents, values and underlying approach to the purpose of art, this contemporary criticism is remarkably similar to that adopted after the 1880s by the critics of Joseph and other genre artists.

Graham Reynolds

Graham Reynolds (1987) in his 'Victorian Painting' presents a more thoughtful and balanced view of the characteristic strengths and weakness of mid-Victorian painting offering a relatively modern framework for appreciating Joseph's works.

Reynold's (1987) starts by saying that the snobbish basis for later criticisms of genre works were already apparent in the eighteen sixties. Critics writing in 'The Athenaeum' and 'The Art Journal' often took artists to task for squandering their talents on 'low subjects' and from time to time expressed the view that contemporary nineteenth century dress was so ugly that it should never be portrayed. Joseph and others ignored this advice as they developed their artistic reputations.

Reynolds then points out that later in the century genre came under attack from art theorists taking their lead from the Aesthetic Movement. Their perspectives dominated critical thinking for most of the twentieth century. They accepted the idea that a portrayal of external appearance of an artist's subject should also reveal its inner qualities. The step change that occurred after the eighteen sixties was about how best to achieve this. Joseph's generation provided the visual clues and expected their audience to draw their own conclusions about the underlying inner qualities and emotions of the work's subjects. The art theorists felt that the artist had to present explicitly the underlying emotions to the audience. They also dismissed the careful presentation of mundane life in art.

Another line of attack on genre was that it created an unrealistic impression of order, self-control, material prosperity, external graciousness and rigid class distinctions in society. This saw genre artists as presenting a false view of contemporary life and of being apologists for the injustices suffered by many. These critics maintained a literalist viewpoint that failed to address the possibility that genre artists were depicting an alternative to contemporary life thereby challenging its values, ethics and practices.

Reynolds concluded that although the theorists had little direct effect on the practice of painters, their impact was on later generations of art critics and patrons; and that lasted at least a century. The continual critical onslaught contributed significantly to the decline in the market for contemporary genre lasting well into the twentieth century. Despite the critics' efforts, genre works remained popular with the public throughout the twentieth century.

Alain de Botton and John Armstrong – 'Reading Art'

It is far too early to talk of a distinctive twenty first century approach to appreciating art. That said, Alain de Botton and John Armstrong (2013) provide a helpful approach when they talk about five ways of reading a work of art, and by extension evaluating the output of a single artist over time. Their ideas provide a good basis for an appreciation of Joseph's work.

They argue that the first way of reading art is a *'technical reading'*. This views art history as a series of technical inventions and discoveries, perhaps inevitable, that privilege those taking the first step towards each new stage. As mentioned already Joseph's work as part of the mainstream of his generation and he did not aim to innovate in either the range of subjects portrayed or the artistic techniques employed.

The second way is the *political reading*. This approach values art that contributes to important stages in mankind's search for dignity, truth, justice and the fair allocation of resources within society. By extension it is possible to distinguish between the impact of a single work of art and that of an artist's works throughout his career. Likewise, it is helpful to distinguish between the impact on an individual viewer or on 'society' more widely. It would be unrealistic to expect a single work or an individual artist to change the perceptions of society as a whole. Very few works have been highly influential in this way: Piccaso's Guernica (1937) is a notable example. This work capured the horror of the Spanish Civil War at a particular moment and influenced public opinion across Europe and beyond. Few artists have a 'Guernica moment'.

Joseph's works made important points about dignity, trust and justice at the individual and family levels; and by extension at the societal level. This reflects his strong concern with individual behaviour. The focus on 'individual action' allows his works to speak to each new generation, or at least those able and willing to take the time to understand both the underlying and the superficial meanings in his pictures. The effort needed to achieve this becomes steadily more demanding as each successive generation faces new situations with novel moral, ethical and social challenges. Inevitably, as time passes the power of particular works to speak to the public shifts as the dominant values, culture, political and legislative frameworks change. As we have seen already, Joseph's works do not make explicit comparisons about widespread inequalities in income or wealth during his life time; or about gender, age, racial or disability based inequalities.

The third approach is the *'historical reading'* concentrating on what an artist's otput tells us about the past that might otherwise have been lost for ever. The 'historical genre' school active during Joseph's lifetime tells us about the ways Victorians tried to made sense of the the changing world around them by reimagining their past. In contrast, Joseph's works were about the time in which he lived and the 'rural' world from which many of his audience or their parents came. In the second half of his career he extended his output to depict the urban middle class world in which he lived. One underlying theme in Joseph's work was the risk of losing the positive humane aspects of 'rural' past amid the chaos and challenges of the emerging world. As noted earlier, Joseph's works provide an unrivaled insight into the fashions, values and tastes of the nineteenth centry world. Jeremy Paxman (2009) based his 'The Victorians – Britain through the paintings of the Age' on this potential inherent in genre art. He refers to a range of works, though none by Joseph Clark, and the changing responses to them ranging from 'comfort food' to 'bitter medicine'. This approach allows the modern audiences to reassess aspects of twenty first century life from a new and at times challenging perspective.

A *'shock-value'* reading focuses on the way in which some artists challenge complacency in the society by using startling visual images. This was not Joseph's style. Rather he sought to challenge complacency about personal behaviour by presenting idealized views of how personal relationships could make life better.

The final reading introduced by Alain de Botton and John Armstrong (2013) is that of a *'therapeutic reading'* of art. They suggest that a work can be good or bad depending on how well it meets the audience's 'inner needs' and responds to one or more of seven psychological frailties human beings exhibit. In this approach 'good art' helps people to counter seven psychological frailties so people can:

- Remember both important incidents and aspects of their lives allowing them to concentrate on 'what really matters' in busy and stressful lives.
- Sustain a hopeful outlook to counter the risks of excessive 'gloom' and recover the capacity to act in the face of debilitating feelings of smallness, powerlessness and weakness amid complexity and injustice.
- Offer support and consolation in the face of great sorrow and loss especially feelings of isolation and loss of perspective.
- Regain balance in their lives when facing too much intensity, stimulation and distraction, not least because of the intrusive spread of computer based technologies. These technologies, like the pressures Joseph's generation faced from industrialisation, urbanisation and imperialism, tend to prioritise the immediate and trivial while squeezing out the truly important things in life.
- Encourage self-understanding and the ability to communicate who they are and their feelings.
- Stimulate personal growth by presenting 'alien views' that challenge their understanding of the world in which initial responses are often ones of defensiveness.
- Appreciate what they have and those around them. Habitually people fail to notice their immediate surroundings and respond without conscious thought of the value of what they have and experience in their daily lives. Good art can overcome the tendency to aspire to have the novel and glamourous while downplaying what people already have.

In using the term 'threaputic' it is important to distinguish a therapeutic reading of art's purpose from the widespread use of art as a formal therapy that the British Association of Art Therapists (2014) defines as:

> "… a form of psychotherapy that uses art media as its primary mode of communication. It is practised by qualified, registered Art Therapists who work with children, young people, adults and the elderly. Clients who can use art therapy may have a wide range of difficulties, disabilities or diagnoses. These include, for example, emotional, behavioral or mental health problems, learning or physical disabilities, life-limiting conditions, brain-injury or neurological conditions and physical illness. Art therapy may be provided for groups, or for individuals, depending on clients' needs."

It is helpful to consider Joseph's works alongside the five different 'readings' and assess their capacity to counter the seven 'psychological frailties'. It is possible to think of the dominant approach for an individual artist, a critic, art lover or socity as being about the balance struck between these different 'readings'. As suggested earlier, Joseph, although he would not have recognised the term, focused on the therapeutic aspect of art and its potential to offer healing for troubled minds and a stimulus for those who have lost touch with what they could do for those in less fortunate circumstances. Equally he did not seek to communicate his ideas through a 'technical' or 'shock value' approach.

Although Joseph would not have expressed his aims or impact in these terms, he would have understood Alain de Botton's (2012) critique of the traditional approach of Christians to the purpose of art within society and his views on the inadequacies of secular approaches to gallery management and by extension to other aspects of the art world.

Alain de Botton (2012) argues that gallery managers struggle to artriculate the fundamental purpose of art whereas Christrianity leaves us in no doubt that its purpose is to remind people about really matters in their lives. Alain de Botton refers to Hagel's (1770–1831) view that art was about conveying concepts by engaging people through both their senses and mind, and modifies this to focus on art's power to direct our attention to the ideas that matter for the well being of our souls. Christianity gave art an educative and therapeutic mission to enhance our receptivity to modesty, friendship and courage. In Christianity, human beings are seen as inherently vulnerable and unable get through life without great griefs of mind and body. It also recognises that any pain is aggravated by a sense that we are alone in experiencing it. Art can help overscome this and remedy our lack of skills in communicating our troubles to others. Likewise art can help people recognise their neglected hurts and to withdraw into unproductive isolated situations. Religion also teaches us to be gentle on ourselves in times of crisis, and when desperate or afraid to cry out for help needed to pull back from dark moods.

Alain de Botton (2012) highlights the unreliability of our imaginative powers as magnifying the need for art. Consequently, we depend on artists to stimulate moments of compassion and excite our sympathies so that we can practice what we might one day feel towards others in our lives. Finally, art also helps us to sense and respond to the sorrows of others as they hide behind stoic facades; and understand that responding compassionately depends on 'our angle of vision' to their pain. Good art can help us see events from several angles.

Developing this argument, we can see that Joseph used his artistic skills to give us ways of seeing things from different perspectives. Many modern artists try to capture different perspectives within compound images leaving less to the imagination of the audience while obscuring the message for those without the skills to interpret easily the artist's message.

This line of arguament captires nicely from a philosopher's perspective what a painter with deeply held beliefs might want to achieve with his life. Joseph's works were unashamedly didactic and intended reawaken in his audience many of those finer sentiments which he, like many of his contemporaries, thought had been diminished by the advnce of industry, science and commerce.

ELEVEN

Postscript

It is a century since Joseph Clark sent his last picture to the Royal Academy and over ninety years since he died.

I hope that his life and works covered in this book have enriched and deepened your understanding of how our ancestors lived. At one level Joseph's works tell us something of their daily life, the clothes they wore, the homes in which they lived and the relationships between people in a range of 'respectable' households. At a deeper level, his emphasis on individual behaviour remains valid for today's complex, confusing, chaotic and deeply unequal world.

Although, Joseph's works are widely regarded for his treatment of children, they also challenge other aspects of our experience of family life. Many of his works depict the older generation playing a major part in family life, not least in caring and educating the younger generation and supporting their adult children. These insights are of significance in an 'ageing' society where too many older people live isolated lonely lives, too many parents suffer stress from combining family and work roles, too many children have limited contact with their grandparents, and many governments feel unable or unwilling to invest enough to tackle these problems.

This is in no sense saying that we should return to a Victorian society or values; rather that we need to learn from how earlier generations dealt with major changes in their economy and society. Joseph and other artists help us to do so. They demonstrate that there are other ways to think about change that might help us tackle today's challenges. Similarly, his works show that securing an ever-increasing range of material goods, economic growth and the associated growth in inequality within and between nations across the globe are not inevitable nor part of living 'a good life'. Rather Joseph recognised that individuals focused on the quality of their relationships are central for achieving a fulfilling life for everyone. The challenge is how we can do this in our increasingly divided and fractious societies.

Perhaps deepening our understanding of what nineteenth and twentieth century arts could help each of us meet this challenge. There are four things readers might do:

- Firstly, I have only been able to present a limited range of images of Joseph's works in this book. It is relatively easy to build a wider collection of images using internet sources and use these to deepen our understanding of the themes embedded in his work and the experiences he bought to his canvasses.
- Secondly, you may be able to locate and make more widely available images of the 'missing' works exhibited by Joseph – and works that never reached the walls of the major exhibition societies.
- Then, similar sources to those used in preparing this book, would allow you to explore what other artists from around the world working in realist contemporary genre traditions had to say about the societies in which they lived. Many of their works are readily available on the internet and information about their lives in the many books and academic journals, freely available on the internet.
- Finally, you may like to share the insights you gain with others through the expanding range of 'social media' interest groups.

For my part, I will be donating the proceeds from the sale of this book to the Teso Educational Support Services – an international development charity working with poor and highly disadvantaged young people in Uganda. TESS sponsors about 130 young people at any one time through their education from the start of secondary education until they are established in work. We aim to double this number within the next few years. There is also a growing problem of youth unemployment in Uganda. TESS plans to open the Shalom Centre in Kapir, Uganda to provide practical skills and work experience for these young people. I am TESS's Vice Chair. This charity seems particularly apposite given Joseph's interest in education and his strong Christian commitment

If you have enjoyed this book, please consider making donation to help TESS's work. More details of TESS's work and how to make a donation are available from:

By post:
Stuart Rutter
TESS UK Country Manager
PO Box 287
Nantwich
CW5 9DP

Online:
Website: www.tess.uk.net
Twitter: @TESSUganda
Facebook: https://www.facebook.com/tessuganda
Just Giving for donations: https://www.justgiving.com/tesoeducational/

Phone:
Landline: 00 44 (0)1829 733731
Mobile: 00 44 (0)7890 106103

UK Charity Number: 1131999

Website
A dedicated website – jclark1834.website – provides more information about Joseph Clark and his work. It also gives readers the chance to share their thoughts about Joseph's work or images of works not included in this book. You can also join in the hunt for 'missing works' that are not in the public domain.

I would welcome your thoughts, comments, additional information and questions inspired by this book especially if you have a painting or print that may be by Joseph Clark. I can be contacted through info@jclark1834.website

List of Illustrations

TABLES

PLATES
(between pages 18–19)

1. Joseph's parents (1825). (Courtesy the artist's family)
2. Joseph Clark's Water Colour of Cerne Abbas (1870s). (Courtesy of the Victoria and Albert Museum)
3. 'A private view 1881' (exhibited at the RA 1883) William Frith. (Source: Wikipedia Commons)
4. 'Our New National Gallery: Inspecting the Pictures at Millbank'. (Source: The Daily Graphic, 1897)
5. Joseph's signature from Sketch for oil painting 'The Word of Life' (1881). (Courtesy Victoria and Albert Museum)

(between pages 74–75)

6. Trafalgar Square (1852). Showing the National Gallery – home to the Royal Academy Schools until 1868. Walker, E. (artist), Thomas Picken (lithographer), Day & Son (printers) and Lloyd (publishers). (Courtesy of the Victoria and Albert Museum)
7. Portrait of a Young Man: Joseph Benwell Clark (1870s). (Courtesy of the Victorian and Albert Museum)
8. 'The Draught Player' (1859). (Courtesy Sarah Galvin)
9. 'The Doctor's Visit' (1858) also known as 'The sick boy'. (Source: 'I am a Child' website)
10. 'The Chess Players' (1860). (© Peter Nahum At The Leicester Galleries)
11. 'Return of the Runaway' (1862). (Courtesy Sarah Galvin)
12. Mother washing little girl (*c.*1860). (Courtesy Victoria and Albert Museum)
13. Christina Mary Clark (1860). (Courtesy Maas Gallery)
14. 'Hagar and Ishmael' (1860). (Courtesy the artist's family)
15. 'Crumbs from a poor man's table' (1869). (Source: Wikipedia)
16. Drawing for 'Job for the carpenter' (1863). (Courtesy of the Victoria and Albert Museum)

(between pages 132–133)

17. Drawing for 'Checkmate' (1876). (Courtesy of the Victoria and Albert Museum)
18. Henry Butter (*c.*1870). (Courtesy the artist's family)
19. Sketch for 'Private and Confidential' (1875). (Courtesy of the Victoria and Albert Museum)
20. Drawing for 'Up to her lips the rosy palm she raises' (1878). (Courtesy of Victoria and Albert Museum)
21. 'Chimney Corner' (1878). (Courtesy WikiGallery)
22. 'Buying a new hat' (1880). (Courtesy Wikigallery)
23. 'Children at Play' (1881). (Courtesy Big Sky Fine Art, Nottingham, UK)
24. Facsimile of 'The Very Image' (1884). (Courtesy WikiGallery)
25. 'Three Little Kittens' (1883). (Courtesy WikiGallery)
26. 'No Place like Home', *c.*1890.
27. Portrait of John Clark (1885). (Courtesy Sarah Galvin)
28. 'Golden Days' (1886). (Courtesy Christies)
29. Sketch for 'Home Again' (1885). (Courtesy Victoria and Albert Museum)
30. 'Blowing Bubbles' (1889). (Courtesy WikiGallery)
31. Photograph of 'Christmas Dole' in Hazelbury Plucknett Church. (Courtesy Teresa Galvin)

(between pages 172–173)

32. Sketch for 'Familiarity Breeds Contempt' (1890). (Courtesy Victoria and Albert Museum)
33. 'Scraping an Acquaintance' (1897). (Courtesy Sothebys)
34. 'Jubilee Rejoicings' (1897).
35. 'War News at St Cross' (1899). (Courtesy Christies)
36. 'Daddy's Darling' (1904). (Source: Cassel & Co)
37. 'Dancing Children' (1900). (Courtesy Victoria and Albert Museum)
38. 'For Daily Bread' (1907). (Source Pall mall Gazette)
39. Sketch for the oil painting 'Vaulting Ambitions' (1901). (Courtesy Victoria and Albert Museum)

Bibliography

Argyle Primary School (2014) Accessed 11 October 2014 at *http://www.argyle.camden.sch.uk/curriculum-a-learning/art*

Alexander, Cecil Frances (1848) 'Hymns for little children'. The modern paperback edition is published by the Rare Book Club (2012) ISBN-10: 1154376265

'Art and Artists' website accessed 14 July 2014 at *http://www.artistsandart.org/2010/06/blowing-bubbles-in-painting.html*

Art Journal (1845) Vol. 68 for *'Conservative by education, habit, and principle, we shrink from the idea of aiding the adversaries of any established institution'*

Art Journal (1858) 20: 161 *'Frith's 'Derby Day'*

Art Journal (1861) 23: 161 'Exhibition of the Royal Academy'

Art Journal (1863) 'British Artists: Their style and character – No LXIII JOSEPH CLARK pp 49–51 George Virtue, London, England

(American) Art Journal (1876) 'London Exhibitions' New Series, Vol. 2 (1876), pp. 62–63. Accessed: 10th April 2014 at *http://www.jstor.org/stable/20568851*

(American) Art Journal (1876) 'Paintings at the Centennial Exhibition: The English Pictures' by S.N.C. Art Journal (1875–1887), New Series, Vol. 2 (1876), Accessed: 28 September 2013 at JSTOR *http://www.jstor.org/stable/20568928*

Atkinson, J.B. (1859) 'London Exhibitions – Conflict of the Schools,' (Blackwood's 86: 128)

Atkinson, J.B. (1862) 'Pictures British and Foreign: International Exhibition,' (Blackwood's 92: 360)

Atkinson, J.B. (1863) *'The power of the British Press has been as great as that of the Royal Academy, and it has been much more abused'*, (Blackwood's, 94: 71)

Atkinson, J.B. (1865) 'Review of the art season' (Blackwood's 98: 336)

Atkinson, J.B. (1867) 'The Royal Academy and other exhibitions' Blackwood's (Blackwood's 102: 80)

Atkinson, J.B. (1885) 'Decline of Art: Royal Academy and Grosvenor Gallery' (Blackwood's 138)

Baldry, A.L. (writing as Alfred Lys) (1896) 'The life and work of Marcus Stone, RA 'The Art Journal, London. Accessed on 28 September 2013 through Internet Archive at *http://archive.org/details/lifeworkof marcus00baldrich*

Barrington, Mrs Russell (1906) 'The life, letters and work of Frederic Leighton'. London, Allen. Accessed 23rd April 2013 through Internet Achieve at *http://archive.org/details/lifelettersworko01barruoft*

Baxter, Lucy (1887) writing as Leader Scott 'The life of William Barnes – poet and philologist'. London, MacMillan and Co. Available online at the Internet Archive *http://archive.org/stream/lifewilliam barnooscotgoog#page/n10/mode/1up*

Bayes, A.W. (1860) 'The Studio'. [Unpublished extensive manuscript material in the possession of Mrs. Clare Ash, Bayes great granddaughter, Portsmouth, England.]

Bindman, David (ed) (2008) 'The history of British Art 1600–1870', London, Tate Publishing. ISBN-13: 978-1854376510

Blackburn, Henry (ed) (1895) 'English Art in 1884: illustrated by facsimile by the artists', New York Appleton

Booth, Charles (1889) Charles Booth Online Archive, Booth Poverty Map & Modern map, London School of Economics & Political Science. Accessed on 4 August 2013 online at *http://booth.lse.ac.uk/cgi-bin/do.pl?sub=view_booth_and_barth&args=531000,180400,6,large,5*

Boswell, James (1791) 'The Life of Samuel Johnson',Vol. 3 April 5, 1776. Available in many modern editions.

Botton, Alain de (2012) 'Religion for Atheists'. London, Penguin. ISBN 978 0 141 04360 0

Botton, Alain de and Armstrong, John (2013) 'Art as Therapy'. London, Phaidon. ISBN 978 0 7148 6590 1

Bradshaw's Handbook (1861) 'Bradshaw's descriptive railway handbook of Great Britain and Ireland – Section One: Bradshaw's tours through the counties of Kent, Sussex, Hants, Dorset Devon, The Channel Islands and the Isle of Wight'. Reprinted edition (2015) Glasgow Collins ISBN 978-0-00-759189-3

British Association of Art Therapists (2014) 'What is art therapy' Accessed on 1 November 2014 at *http://www. baat.org/About-Art-Therapy*

Bucknell, Roger (2013) 'Wulfric of Haselbury and other West Country Tales'. Somerset (TA18 7RJ), Tinkertails Publications.

Bulletin of the American Art-Union (1849) 'Changes in Art patronage in England' vol. 2, 1st July 1849 available from Internet Archive at *http://archive.org/details/jstor-20646617*

Carter, A.C.R. – compiler – (1898) 'The year's art: A concise epitome of all matters relating to the arts of Painting, Sculpture and Architecture and the Schools of Art'. London, J S Virtue Limited, 16 Ivy Lane, Paternoster Row. Accessed online at *https://archive.org/details/yearsartoolonduoft* on 2nd March 2014 – and editions for earlier years held in the City of Westminster Art Reference Library, London.

Centennial Board of Finance (1876) 'Visitors' guide to the Centennial exhibition and Philadelphia' Philadelphia, J.B. Lippincott & Co. Accessed on 3 October 2013 through Internet Archive at *http://archive.org/details/ visitorsguidetocoophil*

Chiles, Rosemary (2010) 'Joseph Clark R.O.I. (1834–1926): Victorian artist'. London. Unpublished but copy available in the National Art Library, London.

Chiles, Rosemary (2011) 'The Immediate family of the artist Joseph Clark (1834–1926) and his wife Annie Clark (nee Jones). Unpublished

Clark, Alfred (1918) 'My erratic pal' London, John Lane, The Bodley Head

Clark, Alfred (1919) 'The Margaret Book' London, John Lane & The Bodley Head

Clark, Graham (2013) 'Cerne Abbas Properties associated with the Clark Family'. Unpublished

Clark, Joseph (1910) Reply to a letter from Alfred B Cooper held in The Getty Research Institute, Research Library, Special Collections & Visual resources, Los Angeles California. Copy supplied March 2014.

Clark, Kenneth (ed) (1964) Ruskin Today: London, Murray

Clinton-Brock, A (1919) 'Essays on Art'. London, Methuen & Co Ltd., Essex Street, WC. The essays were first published in the Time Literary Supplement

Cook, Edward and Wedderburn, Alexander (eds) (1906–1912) 'The works of John Ruskin'. London, G. Allen; New York, Longmans, Green, and Co. 39 volumes. Accessed 1 June 2013 at *http://archive.org/search. php?query=cook%20and%20wedderburn*

Cooke, Simon (nd) 'Art-training in mid-Victorian Britain: Leigh's/Heatherley's'. Accessed on 21st February 2013 at *http://www.victorianweb.org/art/institutions/leigh.htm*

Codell, Julie F. (2003) 'The Victorian Artist: Artists' Life Writings in Britain, *c*.1870–1910' Cambridge, Cambridge University Press ISBN-10: 0521817579

Dixon-Spain, Thomas (1876) 'A Practical Guide for the formation and management of district and parochial branches of the Church of England Temperance Society' London

Dorset History Centre (1850) '*a bill and receipt, written and signed by the Rev William Barnes, for schooling of the masters Chick, major and minor (Thomas Chick IV and his brother William) for … The half year ending Christmas 1850*'. (County Archive Reference D.475/F/14 accessed 4th October 2013).

Drummond, Margaret (1950) 'Notes for a talk given to the Women's League of the Swedenborgian House in the 1950' quoted in Chiles (2010)

Edge, Frederick Milnes (1859) 'The Exploits and Triumphs, in Europe, of Paul Morphy, the Chess Champion' New York: D. Appleton and Company, 346 & 348 Broadway. The Project Gutenberg EBook accessed 12 March 2016 at *http://www.gutenberg.org/files/34180/34180-h/34180-h.htm*

Encyclopaedia Britannica (1911) – Artists biographies – Accessed on 18 February 2013 online at *http:// encyclopedia.jrank.org/*

Fletcher, Pamela and Helmreich, Anne with David Israel and Seth Erickson (2014) 'London Gallery project' reported in 'Local/Global: Mapping Nineteenth-Century London's Art Market'. Accessed online on 1 March 2014 at *http://www.19thc-artworldwide.org/autumn12/fletcher-helmreich-mapping-the-london-art- market*

Finch, E. Mrs (1865) 'Memorials of the late F.O. Finch … with selections from his writings.' London, 1865.

Frith, William (1888) 'My autobiography and reminiscences' New York, Harper & Brothers – p. 160. Accessed on 22 February 2013 at the Internet Archive, University of California – *http://archive.org/details/myautobiographyr00fritiala*

Galvin, Eric (2003) 'Leading for creativity in the public sector' University of Exeter/ Unpublished.

Gillett, Paula (1990) 'The Victorian Painter's World', Alan Sutton Publishing Company, Gloucester. ISBN 0-86299-724-0

Goodall, Frederick (1902) 'The reminiscences of Frederick Goodall RA' London and Newcastle-on-Tyne: The Water Scott publishing Co., Ltd. Available at Internet Archive at *https://archive.org/details/reminiscencesoff00good* accessed 15 May 2013

Graham-Dixon, Andrew (1996) 'A history of British Art' London, BBC Books ISBN 0 563 370440

Graves, Algernon (1918) 'Art Sales from early in the eighteenth century to early in the twentieth century (mostly old master and early English pictures). Vol 1 A-G' London: A. Graves, 1918–21. (Limited ed. of 300 copies.)

Harrison, Frederic (1888) explained in 'A Few Words about Picture Exhibitions' Nineteenth Century, Vol. 24

Haskins, Katherine (2012) 'The Art-Journal and Fine Art Publishing in Victorian England, 1850–1880' Ashgate: Burlington, Veremont, ISBN-13: 978-1409418108

Hawthorne, Mrs Julian (1876) 'Art in London. The Winter Exhibitions' Art Journal, Vol 8, 1 January 1876) The Aldine Press. Accessed on 28 September 2013 at Internet Archive at *http://archive.org/stream/jstor-20637218/20637218#page/n1/mode/2up*

Hearl, Trevor (1966) 'William Barnes – 1806–1886 'The schoolmaster.' London, Longman's

Heaton, Mrs. Charles (1893) 'A Concise History of Painting' London: George Bell & Sons, York St., Covent Garden & New York: 112, Fourth Avenue.

Heywood, John (1887) 'Fifty years of British Art as illustrated by the pictures and drawings in the Manchester Royal jubilee exhibition', Manchester and London, Paternoster Row. Deansgate and Ridgefield. Accessed on 4th March 2014 through Internet Archive at *https://archive.org/stream/fiftyyears00hodg/fiftyyears00hodg_djvu.txt*

Hilton, Timothy (1970). The Pre-Raphaelites, Oxford University Press – Thames and Hudson Ltd; Reprint edition ISBN: 978-0500201022

Howe, Rev. E.C. (1935) '100 years of the New Church Sunday School Union', London – Revised edition. Copy held at Swedenborg Society Archive, The Swedenborg Society, 20–21 Bloomsbury Way, London, WC1A 2TH

Inglis, Alison (2011) 'Art at second-hand': Journal of Art Historiography, Edgbaston, Birmingham ISSN 2042-4752. Accessed 18 May 2013 and available at *http://arthistoriography.files.wordpress.com/2011/10/inglis-art-at-second-hand-article.pdf*

Irwin, Robert (2013) ' Local Colour – a review of M. Shafik Babr's work 'Masterpieces of Orientalist Art' in Times Literary Supplement, London, 12 April 2013

Jameson, Anna (1842) 'Handbook to the Public Galleries of Art in and near London: with Catalogues': London John Murray, Albemarle Street Accessed 25 July 2013 Available online at *http://archive.org/stream/handbooktopubli02anngoog#page/n6/mode/2up* (Vol 1) and *http://archive.org/stream/handbooktopubli03anngoog#page/n6/mode/2up* (Vol 2)

Jameson, Anna (1844a) 'Companion to the Most Celebrated Private Galleries of Art in London; Containing Accurate Catalogues, Arranged Alphabetically, for Immediate Reference, each proceeded by an historical and critical introduction, with a Prefatory Essay on Art, Artists, Collectors and Connoisseurs': Modern edition (2012) Rarebooksclub.com ISBN-13: 978-0217813396 [The Rare Book Club is a US based membership organisation offering a facility to download rare books for a monthly subscription. Accessed 25 July 2013]

Jameson, Anna (1844b) 'Handbook to the Public Galleries of Art in and near London: with Catalogues': London John Murray, Albemarle

John of Salisbury (2010) 'Metalogicon: A Twelfth-Century Defence of the Verbal & Logical Arts of the Trivium.' Originally written in 1159 and translated by Daniel D. McGarry. Philadelphia, Paul Dry Books, Inc. ISBN-13: *978-1589880580*

Johnstone, H.F.V. (1961) 'Joseph Clark of Cerne Abbas – The artistic counterpart of William Barnes' Dorset Yearbook 1961–62

Laver, James (1930) 'Whistler' London, Faber and Faber – reprinted 1951 and 1976)

Leslie R.A., Charles Robert (1856) 'Handbook for Young Painters' London: John Murray, Albemarle Street. Accessed online on 28 September 2014 at Internet Archive *https://archive.org/stream/gri_33125008253409/ gri_33125008253409_djvu.txt*

Leslie, Charles Robert R.A. (1860) 'Autobiographical recollections: By the late Charles Robert Leslie, R.A. edited, with a prefatory essay on Leslie as an artist, and selections from his correspondence, by Tom Taylor, Esq. Boston: Ticknor and Fields. Accessed on 28th September 2014 at Internet Archive *https://archive.org/ stream/autobiographicaloolesl_0/autobiographicaloolesl_0_djvu.txt*

Leslie, George Dunlop (1914) 'Inner life of the Royal Academy' London, John Murray & Co. Accessed on 15 February 2013 at the Internet Archive, University of California. *http://archive.org/stream/ innerlifeofroyalooleslrich#page/n7/mode/2up*

Liddy, Brian (2006) 'The Origins and Development of Pictorial Photography in Britain.' in Patrick Daum (Ed.) Impressionist Camera: Pictorial Photography in Europe, 1888–1918: Merrell Publishers Ltd ISBN 978-1858943312

Linkof, Dr Ryan (2010) review of *The Edwardian Sense: Art, Design, and Performance in Britain, 1901-1910*, edited by Morna O'Neill and Michael Hatt: New Haven, CT, Yale University Press, 2010, ISBN: 9780300163353 Available online at *http://www.history.ac.uk/reviews/review/1121* Date accessed 17 May 2013.

London Gazette 19 May 1899. Available online at *http://www.london-gazette.co.uk/issues/27081/pages/3186 accessed 23rd August 2013*

MacColl, D.S. (1904) 'The administration of the Chantrey Bequest'; London, Grant Richards, 48 Leicester Square. Accessed through the Internet Archive on 19 February 2015 at *http://archive.org/details/ administrationofoomaccuoft*

MacColl, Dugald Sutherland and Gibson-Carmichael, Thomas David (1902) 'Nineteenth century art' Glasgow, J. Maclehose & Sons. Available online at *http://archive.org/details/cu31924020701748*

Macdonald, Stuart (1970) 'History and philosophy of art education' ISBN 0 718 89 1538 Lutterworth Press, Cambridge (reprinted 2004)

Mayhew, Henry (1851) 'London labour and the London poor: a cyclopaedia of the condition and earnings of those who can work, those who cannot work and those who will not work': The Office, 16 Upper Wellington Street, Strand Accessed 26th April 2013. Available online at *http://archive.org/stream/ londonlabourand03mayhgoog#page/n6/mode/2up*

Monkhouse, Cosmo (ed) (1893) revised edition of 'A concise history of painting' by Mrs Charles Heaton (1878), London, George Bell and Sons, Covent Garden and New York, 114 Forth Avenue Accessed 23rd March 2014. Available on line at Internet Archive at *https://archive.org/details/cu31924008743365*

Moore, George (1893) 'Modern Painting' London, Walter Scott, Limited, 24 Warwick Lane. Available online at *http://archive.org/details/modernpaintingoomoorrich*

New Church Magazine (1926) copies held in the library of the Swedenborgian Society, Bloomsbury, London. Accessed 30 May 2013 *http://www.swedenborg.org.uk/*

New Church UK Website, See *http://www.newchurch.org/index.html accessed 16th September 2013*

Nizer, Louis (1948) 'Between You and Me', New York, Beechurst Press, 1948.

Palgrave, Francis Turner (1866) 'Essays on Art'. London and Cambridge, Macmillan & Co. Accessed on line on 1st August 2013 through Internet Archive at *http://archive.org/stream/essaysonartissuoopalggoog/ essaysonartissuoopalggoog_djvu.txt*

Panton, Mrs James (1908) nee Jane Ellen Frith – 'Leaves from a Life' London, Everleigh Nash, Fawside House available online through Internet Archive at *http://archive.org/stream/cu31924013660984#page/n375/ mode/2up*

Paris Universal Exposition of 1878 (1878) 'Catalogue of the British Fine Art Section' London; Paris: Offices of the Royal Commission. Accessed on 3 October 2013 at Internet Archive *http://archive.org/stream/parisuniversalex00pari#page/10/mode/2up*

Pascoe, Charles E. (1877) 'Art in London' in The Art Journal, 1st January 1877. Accessed 6 June 2013 online at *http://archive.org/details/jstor-20569062*

Pascoe, Charles Eyre (1887) 'London of To-day – an illustrated handbook for the season 1887'. London, 188 Fleet Street; Sampson, Low, Marston, Searle & Rivington.

Paxman, Jeremy (2009) 'The Victorians – Britain through the Paintings of the age' London, BBC Books. ISBN-13: 978-1846077449

Peterson, Linda (2004) Review of Julie Codell (2003) 'Artist Life Writing in Britain *c.*1870–1910' Victorian Studies Vol. 46 No. 4, pp 711–713

Pevsner, Nikolaus (1936), 'Pioneers of Modern Design' London, Faber – currently available in an edition published by Palazzo Editions Ltd (1 Sept 2011) ISBN-10: 0956494269

'Pictures 1904 – illustrating the hundredth and thirty sixth Exhibition of the Royal Academy', Cassell and Company, London, Paris, New York and Melbourne. Accessed on 23 August 2013 through the Internet Archive at *http://archive.org/stream/royalacademyillu1904royauoft#page/n7/mode/2up*

'Pictures of 1907' London, Pall Mall Press. Accessed on 23 August 2013 through the Internet Archive at *http://archive.org/details/picturesof1907pa00lond*

Poë, Simon (2007) Review of Elizabeth Prettejohn (2007) 'Art for Art's Sake: Aestheticism in Victorian Painting' in The British Art Journal Vol. 9, No. 3 (Spring 2009), pp. 92–93 DOI: 10.2307/41614850. Accessed on 30 May 2013 at *http://www.jstor.org/stable/41614850*

Post Office (1852) Post Office Directory of London with Essex, Hertfordshire, Kent, Middlesex, Surrey and Kent London Directory (Small Edition, 1852) London; W Kelly and Co. Accessed 20 May 2013 at *http://www.historicaldirectories.org/hd/c.asp?ZyActionD=ZyDocument&Client=Test+Web+Site&Index=Historical%20Directories&UseQField=County&QField=County^London&Query=&File=E%3A%5CZYIMAGE%5CDATA%5CHISTDIR%5CTXT%5C00000000%5C00007VIB.txt&User=ANONYMOUS&Password=anonymous&SortMethod=f%3ADecade&MaximumDocuments=10&FuzzyDegree=0&ImageQuality=r80g5/r80g5/x150y150g5/i500&Display=hpfr&DefSeekPage=f&Back=ZyActionS&BackDesc=Results%20page&MaximumPages=1&ZyEntry=1&SeekPage=f&id=00007VIB.txt*

Post Office (1854) 'History, Gazetteer and Directory of the County of Huntingdon' London, Kelly & Co., Old Boswell Court, Temple Bar

Prettejohn, Elizabeth (2007) 'Art for Art's Sake: Aestheticism in Victorian Painting' Yale University Press for the Paul Mellon Centre for Studies in British Art, ISBN 978-0-300-13549-7

Puloy, Monika Ginzkey (1998) 'High Art and National Socialism' in the Journal of the History Collections 10, No. 2 (1998)

Redgrave, Richard (1857) 'Inventory of the pictures, drawings, etchings, &c in the British Fine Art Collections deposited in the new gallery at Cromwell Gardens, South Kensington, – being for the most part the gift of John Sheepshanks Esq'; London; George E. Eyre and William Spottiswood, printers to the Queen's most excellent Majesty, for Her Majesty's Stationery Office. Accessed on 14 April 2013 at Internet Archive *http://archive.org/details/inventorypicturoomusegoog*

Redgrave, Richard and Samuel (1866) 'A century of Painters of the English School 2 vols. London: Sampson Low, Marston, Searle & Rivington, Limited. The second edition of 1893 is available online at *http://archive.org/details/centuryofpainteroooredg*

Reynolds, Graham (1953) 'Painters of the Victorian scene' London, B.T. Batsford

Reynolds, Graham (1987) 'Victorian Painting' (2nd edition) The Herbert Press Ltd, Northchurch Road, London N1 4EJ. ISBN 0 906969-72-7

Reynolds, Sir Joshua (1842) '*Discourses on Painting and the Fine* Arts' (delivered between 1769 and 1790 at the Royal Academy) London, Bond Street: James Carpenter. On line versions available at *http://archive.org/details/discoursessirjoooreyngoog*

Richardson, H.C. ed. (1877) '*Academy criticisms 1877*', Published by the Auxiliary Steam Printing Co, New Broad Street, London EC – available online *http://archive.org/details/academycriticis01artsgoog*

Robson's Commercial Directory (1839) of the six counties forming the six counties forming the Norfolk Circuit (1839), William Robson and Co., London Directory and Circuit Guide Office, Cloak Lane, Cheapside, London.

Rose, G.B. (1900) 'Review of English Contemporary Art,' by Robert de la Sizeranne, translated by H.M. Poynter. New York: Frederick A. Stokes Company. Appearing in *The Sewanee Review*, Vol. 8, No. 2 (Apr. 1900), pp. 193–206 Accessed online at *http://www.jstor.org/stable/27528098* on 28 September 2013

Rossetti, William Michael (1858) 'The Externals of Sacred Art,' Crayon, 5: 334.

Royal Academy of Arts (1854a) 'Laws relating to the Schools, the Library and the students' W. Clowes, 14 Charing Cross, London. Available in the Royal Academy's Archive, Burlington House, Piccadilly, London and accessed March 2013

Royal Academy of Arts (1854b) 'Minutes of the Royal Academy Council' held at the Royal Academy Archive, Burlington House, Piccadilly London and accessed March 2013.

Royal Academy of Arts (1910) 'Royal Academy 1910 – Published at the office of 'Black and White' Fleet Street, London' Cassell, London. Accessed on 23 August 2013 through the Internet Archive at *http://archive.org/details/royalacademyil1910royauoft*

Ruskin, John (1858) 'Academy Notes' in E.T. Cooke and Alexander Wedderburn (eds) (1904) 'The works of John Ruskin' Vol. 14, George Allen, London pp 151–155

Ruskin, John (1859) 'Notes on some of the principal pictures in the rooms of the Royal Academy, the old and new Societies of painters in water colours, the Society of British Artists, and the French exhibition', London: Smith, Elder Accessed through Internet Archive on 8 April 2014 *http://archive.org/stream/onsomeofprincipaooruskiala#page/n5/mode/2up*

Ruskin, John (1875) 'Academy Notes' in E.T. Cooke and Alexander Wedderburn (eds) (1904) 'The works of John Ruskin' Vol. 14, George Allen, London p. 279

Russell, James (2011) 'The pocket guide to Victorian Artists and their Models' Barnsley, Remember When, an Imprint of Pen & Sword Books ISBN 978 1 84468 095 5

Rutter, Frank (1922) 'Contemporary Artists'. London Leonard Parsons Ltd Devonshire Street – Available online at Internet archive. Accessed on 15 February 2015 at *https://archive.org/stream/somecontemporaryooruttuoft/somecontemporaryooruttuoft_djvu.txt*

Rutter, Frank (1926) 'Evolution in modern art: a study of modern painting, 1870–1925' London, Calcutta, Sydney George G. Harrap. Accessed at the Internet Archive on 25 August 2013 at *http://archive.org/details/evomoderooruttt*

Rutter, Frank (1930), in the preface to 'The Camden Town Group: A Review' – exhibition catalogue. London Ernest Brown & Phillips, The Leicester Galleries.

Rutter, Frank (1933). 'Art in My Time', London, Rich & Cowan

Sachs, Jeffrey (2010) 'The Price of Civilization – Economics and Ethics after the Fall'. The Bodley Head, London. ISBN 978 1847920928

Sandby, William (1862) 'History of the Royal Academy of Arts from its foundation in 1768 to the present day' London, Longman, Green, Longman, Roberts, & Green. Available at Internet Archive *http://archive.org/details/historyroyalacaoosandgoog* accessed 26 March 2015

Saturday Review (1886) 'William Barnes Obituary' quoted on The Poetry Foundation's web site at *http://www.poetryfoundation.org/bio/william-barnes* Accessed on 30th May 2013

Sickert, Walter (2002) 'The complete writings on art'. Edited by Anna Gruetzman Robins. Oxford University Press ISBN 0 19 9261 69 5

Shinn, Earl (1876) The masterpieces of the Centennial international exhibition of 1876. Volume 1 Philadelphia, Gebbie & Barrie. An online version at Internet Archive Accessed 3 October 2013 at *http://archive.org/details/masterpiecesofce01shin*

Smith, Charles Saumarez (2009) 'The Institutionalisation of Art in Early Victorian England'. Text of the Joint Royal Historical Society/Gresham College Annual Lecture, 11 November 2009. Text and video available on line at *http://www.gresham.ac.uk/lectures-and-events/the-institutionalisation-of-the-arts-in-early-victorian-england*. Accessed 19 February 2015

Somerset and Dorset Family History Society (nd) 'Dorset Militia Ballot Lists – Vol. 2 West'. [Fiche]. PO Box 4502, Sherborne, DT9 6YL

Sperling, Joy (2002) 'Art, Cheap and Good: The Art Union in England and the United States, 1840–60' Nineteenth Century Art Worldwide'. Vol. 1 No. 1, Spring 2002, available online at *http://www.19thc-artworldwide.org/index.php/spring02/196--qart-cheap-and-goodq-the-art-union-in-england-and-the-united-states-184060*

Standage, Tom (1998) 'The Victorian Internet: The Remarkable Story of the Telegraph and the Nineteenth Century's On-Line Pioneers' London Phoenix; New Edition (1 April 1999) ISBN-13: 978-0753807033

Stephenson Andrew (2013) 'Introduction to 'Edwardian Art and its Legacies' Visual Culture in Britain' Volume 14, Issue 1 Routledge ISSN 1471-4787 (Print), 1941–8361 (Online)

St Michael and All Angels (2009) 'Some Historical Notes with mention of Wulfic, Haselbury's 12th century Anchorite Priest'. Third edition. Confirmed by a reference in the website of the Hazelbury Plucknett Church, accessed 26 August 2013 at *http://www.haselburystm.org/history.html*

Stourton, James and Montefiore, Charles Sebag (2012) 'The British as Art Collectors: From the Tudors to the present'. London Scala Publishing Ltd. ISBN-13: 978-1857597493

Swedenborg, Emmanuel (2012), Arcana Caelestia; The Heavenly Arcana Contained in the Holy Scriptures, or Word of the Lord, Unfolded, Beginning With the Book of Genesis: Together … Heaven of Angels, 1890. Forgotten books, London 2012

Temple, A.G. (1918) 'Guildhall Memories'. London John Murray, Albemarle Street, W.

Treuherz, Julian (1999) 'A brief survey of Victorian Painting' in 'Art in the Age of Queen Victoria ed. Helen Valentine (1999): London, Royal Academy of Arts ISBN 0 9000 94669 5

Treves, Sir Frederick (1906) 'The Highways and Byways in Dorset'. Macmillan and Co. Limited, London. St Martins Street – reprinted 1914 and 1920

Trumble, Angus (2013) 'Six Half-Lengths' London. Times Literary Supplement, 6 July 2013. Accessed 25 July 2013 at *http://www.the-tls.co.uk/tls/reviews/other_categories/article1282925.ece*

Truth (1905) 'Art Notes: An Artistic Hotchpotch' 22 February 1905 p 502.

Tupper, G.F. (1850) 'The Subject in Art' in 'The Germ' Issue 3. London, Aylott and Jones. Copy available at 'The complete writings and pictures of Dante Gabriel Rossetti – a hypermedia archive'. Accessed online on 2 November 2014 at *http://www.rossettiarchive.org/docs/ap4.g415.1.3.rad.html#p118*

Turner, Francis C. (1906) 'A short History of Art' London – 25 High Street, Bloomsbury. Swan Sonnenschen & Co Ltd. Available online at the Internet Archive – Accessed 1st August 2013 at *http://archive.org/details/ashorthistoryar02turngoog*

UCL Bloomsbury Project (nd) copy of advertisement for Sass's Academy from 1840. Accessed on 2 January 2014 at *http://www.ucl.ac.uk/bloomsbury-project/institutions/sass_academy.htm*

United States Centennial Commission (1876) 'International Exhibition, 1876: Official Catalogue, Volume 2.' Publisher: Nagle – accessed 3 October 2013 through Internet Archive at *http://archive.org/details/internationalex01commgoog*

University of Glasgow (2006) 'Exhibition Society in London, 1878–1908', accessed 3 May 2013 at *http://www.exhibitionculture.arts.gla.ac.uk/*

University of Glasgow (nd) Arts Faculty listing of exhibitions in London in the nineteenth century. Accessed on 11 May 2013 and at *http://www.whistler.arts.gla.ac.uk/correspondence/exhibit/*

Vaizey, Marina (2015) In the Public Eye' a review of **Waterfield, Giles** (2015) 'The People's Galleries: Art Museums and Exhibitions in Britain 1800–1914' (Yale 2015) in Art Quarterly – autumn 2015, pp 32–34, Art Fund, Islington, London

Vale, Vivian and Patricia (2000) 'The Parish Book of Cerne Abbas: Abbey and after'. Tiverton, Devon. Halsgrove. ISBN 1 84114 005 4

Visitors' guide to the Centennial exhibition and Philadelphia (1876) gives details of H.J. Turner. Philadelphia, J.B. Lippincott & Co. Internet Archive copy is available online at *https://archive.org/details/visitorsguidetocoophil* accessed 3 October 2013

Wallis, Neville (ed) (1957) 'A Victorian Canvas – the memoirs of W.P. Frith', London, Geoffrey Bles, Doughty Street

Waterfield, Giles (2015) 'The People's Gallery: Art Museums and Exhibitions in Britain 1800–1914'. Yale University Press. ISBN 9780300209846

Weale, John (1854) 'The Pictorial handbook of London: comprising its antiquities, architecture, arts, manufacture, trade, social, literary, and scientific institutions, exhibitions, and galleries of art: together with some account of the principal suburbs and most attractive localities; illustrated with two hundred and five engravings on wood, by Branston, Jewitt, and others and a new and complete map, engraved by Lowry (1854); London, Henry G. Bohn. Accessed 23 April 2013. Available from Internet Archive at *http://archive.org/stream/pictorialhandboo00weal#page/62/mode/2up*

Webb, Beatrice and Sidney (1917). London, New Statesman, 21 April 1917

Webb, R.K. (1963), 'The Victorian Reading Public' in From Dickens to Hardy (London: Pelican Books). Accessed online 27 September 2014. Available at *http://www.fee.org/the_freeman/detail/the-spread-of-education-before-compulsion-britain-and-america-in-the-nineteenth-century#ixzz2olD8CNrO*, on 28 December 2013

Wedmore, Fredrick (1880) 'The masters of Genre Painting' C Keegan Paul &Co, Paternoster Square, London. Internet Archive *https://archive.org/details/cu31924008631115* Accessed 28th January 2015

White, Harrison C. and White, Cynthia A. (1965) 'Canvases and Careers: Institutional Change in the French Painting World,' New York: Wiley. Second edition (1993) published by the University of Chicago Press. ISBN-13: 978-0226894874.

Whitford, Frank (2013) 'White light' a review, published on 9 August 2013 in the Times Literary Supplement, of 'Lowry and the Painting of Modern Life' exhibition: Tate Britain, until October 20 (2013) and the curators' book **T.J. Clark and Anne M. Wagner** (2013) Lowry and the Painting of Modern Life: London Tate. ISBN 978 1 84976 091

Wikipedia (2015) extract relating to William Frith's 'Private Viewing 1881' Accessed 16 January 2015 at *http://en.wikipedia.org/wiki/A_Private_View_at_the_Royal_Academy,_1881*

Wilde, Oscar (1889) 'London Models'. London and Bungay. Richard Clay and Sons. Accessed on 4 March 2014 through Internet Archive at *https://archive.org/details/londonmodels00wildrich*

Willesden New Church Register of baptisms according to the form directed to be used by the Seventeenth General Conference, New Church, Birmingham 1824. London, H.C. Hodgson, 15 Cross Street, Hatton Garden. Copy held by the Swedenborg Society Archives.

Wilton, Andrew (2009) review of David H. Solkin (2008) 'Painting out of the Ordinary: Modernity and the Art of Everyday Life in Early Nineteenth-century Britain'. The Paul Mellon Centre for Studies in British Art. Yale University Press, ISBN 9780300140613

Wood, Christopher (1995) 'Dictionary of British Art, Vol. IV Victorian Painters' Woodbridge, Suffolk, Antique Collectors Club ISBN 1 85149 1716

Wood, Martin (1912) 'Genre Painting': Art and Progress, Vol. 3, No. 4 (Feb. 1912), pp. 469–474 Published by: Stable for the American Federation of Arts, Accessed on 28 September 2013 through the Internet Archive at *http://www.jstor.org/stable/20560580*

Wordsworth, William (1844) Letter to the editor of the Morning Post of 9 December 1844 included in Julian Holland (ed.) (2013) 'Voices from the Railways: How the railways changed our lives' AA Publishing, Basingstoke, Hampshire. ISBN 978-0-7495-7408-6. It appeared originally in (1876) 'The Prose Works of William Wordsworth in three volumes' Edward Moxon, Son and Co. London

Acknowledgements

I am grateful for assistance from:

Members of the Clark family especially Rosemary Chiles, Graham Clark, Peter Benwell Clark and Richard Neal

James Wilson, Librarian at the Swedenborg Society, 20–21 Bloomsbury Way, London, WC1A 2TH

The National Art Library and Archives

Victoria and Albert Museum,

Royal Academy Archives

Bishopsgate Library

City of Westminster's Art Reference Library

The Dorset History Centre

Metropolitan Archives

Royal Institute of Oil Painters

US Library of Congress (Philadelphia)

Nottingham and Exeter University Libraries

Jane Oakley, Sotheby's

Christies

Bearnes, Hampton & Littlewood Limited, Exeter – Auctioneers

Trevor Vacher-Dean, former editor of the 'The Dorset Year Book'

George Mortimer, Cerne Abbas Historical Society

Hilde and Roger Bucknell of St Michael and All Angels Church, Haselbury Plucknett, Somerset.

Big Sky Fine Art, PO Box 9956, Nottingham, Nottingham, NG12 3SZ

Rupert Maas, Maas Gallery 15a Clifford St, London W11 4SL

Peter Nahum, At the Leicester Galleries, 5 Bloomsbury Square, London WC1A 2TA

Hallsgrove Publishing, Wellington, Somerset

The main web sites used in preparing this book were:

Find My Past (http://www.findmypast.co.uk)

Internet Archive (for electronic versions of rare Victorian and Edwardian art books) (https://www.archive.org)

JSTOR (for academic journals and books) (http://www.jstor.org)

Measuring Worth (for converting Victorian monetary values to those of the early 21st Century) (https://www.measuringworth.com/ppoweruk/)

The British Newspaper Archive (for contemporary press coverage of the art world) (www.britishnewspaperarchive.co.uk)

The Victorian Web (for scholarly coverage of many aspects of life between 1837 and 1901) (http://www.victorianweb.org/)

Wikigallery (for images) (http://www.wikigallery.org)

Wikipedia (for background information) (https://www.wikipedia.org)

Index